State Failure and Human Miseries

A Study with Special Focus on Famines In British Malabar

State Failure and Human Miseries

A Study with Special Focus on Famines in British Malabar

M. Raghavan

KALPAZ

ISBN: 978-93-5128-168-9

Price: ₹ 990

First Published, 2016

Published by

Kalpaz Publications
C-30, Satyawati Nagar,
Delhi – 110052
E-mail: kalpaz@hotmail.com
Ph.: 9212142040

Printed at: G. Print Process, Delhi

Cataloging in Publication Data—DK
Courtesy: D.K. Agencies (P) Ltd. <docinfo@dkagencies.com>

Raghavan, M., author.
State failure and human miseries : a study with special focus on famines in British Malabar / M. Raghavan.
pages cm
Includes bibliographical references.
ISBN 9789351281689

1. Famines—India—Malabar—History. 2. India—History—British occupation, 1765-1947. I. Title.

HC437.M35R34 2015 DDC 363.8095483 23

"It has long been my feeling that the lessons of economics that ride in economic history are important and that history provides an interesting and even fascinating window on economic knowledge."

John Kenneth Galbraith (1954)

"If the study of history cannot help us to solve the immediate problems confronting humanity, then the time spent studying it were better employed doing something more practical".

William Paul (1918)

To

MY LATE PARENTS

Contents

Acknowledgement 11
Preface 13

Chapter 1

Introduction **19**

Chapter 2

Famines in Malabar: A Historical Sketch **53**

Chapter 3

Food Availability Crisis and Famines **126**

Chapter 4

Famines and British Land Revenue Policy **152**

Chapter 5

Epidemics and Famine Mortalities **181**

Chapter 6

Entitlement Approach to Famines: Some Comments **221**

Chapter 7

The 1943 Famines: Comparing Bengal and Malabar **252**

Chapter 8

A Postscript **274**

References **287**

Index **299**

Acknowledgement

Having little or no exposure to historical research, I was a bit nervous to plunge into this venture. Prabhat Patnaik and Abhijit Sen encouraged me to take up this study, assuring any form of help required for its research. M.G.S Narayanan, former Chairman of the Indian Council of Historical Research (ICHR) initiated me to the history of Malabar and helped to pick up the major writings in this area. He gave me introductory letters to the Kerala State Archives and the Regional Archives at Kozhikode for permission to refer their records. M.G.S has always been available for discussion whenever I confronted any problem in preparing this monograph. Equally helpful was Utsa Patnaik, with whom I had a long discussion on various theoretical and empirical issues relating to hunger and destitution in the context of the vast famine literature and archival data. If this monograph has emerged somewhat differently in the analytical insights from most other existing works on famine, it was basically because of my discussion with her.

One serious problem that I confronted while preparing this monograph was how to get hold of basic references on the subject, lying in old journals. Jayati Ghosh, in spite of her busy schedules, organised and sent quite a number of those papers. Peter Bowbrick of UK forwarded a few articles and excerpts from books, mainly on Bengal Famine, in addition to his own critiques of Amartya Sen's *Poverty and Famines*. Akshya Panda, my former colleague in Planning Commission, helped me with photocopies of some of the well-known works on famine. At the Regional Archives of Kozhikode, Abdul Majeed, the Archivist and his colleagues, Sugesh Das and Varghese Samuel were highly helpful in laying hands on most of the historical documents needed to draft this monograph. I also received unstinted support at the National Archives of India, New Delhi, from Vandana Kamalvanshi, Pradeep Kumar and Sadaf Aktar. At home, my wife Thankamani (Mani) extended all supports for a congenial atmosphere needed to do this work and my daughter, Vandana, was always available to solve the persistent problems that I confronted with my computer.

It is an undisputable fact that any discussion on famine is incomplete without reference to epidemics and mortalities. In British Malabar, which was the breeding ground of a large number of water-borne and air-borne diseases, the age-old indigenous healthcare system and rejuvenation practices like *Ayurveda* and *Kalarippayattu* were instrumental in protecting the people from seasonally erupting fatal and not-so-fatal epidemics. Discussions with P. Madhu, Amruth M, and C.K Raju revealed how the British administration's ruthless suppression of these indigenous systems by the use of a Gramscian type hegemony dragged Malabar into repeated epidemics and famines. Brahmaputhran, a social activist and practicing allopathic physician enlightened me about debility diseases and the significance of social medicines in combating them.

C.K. Raju and Mumthas Thampi read through the entire draft and pointed out certain stylistic blemishes and apparent logical inconsistencies in the monograph. Jean Dreze was kind enough to read one of the core chapters of this book dealing with entitlement approach and the role that the state played in the prevention of famine, and complimented me for attempting 'this original and well written piece of work'. He underlined some of the crucial points in the chapter and advised me that I should be sure about the veracity of my references relating to Professor Amartya Sen. Afterwards, the newly established Institute for Social and Ecological Studies (ISES) at Kozhikode that specialises in multi-disciplinary researches, organised an internal discussion on the monograph with the participation of Professors M.G.S Narayanan, K. Gopalan Kutty, Jayaprakash Raghaviah, C.K Raju, P.V Smitha and a few other retired and serving teachers in the neighbouring universities and post-graduate colleges. Their comments were highly helpful in sprucing up the manuscript. Last, but not least, I am extremely thankful to Amit Garg and his editorial team at Kalpaz Publications for bring out this book with utmost care in removing my otherwise unintended errors. I have no words to express my sincere gratitude to each and every one of them. Even after these helps and supports, if any lacuna is still remaining in the work, the blame should go to me and me alone.

M. RAGHAVAN

Preface

This monograph deals with a discarded piece of history relating to British Malabar, a region that presently constitutes mainly the districts in the northern and central parts of Kerala. I stumbled upon this theme by sheer accident, while reading a statement in Jawaharlal Nehru's *Discovery of India* (1946): "Famine came, ghastly, staggering, (and) horrible beyond words. In Malabar, in Bijapur, in Orissa, and, above all, in the rich and fertile province of Bengal, men and women and little children die in their thousands daily for lack of food." The reference was about the 1943 famine, which researchers across the world characterise as the Great Bengal Famine and, according to them, the only famine that British India witnessed during the first half of the twentieth century. The 1943 famine in Bengal and its after-effects were minutely investigated by several social scientists, including such eminent scholars like Mahalanobis and Amartya Sen, and are still being subjected to newer spheres of scrutiny. There are also research studies on the history of famines in Orissa. However, this or any other famine that repeatedly stalked Malabar for centuries is intriguingly absent in the numerous historical discourses available for the region.

There is no convincing reason for this. The regional archives set up to bring together the historical records of British Malabar have been working at Kozhikode for around five decades; and it continues to be one of the busiest reference centres. Furthermore, after the publication of Amartya Sen's path-breaking work, *Poverty and Famines* (1981), innumerable historical studies on famines have come up, and are still coming up, not only in respect of the generally backward and malnourished regions of Africa, Asia and Latin America but also of China, Russia, and many countries in Europe. Even these widespread debates failed to move the social scientists of the region.

Perhaps the blame lies elsewhere. William Logan who served British Malabar for more than one and a half decades in various capacities during the closing decades of the nineteenth century had insisted in his influential historiography, *Malabar Manual* (first published in 1887) that the district does not have any record of famine ever since it was brought under the British rule. Some of his distinguished successors in the bureaucracy, particularly C.A. Innes and F.B. Evans, who together prepared a district-wise gazetteer of the Madras Presidency also reiterated that, Malabar being blessed with regular, copious monsoons and produced enough food, it was impervious to famine. Similarly, in recent times, several economic historians have argued that, in the first half of the twentieth century, except the Bengal Famine of 1943, the British India did not witness any other famine.

Contrary to these assertions, our survey reveals that, during 1876-78, when Logan himself was the Collector of Malabar, the district had experienced one of the most harrowing famines in its history and the periodic reports about it from his lower formations were received by him under his official seal and date. Likewise, in the first half of the last millennium, we came across four grievous famines in Malabar alone (as the years indicated in parentheses) from the writings of N. Ram (1918), Gandhiji (1924), A.K Gopalan (1933), and Jawaharlal Nehru (1943). What is interesting is that, all these episodes of famine have robust empirical support in the archival records.

Nevertheless, there were real hurdles for the preparation of this monograph. In the absence of any direct work on the famines in Malabar *per se*, we had to adopt a two-pronged strategy to develop our frame-work of research. To begin with, we compiled the central features of famines, including their causes and consequences as are available in the vast literature on the subject. The second step involved the identification of famines in Malabar from the period when the East India Company (EIC) was a commercial organisation to the end of the British rule in 1947 and connecting them with the features of famine that we compiled at the outset. This methodology enabled us to narrate famine on a wider canvas, integrating: (i) the hitherto unused empirical material from archival records; (ii) existing theories postulating the causal mechanisms underlying famines, (iii) flawed policies that plunged the colony into famines, mainly the assessment and collection of land revenue, environmental sanitation and health-care practices imposed ruthlessly by the British rulers; (iv) extreme parsimony in public expenditure intended for the implicit objective of imperialist aggrandisement; (v) prevalence of a persistent pre-famine condition due to shifts in large areas of land for commercialisation of agriculture, long-term decline in food availability, speculation, hoarding and escalation in the prices of food and other essentials; and (vi) the social unrests leading to sale of children, petty crimes, and outmigration.

These developments are brought out in eight chapters, broadly divided into two parts. Part-I comprises five chapters: a comprehensive introduction, the historical sketches of the major famines in Malabar during the British period, and issue-based narrative of famines in the district within a macro-historic frame-work. Part-II has three chapters. The first of these is a survey of the critiques and counter-critiques surrounding Amartya Sen's exceptionally innovative and widely debated 'entitlement' theory of famine, and then takes off to an examination of the role of state in combating famines from the period of the Roman Empire to British imperialism to some of the domestically formed sovereign states during the closing phase of the last century. The next chapter is a comparison of the intensity of the 1943 famines in Bengal and Malabar, with the implicit objective to get to know why this famine in Bengal evokes spine-chilling recollections even today while that of Malabar is completely ignored. Finally the last chapter summarises the main findings for a conclusion.

Before closing this note, a word about why this monograph has taken a form relatively different from most other works on the subject. This has not happened entirely intentionally. Nonetheless, there was a feeling in the back of the mind that today it is not easy to write a book on famine with any semblance of originality. After the publication of Amartya Sen's *Poverty and Famines*, innumerable books and research papers have appeared on the subject and, as stated already, are still appearing in different parts of the world. During the last decade of the twentieth-century, Professor Sen himself had brought together some one hundred experts on behalf of the United Nations University and World Institute for Development Economic Research (WIDER) to conduct wide-ranging, issue-oriented as well as multi-disciplinary inquiries on famine. Most of these studies, while probing the causes, consequences, features and prevention of famine, rely largely on the notion of the 'failure of exchange entitlement' ideally in a private ownership market economy. As this monograph attributes famine prevention as the basic responsibility of the State, be it democratic, authoritarian or imperialistic, we expect that scholars should find the polemics interesting for a relook at the whole debates on the subject.

Another insight came from the post-graduate students and doctoral researchers of the neighbouring universities and colleges, with whom I used to interact at the Regional Archives at Kozhikode from where most of the research for this monograph was carried out. As famine and related aspects are presented here in a macro-historic frame-work along with elaborate notes, references and easily accessible but hitherto unused empirical data, the present study should be highly useful for the new generation students in the selection of topics for their research, not necessarily relating to famine, or to Malabar, alone.

PART-I

Chapter 1

Introduction

1.1 The Background

For centuries, mass starvation, leading to outbreaks of diseases and excessively large number of mortalities were a recurring phenomenon in several parts of the Indian sub-continent. Being perpetually deficient in food, the condition of the old Malabar district of the Presidency of Madras under the British rule, and presently situated mostly in the northern part of Kerala, might not have been different. Even when other regions of the Presidency developed irrigation facilities, Malabar had to depend solely on natural precipitation for cultivation. If the monsoon failed, sowing would be affected, despite the district being blessed with many rivers, backwaters and canals. On the other hand, if monsoons were regular, farmers could produce as many as three rice crops, minor cereals and commercial crops in a year. Being a hilly region, sloping from the Western Ghats to the Arabian Sea, the rain-water stored in rivers and rivulets of the district got easily drained off. Consecutive failure of monsoons in two or three seasons created drought-like conditions, resulting in disastrous crop failures, shooting up of grain prices and access to food extremely difficult for the people at large. The land revenue system adopted in the region by the British East India Company (EIC) and continued under the Crown rule further accentuated the situation. If the neighbouring Mysore state spared its surplus foodgrains or permitted imports from Burma (now Myanmar) through its port, there might not have been much problem. Quite often, however, conflicts between local rulers of Mysore and the British administration, or the native rajas of Malabar, made 'imports' through Mysore-border difficult. That was why this region came repeatedly under sharp bouts of famines, famine-related epidemics and large-scale mortalities. Nonetheless, these human miseries have never been studied despite almost all other aspects of the history of Malabar are extensively researched.

Interestingly, a perusal of the historical writings from other parts of the country or abroad would reveal that some of the worst famines in India during the British era had not spared this district. To cite an example,

Jawaharlal Nehru in his *Discovery of India* wrote: "*Famine came, ghastly, staggering,* (and) *horrible beyond words. In Malabar, in Bijapur, in Orissa, and, above all, in the rich and fertile province of Bengal, men and women and little children die in their thousands daily for lack of food*" (Nehru, 1946). Nehru's reference was about the worst famine of 1943. Though the Bengal famine and its after-effects were minutely investigated by several social scientists, including such eminent scholars like Mahalanobis and Amartya Sen, and of Orissa by some of the researchers from that state, famines in Malabar failed to attract attention of the scholars in this region.

The purpose of the present study is admittedly modest. It is intended only to make a beginning in filling this research gap, rather than preparing a gazetteer of famines in Malabar during the British period. Two approaches were felt necessary to sketch the groundwork for undertaking our task: The first was to bring together the dominant features of famines as are brought out in some of the scholarly works on the subject; and secondly, to compare these features with the historical episodes of malnutrition, morbidity and mortalities in Malabar region. Generally, sources of reference for comparison are available in folklores and creative writings of the selected area. In our case, the archival records came in handy. The British period covered in the investigation begins from the trading activities of the EIC by setting up 'factories' or export processing centres in different parts of the country to the end of the British Crown rule in 1947. Studies show that, during this period, not only Malabar but also the entire Indian sub-continent had witnessed the worst famines in its history though, for centuries before that too, famine was not unknown here. According to Brian Murton, there were eighteen major famines in India during a long period of six and a half centuries before the British era, covering 1000 AD to 1745 AD. The number of lives lost in these famines was rather trivial. After the advent of the British, either for trade or for direct rule since 1745, as many as 40 major famines were recorded with a death toll of more than 70 million people in India (Murton, 2000). Another account places the number of deaths from famines during the eighteenth, nineteenth and early twentieth centuries at 60 million (Lancaster, 1990). These famines were not only excessively gruelling in terms of human miseries but the gap between one spell of famine and the next became relatively shorter. This was particularly so since 1858, when the EIC was dismantled and the powers of governance shifted to the British Crown with the result that the Indian administration, in effect, became remote-controlled from England (Stein, 2001).

Bhatia (1967) summarises the frequency of famines in Indian history in a different way: (1) in the pre-British period from the eleventh century AD to the end of the seventeenth century AD, there was one major famine in every 50 years; (2) during the 93 years between 1765, when the EIC took over the *diwani* of Bengal and 1858, when the EIC surrendered the administration to the British Crown, there was one famine in almost every 8 years; (3) in the first 50 years of the direct Crown-rule in India from 1860 to 1908, there was one famine every two years; and (4) in the last phase of the British rule from 1908 to 1947, there was only one major famine in India, the 1943 Bengal famine. One unanimous opinion in all these historical sequencing is that, for nine and a half centuries from the pre-British period to the end of the British rule, the frequency of famines in the country had reduced fast during the latter period. Another point of unanimity among these historians is that Malabar did not experience any famine throughout this era. We will come to this later. As regards the reducing frequency of famines during the British period, there were specific reasons.

After the EIC shifted its focus from commercial activities to governance as its main pre-occupation, the administration of the country looked like that of an Indian state. During this historical phase, even while continuing with its commercial aspirations, some of the EIC rulers had exhibited reasonable sensitivity to local problems. They initiated a few developmental schemes, which could benefit the local economy in the long run so that the recurrence of famine was delayed and its intensity muted Afterwards, these were subverted by Queen Victoria's ministers in charge of India so that famines repeated faster than earlier (Stein, 2001).

With the transfer of Indian administration from EIC for the direct rule of the Crown, it was the Secretary of State for India, stationed at London, who controlled the overall governance of the colony, including recruitments to the Indian Civil Service (ICS). Only a very few Indian nationals, who could go to England for higher education and write the competitive examination for ICS from that country could get into the civil service in India. Therefore, most of these posts were occupied by British citizens. The task of the ICS officials was to assist Britain in its empire-building mission. They were in fact truly sanctimonious in carrying out this job while utterly indifferent in attending to problems of common people, irrespective of whether these officials were of Indian origin or British nationals (Misra, 1977; Guha, 1977). As regards famine prevention, there were clear-cut guidelines in place. Nonetheless, these officials refused to implement the guidelines. Even otherwise, given their authority in British India as also over the local kings, they could have mobilised food stocks from surplus areas and distributed to the malnourished people in famine stricken regions. Instead, these bureaucrats, with implicit approval of their political bosses, encouraged private traders to mop up the available foodgrains from domestic markets and export to Britain, British war-theatres, or elsewhere in Europe.

It would appear that these activities were going on without the knowledge of the British parliament. Some of the Secretaries of State appointed in British cabinet to deal with Indian affairs reportedly tried to suppress all information relating to famines taking place in different parts of the colony. They even prohibited journalists of foreign print media working in India to cable any information about food crises, famines, debility diseases and large-scale deaths. As a result of this, there was no discussion in British parliament or in the popular press anywhere in England about famines and other human miseries (Mitra, 1989).

To make matters worse, the imperialist administration gave draconian powers, including the powers of police and judiciary to the revenue collectors and foreign plantation owners with a view to extract more and more resources for the empire. These powers were brutally used in the colony. The revenue collectors snatched away from the cultivating households their belongings like land, livestock, food stocks and other movable household-articles to recoup land revenue arrears. Similarly, the plantation owners forced the employees to do longer hours of work at below survival wage. The peasants and workers were thus reduced to the level of under-nourished slaves in perpetual starvation, increased morbidity and early mortality (Chandra, 2009; Kolsky, 2010).

One reason attributed to this attitude in dealing with poverty and famines in India during the colonial period was that the British administration was carried away by the economic thinking in England in the nineteenth century, particularly of the Scottish Economist, Adam Smith, who advocated the pre-eminence of *laissez faire* in solving all economic problems. Sticking to the free-market ideology, Robert Bulwer-Lytton (Lord Lytton), the governing British Viceroy in India (1876–1880) rejected all appeals to extend relief to victims of one of the worst Indian famines of 1876-78 on the specious ground that such assistance amounted to acting on 'cheap sentiment'. The Viceroy issued strict orders that "there is to be no interference of any kind on the part of Government with the object of reducing the price of food." The district officers were instructed to "discourage relief works in every possible way" because, he averred, "mere distress is not a sufficient reason for opening a relief work" (Davis, 2001).[1] It was not only Lytton but the entire British administrative hierarchies in India and England believed that money and goods in a free-market moved by themselves in ways beneficial to the mankind so that the less the government interfered with this process, the better. Going by this belief, they refused to interfere in the market even during the worst famine times. There were reports about fleets of ships bringing rice to India, when people were reeling under famine but simultaneously another fleet of ships carrying the same rice out of India. Materially, therefore, the free movements of food made no difference to the starving millions (Mason, 1985).

Some of the economists in the West held still harsher views against the state intervention as a policy-instrument in preventing famines. For instance, in 1816, when the British weather became extremely bad and a famine was imminent, James Mill, a utilitarian economist and a personal friend and supporter of David Ricardo, in a letter to the latter wrote: "….there must now be of necessity a very deficient crop, and very high price – and then with an unexampled scarcity of work will produce a degree of misery, the thought of which makes the flesh creep on one's bones – one third of the people must die." Rather than advocating for immediate action by the government to halt the impending tragedy, Mill wrote, "it would be a blessing to take them into the street and highways, and cut their throats as we do with pigs."[2] This attitude was evident, though apparently not with the same cruelty, in dealing with famines under the British rule in India. Whenever famines broke out here, the colonial government took the position that "market forces alone would suffice to feed the starving Indians." The officials were instructed by the government that "absolute non-interference with the operation of the private enterprise must be the foundation of their famine policy" and warned that "any government which, by indiscriminate alms giving, weakened the fibre and demoralised the self-reliance of the population, would be guilty of a public crime" (see Ferguson, 2004).

This was the time when British India witnessed the emergence of an all-powerful imperial bureaucracy, whose members were, in the words of Burton Stein, "immovable, irresponsible and amenable to no other authority but their fellow members." When various regions of the country were facing severe food shortages, "these officials remained doggedly attached to principles of free-trade and non-interference with markets. Bureaucratic cowardice also entered. Fearing for their careers, most officials were reluctant to recommend that the revenues of the country be reduced to deal with the dearth or that investment be made in public projects, such as irrigation works" (Stein, 2001). Instead, they were more anxious to quicken the process of free market through the construction of roads and railways. They even permitted forward-contracts in foodgrains, an extreme device to strengthen the free market, which led to steep rise in prices during famines. The English civil servants, who had the power to take independent decisions, kept an element of racialism against Indians. This strengthened their inertia in extending famine-relief as needed. Their Indian-born counterparts had more duties than authority to deal independently with local problems. Many of them were however reportedly more irresponsible in discharging their assigned duties, particularly those beneficial to the masses.

A shocking example of the official attitude is available in the biographical note by Asok K. Mitra, who himself had served as a civil servant under the British government in the presidency of Bengal during the closing phase of the colonial rule. In 1943, when the Bengal famine was devastating the presidency, the district collectors were directed by the government to take care of relief works in accordance with the Famine Code of 1883. One R.S.T John was the Collector in charge of the famine-relief work in Vikrampur district on the Dacca side of Bengal. Mitra writes that "John seemed more unsympathetic than the masters in Calcutta. He developed a total lack of empathy as the famine approached its critical stage.......Much to my dismay I found a sandwich board with notices painted on either side propped up on a stand on the half landing of the staircase leading to John's *khas karma* in the Collectorate. On the one side the notice read: *The Collector Sahib Bahadur will not come to office today.* The other side read: *The Collector Sahib Bahadur will be in office today from 11 am to 12 noon but will receive no visitors* (emphasis added). I traced him to the corner of the Dacca Club at twelve thirty to find him ensconced with his second glass of pink gin." When asked about the relief works, he retorted that these people who are multiplying without control will not be able to survive by the food distributed with his hands (Mitra, 1989).

The attitude of the British authorities and their bureaucrats towards the plights of the people in Malabar during famine times, though not openly as harsh, was not very different. Some officials who worked in Malabar reported that this region was unlikely to face famine because of its climatic and rainfall patterns. This was the basis on which the presidency left out Malabar from advance preparations for famine-prevention activities, as provided under the 1883 Famine Code. Evidences marshalled from archival records for the present monograph show that this claim was factually unfounded. In fact, the very geographical position as well as the rainfall and climatic conditions of Malabar are more favourable for epidemics and famine. This will be clear if we make a cursory survey of the region, particularly of its physical features, soil, climate, population and agricultural production. These features, including its political history are briefly brought out below to get an idea about how far the argument that Malabar was impervious to famines could sustain.

1.2 History, Geography and Population

At present, Malabar, which forms the focus of our study of famines, has no existence on the political map of India. After independence, when states were reconstituted according to the main language of each region in terms of the recommendations of the States Reorganisation Commission, Malabar was detached from Madras, divided into a few new districts and attached to the northern part of Kerala. Nevertheless, to the people of this region Malabar 'still exists', to quote the poet Anita Nair, 'as a state of mind.'[3] Several private buildings, service activities and cultural fetes in this part of the state are even now adorned by this name.[4] Before the EIC's annexation, Malabar was a part of the Mysore kingdom. Haidar Ali, who was a petty officer in the Mysore army, overthrew the ruler and established his authority over the kingdom. Subsequently, when he came into contact with Malabar, he found that it was sub-divided into a number of tiny principalities fighting against one another. Using the on-going rivalry among the local chiefs as an opportunity, he invaded Malabar in January 1766 and by about mid-April that year succeeded in subduing the competing chiefs of various principalities (Hasan, 1951). Though known in history as illiterate, Haidar Ali could effectively introduce the Mughal system in his general administration, revenue rules and public finance, and convert Mysore state from the position of a weak kingdom to that of a leading Indian regional power (Chandra, 2009).

After the death of Haidar Ali in the course of the Second Anglo-Mysore War of 1782, his son Tipu Sultan took over the reigns of the kingdom. One of the major reforms that Tipu introduced was to remove the intermediaries between the state and cultivators in collecting the land revenue. This is believed to have paved the way for the *ryotwari* system in South India. Tipu was also instrumental in restraining several illegal practices in the collection of land revenue, especially imposing on the farmers a cess in excess of the assessment without administrative authority. Unlike other contemporary rulers, he was liberal in granting remission of the land revenue whenever there was an agrarian distress. These practices are believed to have a lot to do with non-recurrence of famines and excess mortalities in Malabar when it was under Mysore state.

In the Third Anglo-Mysore War, Tipu Sultan had to broker peace with the EIC's Cornwallis. By the Treaty of Srirangapatam concluded on 19 March 1792, Tipu surrendered half of his territory, including Malabar to the EIC.[5] Initially, though Cornwallis placed Malabar with the presidency of Bombay later, in 1800, it was transferred to the Madras presidency. The EIC rulers, on taking over its administration, were surprised to see that, under Tipu Sultan, Malabar had become more prosperous than the presidency of Madras (Logan, 1887; Raychoudhary, 2009; Chandra, 2009). For the purpose of administrative convenience, the government divided Malabar into nine *talukas*,[6] each of which was further sub-divided into parishes or *amsams* and hamlets or *desams*. Subsequently, Malabar received the *taluk* of British Cochin consisting of 19 isolated bits of territories; two villages of Tangasseri; Anjengo of Travancore; and the Islands of Laccadives and Minicoy.

Topography

Geographically, the Malabar district proper was bounded on the northern side by South Canara; on the east by Coorg, Mysore, Nilgiris and

Coimbatore; on the south by the native state of Cochin; and on the west by the Arabian Sea.[7] The total area of Malabar was 5,583 sq. miles[8] with a sea-board from the north-north-west to south-south-east measuring about 150 miles, and an extreme breadth of just 80 miles. On the opposite side of Arabian Sea bordering the district situates the Western Ghats, otherwise known as *Sahyadri*. A large part of the region is filled with mountain-peaks. Between the Western Ghats and the Arabian Sea, there are extensive ravines, dense forests, tangled jungles, cultivable valleys and plains of paddy fields, rivers, backwaters and canals.

The climate of Malabar is hot and damp. At the beginning and closing of each season, the region was afflicted by water-borne or air-borne diseases of epidemic nature. The monsoons in Malabar are by and large regular. The south-west monsoon starts at the end of May and there will be copious rains between June and October. Then there is the north-east monsoon for a short period between October and December. Normally, Malabar witnessed the highest rainfalls as compared to other regions in the country. The recorded long-term mean annual rainfall in the nineteenth century was as low as 20 inches in Punjab, 27 inches in western India, 48-92 inches in eastern India, and between 33 to 52 inches in south India as a whole. Taking Malabar separately, the corresponding average was 104 inches (Roy, 2006). The relatively high rainfall could result in flash floods leading to epidemics and famine, affecting the entire population without class distinction. As we shall see below, the soil type in larger parts of Malabar is such that it can drain off rain-water in no time. The accompanying run-off of the top soil leads to poor crop yields. This apart, the high level of rainfall and the influx of salt-water destroy standing crops and pave the way for a food crisis.

Surface Soil

The surface soil in Malabar is mainly of two types:[9] (i) the laterite soil, and (ii) alluvial soil. The laterite soil is seen mostly in hilly areas. Though incapable of holding water, this type of soil is appropriate for low water consuming plantation crops like coconut, rubber, and arecanut as also for condiments and spices. In low lying areas, the laterite soil is suitable for paddy cultivation. Being less fertile, laterite soil does not give better yields. As the food production is low, the density of population in such areas would also be relatively low. The people living in these areas normally grow millets (mainly ragi, maize and jowar) and engage in animal husbandry for livelihood.

The alluvial soil in Malabar region is classified as 'non-coastal alluvial soil', and 'coastal alluvial soil'. The former is seen mainly on the river banks. This type of soil is capable of preserving the precipitation from rainfall better. It is also highly fertile. Even when the rainfall is scanty or somewhat delayed, the cultivation is not seriously disrupted in the 'non-coastal alluvial soil' because of its retained precipitation. The levels of yields of foodgrains in these tracks are normally high. The density of population also being relatively high, the possibility of producing surplus food over consumption in this type of soils is rather bleak. Even then, during periods of better rainfalls, bumper harvests that ensue would generate some surplus so that famines engulfing other areas in Malabar visit these tracts with a delay.

The 'coastal alluvial soil' is rather sandy, having very low water-holding capacity. Its nutrient status is also poor. The rain-water received on this type of soil is absorbed by the soil, or evaporated to the sky, or drained off into the sea. Whenever the rainfall becomes meagre, cultivation and availability of food from local harvests in the tracts of coastal alluvial soil could be seriously hampered. The production of food in such areas being relatively low, normally, the density of population would also be relatively low. The people living in these areas are generally poor. In times of severe scarcity of staple cereals, they used to live on tapioca, ragi, mango kernels and even wild plants.

Crops

Malabar was well-known for its commercial crops. The history of this region was marked by repeated struggles between the Portuguese, Dutch, French and English settlements for more than a century to capture the monopoly of trade in spices such as pepper, cinnamon, cloves, ginger and cardamom. Cotton piece-goods constituted another highly profitable product of the region for which there was inter-imperialist competition (Logan, 1887). The British EIC appeared shrewder among the other European settlers in this respect. Not only did it engage in the lucrative trade in spices but also in setting up of cotton textile mills in certain parts of Malabar and attracted traditional spinners and weavers to work in these mills. The weavers were happy to leave their customary enterprises and join the newly established factories as wages and working conditions in these establishments were more attractive. Apart from spices and cotton, the other commercial crops cultivated in Malabar included coffee, tea, sugarcane, tobacco and castor. Extensive coconut plantations, areca-nut, mango, cashew, jack, and palmyra trees formed a unique feature of Malabar. The hills were clad with a variety of extremely valuable trees like sandalwood and timber that created proliferating industries. Honey and bee-wax, the nutritious forest produces of Malabar, were highly in demand throughout Europe. The commercial crops and forest produces gave large incomes to their owners and attractive wages to the employees. These commercial crops also provided exchange entitlements to food for the population.

The region is well suited for the cultivation of highly water-consuming rice crop because of its fabulous monsoons. Coinciding with rainy seasons, as stated earlier, Malabar raised three crops in a year: (1) The *autumn crops* were cultivated in most parts of Malabar, except Kurumbranad, and certain areas of Kottayam, Chirakkal and Calicut. (2) The *winter crops* could not be cultivated in Wayanad, Kottayam, Chirakkal and Calicut. In other parts, these were taken up every season. (3) The *summer crops* constituted a very small portion of the three field crops and were cultivated in some pockets of Eranad and Valluvanad *taluka*s; the success or failure of summer crops had no noticeable impact on the food availability of the region. Other food crops cultivated in Malabar during almost all seasons were tapioca, ragi, small millets and horse-gram, which formed the staples of the relatively poor in all times and substitutes to rice for the richer people in times of scarcity and famines.[10]

Population

In olden times a village in Malabar (for that matter, any village in India) comprised a set of population-groups with specified occupations: priests performed worships in temples; calendar-Brahmins, or astrologers, predicted propitious periods for individuals, and for sowing and harvesting; smiths and carpenters made farm implements and built dwellings for ryots; cow-keepers looked after the cattle; potters, washer-men and barbers engaged in their specific services; dancing girls attended rejoicings; and there were also distinct professionals like poets, musicians and so on (Dutt, 1904). Their occupation-wise number was not however recorded until the census of 1871,[11] which, for the first time, brought out a trustworthy district-wise head-count population data. The next decennial census of 1881 enumerated detailed break-ups of population with average family-size and occupational categories. The total population of Malabar, estimated at 2.26 million in 1871, rose to 2.36 million in 1881, comprising 1.17 million males and 1.19 million females. The average family size in the district was 5.8, with the highest of 10.1 in Wayanad and the lowest of 5.3 in Kurumbranad. The children under six years of age constituted about 15 per cent and the elderly above sixty, 14.6 per cent of the total. Thus, around thirty per cent of the population in Malabar required feeding by the working age population even while there were no calamitous conditions like famines.

The agriculture-dependent population accounted for over 55 per cent of the total population in the district. Among them almost ten per cent were landholders with proprietary rights on land. In north Malabar, the average area under ownership-holding was comparatively small so that the proprietors themselves undertook cultivation without much hired labour.

As against this, in south Malabar, the land holdings were larger in size. The owners leased out their lands in parcels to tenant farmers. This category of farmers in Malabar worked out to more than two-fifths of the total agriculture-dependent population. Since 'land-hunger' was rather acute in the region, prevalence of rack-renting was very common. Compared to tenant farmers, agricultural labourers without any land were proportionately less, i.e. almost 38 per cent of the agriculture-dependent population.

Among the non-agricultural population in the district, the most noteworthy were those engaged in trading activities as well as in plantation and timber industries, cotton weaving, coir works and umbrella making. The traders dealt with food and drinks, fuel and forage. They advanced farm credits to the needy cultivators, mainly tenant-farmers for the purchase of inputs at the time of sowing. They also gave loans liberally to the cultivators for other needs like marriages of their daughters or traditional celebrations in the family. One of the common conditions for availing these loans was that they should surrender their crops immediately after the harvest, equivalent to the value of the credit plus interest thereon, estimated at the price prevailing during the peak arrivals of the crop. Since post-harvest prices at the peak arrival period would be the lowest of the seasonal price cycles, quite often, the produce harvested in a season might not be sufficient to repay the credit with interest in full. Still, the peasants had to again-and-again depend upon rural moneylenders for meeting their livelihood-charges and cultivation-expenses. They were thus continuously indebted to the moneylenders. In times of scarcities and famines, indebtedness exacerbated the crisis. Wherever the land and other belongings of the peasants were forfeited by the moneylenders against defaults, their conditions became more pathetic.

1.3 Susceptibility to Famines

Unhygienic surroundings and lack of public health facilities generated several epidemic diseases in Malabar, both water-borne and air-borne. These diseases generally disabled bread-winners of the households from going out for works. Unemployment reduced family income and purchasing power, so that invariably starvation and destitution ensued. When under-nutrition and starvation weakened the resistance capacity of the body, attacks of other fatally dangerous epidemics became easier. The result was a large number of unnatural deaths. Charities by philanthropists helped for a while but not always. Conventionally, famine is attributed to a steep decline in the availability of food, arising mainly from monsoon failures. However, studies have established that, whenever a monsoon fails, it need not necessarily end up in famine because people might fall back on 'carry-over stocks' from the preceding harvests, or there might be arrangements by official and private agencies to bring food from other surplus areas. The latter source could be impeded in case of underdeveloped transport system, or if the movement of grain was obstructed by wars or other local disturbances. Nonetheless, even if we assume that such bottlenecks did not exist, famine could be most likely if monsoon failures continued for two or three seasons at a stretch and disrupted the rural economy (Dreze, 1995).

It was Adam Smith who explained for the first time in his *Wealth of Nations* that there is a process through which famine spreads from the lowest class of poor landless labourers to other strata of population over time. According to Smith, when monsoons fail continuously, the area under cultivation goes on declining. Consequently, the demand for various types of employment in agriculture diminishes. Then, whatever employment is available would be snatched away by the 'superior classes' of influential labourers in rural countryside. "The lowest class being not only overstocked with its own workmen, but with the over-flowings of all other classes, the competition for employment would be so great in it, as to reduce the wages of labour to the most miserable and scanty subsistence of the labourer. Many would not be able to find employment even up on these hard terms, but would either starve, or be driven to seek a subsistence by begging, or by the perpetration perhaps of the greatest enormities. Want, famine, and mortality would immediately prevail in that class, and from thence extend themselves to all the superior classes" (Smith, 1776).

The process of famine that Adam Smith postulated has three facets: (i) the area under cultivation shrinks due to monsoon failures and results in the scarcity of food availability; (ii) large number of agricultural labourers who depend on farm works go out of employment and therefore lose their wherewithal to access food; and (iii) wages of those who manage to get employment come down owing to the rising competition in job markets and their food purchasing power takes a beat. This was further elaborated by Amartya Sen, according to whom, what Adam Smith kept in mind while explaining the process through which famine spreads was that, consequent on loss of employment and real wages, workers would plunge into famine due to the failure of their market-based entitlement. Sen further argued that, in this scenario, the famine is likely to aggravate as the 'collusive traders' engineer artificial scarcity in the market and push up prices. However, being a free market economist, Smith had ruled out such a possibility and it was David Ricardo who later elaborated and established this possibility (Sen, 1995).

Adam Smith also rejected the possibility of famines in the colonies established by England. His reason was that "the colony of a civilised nation advances more rapidly to wealth and greatness than any other human society." One source of this advancement, according to Smith, came from the export market that Great Britain opened up for the colonies. "In the disposal of their surplus produce.....the British colonies have been more favoured, and have been allowed a more extensive market, than those of any other European nation." And, back home, the workers in the colonies received "liberal wages" and became prosperous; their "children are well fed and are properly taken care of unlike in the Spanish or French colonies, or during the pre-colonial era." Referring to India, Smith was emphatic that England could not prosper from the activities in that colony as whatever it earned from there was spent either on local development, or for waging wars with local kings (Smith, 1776).

There are however several other studies, which contradict the claims made by Smith. We have already noted Murton's widely quoted figures from 1000 AD to 1947 AD that the number of famines and their intensities in terms of death-tolls had recorded a tremendous increase after the advent of the British Crown rule in India. This was essentially because, after 1858, the British Empire imposed strict rules of obligation on the colonial economy that did not allow the people at large to come out of poverty and pestilence. In terms of these obligations, the revenue collected from the colony was the 'wealth' of the empire that could be used as it liked. If it was used for the construction of railways or for the creation of irrigation networks, that was considered as investments of British capital and that India had to pay the money along with the interest thereon from its export earnings. On this fictitious argument, the sale proceeds of Indian goods exported to England were retained there towards 'home charges' arising from the payments of salaries and pensions to the Secretary of State for India and his staff.

Moreover, India had to provide free market for British manufactured goods, and serve as the source of agro-based industrial raw materials for the production of those goods. The British goods were also to be exempted from import duty on the insistence of the Lancashire lobby, which argued that free import to the colony was 'our right'. These obligations were strictly enforced so that, between 1858 and 1914, India consumed as high as 85 per cent of the cotton piece-goods produced in Lancashire, and the Indian railways absorbed almost 20 per cent of British iron and steel.

Apart from usurping the natural resources and market, the British administration took it as its right to deploy Indian citizens in the army and wage wars against local kings as well as against Burma, China, Afghanistan or other far-flung areas. The people in the colony had to also shoulder the expenses on such wars. As agriculture was the main economic activity of the period, though technologically backward, it was land revenue that became the main source of fund for these expenses. In short, the deindustrialisation stimulated by Lancashire and the agrarian distress inflicted by the imperialist land revenue policy generated poverty and hunger in the colony and, during harvest failures, pushed the people into calamitous famines in different parts of the country (Srivastava, 1968; Bandyopadhyay, 2004).

Thus, there were two schools of thought on famines in India under the British imperialism. One claimed that, being a more 'civilised nation' than other European colonialists, the Great Britain reinvested whatever revenue was collected from India for developmental works like construction of railways, irrigation networks etc., employed the local people on these works, paid liberal wages, and opened up Britain's import-market for their products on favourable terms. Consequently, there was no possibility of famines during the British rule in India. The second school of thought argued that, as the British administration had allowed 'free market' in foodgrains without any control, 'collusive traders' had a field day to indulge in speculative practices and escalate prices beyond the purchasing power of the common people. This was one major reason why, according to this view, famines recurred more frequently during the Crown rule in India than during the pre-British era. These opposing claims call for an investigation into the types of investments made by the British administration in economic and human development sectors, and their impact on famine-prevention; or if they could not prevent or mitigate famine, the reasons thereof.

1.4 Public Investments and Famine Prevention Policy

The Indian Famine Commission 1880, the first official body that British administration set up in the backdrop of one of the worst famines that shook the country during 1876-78 had stated that famine was a calamity beyond the control of single individuals. Being a collective human misery, only the state could prevent it. The Commission further stressed that the basic strategy of famine-prevention should be provision of subsistence wages to the needy through investments for the creation of permanent public assets like roads and irrigation-canals.[12] This strategy had in fact existed even before the Famine Commission submitted its report. The Commission also recommended that the government should promulgate a Famine Code and extend famine-relief to the affected people with uniform principles applicable for all provinces. In what follows we will briefly survey some of the long term measures initiated by the imperialist government and to what extent these were effective in famine prevention.

Irrigation

When the EIC enlarged its activities from commerce to administration, it was aware of the ecological constraints obstructing the food availability and causing repeated famines in the colony. A solution that it felt feasible was to construct irrigation net-works. In its view, these would on the one hand reduce the susceptibility of the people to attacks of famines and famine-related epidemics, and on the other hand raise the revenue collection for the government. It had only one worry: what might be the extent of revenue outgo vis-à-vis the anticipated revenue collection, if public funds were used for investment in irrigation? This worry seemed to have continued for years. For instance, one of the terms of reference given by the government to the second Famine Commission of 1901 envisaged to identify the scope for extension of irrigation projects with "state assistance", and "the utility of irrigation under local conditions of agriculture whether in generally increasing the produce of the land or in securing from the effects of failure of rainfall." In considering the proposal for new irrigation projects, the government asked the Commission to recommend: (a) whether these would be likely to prove financially profitable; and (b) whether the future net-burden that these might impose on the state by way of charges for interest and for repair, maintenance and other recurring expenses would be "too high a price to pay for the protection against famine" (see Ray, 1909).

The Commission conducted a study and found that "a wide but not an unlimited extension of irrigation works" in crucial agricultural tracts would entail an aggregate cost of Rs 44 crore at current prices so that it should be spread over a number of years. With respect to "the question of profitability versus protective value of irrigation expenditure", the Commission stated that the state would be relieved by: (i) a reduction in the future cost of famine-relief resulting from the increased food output that investments in irrigation could bring about; and (ii) contributing its share to increase the wealth of the community and would indirectly accrue to the state. For these beneficial effects to be reaped in full, the Commission recommended that the state should also extend liberal loans to farmers "at a universal rate of 5 per cent for private irrigational improvements such as the construction of wells, water-course etc" (Ray, 1909).

When the EIC decided to undertake construction of irrigation projects, it found that the extensive irrigation net-works created centuries ago, such as the grand 'anicuts', or low barrages on river beds, constructed during the period of Cholas in south India and the irrigation channels developed by Mughal emperors in north India – were lying dysfunctional. As an expenditure reduction strategy, the EIC thought it fit to repair and restore these irrigation structures before taking up construction of new ones. For the achievement of quicker results, the repair works were entrusted with the engineering department of its army. Later, in 1854, Dalhousie set up a new Public Works Department for the purpose of both renovation of the old canal irrigation systems and the creation of new large-scale irrigation works (Roy, 2006).

With the establishment of the Public Works Department and particularly after the promulgation of the Government of India Act in 1858 that replaced the EIC by the Crown rule, the British administration in India took up irrigation as one of its developmental priorities. While drawing up plans and undertaking feasibility studies of irrigation works, the administration classified the projects as: (a) 'protective' irrigation works purely for famine-relief; and (b) 'productive' irrigation works primarily to increase per hectare agricultural yields. In the British view, while protective irrigation facilities would save public funds from frittering away on famine relief, productive irrigation net-works would help to generate commercially profitable export-surpluses and bring in additional revenue for the government. At the level of implementation, however, these distinctions were hardly in evidence. What is significant to note here is that the irrigation policy of the British government in India had led to an appreciable increase in the area under irrigation. The irrigated area as a proportion of the total area under cultivation in British India was estimated to have increased from as low as 5-6 per cent in the early nineteenth century to 22 per cent in the beginning of the 1940s. Out of the total, about 60 per cent was contributed by government canals (Roy, 2006). These public canal-irrigation works were concentrated mainly in Punjab, western Uttar Pradesh and Madras which in due course became the granaries of India.

The views about the British government's emphasis on canal irrigation and its impact on famine relief or the level of living of the cultivating classes were not uniform. One view was that at the close of the nineteenth century, the area under canal irrigation as a ratio of total cropped area was not noticeably different in Madras and Punjab. Yet the people of Madras presidency suffered far more grievous famines than the people of Punjab. It is argued that canals could not prevent water scarcity during dry months because of their dependence on rainfall for sustenance. In other words, canal irrigation and water supply from rainfall being positively correlated, the former's ability to produce enough food and prevent famine is closely dependent on normal rainfalls (Roy, 2006).

Elizabeth Whitcombe who conducted research on the Ganga-Jamuna Doab (western Uttar Pradesh and Haryana) expressed considerable doubts on the efficacy of British irrigation system on cultivation. Because of defective engineering, these canals tended to block natural drainage routes. The resultant water logging allowed mosquito breeding and increased the incidents of epidemics like malaria around the irrigation tracts. It also led to saline deposits, which affected the fertility of large areas of land around the canals. Furthermore, the benefits went to a minority of rich farmers who could afford to pay the excessively high rates charged for the use of water from these canals. Along with the development of artificial irrigation, the government encouraged cultivation of commercial crops like cotton and sugarcane, at the expense of millets and pulses comprising normally the staples of the poor (Whitcombe 1983). Supporting this view, Sarkar (1983) argued that the canal irrigation system devised by the British rulers in India was less favourable than traditional *kaccha* wells to local conditions of cultivation.

In a more detailed study on canal irrigation, Ian Stone asserted that, compared with the existing conventional irrigation methods, exploitation of irrigation potential through major and minor projects, as also creation of facilities for intensive use of ground-water resources, is an alternative to the deteriorating precipitation in soil. Stone found these projects offering several direct and indirect benefits, the most important among them being their efficiency to substantially reduce harvest fluctuations and improve the productivity of land. Another positive effect that he witnessed around the irrigation tracts was their ability to convert settlement patterns. Before the introduction of canal irrigation, these places were largely barren and mostly uninhabited. With irrigation projects in place, several colonies came up around the vicinities not only of the cultivating classes but also of a large number of ex-servicemen. Over time, along with crop farming, other economic activities like livestock rearing and small-scale rural industrialisation, mainly sugarcane crushing, made a beginning around the northern canal irrigation tracts, though on limited scales (Stone 1984).

What Ian Stone or even the critics of British irrigation failed to notice is the negative effect of an otherwise well thought out policy for irrigation development. For instance, at the project preparation stage itself, the British administration had decided to exclude the areas blessed with proper 'seasonableness' and better rainfall, and gave preference to those agricultural regions which were susceptible to droughts. While nobody could find fault with such a policy, Malabar became its victim. Throughout the imperialist rule, the district never received any irrigation project. From the figures noted in the Malabar District Gazette, it could be observed that, as at 1930, out of more than 9.25 million acres of land irrigated in the Madras presidency, not a single acre belonged to Malabar district Thus, the British administration kept Malabar outside 'flood and drought proofing' facilities, which are essential to safeguard crop failures that result in food scarcities and famines.

Railways

Before the mid-nineteenth century, the main modes of transportation in the colony were pack animals and small sailing vessels. These were not very effective in carrying food from surplus centres to famine afflicted areas because of the enormous transport costs. During the second half of the nineteenth century the business communities in London, Liverpool, Calcutta, Bombay and Madras lobbied vigorously for extension of the generally port-centred railways into other interior regions of British India. That marked the beginning of the expansion of Indian railways. By 1875 most of the cities and ports were connected with agricultural production centres by the newly created railway lines.

The construction of railway lines in Madras presidency started in 1853 and in Malabar district, as late as 1861, when the first railway track was operationalised between Beypore and Tirur. In 1888, it was extended to Calicut. In the same year the Palghat branch of railways was opened and the Beypore line relinquished. Then the British administration decided to construct six more railway lines aggregating 186 miles. Contrary to its earlier stand, the government declared that Malabar was famine-prone and earmarked 'famine insurance fund' in the annual budget. Announcing the six newly proposed railway tracts as 'famine lines', it diverted the entire 'famine insurance funds' for the construction of these tracts.[13] While doing so, the administration assured that, once the railway lines were completed, famine would automatically disappear, as these lines helped to carry food from surplus producing regions to Malabar at the earliest symptom of shortages.

This was widely welcomed as construction of railways was then generally perceived as the best long-term guarantee against food scarcity and famine. Even the report of the 1880 Famine Commission had stressed the need for creating large-scale railway network on the justification that the greatest mortality due to famine was witnessed in those tracts where transport facilities were underdeveloped. Apart from putting an end to famines, according to the Commission, it would catalyse internal and external trade so that whatever they produced could bring in better returns and vastly improve the economic conditions of the people. Strengthened by these recommendations, the British rulers extended railway lines to all possible areas in the country not only by diverting famine insurance fund but also by raising taxes and throwing attractive terms to private parties who were ready to take up construction of approved tracts (Gadgil, 1924; Stein, 2001).

The development of railways in India had passed through four stages during the British period: The first stage comprised the period between 1845 and 1869, when private enterprises were involved in its construction and management. These enterprises were given liberal interest-free loans as operational capital from the revenue (mainly land revenue) collected within the country. They were also assured a minimum guarantee of 5 per cent return on the operation of railways they constructed. The second stage covered 1870 to 1880 when the government took over the ownership and management of railways on payment of compensation to the private enterprises. The third stage encompassed the years from 1881 to 1924 when the management of railways was given back to the private operators, keeping the ownership with the government. In the fourth stage that started from 1924, both the ownership and control were brought under the direct control of the government. By that time, Indian railways had become one of the world's largest transport services, which expanded from 838 route-miles in 1860 to 41,852 route-miles in 1940 (Roy, 2006).

In the initial stage, the railways were not designed on the basis of any cost-benefit analysis. The immediate objective of railway construction was not to earn a profit over investment. Its stated purpose was to act as an institutional safeguard against frequent famines that devastated regions after regions in the colony. Considering the quickness with which railway lines were constructed, drawing funds from all budgetary heads in addition to specific funds allocated for railway development, the declared objective of transport networking as prevention of famine could not have been doubted. However, to what extent that objective was materialised remained unclear (Gadgil, 1924).

When the railways were restructured to expand from a port-centred system to an intra-Indian transport service, the expectation was that it would effectively play the role of an institutional apparatus for equitable distribution of grain at the least possible cost from food surplus regions to food deficit and starvation-stricken areas at the shortest possible time. Instead of fulfilling this role, the Indian railways served as handmaids of large grain merchants to carry away stocks from food-scarce areas to distant centres on the alibi that otherwise the food-rioters would attack and defraud them. The real reason however was to use the scarcity condition to indulge in profiteering through speculative activities in connivance with the officials. There was an undeclared additional purpose behind this. If the traders increased their revenue, the administration could get an increase in their tax revenue. They could also get from these traders their subscriptions for the 'war bonds' issued by the British administration to meet the additional expenses needed to wage wars with local rulers or with neighbouring countries. That is why some authors argued that the Indian railways were constructed not to prevent famines as officially declared but with the logic of imperial benefit (Davis, 2001; Stein, 2001).

By the time the Indian railways were being expanded, two other developments took place elsewhere, complementing the acceleration process of free-trade across the world: (a) opening up of the Suez Canal in 1869 that reduced the navigable distance between India and Europe, and cut down transportation costs substantially; and (b) possession of a large number of steamships by the British empire which enabled it to undertake bulk-transport from England to its colonies and back. It was during this period that India witnessed some of the most disastrous famines. The British government could have imported foodgrains from other parts of the world and fed the needy at affordably lower prices in India at least during famines, as imported foodgrains were cheaper than the grain available in domestic markets. This could have two desirable results: (i) as soon as domestic prices stabilised at pre-famine levels, government could stop imports; and (ii) its free market policy remained intact while mitigating the sufferings of the people and thereby earning their goodwill. However, even during famines, government encouraged exports of foodgrains from India to augment and stabilise food prices in England (Gadgil, 1924).

Side by side with the expansion of the railway-network, metalled roads were constructed to take advantage of the surface transport. Thus roads and railways started expanding almost at the same pace. One beneficial effect of the roads was that it increased the importance of weekly markets. The village artisans who made handicraft items were not required to wait for merchants to approach them for disposing of these items; instead, they could take their products to these markets and sell at ready cash. This benefit was however more than displaced by another development. The expansion of transportation system raised and levelled the prices of essential items of consumption, especially food, everywhere. During famine times, equalisation of food prices at very high levels made the plight of the people worse (Gadgil, 1924).

The railway-network, complemented by road transport allowed Great Britain to enforce larger and larger penetration of its industrial products, mainly the high quality Lancashire cotton piece-goods, deep into interior Indian markets. These goods being price-wise cheaper and quality-wise superior, they could easily compete out the traditional cotton textile industry in the country (Bagchi, 1972). Continued decline in demand compelled the domestic industries to close down. In the absence of alternate employment, those who lost their jobs in these industries migrated along with their families to neighbouring villages. Being already stagnated, these villages could not bear the rising burden of the population in the provision of employment or food. Poverty, malnutrition, epidemics, and famine became part of the village life.

To make matters worse, commercialisation of agriculture promoted by the British administration reduced the area under food crops and therefore the overall production of foodgrains. With the development of railways, this process became faster. The factors that supported this process *inter alia* included: (i) Industrial Revolution in England that stimulated demand for agro-based industrial raw materials and superior foodgrains like wheat; and (ii) an increase in world prices and external demand for Indian raw-cotton and other commercial crops because of the abrupt stoppage of these commodities from the U.S. after the outbreak in 1861 of the American Civil War. With the new found demand, farmers in India were encouraged to shift cultivation from food crops to the high-value commercial crops in several parts of the country. The railways acted as a catalyst in this process. As far as Malabar was concerned, the shift in the areas under food crops to spices, which were highly in demand in Europe and Arabian countries, had started long before this development but the newly emerging demand gave further boost to their production. This process however received a massive blow when the American Civil War was over and the U.S. agricultural exports resumed as earlier. Its immediate impact was: (a) plummeting of international prices of exportable agricultural produces; and (b) a sharp decline in the foreign demand for India's short-staple raw cotton. The rural life once again slumped into the old miserable condition as (i) the lands put under cotton cultivation could not be converted for production of foodgrains, since the texture of the soil had undergone a change in favour of the cultivation of cotton. It is believed that shifting back the texture of soil from the cultivation of a commercial crop to food crop would, if possible, take longer time and heavier costs (Gadgil, 1924; Roy, 2006).

Health Care

Famines generally coincided with epidemics and unnatural mortalities. British Malabar was particularly vulnerable to various contagious diseases, like cholera, malaria, plague, smallpox, typhoid, tuberculosis, dysentery and diarrhoea because of its nearness to the sea, heavy rains, humid weather persisting most of the year, contaminated drinking water, and lack of sanitation. In times of famines, these diseases flared up and took away large number of lives. Available historical records would show that the government was least responsive in providing health-care facilities to the people. Though Malabar contributed to the treasury by way of land revenue, taxes and cesses more than what was needed to maintain basic necessities in the district (after meeting its administrative expenses), the government was reluctant to spend on such basic needs of the people. At times it imposed the responsibility of keeping the municipal roads and sewerages, the epicentres of epidemic diseases, on the lower level employees in the district. Without allocation of funds, and in the face of their own normal workloads, the employees failed to do the job.

The night-soil lying all over the land-surface without suitable arrangements for its disposal acted as a perennial source of various contagious diseases in Malabar. The local administration refused to appoint sufficient number of carts and scavengers to remove the filth to the incinerators, which were also extremely insufficient. In Calicut, lack of space was cited as a reason for not creating sufficient number of incinerators. The municipal authorities declared that if the local households could deposit the payments for private scavengers, arrangements could be made to remove night-soil from their residences. Archival records would show that, attracted by these assurances, several middle-class households deposited the requisite amount to the municipality. Nonetheless, even after more than five years, no scavenger visited their homes.

The diseases created by these surroundings became worse in the absence of hospitals to admit and treat the infected patients. The government's response to deal with these diseases were: (i) getting the people vaccinated by unqualified municipal sweepers and peons who were not to be paid any extra remuneration; and (ii) keeping infected persons away from their families and neighbourhood without any arrangement for medicine, food or drinking water. As regards setting up of general or contagious disease hospitals, the government stated that: (a) the size of the population requiring such treatments were too large and the resources at its disposal too meagre to meet the health care needs; (b) the people were generally antagonistic to western medicine and refused to accept it in the treatment of ailments; and (c) local people were averse to using the facilities available in civilian hospitals maintained by government. However, the actual fact was that these hospitals and dispensaries were not only too meagre to meet the existing requirements but also always filled with beggars who came not only for medicines but also for the food being freely supplied to patients. Moreover, since police used to bring street prostitutes apprehended for immoral activities in public places, women from conservative families thought it below their dignity to visit these hospitals. Citing this as a negative attitude, the government argued that there was no point in wasting the scarce public funds on building more and more civilian health care centres.

Famine Code

The famine relief measures adopted in British India before and after the report of the Famine Commission 1880 had differed at least in one respect. Before 1880, there was no well-defined famine relief policy. Whatever the EIC did was *ad hoc* in nature, just to meet the immediate needs arising from a famine. The whims of the Governor-General, who was in charge of the colony at that time, had much to do with the relief operation. The guiding principle of famine relief was that, while it should preserve the life of the affected people, the money spent on the task should not be exorbitant. While poor-homes were permitted to be opened for feeding the economically down-trodden sections, there was no uniformity in the rules governing the gratuitous supply of food. In Bengal, whoever came to the poor-home begging for food was accommodated and the relief was granted partly in cooked-meal and partly in cash. In the presidency of Madras, on the other hand, gratuitous famine-relief was extended only to selected people who were packed in an enclosure and given tickets as a mark of identification. They were served only cooked-meal – *rice* on Sundays and sorghum (*cholam*) or *ragi* on other days. Initially food was distributed once in a day and later increased to two meals per day. The presidency was very particular that this did not unduly increase public fund. In order to abide by this instruction, while continuing with this humanitarian service, the district level officials persuaded landlords and other wealthy persons in the locality to come forward and offer charitable food to the affected people (Srivastava, 1968).

The situation changed after the Richard Strachey headed Famine Commission submitted its report in 1880. As we noted earlier, the report was prepared in the backdrop of a disastrous famine of 1876-78. The Commission squarely imposed the responsibility to deal with famines on the government of the day when it stated that "there can be no doubt that a calamity such as famine, exceptional in its nature and arising from causes wholly beyond human control, which deprives an entire population of its customary food supply, and arrests the ordinary employments of the wage-earning classes, is one which in a country such as India wholly transcends individual effort and power of resistance. It accordingly becomes a paramount duty of the State to give all practicable assistance to the people in time of famine, and to devote all its available resources to this end." The report also warned that since the relief measures to be implemented being "complicated and multifarious….they cannot be left to individual energy and resources." What action should be taken in the event of a calamity like famine should be decided well in advance. In this context, the Commission recommended that "the Government of India should, as soon as possible, issue a set of rules embodying the main principles that should govern the administration of famine relief and that these rules should be authoritative in all parts of British India."

The Commission prepared a model Draft Famine Code (DFC) containing a set of rules for famine relief activities and circulated among the local administrations for comments. But it could not pursue the matter as, in the meanwhile, the government wound up the Commission. The DFC was therefore revised by the British administration, taking into account the opinions of the ground level officials, and issued an eleven-chapter Provisional Famine Code in June 13 to the presidencies, directing them to prepare their own famine codes without, however, deviating from the basic principles laid down in the model code.

The Code rules prepared by the Madras presidency, based on the model code circulated by the central government, entrusted the district collector with the responsibility for 'standing preparation' of a comprehensive plan of action before hand and implement it as and when called for, after taking permission from the Board of Revenue. The code rules provided that the district collector, with the help of his lower formations should develop a 'system of intelligence' on a continuing basis and initiate prompt action at the first sight of famine. The preparation of the intelligence system was to be an ongoing process, according to which: (a) the Village Accountant would maintain registers of cultivation, harvests, rainfall, water supplies, condition of the people and cattle, as well as the works needed in the village that could act as an instrument of famine prevention, (b) Village Headman would maintain a register of births and deaths, epidemics to human and cattle population, and submit daily reports to the Tahsildar, who would in turn forward these reports to the collector, (c) the Revenue Inspector to oversee the works of the Village Accountants and Village Headmen and prepare monthly reports for the district collector, and (d) the collector, working with his lower level officials, submit a comprehen-sive monthly report to the Board of Revenue, covering *inter alia* market prices of foodgrains and non-foodgrains, climate and monsoon, water supply, conditions of the standing crops, availability of pasture and fodder, epidemics and mortalities of both people and cattle.[14]

The other duty assigned to the district collector included watching the market price movements of foodgrains from 'normal rate' to 'warning rate' and to 'scarcity rate'. By the time prices reached the 'scarcity rate', he should immediately inform the Board of Revenue that a famine was imminent in the district. While doing so, he was to also see: (i) the trend in the number of wandering paupers, (ii) the extent of 'feverishness' in the activities of grain markets, (iii) restlessness in the society as indicated by an increase in petty thefts and other crimes, (iv) movement of herds in search of pastures, and (v) unusual migration of people.

If, in the judgement of the district collector, a famine was imminent, he could take up the relief works already prepared in the order of priorities, that is, "the complete programme of sanctioned works of utility" first and then, if needed, "the subsidiary emergency programme of unsanctioned works." The Famine Code of Madras stipulated that, "the programme shall provide employment as nearly as possible for 20 per cent of the population for six months for all districts." While clarifying the provision further, it stated that this instruction was not applicable to Malabar.[15] The British rulers and experts on famine were of the view that, being a high rainfall area, Malabar was not susceptible to famine. Nevertheless, the history of the district, as revealed by the administration reports available in the archival reports, is full of tragic tales of repeated hunger and famines. As we shall see in the following, these human miseries had led to the worst form of social disintegration and social upheavals that any disastrous famines anywhere in the world had created.

1.5 Social Stresses

Whenever famine breaks out its most visible repercussion appears in the form of social disorganisation, family disintegration and all-round anarchy. In several families, at the initial signs of famine, the bread-winners migrate to other regions unaffected by drought or flood in search of food for the family and forage for cattle. They may also migrate to other countries, which are expected to provide ample opportunities for livelihood and, in most cases, to become their permanent residence. Another common practice noticed during famines in economically poorer regions, like Malabar, was the sale of children. This was not necessarily for money, though several observers have taken such a view. Bread-winners who were unable to feed all the members in the family wanted at least their children survived in the hands of those who could give them food. A third ramification of famine was that individuals, who were not until then known to have indulged in any unlawful activities, entered into petty thefts and other crimes in the hope that, if the law enforcement authorities picked them up and put in jail, they could get their food despite other adverse consequences of incarceration. Let us briefly consider these developments emanating from famine.

Sale of Children

Burton Stein in his *A History of India* had stated that, if the most significant social reform that the British rule introduced in India was the abolition of 'sati' and child marriage, the most disgusting human degradation that it deliberately permitted to intensify was slavery. When the Parliament of England decided to amend the British Emancipation Act, 1833 and extend its provisions to the British colonies so as to stop this dehumanising practice, India was kept outside its purview. This was a deliberate decision to perpetuate slavery for the benefit of the elitist sections in British India, including the European planters and officials from England employed here. Slavery originated from trafficking. It was a general sight in the poverty-ridden regions in India where indigent parents sold their children, and earning men, their wives and sisters. They also sold themselves for food and discarded the aged parents. This practice was on the rise in times of famine and the most heart-rending part of it was the sale of children (Stein, 2001).

The report of the Select Committee on the Affairs of the East India Company (1832) had given a detailed account of the sale of children, human trafficking and slavery in India.[16] It is stated in the report that these practices were widely prevalent in all parts of Madras presidency. As the West Coast provided the easiest facility for trafficking, the sale of children flourished in Malabar more than any other parts of the presidency. Such sales were reported predominantly from several parts of the district like Pazhayangadi, Balliapattam, Cannanore, Tellicherry, Quilandi, Calicut, Condotti, Parappanangadi, and Ponnani.[17] "The children so sold out were brought up", according to Stein (2001), "by buyers to be used as agricultural labourers, domestic servants, seamstresses, musicians, dancers, weavers, dyers, scribes, business agents, carpenters, ironmongers, brick-layers and above all as body servants and menials." British civil servants in India bought them as domestic servants and the European plantation owners, to work in their estates without payment of wages. There were cases where boys purchased from poor parents were castrated and transported inside and outside the country to be used as harem keepers. Most of these children died in transit.

In Malabar, sale of children continued among poorer sections even when there was no famine. Three such cases were mentioned in the 1832 Select Committee report referred above: (i) women who became widows, having no source of income or means of livelihood, sold their children to procure some food; (ii) females engaged in prostitution sold their children, either as their share of income from the profession was insufficient to bring up the children or because the limited space in which they lived obstructed their profession in the presence of children; the female children among them were bought by brothel-keepers who gave training to be dancing girls and, then, forced into prostitution; and (iii) there was a practice among indigent parents to hire out their children during famine against a small sum of money for a considerable period of 70 to 80 years; under this pretext, the buyers kept them and their progenies as slaves forever.

Some of the analysts felt that had the British administration in India practised at least what it proclaimed, famine could have been prevented and this obnoxious and dehumanising practice banished from the colony. The very fact that parents sold their children for a paltry sum of money to the extent of one observer stating that if children in Malabar were the cheapest, it was a proof to the fact that the underlying purpose of selling children were not to make money but to see that their lives were saved from starvation and death. "During a famine or a dearth parents have been known to sell their children for prices so very inconsiderable, and so little more than nominal, that they may in frequent instances have credit for a better motive than that of monetarily relieving their own necessities, namely, the saving of their children's lives by interesting in their preservation persons able to provide nourishment for them. The same feeling is often the motive for selling children when particular circumstances of distress, instead of a dearth, disable the parents from supporting them" (Adam, 1840: 139)

The district collectors of Malabar used to look after orphaned or deserted children during famines as per the directive of the presidency headquarters. Once the distress came to an end, the general practice was to make a search for the parents of the children, who could pronounce their parents' names or the name of their residence. Otherwise, the Collector handed over the children to orphanages established by the Missionary Societies or to those who approached for adoption. According to the Famine Commission 1880, "there were so many cases of such children being brought up to a life of prostitution or of semi-domestic slavery." The Commission warned that "an officer would not be justified in making over a child, especially a female child, without inquiry, to *any* applicant" (emphasis added).[18]

Migration

Mass migration was a key-feature of every famine everywhere in the world (O'Grada, 2010). Hundreds of starving men, women and children of all ages emigrated from famine-infested regions to safer places in other parts of the country or abroad and escaped from imminent death. In many cases, the people who migrated never returned. They continued to live in the new place of migration as indentured labour in agriculture and plantation estates. The impact of such irreversible migration was that, houses of the areas from where they left during famine looked empty even after the famine was over (Gadgil, 1924). In Madras presidency and western India, one of the earliest famine-migration was recorded during 1876-78. All bread-earning male members, while leaving their houses, could not take their dependents with them as they were not sure about getting some food on the way, or on reaching their destination. It was in such cases that sale of children, wife and sisters as well as discarding of the elders happened. Speaking about the disastrous famine of 1876-78, Gadgil (1924) stated that the imperialist rulers in India were patently indifferent about such problems and the people were totally unprepared to face that calamity. Food stocks were mostly depleted by exports to Europe. The droughts in many parts of the country that preceded the famine led to complete lack of fodder. Large streams of people steadily migrated to Western Ghats, which had no dearth of fodder and forest produce that could be used as 'famine food' by the migrants.

According to the Famine Commission of 1880 (which was set up in the backdrop of the 1876-78 famine), unlike from other areas in the Madras presidency, the mass migration from Malabar was not significantly large. The people in general regarded it as an honour to stick closest to their homes. While male members of the families in Malabar used to migrate freely, their women rarely went out with them. Among the adult males who left their homes, the Famine Commission stated, only a small section went to other places within the country. Most of them had migrated abroad, mainly to the British colonies in Asia and Africa. The Commission however does not indicate the countries to which they migrated. Unfortunately, we could not lay hands on any useful study on the history of migration *from* Malabar though there are empirically sound works on migration *to* Malabar. The very fact that Malayalees, including from Malabar, had been living in different parts of the world, participating even in politics to reach on the top of the government in some of those countries, we can only assume how migration from Malabar might have taken place. For instance, it was known that during periods of farm distress when the *janmi*s (landlords) who could not pay land revenue in time were threatened by the administrators of Tipu Sultan and by the British rulers in Malabar that, in case of defaulting in the payment of dues, they would be put in jail before auctioning their properties to recoup the defaulted amounts. In order to escape from the ignominy of such extreme steps by the rulers, these landlords had run away from Malabar to Trivandrum and, from there, ferried into other countries. This might be one reason why dependable official data on emigration *from* Malabar were not available.

Furthermore, the British administration in India had debarred the unskilled youth from Malabar to leave their premises without permission and conscripted them into the army whenever it engaged in wars with local kings or with the neighbouring countries. Thus, in 1883, it passed a comprehensive Emigration of Natives of India Act laying down conditions under which the people from the colony could migrate to other countries. This Act was amended from time to time for invoking the Defence of India Rules to prohibit unskilled youth from leaving the country. Archival records show that such prohibitive orders were issued in 1915 and 1917 for conscription and once at the beginning of the Second World War. These orders were withdrawn only in October 1944. From this, it has to be presumed that most of the immigrations from Malabar during the British period had taken place illegally.[19]

Petty Crimes

The famine crimes are a class apart. A large number of petty-to-not-so-petty crimes take place during food scarcity. These are not committed by 'criminals' in the ordinary sense of the term. These are committed by hungry people who find it difficult to get food except by stealing. Even police records treated these crimes in the category of 'cognisable offences', i.e. 'ordinary theft cases'. As these were not generally of very serious nature, the law enforcement authorities apprehended them, gave a warning and let them off. Some of them did it with the hope that, in case the police arrested and put them in jail, they could get their food there. Such people, as and when they were released from jail, repeated the same offence and went back to jail. This happens in all poverty stricken societies, not necessarily during famines alone though in times of famine the number of such 'crimes' goes up. The very fact that this category of offenders, when apprehended, were found to be extremely feeble and suffering from some epidemic disease, it has to be presumed that these offences were not committed out of criminal intentions.

The annual administration reports of Madras presidency used to give a chapter on 'law and order'. The following are some of the points that various administration reports had been giving about 'cognisable offences' or 'ordinary theft cases'. During food distresses, petty thefts were being committed by both males and females of all ages, viz., adolescents, teenagers, adults and even the elderly. The type of offences that they indulged in included ordinary thefts like lifting of cattle, coconuts or bags of rice and, in exceptional cases, dacoity, robbery, house-breaking, and so on. These 'cognisable offences' had a positive correlation with the prices of staple cereals. When the prices of rice went up, these theft cases also recorded an increase. With a decline in prices and an increase in employment and income, such cases came down of their own.

Another significant point recorded in these reports was that, among all districts in the presidency, Malabar recorded the largest number of cognisable offences during famine times. It was also reported that, apart from thefts, the people of Malabar were in the forefront for protesting against the want on indifference of the imperialist government in controlling speculation and hoarding of foodgrains. The nature of protest was mostly in the form of 'food-riots'. The main characteristic of 'food-riot' was organised smuggling of rice from the stocks piled up by shop-keepers for speculation, presumably with the implicit approval of officials. In case the police applied force to keep the rioters away, there were reports of their becoming violent and even using country-made bombs on the police.

1.6 The Issues

By consolidating the points somewhat haphazardly spread out in the foregoing, it is now possible to identify the issues relevant for a detailed analysis. Traditionally, famines were attributed to irregular and uneven rainfalls leading to pervasive droughts, or floods hampering cultivation and culminating into severe food availability crises. Large tracts of agricultural lands in India (like Malabar in the southern presidency under the British rule) being left out of artificial irrigation facilities, farmers had to depend exclusively on rainfall for agricultural operations. If the principal south-west monsoon between June and September failed, there would be a major shortage in kharif crops, which provided the predominant portion of cereals, pulses and edible oils for the people not only in Malabar but also in larger parts of the country. If the next south-east monsoon between October and December also failed, there could be acute food crisis so that famine became inevitable, especially in food deficit areas like Malabar. Of late, though doubt has been cast on the food availability decline or FAD as a sufficient cause of famine, there are historical studies, which have established that every major Indian famine during the imperialist period had preceded one or two monsoon failures. According to these studies, if adverse climatic conditions coincided with human factors like wars, local disturbances, movement restrictions, and speculative practices by private traders, famine and excessive unnatural mortalities became exceptionally acute (see Srivastava 1968).

Second, the flawed systems of land tenure and revenue assessment introduced by the British administration led to forfeiture of the ownership in land of actual cultivators and their herding into the flocks of agricultural labourers. The exorbitant land revenue demands, widespread corruption in revenue settlements, and coercive methods adopted for revenue collection impoverished the rural population and weakened the institutions of village communities, which had, for ages, provided social insurance to the people in times of food crises. Several observers had placed the responsibility for frequent famines in British India on the thoughtless land revenue policy of the colonial administration. If their arguments are tenable, the causes of frequent famines in British Malabar could not be otherwise.

Third, flaring up of food prices, a constant tendency witnessed during the British imperialist period, made access to food beyond the purchasing power of the local people. The condition became worse when large-scale commercialisation of agriculture increasingly shifted the areas under food crops to export-oriented cash crops and reduced the availability of foodgrains, especially minor cereals like jowar, bajra, maize and ragi, which the poor people consumed during normal times and the richer segments during the availability crisis of major foodgrains. Along with this, the destruction of indigenous industries in India due to imports of low-priced, high quality substitutes from Britain led to exodus of workers from urban centres to rural countryside. The resultant increase in the reserve army of unemployed workers in the already stagnated agriculture sector had further depressed the level of rural wages on the one hand and in the per head food availability on the other. The combined effect of all these factors pushed the colonial population to the brink of starvation, which in times of crop failures steeped into famines.

Fourth, famines often lead to widespread panic among the affected population. Faced by helplessness, there were rampant sale of children, wives, sisters and discarding of old-aged parents. Food riots became common, primarily to air their anger against the insensitivity of the state and not to really snatch the food-stocks from traders. Many of them, mainly young, who failed to get some food, committed petty thefts in their neighbourhood, not because they wanted to defraud its owners but to get them imprisoned so that they could get food from the jail, albeit other ordeals associated with incarceration. Bread earners migrated to the neighbouring regions or abroad in search of employment that created disintegration of families and disruption of social cohesion. Even after famine subsided, the anarchy that it unleashed failed to fade away for a long while.

Fifth, continued under-nourishment and starvation weakened the resistance power of the affected people who became easy victims of various epidemic diseases, like smallpox, cholera, plague, malaria and other fevers, tuberculosis, diarrhoea and dysentery. In areas like British Malabar where humid conditions and lack of sanitation prevailed, many water-borne and air-borne diseases were common. These diseases disabled the infected persons from going out to work and earn the livelihood needs of themselves and their families. For a while they depended upon what is called 'famine food' and the charitable food distribution by the better off. Ultimately, the affected people ended in famine and unnatural deaths.

Sixth, the Famine Code of 1883 affirmatively imposed the responsibility to feed the hungry on the state, rather than on private charity. The code rules required the district level officials to keep a system of intelligence gathering on a continuing basis from famine-prone areas and prepare a work programme that could simultaneously provide relief to the people and create permanent public assets that could prevent or mitigate the possibility of future famines. However, the code rules were prepared on the assumption that the trigger for any famine was the drought caused by monsoon failures. In that case, it was presumed that Malabar could not have famine as it was a high rainfall area. The district was thus kept outside the requirement of advance plan preparations to prevent anticipated attacks of famines, though it was always on the brink of famine.

1.7 Plan of the Book

Broadly, the preceding section has summarised the major issues involved in the causes and consequences of famines. The subsequent chapters of this book will take up - depending on the availability of information - some of these issues for detailed discussion. While our focus is on British Malabar for a relatively longer period of more than two centuries, it should not be ignored that, as a human misery, the impact of famine applies equally to anywhere in the world; so are their essential features. Considering this fundamental reality, the issues are discussed somewhat generally in macro-historic terms, incorporating the micro-historic features of famines specific to British Malabar. For instance, conventionally, famines are supposed to follow a hierarchical pattern: initially it attacks the poorer segments of population, i.e. workers, peasants and mendicants. If it continues for another two or three seasons, those belonging to middle-class and, subsequently, the upper-middle-class would fall its victims. In Malabar, famines mostly preceded a flash flood, washing away most of the houses and other belongings of the entire inhabitants of the area, without differentiating the rich and the poor.

The following assumptions have been kept in mind, while drawing up the plan of the book: First, if poverty and hunger have no caste or religion, but only class bias, famine need not have class distinction either. To an extent, it may not be wrong to say that, in extreme cases, famine does not even distinguish between the rulers and the ruled or the patricians and the plebeians. For example, it was believed that, in 1605, Akbar the Great died due to dysentery spread from his malnourished subjects around the way he used to make regular strolls and was buried at a mausoleum in Sikandra (Agra). Similarly, in 1827, Thomas Munro, who was Governor of Madras between 1814 and 1827, died of cholera infected while on tour in the ceded districts. A third example being cited in this regard is that of Rudyard Kipling, the English poet, story teller and the bard of the British Empire. One version of his death is that Kipling died of pneumonia. Along with cholera and dysentery, this epidemic was also considered until the nineteenth century as originating from hunger and malnutrition, spreading to others living around the affected areas and radiating outward without class difference. Though apparently overstretched, these examples cannot be ignored while discussing famine.

The book is divided, despite not thematically water-tight, into two parts consisting of eight chapters, including this introduction and a postscript. Of the remaining four chapters in Part-I, Chapter-2 sketches selected famines in Malabar from the EIC period through the end of the British Crown-rule. One of the widely held views that famine takes place in a region because of the food availability decline, which is otherwise called the FAD approach to the study of famine, is critically scrutinised in Chapter-3. Among the other causes of famines, there was an empirically unmistakable argument that famines frequented India in the nineteenth and the first half of the twentieth centuries, essentially because of the flawed land revenue policy of the British administration. Chapter-4 examines this issue. It is well known that famine and epidemics occur simultaneously, reinforcing each other. Chapter-5 discusses the nature of epidemics and their relation with famines in a non-specialist perspective, with reference to the imperialist healthcare policy in general and, in particular, the types of famine-related epidemics that British Malabar witnessed repeatedly.

After the publication in 1981 of Amartya Sen's highly influential work, *Poverty and Famines*, the focus of famine-analysis has shifted from the conventional notion of FAD to an exceptionally innovative and extremely comprehensive 'failure of exchange entitlement' or the FEE theory. The fresh insight that Professor Sen offered to the researchers with his entitlement approach has generated a flood of studies on the famines in South Asia, Africa, Latin America, China, Russia and several European countries, primarily to ascertain to what extent the FEE theory is tenable. When a theory is subjected to closer examination by a wider spectrum of researchers, it is not unusual to crop up certain doubts on its validity. Thus, some authors express reservation about the relatively minor role that Professor Sen offers to non-market institutions, especially State, in the prevention and eradication of famine. One of the aims of the present study is to explore whether a collective human misery like famine should be analysed in relation to the exchange entitlement of individuals in a private ownership market economy, largely bypassing or minimising the role of the state machinery. This is the undertone of Chapter-6. Another issue that could agitate the mind of any new researcher is why famine, which was a recurring phenomenon in British Malabar, hardly attracted the attention of historians in this region. A sober view might be that these were too insignificant to call for any serious study. However, in 1943, when a widely noted famine scorched the length and breadth of Bengal, a large number of people belonging to all ages had reportedly perished everyday in British Malabar also. This famine too failed to attract the attention of scholars in the region, though Malabar is known in academic circles as the playground of historians. In Chapter-7 we attempt to make a comparative account of the 1943 famines in Bengal and Malabar with reference to the readily available information to ascertain why in Malabar it should remain a discarded piece of history. Finally, Chapter-8 summarises the main findings of the investigation for a conclusion.

Notes

1. In spite of this attitude, it was Lytton who appointed a Commission with Richard Strachey as chairman to inquire into the causes of famines and to recommend how to overcome them. The result was the widely known, first-ever Indian Famine Commission Report of 1880 which recommended that the State should recognise that it was its duty to organise relief operations as and when famines struck the people. The Famine Commission had also prepared a model Famine Code, with the suggestion that the three presidencies of Bengal, Bombay and Madras could adapt it with necessary modifications to suit their local needs. However, the implementation of Famine Code had to wait for Lytton to depart from India

because of his strong objection to State intervention in dealing with famine (See, Raychoudhary, 2009)

2. Reproduced from the letter written by Mill to Ricardo, as quoted in Dreze and Sen (1989); op.cit.
3. The footnote to the poem, captioned *Malabar Mind* in the collected poems of Anita Nair with the same title, published by Harper Collins and reproduced in his review article by Rajeevan (2011), op.cit.
4. For example, Hotel Malabar Palace, Malabar Mahotsavam, Malabar Tours & Travels, and so on.
5. The other territories surrendered by Tipu Sultan were Dindigul, Baramahal, and Coorg. See, The Gazetteer of India, Vol II: History and Culture, New Delhi: Publication Division, Government of India; p. 509.
6. These *talukas* were Chirakkal, Kottayam, Kurumbranad, Wynad, Calicut, Eranad, Walluvanad, Palghat, and Ponnani (see Logan, 1887).
7. Unless otherwise indicated, Section-2.1 is heavily dependent on William Logan's *Malabar Manual* (1887) and the *Statistical Atlas of Malabar* published by Madras presidency in 1908.
8. The Census Handbook, published by the Superintendent of Census Operations, Government of India gives the total geographical area of Malabar at 5794 sq. miles in 1911, 5790 sq. miles in 1941, and 5844 sq. miles in 1951.
9. See, the *Statistical Atlas of Malabar*, 1908 (op.cit); and *Handbook of Agriculture* (Chapter 2), Indian Council of Agricultural Research, New Delhi, 1967 (reprinted 1997).
10. Taken from *Statistical Atlas of Malabar* 1908, op.cit.
11. The first census data relate to 1872. The difference between this and the next census of 1881 was only nine years, though these are called decennial censuses.
12. Reproduced from Hamilton's East India Gazetteer, 1829 by Adam (1840), which is our source here.
13. *Ibid.*
14. See, Report of the Indian Famine Commission 1880: Part-I *Famine Relief* (Printed at the Home, Revenue and Agricultural Department Press, Calcutta, 1880).
15. See (a) Part I of ACT XXI of 1883, as amended in 1898, (b) Malabar Collector's Office Record No. D 730/m 17 dated 18-04-1917; and (c) Madras Administration Report for 1944-45 (Part-II), published by the Superintendent of Government Press, Madras (1946).
16. See, Report of the Indian Famine Commission: Appendix-I; p.117 (Printed by the Home, Revenue and Agricultural Department Press, Calcutta).
17. See, the Administration Report relating to the Railway Branch of the Public Works Department of Madras Presidency, 1897–98.
18. Famine Code: Madras Presidency, 1883 (Printed by the Superintendent of Government Press, Madras, 1905).
19. *Ibid*, Chapter 1, para 11.

Chapter 2

Famines in Malabar: A Historical Sketch

2.1 The Context

The report of the Indian Famine Commission 1880 had stated that "in the Western district of Malabar, rain never fails so that its population....are safe from famine."[1] This was later echoed by Innes and Evans in their well-known Madras District Gazetteer, when they claimed that "Malabar is protected from famine by the unfailing south-west monsoon, and the prices of food stuffs.....do not fluctuate so much as in other less fortunate districts. Agrarian depression due to rack-renting, evictions and oppression of the *janmi*, has occasionally in the past led to outbreaks of violent crime; but on the whole labour is plentiful, wages are high, and actual want derives fewer people to crime than is the case elsewhere" (Innes and Evans, 1908). On the other hand, William Logan, who was the earliest to comprehensively document the historiography of the district in his widely read *Malabar Manual* had noted that this region was constantly on the 'brink' of famine but after the first half of the eighteenth century there was no record of any famine in the district (Logan 1887). The reasons that Logan attributed to this district remaining in perpetual pre-famine conditions were the following.

Despite being a very high rain-fall area, Malabar could not produce enough food needed for the consumption of its population even during normal years. The condition became worse after the arrival of the European coffee planters in Wayanad taluk, which was until then a major surplus producer of rice and could mostly bridge the gap in the food requirement of other parts of the district. Large-scale coffee plantations took away a part of the high-land areas under rice and other grain cultivation in Wayanad. Along with this, there was a sharp decline in the availability of labourers to work in paddy fields as they were also absorbed in the better-paid coffee estates.

This might not have created any problem to the extent of dragging the district into famine, had the surplus food available in other parts of the presidency been used to compensate the shortage. Instead of feeding the deficit areas like Malabar, the presidency diverted a sizable part of the rice for exports to England, or to other European countries, or for the use of the defence personnel increasingly deployed in the British war-theatres of Indian sub-continent. The people of Malabar had generally depended on the neighbouring Mysore state for rice, or on imports from Burma, the largest producer of rice in British India. As the rulers of Mysore were at loggerheads with the EIC and some of the local kings of north Malabar, they prevented bulk movements of rice from Mysore to this region, especially when there were shortage situations in the district. Similarly, the port of Mysore through which Burmese rice was imported to Malabar was under the control of the King of Bednur. In times of extreme food crises in the district he would put an embargo on the port against off-loading of the grain brought from Burma as his revenge against one of the *raja*s in north-Malabar.

Malabar was well-known for its commercial products, like coconut, coir, coconut oil, arecanut, pepper, ginger, cardamom, and timber. These were highly in demand in other parts of India and abroad. Money earned from the sale of these products determined the ability of the people for their 'entitlement' to food. The Mysore rulers not only prevented the movement of rice across its territories to Malabar but also objected transporting of commercial products from Malabar into or across their territory. The district, thus, lost an important trade-route for external commerce. The resultant internal glut led to steep decline in prices of these products and, therefore, of the income and food purchasing power of the producers of these items. One of the main reasons why the agriculture-dependent population in Malabar became relatively poor and succumbed to starvation and famine was the artificial slump in market prices of its commercial crops.

The recurring food shortages and entitlement failures were compounded by the change in land-tenure and land-revenue systems that the British rulers introduced in Malabar, the impact of which created 'pre-famine' conditions and deepened into famine whenever any crop failures occurred. Before the advent of the British, there was a peculiar system of land tenure in Malabar where a *janmi* (landlord) held hereditary right on land. He appointed a *kaanakkaar*, or supervisor, to look after his field. With this power on hand, the *kaanakkaar* leased out parcels of the land under his control to ryots against payment of a predetermined *paattom* or rent. When the *ryotwari* system was introduced by the British administration, it made two major changes: First, the land revenue was converted from the traditional kind-payment to cash-payment. Second, the output valued in cash was divided into three shares, (i) for the government as land revenue, (ii) for the *ryot* as reward for cultivation, and (iii) for *janmi* or *kaanakkaar*. This immediately reduced the farm retention from four to three portions of the output. Earlier, the portions shared by the *janmi* and the *kaanakkaar* were partly recycled to the poor farm-workers in the village in times of distress. The latter also received paddy/rice from the former during the region's social ceremonies like Onam, Vishu etc. With the new system of land revenue, these facilities enjoyed by the poor had automatically shrunk. Apart from this, the unethical practice of over-assessment, fabrication of accounts, and forfeiting of land in case of default in payment of revenue by the officials further reduced the farm retention and created perpetual poverty in the district (Logan 1887).

These changes under the British rule not only pushed the colony into famines but the time span between one famine and the next also reduced over time. Ramesh Dutt, in his well-known *Letters to Lord Curzon* had cited that within 130 years from 1770 to 1900, there were 22 famines of severe magnitude in India, some of which were felt all over the country and some, in specific regions. Of these, the most serious nine episodes were recorded in the Madras presidency (Dutt 1900). He did not say how many of these had afflicted Malabar. In the absence of any known study so far on the history of famines in the district, we can only use these chronological episodes to scan through the archival records and find out whether Malabar had faced any of these famines. Regarding the remaining British period that Dutt could not cover, namely, the first half of the twentieth century, several authors had stated that there was only one major famine in the country – the widely discussed famine of 1943 in Bengal. In what follows, we will have a rigorous scrutiny of the history of Malabar to test the veracity of this view.

2.2 Eighteenth Century Famines

Logan in his *Malabar Manual* had stated that, though Malabar was always on the brink of famine, the first 'recorded' famine that this region faced was in 1727, when the EIC was a commercial organisation operating through export processing centres or warehouses, commonly called 'factories', which were built near the port centres of India. In Malabar, there were three such 'factories'. One was set up at Anjengo, in 1684, on a piece of land received free of cost from the Rani of Attingal. The second was in Tellicherry, built with the permission granted in 1689 by the local raja on the condition that the EIC, in addition to using the 'factory' for commercial purposes, should protect his kingdom from possible attacks of the neighbouring rulers. The third 'factory' was in Zamorin's territory at Calicut along with those of the Portuguese, French and Danes (Logan, 1887). These were among the more than twenty 'factories' that the EIC had possessed in India before it shifted the focus from commercial activities to political and administrative realms. Each factory was put under the supervision of a 'factor'. His duty included, apart from dealing with the day-to-day businesses of the EIC, maintenance of a diary of events taking place in and around the locality. Logan got the information on the 1727 famine from the diary preserved in Tellicherry 'factory'.

The Famine of 1727

As per Logan's accounts of the 1727 famine in Malabar, during the months of August and September, when the season's autumn-sown *kharif* crop was harvested, it became clear that there was an extraordinary shortage of rice in the district. Otherwise also July, August and September being lean months, there would be a seasonal upswing in the prices of rice, making it unaffordable to the poorer sections of the population. In times of bad harvests the situation became worse because, during these months, stocks from the preceding harvests could quickly be decumulated and used up. At the same time, new harvests of paddy converted into rice, after hulling, milling and drying, would start trickling into the market by late or after September.

In addition to the shortage of harvested paddy and the extremely low level of carry-over stocks from the previous year, it was reported that there was also no surplus to spare in Mysore on which the households from north Malabar generally depended for relatively low-priced rice. Even when the Mysore rulers were antagonistic to bulk transport of rice to meet the local shortage, private individuals could bring in small quantities of rice without being intercepted. As a result of the decline in the overall supply of rice, by the beginning of September, a severe starvation broke out. The enormity of starvation could be judged from the fact that the 'factory' gate at Tellicherry was besieged every day by hordes of poor people begging for food. The store-house of the factory had provisions barely for a month. The conditions of the people were so acute that parents started selling their children at Mangalore to obtain money for their own subsistence. Moved by the plight of the people, the factory officials summoned the available surplus-rice from Anjengo for gratuitous distribution to the beggars thronging in front of the gate, or roaming around the street. However, according to Logan, this plight did not continue for long. By the end of September when rice from the new harvest started arriving in the market, Logan noted, the famine slowly receded and the situation became normal.

The narrative of this episode of famine is too paltry. Studies would show that a famine is not characterised simply by starving people loitering on the street or begging for charities, or sale of children by parents, or discarding of elders by the income earning men. Another symptom of famine is the development of widespread epidemic diseases and unnatural mortalities. Areas like Malabar were generally susceptible to contagious diseases because of bad weather, unclean surroundings and contaminated water. If the epidemics proliferating from unhygienic conditions infect the bread-winners, the entire family would plunge into famine. At this stage, the demarcating lines between famine through starvation and famine through epidemics become blurred. Furthermore, the amelioration of famine then requires not only improving food supply but also arrangements for health and medical care. Considering That one of the routes through which famine occur is epidemics, there were at least three more famines in Malabar, according to Logan's own account.

Disease-led Famine: 1730

Logan noted from the diary of Tellicherry 'factory' that, in the third quarter of 1730, an unknown pestilence started cropping up in the surroundings and peaked by October. By then it had spread as far as to Calicut, the headquarters of Malabar. The disease was so fatal that even the garrison soldiers stationed at the 'factory' had died from its attack. The people in the neighbourhood, who were emaciated by the disease, could not go out to earn their livelihood. Most of them had to be relieved by charity. The factory authorities, wrote Logan, had to build new barracks to look after the sick and provide resting places for people engaged in burying the dead. The devastation of lives were so massive that, at the peak of the epidemic, they sent requests to Anjengo as well as to the presidency headquarters at Madras for recruiting soldiers to fill up the vacancies caused by deaths of garrison soldiers, as suitable local youth were all dead due to the disease.

The nature of the 'pestilence' described in *Malabar Manual* and the deaths that followed would indicate that this had actually culminated into a major famine. The area afflicted with the epidemic had no way of getting food, once the bread-winners were bedridden or died due to the disease. As in other famines elsewhere, it was possible that gratuitous supply of food was the only hope for the people who became destitutes. The information culled out by Logan indicated that philanthropists had come forward and set up free kitchens in the affected areas. Considering the severity of the epidemic and mortalities, the 'factors' of Tellicherry had themselves organised charitable relief to a section of the affected people. It is evident from this that there was an epidemics-led famine in Malabar in the second half of 1730. We do not have recorded evidences to strengthen our contention with other usual features of famines, namely, harvest failures, cattle mortalities, inflationary rise in prices, sale of children by parents and wives by husbands, food-riots, thefts, out emigration, and so on.

Disease-led Famine: 1757

The second attack of a disastrous epidemic disease that most probably assumed the scale of a famine occurred in several parts of the district in 1757. That year, the south-east monsoon was excessive. Coinciding with it, a contagious disease, the name of which was not recorded in the factory diary, started raging. From the notings in the diary, the disease had spread to Calicut, Mahe, Tellicherry, and Cannanore. There were terrible mortalities everywhere. No further details were available. From this detail, we cannot know what happened to the livelihood of the families, whose bread-winners died of the epidemic. However, as in 1730, during this time also the factors in Tellicherry, along with private philanthropists had arranged gratuitous food to starving survivors of the epidemic. From this, we have to believe that during 1757, there was an epidemic-led famine in Malabar.

Logan had further noted that there was the likelihood of another contagious disease in Malabar, in 1800, and that the entire region was in scare. In August that year, Bagdad had a massive plague-attack. It was feared that sailors coming from there might have carried the disease and transferred to the people of Malabar, setting the stage for another bout of unnatural mortalities. However, according to Logan, the authorities were very vigilant and all travellers coming by ships were subjected to strict quarantine rules. They were prohibited from visiting local people until a competent doctor certified that they were free from any infectious disease.

2.3 The Nineteenth Century Famine (1876-78)

While explaining the nature of the 1727 famine in Malabar, Logan had argued that, though in the beginning of September that year there was a famine, soon after the *kanni* crops were harvested, the famine disappeared of its own. He further stated that such a situation had developed in Malabar in September 1877 but "one meal of rice *kanji* distributed gratis to all comers daily during this season of the year at many places throughout the district sufficed to stave off actual famine in 1877", and "of real famine in the land there are few records" (Logan, 1887:215). The archival records do not corroborate both these statements. In fact, during 1876-78, when Logan was the collector of Malabar, there was a massive famine in the district and his official desk was flooded with reports submitted by the Tahsildars of Wayanad, Kannur, Palghat and Calicut about the deaths in hospitals and large number of beggars roaming on the roads for alms and food[2].

Interestingly, all these reports were received in the collectorate under his official seal, which read "W. Logan, Dated........"

This famine was not Malabar specific. During 1876-78, several parts of India had witnessed one of the worst famines in its history, covering more than two lakh square miles, extending to presidencies of Madras and Bombay; to Mysore and Hyderabad; to Oudh and the Ganges region of the North-Western Provinces (see Raychoudhary, 2009). Considering the unprecedented magnitude of the famine, Robert Bulwer-Lytton (popularly known as Lord Lytton), the Governor-General and Viceroy (1876-1880) had appointed a Famine Commission, which in its report submitted in 1880 described the holocaust as 'the Great Famine of South India' and that "in respect of area and population affected, and duration and intensity of the distress, it is the most grievous calamity of its kind experienced in British India since the beginning of this century." The report further stated that "the total area which suffered from famine in South India during 1877 was about 200,000 square-miles, with a population of 36 million." In other areas, the intensity of the famine and the calamity that it wreaked was relatively less. Taking the British India as a whole, the 1876-78 famine had caused distress to an estimated 58.5 million people.[3]

The death-toll of Madras presidency being the highest in this famine, Dutt (1900) called it the 'Madras Famine'. The total loss of lives during a famine is estimated with reference to deaths in excess of the normal rate and reduction in birth rates due to a decline in fecundity caused by starvation and distress. The total number of deaths from the combined effects of both these in the 1876-78 famine was estimated differently by different authors, from the lowest of 6.1 million to the highest of 10.3 million.[4] The available archival records indicate that, while Madras presidency in British India suffered the most in this famine, *it was Malabar among the districts in the presidency that suffered the worst tragedy*. This famine was so terrible that British rulers, despite their usual indifference in dealing with such miseries, had to make a beginning for the first time in famine-relief activities. And it was these activities that led to the promulgation of the Indian Famine Code, 1883 (Currey and Hugo, 1984).

As we noted in the preceding chapter, Malabar was kept outside the purview of the Famine Code for advanced preparations to deal with the likely attack of famine on the assumption that the district, unlike most other parts of the presidency, was blessed with copious rains and, therefore, impervious to attacks of famine. Nonetheless, in 1876-78, Malabar plunged into one of the most grievous famines in its history, catapulted by irregular and uneven monsoons. Consequently, food prices shot up beyond the reach of the common man. This was the time when the government should have a sympathetic approach towards the affected people. But nothing was done to relieve the people from the raging morbidity and mortalities. The following sub-sections will deal with the factors that led to the 1876-78 famine in Malabar and how it was exacerbated by a combination of natural causes, which were worsened by government actions.

Monsoons

A year before the actual famine struck Malabar, monsoons became acutely unfavourable for seasonal sowings. Heavy rains and the accompanying floods considerably restricted the area under field-crops, resulting in a drop in the outputs of all major and minor foodgrains. (These details are available in the Annual Administrative Reports of Madras Presidency, and the Land Revenue Settlement Reports of the Madras Board of Revenue.) The starting point of the famine was the recalcitrant monsoon of *fasli* 1285 (i.e. July 1875–June 1876). Paddy cultivation was the main victim of the adverse weather. Farmers had to dispense with large portions of the area under paddy. The *fasli* 1286 (1876-77) was more disastrous than the preceding season. The average rainfall in Malabar was recorded at 83.19 inches, as against 107.95 inches in the last ten years. The rainfall was not only unseasonal but also highly unequally distributed across the district (Table 2.1). The south-west monsoon, the principal rainfall season, failed in most parts of Malabar. Owing to deficient rains, the second crop of the region had also failed almost entirely. The prices of rice and other foodgrains flared up. Loss of employment in agriculture and the resultant loss of the purchasing power led the common people to impoverishment, which, when continued, deepened into a massive famine in the entire stretches of the district.

The monsoon in *fasli* 1287 (1877-78) was somewhat different from that of the previous two *fasli*s. Though above normal, the rainfall was unequally distributed. Availability of water was insufficient during the maturing stage of the crop but became super-abundant when the crop was ready for harvest. The crops harvested during September-October, was the most affected. The total production of foodgrains of all the three seasons taken together in 1877-78 was just two-thirds of the corresponding outputs in the previous year, which itself witnessed a disastrous harvest. Finally, in *fasli* 1288 (1878-79), Malabar received enough rains. The production improved, foodgrains prices came down to some extent and the famine slowly began to recede.

Food Prices

Open market prices of foodgrains in Malabar were lower in 1875-76, i.e. the year prior to the famine started flaring up, than their preceding 10-year averages. The heavy rains from the hostile south-east monsoon inundating large areas of land and preventing tilling of soil in that season were reflected in the level of prices in 1876-77 with the market responding with an inflationary upsurge. The prices of rice, both superior and average varieties, rose by over 35 per cent above their level recorded in 1875-76. Prices of coarse cereals, namely, *ragi, cholam* and *cumbu,* which were generally consumed by relatively poorer households even in normal times, had increased by 80 to 83 per cent over the levels recorded during the preceding year. The rise in prices of coarse cereals much above the increase in prices of different varieties of rice would indicate that, apart from lower production, demand from well-to-do households had also shifted to the poor man's cereals.

In 1877-78, when the famine reached its devastating peak, market prices of rice shot up to 150-153 per cent of their normal levels. The corresponding increase in the prices of *ragi*, the cereal of the poor in normal times, was 150 per cent. The prices of horse gram also registered an increase of 125 per cent. When the rainfall became normal and the usual tilling of soil picked up, the market prices of foodgrains indicated signs of stabilising. Though prices of both the first-sort and second-sort of rice in 1878-79 declined by about five per cent over the preceding year, these were still 40-45 per cent higher than in normal times (Table-2.2). If workers had to keep up their food consumption, wages should have also exhibited the same trend. However, money wage rates for different categories of labourers remained unchanged at their pre-famine levels. According to the report of the average monthly wages of skilled and unskilled labour, published by the Government of India, wages of an able-bodied agricultural labourer in Madras Presidency, between 1876 and 1878, remained the same at Rs 4, with the highest of Rs 6 and the lowest of Rs 2 per day. This indicated that the wages received by those who were fortunate enough to garner an employment could not maintain their food intake as the prices were soaring. The condition of those who could not get employment, or those who got employment in the relief work offered by the government was even worse.

However, Table-2.2 further shows that market prices of pàddy had also moved in line with the trends in prices of rice during the famine. It would appear from this that the 1876-78 famine did not affect the farmers in Malabar as they could receive higher prices for their produce than during 1875-76. Such an impression however might not be out of place in the case of relatively large farmers who undertook cultivation with purchased-inputs and casual labour. In Malabar, most of the cultivators of field-crops were known to belong to the small and marginal category. As outputs produced by this category of farmers were usually insufficient to meet their subsistence

Table 2.1: Rainfall in Malabar, 1875 - 1878 (in inches)

	Malabar District	*Madras Presidency*
1. South-West Monsoon		
Avg. for preceding 10 yrs.	93.71	27.33
1875-76	87.91	25.87
1876-77	78.93	22.44
1877-78	96.11	27.93
2. North-East Monsoon		
Avg. for preceding 10 yrs.	14.24	16.18
1875-76	10.53	11.41
1876-77	4.26	6.67
1877-78	27.38	20.19
3. Total		
Avg. for preceding 10 yrs.	107.95	43.52
1875-76	98.44	37.28
1876-77	83.19	29.11
1877-78	123.49	48.12

Source: Proceedings of the Board of Revenue, Madras for the years 1878 and 1879.

Table 2.2: Market Prices of Foodgrains in Malabar, 1875–79

(Rs / Garce)

	Last 10 yr average	*1875-76*	*1876-77*	*1877-78*	*1878-79*
Rice					
I Sort	548	406	549	612	577
II Sort	498	369	499	564	538
Paddy					
I Sort	212	157	251	272	259
II Sort	192	142	166	221	210
Horse gram	318	226	383	507	381
Cholam	143	196	356	479	340
Cumbu	126	173	313	421	299
Ragi	242	174	318	435	309

Source: Compiled from Board of Revenue Reports, Madras

requirement for the whole year, it was inevitable for them to depend on the market in the latter half of the season when prices peaked. This was the category of farmers who were generally exploited by merchants and rural money lenders. During the 1876-78 famine also this had happened, as per the Revenue Settlement Report of the Madras presidency for *fasli* 1286

(1876-77), which recorded that "the enterprising merchants of Cannanore, Tellicherry and Badagara must have realised handsome profits on their transaction. For the greater bulk of the population, however, the year must be said to have been very bad one." The speculative pressure on the market for foodgrains and other items of essential consumption goods was so high that there were reports of widespread food-riots in almost all parts of the Madras presidency, including Malabar. The government had to call the army to control the riots (Srivastava, 1968).

Coercive Revenue Collection

After the British administration introduced a *ryotwari* system of land revenue in Malabar as soon as it was transferred from Bombay to Madras, the condition of the small farmers became worse. Irrespective of whether they cultivated their land in a season or not, they had to pay the land revenue already fixed by government. Though the *ryotwari* revenue settlement was to be revised only after 30 years, this provision was quite often flouted and exorbitant rates imposed at every revision. If the cultivators failed to pay the revenue, the government imprisoned them before confiscating their lands and auctioned out to recoup the dues. With a view to avoid such a humiliating situation, the cultivator borrowed the required amount from the local money-lenders and paid off the revenue demanded by the government. Quite often he had to borrow additionally to meet his family subsistence and the expenses for the next cultivation. "Once in debt, he found it difficult to get out of it. The money-lender charged high rates of interest and through cunning and deceitful measures, such as false accounting, forged signatures and making the debtor sign for larger amounts than he had borrowed, got the peasant deeper and deeper into debt till he parted with his land" (see Chandra, 2009).

Dutt (1900) had argued that the 1876-78 famine had intensified the sufferings of the people because of the heavy land revenue that Lytton imposed and the oppressive manner in which it was collected. But Lytton, according to Dutt, was astute enough to introduce his ruthless land revenue policy in a very polished manner. For instance, on assuming charge as the Viceroy in 1876, he declared that "the Crown of England should henceforth be identified with the hopes, the aspirations, the sympathies and interests of a powerful native aristocracy." The zamindars and landlords took this message as the recognition of their special status under the British administration. In return, they decided to serve the British interests in whatever way they could. As a part of this implicit, though clearly discernible offer, they obliged the British administration in the collection of land revenue from the *zamindari* and *ryotwari* areas by the adoption of all sorts of unfair means (which are being detailed in Chapter-4). Commenting on this unholy alliance of the imperialist rulers and feudal elements that deepened the livelihood crisis of the people at large, Jawaharlal Nehru wrote in his *Discovery of India*: "Because of this natural alliance of the British power with the reactionaries in India, it became the guardian and upholder of many an evil custom and practice, which it otherwise condemned" (Nehru 1946).[5]

The Famine Code of 1883, as adopted by all the three presidencies, had a provision for the remission of land revenue in times of bad agricultural years as also during other calamities, such as epidemics and famines. The report of the Famine Commission, 1880 had stated that Madras was more pro-active than other presidencies in dealing with the miseries of their subjects. Even before the Famine Code came into existence, the report noted, it was making "reductions on account of remission of revenue made under the ordinary rules." Furthermore, even the reduced imposts were not fully collected and the unpaid balances struck out in times of adverse circumstances. In support of this, the Famine Commission stated that, during 1876-78, the net *ryotwari* land revenue demand in the Madras presidency was estimated at Rs 6.24 crore, while the actual amount collected was Rs 4.22 crore, that is, just 67.7 per cent of the net demand. The amount remitted during these two peak famine years worked out to Rs 1.47 crore, or 23.5 per cent of the net demand and 34.7 per cent of the total collection.[6] There are at least two points that emerge from these figures: (a) the remission of land revenue in Madras presidency was less than one-fourth of the total demand; and (b) if this can be called a 'more pro-active' attitude of dealing with the miseries during an unprecedented famine year, the plight of the people in other presidencies in times of such calamities could be imagined.

An important point to be noted about the revenue assessment and collection was that, contrary to what the Famine Commission claimed, the revenue assessment on *ryotwari* lands had gone up from year-to-year throughout the famine period. On the one hand they allowed remittance but on the other hand they increased the revenue demand in terms of some other accounts so that the amount payable became more than what was remitted. For the purpose of raising the land revenue, according to Logan, the assessment authorities had used deceitful methods. One such method was to inflate the area under cultivation through "fabrication of accounts, over-assessment of produce that did not exist, the assessment imposed on wrong people and the rigid exaction of the revenue" (Logan 1887). Conversely, the official explanation for an unprecedented rise in revenue realisation was that: (a) there was an increase in the quit-rent imposed on individuals who were granted land on favourable terms for the services rendered to the state; (b) quit-rent imposed on *inam* lands scattered in villages, which was earlier left out due to over-sight; and (c) the revenue assessed on lands cultivated by farmers without advance permission. While ruthless coercion resulted in increased revenue collection at the cost of the subsistence of the relatively smaller cultivators, the officials claimed that it was a positive development of the people abiding by the law of the land.[7]

One of the coercive methods adopted to collect the revenue was to threaten the defaulters that in case of failure to pay the revenue in time, they would be imprisoned without bail. Another method was to attach the property of the defaulters. A third method was to sell the attached property at lower than the revenue dues. For instance, compared to the fiscal year 1875-76, which was a normal year in Malabar, the number of defaulters whose properties attached was very high in 1876-78, the peak of the famine-year, when the increase in the number of defaulters whose properties were attached accounted for 54 per cent and those whose properties sold out to recoup arrears, more than 30 per cent, over the preceding year (Table-2.3).

Fearing imprisonment and humiliation, those who could not pay the land revenue, sold off or surrendered whatever was available with them to the revenue collectors, leaving barely anything for their livelihood. The British administration also broke the age-old network of rural relationship by changing the revenue demand from kind payment to money payment so that the famine-ridden poorer households lost their source of help in the form of foodgrains from landlord classes in Malabar. It was the break-down of the network of social relationship that made the 1876-78 famine one of the worst ever human killers in the district.

Temple Wage and Charity

The report of the Indian Famine Commission, 1880 has a long section on the relief operations undertaken by the provincial governments during the 1876-78 famine. Referring to several sources, such as the Parliamentary Blue Book, the proceedings of the Famine Department of Government of India, and the replies submitted by the presidencies in response to the requests sent by the Famine Commission, the report noted that, from the beginning of 1876, when the famine began to appear, the Madras presidency had started initiating relief-works in different districts, albeit on a small scale. However, Malabar does not figure in these names of the districts. When the famine heated up and began spreading to more and more areas, the presidency wanted to take up the relief-works on an extensive scale. But it confronted two problems: (i) the insufficiency of public food stocks, and (ii) shortage of funds. The presidency sent an application to Government of India for additional funds and foodgrains, and seeking permission to procure tentatively some 30,000 tons of foodgrain from the open market to fill the shortage. The Central Government objected to the proposal for the purchase of grain the open market on the grounds that it would be an unfair and uncalled for 'interference with the private enterprise', which was 'extraordinarily active' at that time.

Table 2.3: Evictions from Land in Malabar (1862-1880)

Quinque-Nnium	*Average annual number of*		
	Suits of eviction	*Persons against whom eviction was declared*	*Persons against whom rent was declared*
1862-66	2039	1891	1473
1867-71	2547	3483	2549
1872-76	3974	6286	4314
1877-80	4983	8355	6498

Source: Logan (1887), op.cit. p. 623.

Table-2.4: Deaths by Famine-related Epidemics in Malabar, during 1873-78 (in numbers)

Year	*Cholera*	*Smallpox*	*Fevers*	*Total*
1873-74	10	14858	12166	27034
1874-75	13	7029	13945	20987
1875-76	12288	6479	15208	33975
1876-77	9254	1303	12973	23530
1877-78	7588	5352	19206	32146

Note: Deaths by bowel complaints and 'other diseases' were reported at 22,634 in 1875-76 and 2744 in 1877-78. These figures are not available for other years.

Source: Administration Report for Madras Presidency, 1877-78.

As regards the shortage of funds, the Central Government replied that it was in a 'critical stage of finances' and that since the possibility of famine situation subsiding soon, it was decided that the request need not be accepted. It further asked the provincial government to immediately stop all expensive relief-works and initiate legal action against the officials who refused to do so. Concurrently, in early 1877, the Government of India deputed Richard Temple, who was the Governor of Bengal and an expert in dealing with famines, on a special mission to Madras and Bombay presidencies for giving directives about how to conduct relief operations. On reaching the Madras presidency, Temple visited several relief-work-centres and gave a number of directions. His first directive was that there was no need to bring rice from outside the presidency at reduced railway freights for: (i) the financial position of the government was very weak; and (ii) the on-going famine, in his view, was not that severe (Srivastava, 1968). He stated that there was over-crowding in relief-works and that there was an urgent need for adopting stringent norms in the selection of workers: (a) they should be able-bodied, (b) the workers should be engaged under professional supervisors, (c) if the persons selected under the famine-relief programmes exhibited 'no sign of want' from their physical appearance, they should be immediately dismissed, (d) the daily wage offered at 2 *annas* per adult, or 1.5 lb of grain and 3 *pies*, being very high, should be reduced to 1 lb of grain and half *anna* (or one and a half *anna*s without grain) for an adult, with proportionate reductions for the woman and child labourers, and (e) the quantity of food served in the form of cooked rice *kanji* (porridge) should be reduced, keeping the time of serving in all centres the same, and the distance between one charity centre and the other should be so far-flung that those receiving gratuitous food from one centre could not reach another centre and fill their stomachs.

In the capacity as the then Governor-General, Lytton immediately accepted the recommendations made by Richard Temple. The Madras presidency was therefore obliged to implement them despite its apprehension that the already worse famine situation could further worsen in case these were put into practice. At the initial stage of these recommendations, W.R. Cornish, Surgeon-General and Sanitary Commissioner of the presidency had officially protested against the reduced 'Temple Wage' and steeply reduced 'Temple Charity' of gratuitous food supply. To this, Richard Temple reasoned that "there might indeed be a question whether life cannot be sustained with one pound of grain per diem and whether Government is bound to do more than sustain life. This is a matter of opinion; and I myself think that one pound per diem might be sufficient to sustain life; and that the experiment ought to be tried." Regarding his view on reducing the quantity of grain for charity, Richard Temple stated: "It is to be remembered that, when these people first came on relief, their condition was low, and they needed very full rations. Such rations have been allowed for some time, and the people are in very good case. A reduction might now be demanded in the interests of financial economy and might be attempted for a time at least without danger; at all events the trial might be made for people at task-work, and especially with those who are not really at task-work, and, who, though nominally at some sort of task-work, are doing very light or nominal work. One pound of grain ought to be made to suffice. At the present prices, a rate of one *anna* and a half would purchase a pound of grain and would leave a small margin for condiments, vegetables, and the like."[8]

The actual recommendations of Richard Temple, as approved by Lytton, were more regressive than what is reproduced above. It stipulated that the reduced wage for the relief work should not be shared by the worker's dependants, including children and old people. The dependants should be sent to charity-homes and given still reduced gratuitous food. The civil surgeons should regularly inspect the relief work-site and submit weekly reports whether, "after the introduction of the new rate, they could detect any loss of power or flesh in the coolies." That is, they should record the name, age and weight of each worker in a register and repeat the exercise week-by-week. They should also record, along with the weight, other particulars like anaemia, pulse, heart-beat, muscular power etc. In case there was no much deterioration in any of these scales, Temple thought the wage rate for relief-works could be reduced further.

Lytton ordered that, in the event of those selected for relief works becoming weak after the introduction of the Temple Wage such workers should be asked to stay back at their homes. In addition, Lytton modified the Temple Wage for an able-bodied man at 0.45 kg of grain and one *anna* and a still reduced rate for woman and working child for a 'long day of hard labour without shade or rest' (Hall-Mathews, 2008). When Lytton demitted office and returned to England, his policy of embracing Temple-Wage and Temple-Charity and further tightening these at his whims invited widespread public criticisms that, at those wage rates and level of charity, no body would survive.

Epidemics and Mortalities

Between 1875-76 and 1877-78, the ruinously high prices of foodgrains that the lower segments of population found difficult to afford left them emaciated and succumbed easily to even ordinary diseases. This was recorded in the Annual Administration Report of the presidency as an exceptionally unhealthy period. In 1875-76, when the actual famine was yet to begin, mortalities from epidemic diseases had an unprecedented escalation to 23.24 per thousand from the normal rate of 17.93 per thousand of population. Cholera was the cause of more than one-fifth of the total mortalities. The other diseases that caused high deaths were smallpox, malaria and the enteric group of fevers. Over one-fourth of the mortalities from smallpox in Madras presidency were reported in Malabar alone.

In 1876-77, the general heath condition of the people in the district further deteriorated because of the disastrous rains, defective water-supplies, and unaffordably high prices of provisions. The epidemics conquered the entire length and breadth of the district. The total death rates were frighteningly high, at 34.2 per thousand people, which accounted for eleven points higher than that in the preceding year. Cholera prevailed throughout the year in the three *talukas* of Chirakkal, Kottayam and Kurumbranad, taking away 1770 lives in that year as against 427 in the previous year.

Next year, when the famine reached its peak, the health conditions of the people in Malabar deteriorated further. Though the government had already announced the arrival of famine in the presidency, ameliorative measures were yet to be initiated. Total deaths due to cholera, smallpox and fevers, estimated at 46.2 per thousand people, were more than double that of 1874-75. If loss of lives due to bowel complaints and 'other diseases' recorded in official records were also taken into consideration, the death rates might be still higher. During 1877-78, there were reports of a mysterious, malignant fever that had spread throughout the areas affected by famine, taking away a large number of lives, which were not given out either in the annual administration report or in the revenue settlement report of the presidency. The official explanation was that the actual figures of famine-deaths appeared to be under-reported by the lower level staff 'owing to the imperfect character of the statistical registration'. For instance, if a health worker who reported deaths in an area also died due to any of the epidemics, the appointment of a substitute in his place took a longer time-gap during which the deaths remained unreported (Table 2.4).

Cattle Mortality

Along with the epidemics and human mortalities, the 1876-78 famine in Malabar witnessed widespread outbreaks of rinderpest to cattle. The disease was very acute in Wayanad, which was then the most cattle-concentrated taluk in the district. William Logan, who was the Collector of Malabar, directed the veterinary surgeon of Wayanad to immediately make inquiries and submit a report about the condition of cattle for the purpose of forwarding the information to the presidency headquarters. The surgeon visited a few estates of the British plantation owners, who had kept large number of cattle as a part of their business, and submitted his observations to the Collector[9]. The report as submitted by Logan to the presidency headquarters, did not reveal the total number of animals infected, or the number of cattle died on account of the epidemics.

It is a well-known fact that, generally, human-famines are inter-connected with epidemics and mortalities of cattle. When there is a food shortage, the affected people go for what is called "famine food", which includes feeds preserved for cattle, mainly oil-cakes. Lack of proper feed enfeebles the cattle and makes attacks of diseases easy. The report was silent about such a relationship, probably to conceal the general famine that the people were facing at that time[10]. It only confirms the existence of a severe outbreak of epidemics among the cattle population in southern part of Wayanad. The name of the disease was called 'rinderpest', a typhoid-like, terribly contagious and fatal fever. It had attacked both sheep and goats. The reasons attributed to the attack were: (i) an estate owner of coffee plantations in Wayanad had unknowingly brought a disease-stricken cow from Mysore; it was that cow which spread the disease to his other cattle, and from there to the rest of the animals in the area; (ii) around that time, Wayanad was witnessing a powerful eastern wind, which spread the disease to the cattle elsewhere; and (iii) the pits dug to bury dead cattle were nearer the cattle-sheds where other animals uninfected by the disease were housed; the pits being very shallow, the dead bodies of the animals came out and spread the viruses from the carcasses through the fleas to the healthy animals.

The report submitted to the presidency head-quarters further stated that the animal husbandry division of the taluk had already collected a pamphlet prepared by the Bengal Cattle Plague Commission and circulated among the members of the Plantation Association of Wayanad. With the guidance available in the pamphlet, they were now separating the disease-stricken animals from the rest of the cattle population, as Bengal had been doing in times of infections to cattle. Moreover, the temporary treatment centres established by some of the large cattle owners in Wayanad were very effective in controlling the disease and preventing further cattle mortalities. In view of this, the report emphasised (mainly to satisfy the officials at the top) that there was no need of spending government funds to establish a veterinary hospital for the time being.

Bureaucratic Attitude

At the peak of the famine in 1877 the official position, as articulated by Lytton, was that the state charity would have a general demoralising influence, apart from practical difficulties. In this context, the Secretary of State in charge of India in the British cabinet had written a letter to the Viceroy in India: "The object of saving life is undoubtedly paramount to all other considerations. But it is essential that in pursuing this end your officers should sedulously guard against the danger of inducing the population to rely up on Government aid rather than upon their own industry and thrift. In the interest of the distressed population itself, as well as of the tax-payers generally, you are bound to adopt precautions against indolence or imposition, similar, so far as the circumstances of India will permit, to those with which in this country it has always been found necessary to protect the distribution of public relief from abuse."

Yet another way in which the British administration deliberately avoided its primary responsibility to protect the lives from famine-mortalities was reflected in the Imperial Gazetteer of India: "The people of India are infinitely various in habits, creed, custom, caste, and language .....Thousands would die sooner than resort to relief camps or touch food which they thought was unclean, either in itself or by reason of the agency employed in its preparation. One caste will not feed with another".[11]

The lower level bureaucracy took the imperialist attitude in letter and spirit. The famine records of Malabar have several examples for this. In Malabar, famine mortalities took more than two years since it broke out in 1876 to subside than in other parts of the presidency (where it had eased by the end of 1877) because of the attitude of the local officials to blindly follow the orders of their superior authority in England. This will be clear from the official letters exchanged between the office of the Malabar Collector in Calicut and the Assistant Collectors and Tahsildars under him. To take a case in point, the Special Assistant Collector of Palghat municipality, which was the worst famine-affected area in Malabar, wrote to the district Collector in the second half of 1878, when the famine was still raging, that "there was the promise of a plentiful harvest and hence, it is not necessary to have any relief work." Regarding the emaciated beggars thronging in Palghat town, he wrote, "I have collected all vagrants, fed them and sent back to their native villages, as they were becoming a nuisance."

In Kottayam and Kurumbranad *talukas*, the distress was continuing unabated and there was a need to maintain, if not to increase, the gratuitous relief. The tahsildar of Kottayam insisted for the continuation of relief works in the taluk, whereas the tahsildar of Kurumbranad *taluk* was ambivalent in his assessment of the situation and the need for gratuitous relief: "Palmyras are being sold in pieces in the shops at Tiruvengoor. It is bought by the poor for the starch that can be extracted from its stem." He then stated that "the public opinion in general is that the present pressure is much greater than that of the last year. This is probably correct..... At the same time, there are no signs of any large increase in beggars on the streets and highways. Therefore, I am of the opinion that relief measures are not absolutely necessary, but if they are to be undertaken in South Malabar, they may also be introduced in this region."

The famine condition in Wayanad was worse than in Palghat and Calicut. A special medical report received by Logan from the civil dispensary at Vythiri stated that between March and July 1878, a total of 615 patients were admitted and treated in the hospital. Of these, 243 were due to famine-sickness, and among them 207 proved fatal. "This large mortality, viz. 33.68 per cent of the total treated, was due to people admitted to hospital at the last stages of exhausting from distress, malarial fever, dropsy, diarrhoea, and dysentery. Their exposure to wet and cold, insufficient clothing as well as privation, have a great tendency to accelerate death, in their already shattered and impoverished conditions".

Consolidating the letters received from various lower level officials, the Special Assistant Collector wrote to the Collector of Malabar in August 1878: "The crop has been destroyed by insects to some extent. Still, market appears to be having enough stocks of grain but prices continue to rise very steeply and this fact weighs heavily on the poor. Tahsildars have requested that some *kanji* (rice porridge) houses have to be opened and maintained for some time. They regret their inability to raise any local help for the purpose; the rich people are reluctant to come forward with any help because of the imposition of license tax and the enhancement of local cesses and salt tax."

The records of the correspondences between the Tahsildars and the Collector's office would show that when the permission was granted to set up *kanji* houses for free supply to paupers approaching for food, a large number of tents had sprung up. This helped the officials to submit inflated bills for the release of funds. The bills were shown against "wages of labour, petty establishment, sundries, gratuitous relief, purchase of food from bazaar, clothes, erection of sheds, and burial." Release of funds was also requested for charges incurred for deporting paupers to their native villages. The Malabar Collector's office was regularly writing to the *tahsildars* of Palghat and Wayanad as to why they were submitting most of the bills for expenses incurred against transport charges, while the requests for food charges were insignificant.

By the end of December 1878, famine subsided, and normalcy returned, as was evident from the total absence of beggars thronging at *kanji* houses. The grain-sheds erected for gratuitous feeding stopped functioning but the sheds were not disbanded. On 22 January 1879, the Consulting Engineer of the Railway Department at Madras wrote to the collector of Malabar: "The famine shed put up at Tirur was so close to the railway station. It affords a cover for natives to commit all sorts of nuisances which the station master says has become hurtful to the health of the station. The shed requires removal.....request you to issue necessary instructions for the removal of the shed." Finally, by the last week of January 1879, instructions were issued to the *tahsildars* to stop relief works, disband all famine-sheds and dispose of the tools procured in connection with famine-relief works.

2.4 Famines in Twentieth Century

This section will selectively examine some of the major famines that afflicted Malabar between 1900 and 1947, i.e. the last phase of the British rule in India. As noted earlier, the general opinion among the historians that there was no famine during this period except the localised Bengal famine of 1943 continues even now. This view was articulated initially by Blyn (1966), when he stated: "In 1942-43 cyclones and floods reduced the Bengal rice crop by about a third; this, coupled with absence of imports from Japanese-controlled Burma, and inadequate relief, led to famine, epidemics (of malaria, cholera, and smallpox) aggravated by widespread starvation which resulted in about a million more deaths than would have been normal for that period....*These unusual conditions did not, however, spread to other parts of India*" (emphasis added). Similarly, speaking about the condition of an average individual in British India during the first half of the twentieth century, Percival Spear, who taught history in Delhi University for more than one and a half decades since 1924, commented: "The only certain thing that could be said of him (a man of Indian colony) was that he now had, if not more to eat and wear, more amenities in the shape of general security, transport, public health, and freedom from total famine" (Spear, 1965). Later, this was reiterated by many others too.[12]

A very recent book by Cormac O'Grada, the noted Irish economic historian, argued: "the colonial regime that presided over several major famines in eighteenth and nineteenth century India also helped to keep the subcontinent free of famine between 1900 and Bengal famine of 1943-44. The change was partly due to improved communications, notably through railways, although the shift in ideology away from hard-line Malthusianism toward a focus on saving lives also mattered" (O'Grada 2009). Some authors who were not very sure of this line of argument still took the position that "famines due to harvest failures became rare after 1900" (see Roy 2006). In what follows we will see that, at least in the context of British Malabar, the facts speak otherwise. There are writings – not all related to Malabar – from which we could pick up four grievous famines that occurred respectively in 1918, 1924, 1933 and 1943. As the district was always on the verge of famine, there might have been more such miseries during this period. In the absence of archival records we will not be able to sketch such episodes with surety. Even the four episodes of famines for which there are records, we are not certain as to what extent these were not officially watered down. Generally, lower level officials reported a famine in a particular year only if they had to claim reimbursement of expenditures from the presidency head quarters. Likewise, the revenue collection authorities in the district revealed about a famine, as an explanation of why they could not hit the target fixed for land revenue collection in a particular year. These riders are to be kept in view while dealing with the famines that we have selected for the study here.

A. The Famine of 1918

The first piece of evidence about a devastating famine that shook Malabar in the first half of the twentieth century had taken place in the last year of the First World War. Writing about the role of the press in articulating anti-hunger strategies, N. Ram, former Editor-in-Chief of *The Hindu*, revealed that a famine (which he defined as 'a mass-level food crisis') had struck the presidency of Madras in 1918 and continued sporadically until the end of 1919. The crisis came in the open with 'a sudden rise in the prices of rice and other foodgrains, edible oil, chilli, tamarind, cloth, and other essential commodities'. The worst period was between the middle of May and the end of September 1918, when a 'spate of looting and grain riots' which 'like the influenza, left hardly a town or district of the province untouched'. Three weeks between 3 September and 25 September 1918, when the distress peaked, even villagers came to towns and weekly-markets to loot or just to destroy the grains hoarded by traders for profiteering. *The Hindu* wrote five editorials within these three weeks of mayhem, in addition to publishing numerous reports filed by its correspondents from different parts of the province about the horrors of the on-going famine (Ram, 1995). His narratives indicate that Malabar was one of the many districts in the presidency where looting and grain-riots had turned into its worst forms. From this, it has to be presumed that the impact of the 1918 famine might have been more serious on Malabar than other parts of the presidency. However, this was not a localised catastrophe specific to Madras presidency or Malabar alone. Earlier, Gadgil (1924) had stated that the 1918 famine was as horrible as the disastrous all-India famine of 1876-78.

The 1918 famine was unique in certain respects. The misery started after three years of normal-to-very-good harvests, especially of rice in southern and wheat in northern parts of the country. In 1915-16 and 1916-17, harvests were excellent and in 1917-18, not lower than normal. Whenever the southern region of the country had a bumper paddy harvest, the Indian diaspora in Ceylon (now Sri Lanka) and Gulf Straits used to normally rely on their motherland for food supply. As these bumper harvests coincided with the First World War, there was hardly any export of foodgrains from India to its diaspora or elsewhere. Exports to the allied countries engaged in the war also declined as, in the later years of the war, an armistice was within sight and the countries engaged in war, including the British administration in India, did not feel the need to stock food for the armed forces. Still, by the middle of 1918-19, it was feared that the stocks of foodgrains in the country might be insufficient for the remaining part of the year and that a food crisis could become inevitable (Gadgil 1924).

Monsoons

In 1918, the season was rather unfavourable. The south-west monsoon commenced unusually early in the middle of May. To begin with, the rain was very heavy in Malabar and other areas of the western coast of Madras presidency. However, in June, when the monsoon ought to have been normally heavy, it was considerably deficient. The total rainfall during June-September 1918 was below its long-term average. The situation became worse with the delayed arrival of north-east monsoon. Nonetheless, in November and December, the monsoon turned heavy in Malabar. The uneven pattern of rainfall disturbed sowings in both seasons. The total area under food crops in the entire presidency during 1918-19 was estimated at slightly more than 36 million acres, which was 92.4 per cent of the normal.[13]

After three better-to-not-less-than-normal harvests, with little or no exports, a reduction in the area under food crops in the subsequent season by just 7.6 per cent should not have caused a famine of this magnitude. The situation turned grim when massive attack of pests and diseases destroyed large parts of a whole spectrum of field and tree crops, including paddy, sorghum, ragi, pepper, rubber and coconut plantations.[14] The food crops sown during both the seasons were mostly destroyed by insects and pests. The government domestically procured the 'company seeds', imported better quality seeds from Cambodia, and sold these to cultivators at higher than the existing local market price for standard seeds. Poorer farmers who could not afford to buy these seeds left their lands fallow, knowing very well that keeping the land uncultivated would invite a penalty in the land revenue. The justification given in the annual administration report of the presidency for selling seeds at higher than the prevailing market price was this: "It has been suggested that this (seed) should be sold to the public cheap, but the experience of the department has been that it is much better to charge more than the market rate in order to ensure that it is not wasted and that the grower does not come back for more next time."[15]

Epidemics and Mortalities

In the meanwhile, an influenza epidemic started raging and, by the time the busy sowing season approached, it became virulent. Known as 'Spanish flu' at that time, it was believed to have originated in Spain during the First World War and spread through soldiers accommodated in congested barracks. The victims of this unusually deadly pandemic were mostly young adults, unlike the recent-day influenza, which affects mainly children, elderly and the weak-bodied individuals. The 1918-influenza led to an unprecedented increase in mortalities, and drastically reduced the number of normally available agricultural labourers. The disease was so widespread that it did not even spare officials in charge of agricultural extension services or the paramedical staff in the health-care institutions. Some of the medical service personnel were already deputed for defence duty. In the absence of enough staff and facilities, several influenza cases developed into typhoid, a more fatal disease than other types of fevers. In the municipality of Calicut, where the headquarters of the Malabar district situated, there was one general hospital, one women-and-children's hospital, a smallpox hospital, a cholera shed, and a small dispensary at Kallai. The two hospitals could accommodate about 92 patients. At the height of the pandemic, these hospitals had 1659 in-patients. Including the Kallai dispensary, another 65,768 cases were treated as out-patients in 1918, as compared with 58,622 in the preceding year.[16]

Apart from influenza and other fevers, such as typhoid and malaria, the diseases that started spreading faster than its usual scourge even before the outbreak of the famine were cholera, smallpox, dysentery and diarrhoea. The urban markets, especially the wholesale markets of Calicut and Palghat found an exacerbation of their perennial problem of rats falling dead and generating plague that added to the already devastating miseries. The *taluk* level reports periodically submitted for onward transmission to the headquarters of the presidency had been repeatedly highlighting the escalating deaths from cholera, plague, smallpox and fevers. While consolidating these reports for submission to the presidency, senior officials in the district simply denied that there was any unusual increase in any of the epidemics anywhere within their area of administration. For example, the District Medical and Sanitary Officer of Malabar countered the statements of his field-level junior employees from various *taluka*s that the statements in some of these reports of escalating deaths were mere 'exaggerations' and that, as against what was reported by these officials, 'the deaths were due to natural causes'. The Surgeon General, who put up this report to the Governor-General, forcefully supported the noting of the District Medical and Sanitary Officer: "I inspected the hospitals this morning. Everything was in good order."[17]

During the late nineteenth century, the district-wise annual administration reports used to provide information on healthcare, epidemics and mortalities, if any, with some details of how these miseries had happened. The reports of the Malabar district for the period of the First World War had also given information about epidemics and mortalities in some of the areas within the district, though these were either contradicted by the higher-ups in the official hierarchy or were not properly reported. Apart from these annual reports, the district-wise population census also had published for the first time, the year-wise mortalities by epidemics from 1911 to 1920, in the decennial 1921 census. However, these figures related to the West Coast region as a whole, without district-wise break-ups. A perusal of these figures gives an idea about the enormity of the epidemics and mortalities during the 1918-19 famine. A year before the famine escalated in, total mortalities from cholera, smallpox, plague, dysentery and diarrhoea were reported at 51199, which flared up to 205642 in the next two famine years.[18]

The authorities were not unaware why Malabar was a breeding ground of several infectious diseases and why these became virulent during famines. We have already noted in the preceding chapter that, continuous rains for most of the months in the year would lead to water-logging in Malabar, facilitating the breeding of mosquitoes that spread the diseases. In addition, there were other problems: (i) poor drinking water; (ii) lack of proper drainages; (iii) insufficiency of night-soil disposal facilities; and (iv) the indifference of the administration in taking up disease control measures.

Most people in the district used drinking-water from public or private wells. According to the annual administration report of the presidency for 1918, the people believed that water from wells were good, though quite often it might be bacterially poor. Several of these wells maintained by private households were not regularly cleansed and properly protected. People used these wells for other purposes like bathing and cleaning, in addition to using as drinking water and for cooking food The water in fact became contaminated due to its multifarious uses and served as a source of spreading several kinds of epidemics.

Another source of public health problem in the district was the drains in urban areas. Calicut municipality was the best example for this.[1] Here, the unclean drains filled with muck provided breeding-beds for mosquitoes. To make matters worse, heaps of solid wastes could be seen almost everywhere on the roads, as enough sweepers were never appointed by the district administration. During rainy seasons, wastes would decay and make the areas filthy. A part of these decayed wastes slipped into the drainages and blocked the flow of water. It was these drainages with stationary water on which mosquitoes multiplied and acted as carriers of epidemics.

The night-soil dispersed everywhere on the wayside acted as an even bigger health problem, particularly in the municipal areas of Calicut. The entire municipality had only three incinerators to burn the night-soil into ashes and dispose of as manure. Even for that, the government did not provide funds or appoint enough men and carts to take out the human faeces from residences to the incinerators. The municipal authorities, faced with mounting complaints, went on changing the methods to get rid of the human excreta from houses and roadsides. One method was to dump it in the incinerator, mix with saw-dust, burn and sell the ashes. But the incinerators were not able to procure enough saw-dust for the purpose because the households in the area were using it as cooking fuel. The second method was to make an emulsion of carbolic acid and kerosene oil to burn the night-soil. However, being too costly, this method had to be discarded. The third method proposed was to make trenches and fill the filth in them. On the alibi that there was no suitable space to dig the trenches, this proposal also was dropped.

Superimposed on these, the shortage of scavengers made matters worse. The Calicut municipality announced that it would arrange private scavengers to whichever household could bear the payment for their service. As regards the payment for the service, the municipality announced that "scavenging fees be made to some extent proportionate to the municipal tax paid, namely, that they should be somewhat raised for the richer and lowered for the poorer classes."[19] Though some of the households came forward and deposited the requisite amount with the municipality, there were complaints that, even after five years, no private scavengers visited their houses[20]. Fleas living on the night-soil carried all sorts of contagious diseases to the people living in the area, just as mosquitoes proliferated on stagnant water had been spreading fevers.

Lastly, the British administration had a policy to vaccinate the entire population whenever any fatal epidemic disease was anticipated. But this policy could not succeed because: (a) non-availability of sufficient vaccination staff, and (b) large number of people objected to the method of vaccination. The annual administration report of the Madras presidency for 1918 noted that in the entire Calicut municipality, which was an epicentre of a number of epidemics, there were only one female and two male vaccinators. Women from conservative families did not allow male staff to vaccinate them. Similarly, large number of people vehemently objected to vaccination because of the unscientific manner in which it was administered. Even if some of them had submitted to the persuasion of the officials and got vaccinated, they would destroy its effects immediately after vaccination by applying salt or chillies over the vaccinated area on the body.[21]

Land Revenue

The widespread misery from epidemics and famine was compounded by the excessively high land revenue demand and the coercive manner in which it was collected in Malabar. The officials had to meet additional targets to collect revenue every year. Other countries engaged in the war had raised extra funds through the sale of 'war-bonds'. In India also war-bonds with different denominations and maturities were issued but the government was aware that, being a poor country, only the wealthy, who were a small minority, could be asked to subscribe to these bonds. In order to make up for the shortage in the target of collection, the British administration decided to raise the land revenue from the already higher levels. As the rate of revenue charged from the ryots was saturated beyond the possibility of upward revision, innovative methods had to be devised. Thus, the Madras presidency ordered for a fresh land-survey without revealing that the actual objective. In order to conceal the purpose, different names were given for the survey in different areas within the district. For example, in Wayanad, it was called 'experimental survey', and in other areas, the 'quinquennial revision of touring map'. The survey employees were supported by a Special Settlement Officer, who made quick revision of the revenue assessment as and when the employees completed the survey in each village.[22]

As expected, these surveys, instead of giving any relief to the farmers, inflated the area under assessment and pushed up the revenue payable to the government. But the figures given in the official reports did not reveal the actual increase in the area. As Table-2.5 would show, these reports mentioned only the total number of holdings included for the revenue assessment and the number of villages from which these holdings were identified. The sub-division and fragmentation of land being an unending process in Malabar, the revenue officials knew that people would not doubt the increased number of holdings, instead of areas of land, indicated in the assessment report. Thus, the holdings under cultivation for revenue assessment registered a substantial increase from 1917-18, a monsoon-wise better year, to 1918-19, the year of aberrant monsoons accompanied by attacks of pests and diseases as also a severe famine.

With the increase in the number of holdings, the revenue assessed also registered an increase. This was contrary to the Famine Code of 1883, which stipulated that, during famines, relief should be given to the cultivators by way of remission of land revenue already collected, and suspension of fresh assessment and collection until the end of the calamity. The Madras presidency, while adopting the draft Famine Code, had slightly modified this provision. It added a clause that the administration should carry out a prompt survey in the beginning of every famine to ascertain the intensity of the calamity before deciding whether there was an abnormal situation that warranted remission or suspension of the revenue and, if so, the extent of the relief called for. This clause in the Famine Code allowed the officials to continue with the collection of revenue at the existing rate, even while the famine was raging, until the fresh survey was finalised and a decision taken on the new rate.[23]

During the 1918-19 famine, though the revenue collection was not suspended, deductions were allowed on certain holdings. The rate fixed for the deduction in Malabar was, per rupee, one *anna* on dry lands, two *annas* on registered garden lands, and one-and-three quarter *annas* on wet-lands.[24] However, these deductions in effect became infructuous as the revenue officials took back more than what they allowed by adding additional lands in the assessment under several accounts in such a way that it did not require previous permission of the higher-ups, nor could the cultivators approach the court of law for getting relief. Therefore, the number of holdings on which the revenue demand was estimated registered an increase in 1918-19, even though, as we noted earlier, a large number of small farmers had to leave their land uncultivated, as they could not buy the highly priced seeds for re-sowing their fields in which the crops were destroyed by attacks of insects and pests.

Table 2.5: Assessment of Ryotwari Land Revenue in Malabar, 1917–20

	1917-18		*1918-19*		*1919-20*	
	Extent	*Assessment*	*Extent*	*Assessment*	*Extent*	*Assessment*
1. Ryotwari villages	2223		2223			2223
2. Holdings (Total)	1288165	3303841	1294850	3310117	1303493	3316795
3. Deduction allowed	61565	158499	91906	175033	72034	146010
4. Remainder (Total)	1226600	3145342	1202944	3135084	1231459	3170785
5. Land taken (added)	68250	164775	100549	181711	83032	155788
6. Total holdings	1294850	3310117	1303493	3316795	1314491	3326573
7. Waste remitted	212	368	n.a	n.a	n.a	n.a
8. Final assessment	1294638	3559061	1303493	3565102	1314491	3573424

Just as inflating the revenue demand in the midst of a calamitous famine, coercive methods for collecting the land revenue (a legacy of Lord Lytton) continued unabated during the 1918-19 famine also. Table-2.6 gives an interesting narrative of this practice. When a cultivator failed to pay the land revenue in time, the method adopted to collect the dues, with penalty, became more ruthless. Not only land but his other properties were also confiscated by the revenue officials. These were valued very conservatively so that the confiscated properties could never match the defaulted amount to be paid to the government. As the market prices of the confiscated items, including land, were higher than the estimated values, the authorities had no difficulty to auction these items. In this process, the arrears payable to the government went on accumulating, even after the defaulter lost all his lands and other properties. Finally, he had only two options before him: to borrow from the indigenous money lender at exorbitantly higher rates of interest, or to land up in jail. We have seen that the first option was more dangerous in case he delayed the payment of instalments to the money lender. Then the debtor not only loses his land and other belongings but also, quite often, the honour of the female members in the family.

Food Prices

A general crop failure, coupled with the conditions arising out of the on-going war, led to a sharp rise in the prices of foodgrains. The average wholesale prices of rice reported in Malabar at Rs 51 60 per 10 maunds in 1914, the year in which the First World War broke out, remained firm around that level in the next two years notwithstanding a bumper foodgrains harvest. In 1917-18, the average of the wholesale prices of rice worked out to 5 per cent lower at Rs 49.40 per 10 maunds than in the previous year. In the next two years, prices flared up to unprecedented heights. Compared to 1917-18, the wholesale price of rice was higher by 32 per cent in 1918-19, and by 75 per cent in 1919-20 (Table-2.7).

The run-away rise in prices of foodgrains and other essentials was caused by the massive increase in deficit financing to meet the war expenditures. Though India or even Indian borders were not involved in the First World War, there was tremendous expansion in the recruitment to Indian army. The increase in recruitment was of the order of 1.2 million. Thousands among them were sent to fight and die in alien countries like Mesopotamia. The services of the village chieftains were used to coerce the young men to join the army. The British administration boasted that in some regions they were able to tremendously increase the army-recruitments so that, in a single year, the proportion of defence personnel to the adult males, which was 1:150 before the First World War, became 1:44 in the midst of the war. Such an increase led *inter alia* to an unprecedented increase in defence expenditure, the financing of which called for massive printing of currency notes, which in turn pushed up the prices of foodgrains (Sarkar 1983).

The situation became worse with the shortage created by the massive diversion of foodgrains from civilian use to the army personnel. Even though exports of cereals and other essential items were banned, in the absence of movement restrictions within the country, speculators had a field day. They cornered whatever quantity they could and hoarded for pushing up the prices. When the prices of rice rose, people shifted their consumption to

Table 2.6: Coercive Processes Adopted for Revenue Collection in Malabar, 1917-20

	1917-18	*1918-19*	*1919-20*
1. Number of processes.			
(a) Notice of demand	20100	15753	12796
(b) Notice of attachment	3499	2481	1801
(c) Notice of sale	2967	2129	1671
2. Property attached:			
(i) Personal			
No. of defaulters	3186	1949	1334
Amount of arrears	110985	74492	70228
Value of property distrained	136183	83282	88224
(ii) Real			
No. of defaulters	313	532	467
Amount of arrears	18723	23859	21322
(a) Dry land (area)	4195	4325	2812
Amount	2488	4504	3542
(b) Wet land (area)	1509	2548	2182
Amount	3564	5243	4314
3. Property sold:			
(i) Personal			
No. of defaulters	60	59	18
Amount of arrears	1516	1104	5333
Estd. value of property	1378	1210	2313
Amount realised	1095	1162	2261
(ii) Real			
No. of defaulters	58	74	95
Amount of arrears	2838	3588	3790
Estd. value of property	9117	12027	15902
Amount realised	9636	5934	15130
4. Land sold:			
(a) Dry land (area)	29	11	29
Amount	33	12	51
(b) Wet land (area)	35	45	79
Amount	49	70	118
Govt. bought at	40	6	6
Others purchased at	9631	8928	15124
5. Total amount realised	10731	7096	17391

Table 2.7: Malabar - Average Wholesale Prices of Rice (Rs/10 maunds)

	Rupees	*percentage*
1900	41.60	
1901	44.04	5.9
1902	38.87	-11.7
1903	34.09	-12.3
1904	32.72	-4.0
1905	38.92	18.9
1906	46.62	19.8
1907	49.33	5.8
1908	53.53	8.5
1909	48.84	-8.8
1910	41.98	-14.0
1911	43.55	3.7
1912	50.70	16.4
1913	53.13	4.8
1914	51.60	-2.9
1915	50.05	-3.0
1916	51.92	3.7
1917	49.40	-4.9
1918	64.97	31.5
1919	86.24	32.7

Source: Malabar District Gazetteer, Volume III, 1933.

Table 2.8: Malabar - Retail Prices of Foodgrains (Seer/rupee)

	Norml/Avg	*1916-17*	*1917-18*	*1918-19*	*1919-20*
Rice	8.0	7.4	6.8	5.1	4.3
Paddy	14.3	12.0	11.0	8.3	6.8
Ragi	11.1	15.4	13.9	9.3	6.2
Horsegram	13.0	12.7	10.1	6.8	5.4

Source: Land Revenue Settlement and Season and Crop Reports (Madras)

low-priced minor cereals available in the open market, namely, ragi and sorghum. Consequently, the prices of these cereals also started rising sometimes faster than the prices of rice. *The Hindu*, in one of its editorials wrote about the manner in which prices of essential commodities spiralled up: "the rise in prices of one article leads to a sympathetic rise in the rest. Chillies have gone up abnormally in prices. For what we paid 4 *annas* odd three months ago, today we are called upon to pay Rs 1.10; black grams similarly has risen by about 50 per cent, salt has gone up, we hear, by six *annas* a measure, a rise of 100 per cent; rice also shows a marked tendency to rise; ghee and oils are characterised by the same feature." The editorial further stated that this was going on as "profiteering remains unchecked on an immense scale...The responsibility for eliminating profiteering and reducing the suffering of the people to a minimum rests on the government."[25]

The Famine Code of 1883 required the government to keep a close watch on the movement of foodgrain prices and as soon as these reached the 'warning rate', to start relief works immediately so that the people were rescued from plunging into the rigours of famine. The Madras government had declared for Malabar 8 *seer*s of 80 *tola* each of the second sort of rice per rupee as the 'normal rate', 6 *seers* per rupee as 'warning rate', and 5 *seers* per rupee as 'scarcity rate'. The annual average of the cereal prices of rice in Malabar had risen to the periphery of 'scarcity rate' during 1918-19, indicating that in several centres from where these prices were quoted had reached the 'warning rate' and that the government should have started famine relief operations much earlier. The retail prices of paddy rose faster than directly consumable rice (paddy without husk), and the prices of ragi, which the poorest people ate as their daily cereal, increased faster than the prices of rice or paddy (Table-2.8). *The Hindu*, which was regularly reporting the prices of various foodgrains in different centres had cautioned the government that the 'scarcity' and 'famine' rates were going on in most parts of the presidency and that it was high time the famine relief operations initiated (Ram, 1995). Instead, the government exhibited, in the words of Ram, "a certain Olympian indifference", as revealed by the fact that senior officials in Madras presidency were taking rest in the summer capital of Ootacamund while the crisis was at its peak.[26]

In line with the secondary market prices, the harvest prices of particularly paddy/ rice in the primary market were also going up. It could perhaps be argued that cultivators and others dependent on agriculture had benefited from the war-time inflation and that there were no serious entitlement failures in the district. For instance, the post harvest prices of rice quoted in the primary market, on average, at 4 rupees and twelve *anna*s per *maund* in 1914-15, increased to 7 rupees, 11 *anna*s in 1918-19, and further to 8 rupees, 14 *anna*s in 1919-20 (Table-2.9). However, during the British era, especially after the mode of payment of land revenue was shifted from 'kind' to money terms, any increase in prices of agricultural products immediately raised the land revenue so that the cultivator remained where he was before the prices of his output rose. Because of this the wages for agricultural labourers and payments for rural artisans for the services rendered for farming-operations remained unchanged. Further, as larger sections of cultivators had to borrow from moneylenders against hypothecation of the anticipated harvest, the benefit of any rise in prices accrued to the latter.

Table 2.9: Malabar - Harvest Prices of Rice (Rs / maund)

Year	*Rupees*	*Year*	*Rupees*
1904-05	3.02.0	1922-23	7.00.0
1905-06	3.15.0	1923-24	7.00.0
1906-07	4.13.0	1924-25	7.11.0
1907-08	5.03.0	1925-26	7.02.0
1908-09	5.05.0	1926-27	7.00.0
1909-10	4.13.0	1927-28	7.00.0
1910-11	4.08.0	1928-29	6.12.0
1911-12	5.00.0	1929-30	6.00.0
1912-13	5.06.0	1930-31	5.00.0
1913-14	5.03.0	1931-32	4.00.0
1914-15	4.12.0	1932-33	3.10.0
1915-16	4.12.0	1933-34	2.15.0
1916-17	4.14.0	1934-35	3.06.0
1917-18	5.01.0	1935-36	3.11.0
1918-19	7.11.0	1936-37	3.07.0
1919-20	8.14.0	1937-38	3.10.0
1920-21	7.04.0	1938-39	3.09.0
1921-22	7.04.0	1939-40	3.12.0

Note: A maund = 82 2/7 lbs.)

Source: Prices and Wages of India, Department of Statistics, India (various issues).

Food-Riots

The economic conditions at the closing phase of the First World War were unusually abnormal. The prices of all articles, particularly of food items rose steadily. The distress was so severe among the economically weaker segments of the population that there were food-riots in many places. All sorts of crimes became widespread: house-breaking, theft, robberies, and even murders. Official records stated that the crimes that erupted in the peak of the famine of 1918-19 had reached "a level unsurpassed during the last forty years." Yet another development at that time was the making of fake-coins. Though the annual administration report of the Madras Presidency for 1918-19 had reflected all these developments, it would appear that there was an attempt to under-play the severity of these developments. The shortage of field level staff and the law and maintenance officials, who were mostly deployed for war, was another reason for under-reporting of food-riots. It would also appear that there was some human-touch in the official reports, which explained away these developments in the following words: "most of these (crimes) were small disturbances in which hungry populace turned out to plunder granaries and shops."

David Arnold, who conducted a study on the spontaneous grain-riots of the 1918 famine in the southern part of British India vis-à-vis the government policy, stated that a conjunction of factors were responsible for these developments. "Looting and rioting", to quote Arnold, "were expressions of the bewilderment, panic and anger felt by the poorer classes of the province when faced with abrupt price rises or the sudden disappearances of foodgrains from the bazaars while large quantities of grain were known to be stacked in warehouses or barges and in railway yards ready for export elsewhere" (Arnold, 1979). The grain-riots that broke out initially in a few areas of acute scarcity soon spread to other parts of the presidency. It was reported that 15 out of 25 districts, including Malabar, witnessed three days of continuous rioting and looting. Though it was the poorer segments of the society that started the food-riots, when the agitation progressed, even government employees and others belonging to the middle-class joined the mass movement. In the beginning, the participants in the rioting and looting were from the urban areas. When traders raised the prices of foodgrains every day, even villagers converged to the urban trading centres and weekly-markets, looted or destroyed the foodgrains and other items on sale. According to Arnold, widespread disturbances compelled the traders to close down their shops, mainly after sunset, which was the time when the mayhem aggravated. "Most of the poor obtain their supplies in the evening and have their only hot meal at night. The disturbances stopped all sales, and many families had to starve on Sunday night. Riots were therefore inevitable on Monday, if some plan were not arranged to supply the daily requirement" (Arnold, 1979).

The genuineness of these spontaneous uprisings could be judged from the unusual attitude of the police and the district officials. In several places, the police sided with the rioters and asked the traders to bring down the prices to reasonable levels. Similarly, when the government wanted to repress the rising food-riots ruthlessly, many officials in the district, instead of carrying out the orders, showed sympathy towards the agitators. If at all they intervened, it was in favour of the public to ask traders to sell at lower prices so that the agitation would automatically subside. The district authorities also requested the higher-ups to allow prohibition of grain 'exports' and to permit 'imports' of grain from the northern surplus regions. These requests were flatly rejected on the argument that the whole of India being one unit, such practices would inhibit the freedom of trade. In fact the real intention behind tacit permission that government offered the private traders for unlimited profiteering in the midst of a miserable famine was to collect a portion of the 'super-normal' profit from speculation towards the British war fund against the issue of long-term war-bonds (Ram, 1995).

B. The famine of 1924

The second bout of famine recorded in Malabar occurred during the inter-war period of the last millennium. This was the result of heavy rains, flash flood and devastating cyclone, the ferocity of which was unprecedented in the history of the district. According to the Season and Crop Report of the Madras presidency for 1924-25, the south-west monsoon began on the West Coast from the beginning of June itself and continued almost without break until the 7th September 1924. Between July 15 and 25, the downpour was the heaviest, particularly in Malabar. The severity of rainfall could be judged from the fact that, as against the long-run average of 88.4 inches in the previous fifty years, the rains from the south-west monsoon in 1924 was estimated at 150.5 inches, and the total rain from south-west and north-east monsoons, almost 178 inches. The rain was so excessive that it caused considerable damages to the tea estates even in the hilly areas of the district, in addition to destroying field crops already sown and creating difficulties for taking up re-sowing to compensate the lost crops. The official reports stated that the floods damaged the communication networks and railway traffics, and washed away fodder stacks as well as paddy and rice stored by farm families for their subsistence.[27]

The extent of damages to the life and property in Malabar was so severe that the Reuter reported from Delhi: In a single day in July 1924 the flash flood caused widespread devastation, which was greater than the total damages that could happen to the area during any other adverse season in the past. "Though the loss of life so far reported", according to Reuter, "is small, the loss of property, cattle and crops is very heavy; particulars are meagre owing to breakdown in communications. Railway communication to Malabar has been cut off since July 17.....Calicut, where lives have been lost, experienced a night of terror, the sudden rise of water imprisoning the people in their homes. They were rescued in boats. Over thousand houses collapsed. Thousands of homeless people have been swelled by refugees."[28]

The cyclone and flood had destroyed crops and properties in several areas of Wayanad, Cannanore, Tellicherry, Tirur, Eranad, Palghat and the Malabar portion of Cochin but the impact of the disasters was extremely catastrophic in Calicut. A separate file kept in Collector's office to record the day-today position of the calamity showed that most of the houses of both rich and poor, as well as several provision shops had been destroyed in the municipality by flood and cyclone. The fury of the nature was so devastating that even the well-known saw-mill of Parry and Company at Kallai could not survive. The people belonging to both rich and poor classes without distinction had to vacate, as their houses were inundated, if not washed off. A sizable section among them became refugees. The remaining people were accommodated in the Zamorin's College at Tali.[29]

Production and Prices

Compared to other districts in the presidency, food production in Malabar was seriously hampered. Thousands of acres of wetlands under paddy were silted and became unfit for cultivation. According to official estimates, the area under paddy in 1924-25 was almost 11000 acres less than during the preceding season. Of the minor food crops cultivated in the district, except ragi, other cereals like *Cholam* and *Cumbu* were totally discarded in the presence of adverse climate throughout the year. In normal times, any decline in the local production could be compensated, by 'imports' from surplus areas. As roads were submerged under water and the railways dislocated throughout Malabar for more than a month, neither the government nor the private traders could attempt this possibility.

Just as access to food, another crucial problem that the peasants confronted during the famine of 1924 was how, and where, to procure seeds to replace the lost crops as far as possible. When the Governor asked for its comment on the problem, the Agricultural Department replied: "This is not for the government to worry. The ryots themselves will be able to make independent arrangements for seeds." What the cultivators urgently require is money for which some suitable arrangement has to be found out. "The money lenders are now asking for cent percent interest; if poor ryots are not saved from them at this juncture, their condition will be hopeless." The cooperative societies are understandably the most appropriate source. They can advance money without fear 'as they are of unlimited liability'. There are already a few societies functioning in some of the villages. In others, societies have to be organised expeditiously."[30]

With the shrinkage of acreage under the crops, and the non-availability of inputs for re-sowing, wherever possible, the local production of foodgrains suffered a setback. Consequently, prices of rice and other foodgrains started shooting up since the rainy season began. Contrary to the normal experience, even the post-harvest prices of cereals shot up in Malabar, indicating the sharp decline in the harvested quantity of food supply. However, the official report stated that "prices of the principal foodgrains were at first higher than the previous *fasli* owing to poor harvest" but "fell steadily after October 1924 owing to the fair harvests of the early season crops. Prices at the end of the *fasli* were appreciably lower."[31] The report also stated that the prices of imported foodgrains were still lower whereas "the export-prices of oil-cakes, copra, gingelly, unrefined sugar and cotton piece goods had advanced", meaning that the entitlement to food of the people who produced these items had not affected due to the 1924 flood. Lack of food and shelter in the face of extremely adverse weather, epidemics and famine rampant everywhere in the district.

Epidemics and Mortalities

Usually, the rainy season is the time when a number of fatal and not-so-fatal diseases crops up in Malabar. Being one of the unhealthiest years, 1924-25 witnessed some of these diseases flaring up with unprecedented vigour in several parts of the district. Dysentery and diarrhoea, the ailments that afflict the hungry and spread quickly under low standards of general sanitation continued throughout the year, taking away about 75 thousand lives. The next was cholera, which killed 52 thousand people. Among other diseases, smallpox, malaria and respiratory diseases, mainly tuberculosis, were widely prevalent. In Calicut municipal area, there was an unusual increase in the attack of plague.

Children were the main victims of most of the diseases. The government ordered that, in areas where these diseases were likely to be severe, children should be compulsorily vaccinated. In other areas, attempts should be made to identify children in the families, as per the information readily available in the birth and death registers, and ask the respective local bodies to get them vaccinated. But the annual administration report for the year stated that, in Malabar, vaccination could not be successful even in compulsory vaccination areas (not to speak of other areas), because of "the difficulty to secure the vaccination of unprotected children.........; the reluctance of many local bodies to enforce strictly the provisions of law relating to compulsory vaccination; and the failure to maintain correctly the registers of vital statistics and vaccination registers."[32]

It is not difficult to perceive that, lack of medical care and administrative arrangements for sanitation should have led to excessive unnatural mortalities in the district. However, the 1924-25 annual administration report, instead of giving a rough figure of around 10 lakh deaths during the year in the presidency as a whole, did not give the human mortalities in the flood and famine affected Malabar and other areas. The report simply stated that the mortality statements submitted by the lower formations were not dependable because: (i) these were collected by untrained staff; (ii) as the staff directed to take up this work had to do it in addition to their regular job, they did not show any interest in it; (iii) even if they wanted to do this work, lack of transport and communication as well as the difficulty caused by the floods prevented them from doing the work.[33]

Land Revenue

Considering 'the unprecedented cyclone and flood that led to inundation and loss of crops' in Malabar, the government announced that relief would be granted to the affected farmers in the form of 'suspension or remission' of land revenue as provided under the 1883 Famine Code. Concurrently, the district administration was asked to keep in view the following three points while submitting the claim for relief from the payment of land revenue: (i) the request should be based purely on merit as supported by field-to-field inspection; (ii) as the monsoon in Malabar was 'decidedly favourable' until the flash flood, the crop loss need not necessarily be significant; and (iii) where the land has not been sub-merged or silted, the crops should be above average, calling for a higher revenue assessment, not a waiver or remission of revenue.

The district officials took these orders in letter and spirit. As soon as the field level reports from Tahsildars were received on the extent of crop-loss, the Collector asked the Revenue Divisional Officer (RDO) of Calicut to verify the authenticity of the facts. A sample of the notings in the Collectorate file, as summarised below, would reveal how the RDO treated these reports: (1) In Cochin, the single crop-lands were fully submerged. Nonetheless, as the ryots had attempted to raise a second crop, the question of remission or suspension of revenue does not arise. (2) In Wayanad, heavy rains and flood had completely destroyed the crops on both sides of the Panamaram and Mananthody rivers. Another part of the taluk had faced land slips. Taken together, these two areas constituted a very small portion of Wayanad. Hence, there was no need for any relief to be granted. (3) In Tellicherry, pepper vines, arecanut trees, coconut plantations, and the paddy crops on the banks of the rivers were damaged. But these were not very serious to be considered for any relief. (4) In Palghat, floods destroyed crops on 286.45 acres of land. There was still time for taking up a second crop. Hence, the question of suspension or remission of revenue could be kept in abeyance for the time being. In short, the negative bureaucratic attitude debarred the declared reprieve under the Famine Code from reaching the farming community at a time when flood and famine were raging.

On the basis of these justifications, the government also went on coercing the ryots with increased demand for land revenue and various cesses on the *ryotwari* land. The coercive processes initiated against the defaulters of timely revenue payment were larger during 1924-25 than the next year, when there were no natural calamities or famine. Still the government insisted that it had issued notices 'only when absolutely necessary'. For the large increase in the collection of land revenue in a year when there was an unprecedented natural calamity in the district, the government stated that the increase over the previous year was due to– (i) the introduction of a new resettlement rate, (ii) collection of postponed revenue, and (iii) better compliance by the law-abiding cultivators.

Famine Relief and Famine Insurance

Under Section IV of the Devolution Rules, the Provincial Government was required to make every year, with effect from 1921-22, a sum of Rs 6.61 lakh in the budget estimate for expenditure up on famine relief and famine insurance in the presidency.[34] The amount was to be utilised only for extending famine relief, or for the construction of protective irrigation works, or for any other work which, in the opinion of the administration, would prevent famines in future. The unspent balance, if any, was to be used to build up a Famine Insurance Fund. As this fund was treated, in terms of the Devolution Rules, as invested with the Government of India, the presidency could earn an interest. Influenced probably by this provision, in addition to the bureaucratic indifference towards the plight of the local people, neither the provincial government nor the district authorities of Malabar used the amount for any of the purposes for which it was set apart in the budget. The only outgo from the budget provision was a very insignificant sum towards Taccavi loans. This would be evident from the fact that, as against an opening balance of about Rs 12 lakh in the famine Insurance Funs as on the first of April 1924, the closing balance stood at Rs 14.26 lakh on 31 March 1925.

The district administration appeared very adamant in not using government funds for flood and famine relief. For example, on the directive from the head quarters of the presidency, the Collector had started a Central Relief Fund in Calicut with an initial corpus of Rs 10 thousand. It received another sum of Rs 20 thousand from the budget allocation. The Collector refused to release the fund for gratuitous distribution of food despite the entire population in some of the areas in the district continued to starve without food. Instead, he wrote to the Tahsildars: "If you find any place actually lacking in rice, you should get hold the needed quantity from somewhere and if you are out of pocket, then, let me know; I will meet the deficit so far as we are able."[35]

Gandhiji's Intervention

In this milieu, private charities were of immense help to the people. The most notable among them was Gandhiji's intervention. There are long notes in the *Collected Works* of Mahatma Gandhi, originally published in

Young India and *Navajivan*, narrating how he came across this holocaust and how he could extend a helping hand to the helpless people. Gandhiji wrote that, unlike other famines, which had originated elsewhere and spread to the district, the 1924 famine emerged from the nature's fury mainly in Malabar and spread to other areas. The normal life in the district was completely disrupted. The loss of crops, cattle and houses in the fury of the unprecedented cyclone and flood was so widespread that the famine that followed affected not only the poorer sections but also the otherwise 'clean and tidy middle-class families' (Gandhi, 1924). This was brought to the notice of Gandhiji by some of the women from Malabar, who were active in the national independence movement at Sabarmati Ashram. Hearing about the misery on his release from jail, where he was incarcerated by the British administration for launching the non-cooperation movement, Gandhiji gave an appeal in *Young India* for generous contribution of money and clothes to the helpless people of Malabar.

In the appeal, Gandhiji specifically stated that those who contributed money would be issued receipts by the designated volunteers. If they did not get the receipts, it should be brought to his notice. Regarding the contributions of clothes, Gandhiji asked the donors that: "(a) used clothes may be washed before they are offered, (b) torn garments may first be stitched; and (c) all clothes may be properly folded, bundled and labelled with the name of the donor and the number of garments." A few days after the appeal, Gandhiji wrote that he was extremely overwhelmed by the response received from various quarters: "Readers will be glad to know that some brothers and sisters are missing a meal every day, some have given up milk or other things and they are contributing to the fund.....Even children have joined this work spontaneously" (Gandhiji, 1924).

In one of his *Navajivan* articles, Gandhiji stated that the response from children and students in this case was reminiscent of his South African campaign: A section of pupils from a school collected cotton yarn and contributed. A group of 75 students joined as labourers for the construction of their college-building and the wages earned were pooled together for donating towards relief works in Malabar. Gandhiji further wrote: "Even children have joined this work spontaneously.....A small girl had stolen three pice (paise) which too she paid to the Fund. A sister has donated her four bracelets and a chain of pure gold. Another sister has given her heavy necklace. A child has parted with his gold trinket and a sister with her silver anklets......"

The official report, particularly the annual administration report for the year, however, totally ignored these efforts, as Gandhiji was then leading the independence movement. It simply stated that some of the charitable organisations, including the Servants of India Society, had organised limited relief works. It was mainly the government that came forward with effective famine relief operation. Particularly, arrangements were made with Kovilakam (i.e. Zamorin Raja) to distribute *kanji* for one month.

C. The Famine of 1933

The third famine of the last millennium started in Malabar during the early 1930s and continued beyond the mid-thirties. This famine was characterised by widespread unemployment, hunger and malnutrition, especially in the northern part of the district. The seriousness of the misery came to light when legendary communist leader, A.K Gopalan, organised a large number of affected people and took out a 'hunger march' from Kuthuparamba to the police station at Tellicherry. With the unusual sympathy that the police extended to the peaceful procession, A.K.G. decided to lead another massive 'hunger march' from Kannur to the headquarters of Madras presidency. This unprecedented popular mobilisation was widely reported mainly because of the otherwise unsympathetic police force joining the march from all routes to Madras (A.K.G. 1980).[36] A casual perusal of the archival records would show that the 'hunger march' was the impact of the Great Depression of the 1930s in the U.S. and that the actual famine had reached its peak in Malabar in 1933, as was characterised by the highest level of mortalities in the district. Unlike the 1918 'boom famine', the famine of 1933 was a 'slump famine'. If the former resulted from the deficit financing-led war expenditures, coupled with a major monsoon failure, the latter originated from the Great Depression of the 1930s in the United States and spread like a wild-fire across the world (both developed and developing), except the erstwhile Soviet Union and other planned economies of the socialist block. By that time, the American economy had grown to such a stature that, to recall the adage: "When America sneezes, the rest of the world catch pneumonia."

Innumerable books and articles written on the Great Depression are more or less unanimous about how the symptom of this devastating human misery appeared on the first instance: Beginning from what is called the 'Black Thursday' on 24 October 1929, when the Wall Street crash started, it continued to slip incessantly for the next three years and reached its Nadir in July 1932. The asset price deflation (as it is called in the present day stock market language) infected other sectors of the economy before creating the worst holocaust in human history. In the U.S. the aggregate output collapsed by a third and, contrary to the notions of free market behaviour, prices also followed the same trend. Unemployment climbed up to almost 35 per cent of the civilian labour force in the U.S. The world trade shrank by two-thirds of the level that recorded before the crisis began and the depression became a global catastrophe (Galbraith 1954; Ferguson 2008). And the Indian colony, being the 'periphery' of British imperialism, could not escape.

Monsoons and Food Production

According to the 'season and crop reports' of the Madras presidency, monsoons in the years around the 1933 famine had a peculiar pattern. The south-west monsoon used to set in at least ten days earlier in the month of May on the coastal areas of Malabar. But when, it reached its historically given date of the first June, the rainfall was not only unusually weak but also uneven throughout June to September, known as the months of south-west monsoon. Conversely, the north-east monsoon was very heavy in 1932-33 but normal during the next year. In the previous season, while it caused floods in some areas of the presidency, Malabar was spared by such a natural outrage. Therefore, while in other areas of the presidency it seriously affected the crops, sowing operations in Malabar could be continued uninterrupted during south-west and north-east monsoons. Even the standing crops were not spared by the floods in Malabar, unlike in some other districts of the presidency. Both the early crops sown in the south-west monsoon and the late-sown crops of the north-east monsoon during both these seasons were by and large normal.[37]

It would appear from the behaviour of monsoons in the early 1930s that these were highly uneven and irregular in different parts of the country. The impact of monsoons on output, availability and prices were unmistakable. For the long-term trends in production, we have Blyn's compilation of agricultural trends from 1891 to 1947, which are presented in terms of yield, or output, of individual crops expressed in quantities measured by tons, and the aggregate and crop-wise outputs valued at current market prices, for British India and for different provinces within it. From these figures, if we consider the production of foodgrains from 1928 (the year just before the depression started) to 1934 (the year in which the depression assumed its worst form), instead of recording any increase either in British India or in Madras presidency, it had tumbled by 5.4 per cent. The decline in the production of rice, the staple of the region, was still steeper (Table-2.10). Between 1928 and 1934, while the rice output in British India declined by (-) 6.3 per cent, the decline in the presidency of Madras was estimated at (-) 4.2 per cent. In Malabar, however, the condition appeared somewhat different. According to the figures available from the 'season and crop reports', area under paddy, which was solely rainfed in the district, recorded 22.5 thousand acres more in 1933-34 and per acre yield higher by 126 lbs, or 9.4 per cent, than during the preceding year (Table-2.11).[38]

Farm Prices

The most noteworthy repercussion of the Great Depression of the U.S. on the Indian economy, as Gadgil (1924) narrated, was "the rapid, absolute and relative fall in the prices of agricultural products." The value of outputs of all crops, that is, the outputs estimated at "current" market prices, nose-dived between 1928-29 and 1933-34 to the extent of (-) 54 per cent in both British India and Madras Presidency. The decline was as deep as (-) 60 per cent in Bengal, Bihar and Orissa, though it was only (-) 50 per cent in the presidency of Bombay. Steep downfall in farm prices within a very short period of two to three years was not the experience of British India alone. The economies bitten by the Great Depression had all faced their farm prices crashing to the pre-First World War levels. Even where agricultural produce was not exported but only catered to the home market, the crash in prices could not be prevented. The principal cereals produced in India, namely, rice and wheat can be taken as cases in point. These cereals were mostly consumed within the country. Still, their prices followed the down trends of the world market and remained deeply depressed throughout the first half of the 1930s. This is substantiated by the steep decline witnessed in the value of production (i.e. output multiplied by current market price) of principal agricultural crops throughout the British India (Table-2.12).

Going by the conventional economic wisdom, it was believed that the vertical fall in prices might have been caused by over-production. Those who examined this argument had found that, between 1928 and 1934, there was over-production only in raw-jute and that, in the case of wheat, there was a slight increase in production which could not be considered as excessively high for the price to decline so steeply. All other crops had reported a decline in production. The market logic in this situation had in fact called for an increase in prices. Instead they tumbled across the board. The most important and dramatic fall in prices occurred in the case of wheat and rice. Of late, a good amount of these two cereals was exported mainly to England. According to official reports, the rice exported from India accounted for 2.2 million tons in 1930-31 and 2.3 million tons in 1931-32, but these were not reflected in prices. Next year there was a dramatic decline in the exports of all agricultural commodities, including rice. This was attributed, apart from anything else, to the following two reasons: (i) with the Great Depression engulfing countries after countries, the conventional importers of Indian farm products stopped their purchase; and (ii) in order to prevent external suppliers from vanquishing their markets, the developed countries imposed tariff barriers, quota systems, exchange restrictions etc. Along with this, currency fluctuations and political instability in many countries across the world affected Indian exports of agricultural commodities (see Gadgil, 1924).

The quantity that was not exported on account of the depressed conditions in the global market had found its way into the domestic market. That must be one reason why farm prices dipped in India. However, the share of Indian agriculture in the world trade was extremely meagre. If such a relatively insignificant quantity that could not be exported came back to the domestic market, especially when there was a downslide in production, it could not have depressed the market prices in 1933-34 as reported. Further the growth of population was also expected to have added to the aggregate demand, which should have pushed up the market prices. If that has not happened, the reason for an unprecedented, across the board slump in the market prices of agricultural commodities have to be seen in the 'invisible' exogenous factors imposed by the Great Depression (Gadgil, 1924; Rothermund, 1983).

Table 2.10: Production of Foodgrains, 1928-34 (tons)

	Total foodgrains		*Rice*	
	British India	*Madras presidency*	*British India*	*Madras presidency*
1928	13926	3175	26515	5197
1929	13768	3211	25802	5255
1930	13873	3298	26472	5376
1931	14333	3299	27721	5385
1932	13323	3342	25348	5406
1933	12995	3335	24891	5314
1934	13179	3002	24842	4981
Percentage change (1928-34)	-5.4	-5.4	-6.3	-4.2

Source: George Blyn (1966), op.cit.

Table 2.11: Malabar - Area, Production and Yield of Rice

	Paddy (Area-acres)		*Yield (lbs)*		*Production (tons)*	
	Normal	*Actual*	*Normal*	*Actual*	*Paddy*	*Rice*
1932-33	875000	869368	1400	1344	321620	215485
1933-34	875000	891832	1400	1470	385000	257950
1934-35	875000	864676	1400	1174	378000	253260

Source: Estimated from the Season and Crop Reports of Madras Presidency (for relevant years)

Table 2.12: Value of Production of Principal Crops, 1928-34

(Rs/lakh)

	1928-29	*1931-32*	*1932-33*	*1933-34*
Madras	18078	10125	9933	8317
Bombay	12052	6656	8386	6052
Bengal	23259	10671	9054	9556
Bihar and Orissa	13517	7105	5655	5463
British India	101851	53689	53467	47323

Source: Chapter XV, "The Agriculturist, 1914-39", in Gadgil (1924), op.cit

Of all agricultural commodities, it was food crops that experienced the sharpest fall in prices. This was eminently evident in Malabar, as elsewhere in British India. Grain prices collapsed in both primary and secondary markets. For instance, the harvest prices of rice, after reaching an all time peak at the end of the First World War recorded a moderate decline thereafter and stabilised around that level until 1927-28. Then these prices started declining to reach an all-time low by 1933-34, the worst year of the global depression. A closer look at the centre-wise retail prices of paddy would show that the condition was universally true in the whole length and breadth of the district. We have the retail prices of both first and second sort paddy in 12 and 18 centres, respectively, in Malabar between 1913-14 and 1934-35 (Tables-2.13a and 2.13b). Considering the change in prices between 1913-14 and 1933-34, the average decline in the retail prices of the first-sort paddy was (-) 37.3 per cent in the span of two decades. Of the 12 centres for which these prices were reported, only the surplus producing Palghat accounted for the lowest decline of (-) 10 per cent, another two centres recorded the decline in the range of (-) 22–30 per cent, seven centres in the range of (-) 30–40 per cent, and one centre, *viz.* Alathur, (-) 45 per cent. During the same period the retail prices of the second-sort paddy recorded an average decline of (-) 44 per cent Out of 18 centres from which prices were reported, the decline varied in the range of (-) 35–40 per cent in eight centres, (-) 40–48 per cent in another eight centres and between (-) 56–60 per cent in the remaining two centres.

The retail prices of common variety of rice declined, on average, by (-) 44 per cent in Malabar in 1933-34 over 1913-14, the pre-First World War year. Of the 19 centres in the district for which we have the data on retail prices of rice, the decline was between (-) 30 to (–) 39 per cent in Alathur, Ponnani and Taliparamba, about (-) 50 per cent in Kottayam and Kuthuparamba of north Malabar, and in the remaining 14 centres the decline was between (-) 41– 46 per cent (Table-2.13c). The retail prices of ragi, the cereal that the poorest of the poor consumed remained, on average, firm at

Rs 2.6 per *maund* in the district between the two periods that we considered for our comparison. However, of the 12 centres for which we have the data, the highest price dip of more than (-) 30 per cent was reported only in Wayanad whereas it was less than (-) 3 per cent in Ottapalam, and about (-) 18 per cent in the remaining nine centres (Table-2.13d).

Table 2.13a: Malabar - Retail Prices of Paddy (I Sort) (Rs/ maund)

	1913-14	*1932-33*	*1933-34*	*1934-35*
Cochin	3.30	2.70	2.39	2.51
Alathur	3.40	2.50	1.87	2.41
Palghat	2.20	2.40	2.01	2.46
Ponnani	3.70	2.10	2.05	2.46
Tirur	2.80	2.30	1.86	1.89
Calicut	3.20	2.20	2.10	2.15
Wayanad	2.80	2.00	1.70	2.23
Kurumbranad	3.30	2.30	2.01	2.29
Quilandi	3.30	2.40	2.22	2.44
Kuthuparamba	3.55	2.40	2.03	2.49
Chirakkal	3.50	2.60	2.25	2.68
Taliparamba	3.30	2.60	2.30	2.47
Malabar (avg)	3.30	2.40	2.07	2.37
Presidency (avg)	3.50	2.40	2.12	2.50

Note: A maund constitutes 82 $^{2}/_{7}$ lbs.

Source: Season and Crop Reports of Madras Presidency (various issues)

Table 2. 13b: Malabar - Retail Prices of Paddy (II Sort) (Rs/ maund)

	1913-14	*1932-33*	*1933-34*	*1934-35*
Cochin	3.2	2.7	2.0	2.0
Alathur	**2.9**	2.2	1.5	2.2
Palghat	2.8	2.1	1.6	2.2
Walluvanad	3.0	2.2	1.8	2.4
Ottapalam	**3.2**	2.1	1.8	2.3
Ponnani	3.4	2.1	1.7	2.0
Chowghat	3.4	2.5	1.4	1.9
Tirur	3.4	2.0	1.5	1.7
Eranad	2.9	2.1	1.7	2.2
Tirurangadi	3.8	2.5	2.0	2.3
Calicut	3.1	2.1	1.9	2.1
Wayanad	2.6	1.8	1.5	2.0
Kurumbranad	3.2	2.2	1.8	2.1
Quilandi	3.3	2.3	2.0	2.3
Kottayam	3.4	2.5	2.1	2.5
Kuthuparamba	**2.9**	2.3	1.9	2.3

(Contd....)

Chirakkal	3.3	2.5	2.1	2.6
Taliparamba	3.1	2.4	2.0	2.4
Malabar (avg)	3.2	2.3	1.8	2.2
Presidency (avg)	3.2	2.1	1.9	2.2

Table 2.13c: Malabar - Retail Prices of Rice (II Sort) (Rs/ maund)

	1913-14	*1932-33*	*1933-34*	*1934-35*
Cochin	5.5	3.4	3.0	3.5
Alathur	**4.7**	3.6	2.9	3.5
Palghat	5.2	3.5	2.9	3.5
Walluvanad	5.8	3.8	3.2	4.0
Ottapalam	**5.0**	3.5	2.9	3.4
Ponnani	5.5	3.9	3.8	4.1
Chowghat	5.3	3.9	3.0	3.6
Tirur	**5.0**	3.5	2.9	3.3
Eranad	5.6	3.9	3.3	3.7
Tirurangadi	6.3	4.2	3.5	3.9
Calicut	5.3	3.4	3.0	3.3
Wayanad	5.1	3.3	2.9	3.3
Vythiri	5.8	4.2	3.4	3.8
Kurumbranad	5.4	3.7	3.0	3.3
Quilandi	5.8	3.7	3.1	3.4
Kottayam	5.9	3.6	3.0	3.5
Kuthuparamba	5.9	3.6	3.0	3.3
Chirakkal	5.6	3.9	3.2	3.8
Taliparamba	4.9	3.8	3.1	3.5
Malabar (avg)	5.5	3.7	3.1	3.6
Presidency (avg)	5.3	3.8	3.2	3.8

Table 2.13d: Malabar - Retail Prices of Ragi (Rs/maund)

	1913-14	*1932-33*	*1933-34*	*1934-35*
Alathur	3.4	3.1	3.1	2.9
Palghat	**3.3**	2.7	2.7	3.0
Ottapalam	3.8	3.7	3.7	3.3
Calicut	**3.9**	3.2	3.2	3.0
Wayanad	2.6	1.8	1.8	2.3
Vythiri	**2.9**	2.4	2.4	3.0
Kurumbranad	**3.1**	2.6	2.6	2.8
Quilandi	**3.9**	3.2	3.2	3.4
Kottayam	**2.3**	1.9	1.9	2.5
Kuthuparamba	**2.8**	2.3	2.3	2.1
Chirakkal	**2.3**	1.9	1.9	2.3
Taliparamba	**2.2**	1.8	1.8	1.8
Malabar	2.6	2.6	2.6	2.7

Table 2.13e: Malabar - Retail Prices of Salt (Rs/ maund)

	1913-14	*1932-33*	*1933-34*	*1934-35*
Cochin	2.4	3.5	3.5	3.3
Alathur	2.1	2.8	2.7	2.5
Palghat	1.8	2.6	2.8	2.8
Walluvanad	3.1	2.9	3.2	2.8
Ottapalam	2.8	2.8	2.8	2.8
Ponnani	2.0	3.4	3.6	3.5
Chowghat	2.4	2.7	2.5	2.5
Tirur	2.4	2.4	2.4	2.3
Eranad	2.3	3.1	3.0	2.8
Tirurangadi	2.0	2.8	2.8	2.7
Calicut	2.1	2.7	2.6	2.4
Wayanad	2.2	2.6	3.1	2.6
Vythiri	3.0	3.1	3.4	3.4
Kurumbranad	1.9	2.6	2.7	2.5
Quilandi	2.2	2.6	2.8	2.7
Kottayam	2.0	2.7	2.9	2.7
Kuthuparamba	2.7	2.7	2.7	2.4
Chirakkal	1.9	2.6	2.6	2.4
Taliparamba	1.8	2.6	2.8	2.6
Malabar	2.2	2.8	2.9	2.7
Presidency	2.2	2.7	2.6	2.6

The behaviour of salt prices was a class apart. As against the trends witnessed in the primary and secondary market prices of other food items, between twenty years from 1913-14 to 1933-34, the retail prices of common salt in Malabar rose, on average, by more than 30 per cent. Taking as many as 19 centres in the district, prices of common salt in the pre-First World War year was at a fairly high level and these remained at the same level without change in Ottapalam, Tirur and Kuthuparamba throughout the period under consideration. In another three centres, *viz.* Walluvanad, Chowghat, and Vythiri, prices rose somewhat moderately; in Alathur, Calicut, and Quilandi, the increase was in the range of 25–29 per cent; Ponnani registered the highest increase of 80 per cent, followed by around 55 per cent in Palghat and Taliparamba. In all other centres the increase in the retail prices of common salt varied between 30 and 46 per cent between the same periods (Table-2.13e). It would appear from this that the massive Salt March organised by Gandhiji in March 1930 against the Salt Law passed by the British administration in India, and were extensively reported by the media all over the world, had no discernible impact on the upward movement in the prices of salt. A recent study on the non-violent agitation by Gandhiji against the British Raj, notes that the imperialist government had stoutly refused to take note of the Salt March, as was evident from a communication sent to London by the then Viceroy, Lord Irwin: "At present the prospect of a salt campaign does not keep me awake at night" (Ackerman and Du Vall, 2000).

Whenever a collective human misery like famine occurs, it is the poorest at the bottom, mainly the landless agricultural labourers who are affected first. In the famine of 1933-34 however the scenario appeared rather different. As the Madras Board of Revenue in its explanatory note to the season and crop report for 1932-33 indicated, it was the farmers, including the relatively larger among them, who suffered the most. When the prices of their produce dipped, they tried to compensate the resultant decline in the revenue by bringing in more and more areas under cultivation of that crop. However, in the absence of investible surplus, they had to borrow from money-lenders who, as usual, charged exorbitant rate of interest. With the prices going on depressing and these farmers failing in the repayment of loan, instead of gaining anything, their lands were increasingly confiscated by the money lenders. According to the notings of the Madras Board of Revenue, "they are now overburdened with debt incurred for agricultural expansion and family subsistence. The world-wide depression, in fact, washed away the investments made by large land owners, just as other entrepreneurs in non-agricultural sectors." When the areas under cultivation thus shrank, a predominant section of agriculture-dependent populations lost their employment and source of livelihood.

This situation was what Amartya Sen characterised as famine through 'derived destitution'. That is, the larger farmers whose income from agriculture shrinks and moves to the brink of famine, they evict their dependants, including farm labourers, who slip into famine; the other occupational categories like weavers, craftsmen, service sellers and urban labourers face famine as the demand from the agricultural sector shrinks; when the better off sections are in penury, even the beggars fail to get alms. Thus famine from the top spreads downwards to the lower categories, instead of the other way round as is commonly perceived (Sen, 1981:103). During the 1933 famine, which falls in the category of 'derived destitution', the condition of those who were lucky to get any employment could survive only if they were paid kind wages at least in part.[39] Apart from this, there were other factors that contributed to deepen the crisis, among which the ruthless method adopted to collect the land revenue was the most significant.

Land Revenue

As discussed earlier, the Famine Code of 1883 provides for suspension of land revenue assessment in times of any crisis in agriculture and for remission of the collected revenue until the crisis subsides. In terms of this provision, the Madras government declared in 1933 that, considering the continued fall in prices of agricultural produces, 12.5 per cent of the revenue collected in the preceding year would be refunded and that another reduction of 6.25 per cent would be allowed in the assessment being made for the fiscal year 1933-34. Apart from these across-the-board remissions, the government also announced that it would remit two *anna*s per rupee of assessment of ryotwari lands registered as garden lands in Malabar[40] with a view to help the farmers who either lost the export markets or the prices of their produce steeply nose-dived on account of the global recession.

Concurrently, the presidency administration asked the district authorities to conduct a resurvey of land in Malabar. The declared purpose was to see to what extent the land revenue could be reduced in the on-going bad times.[41] However, instead of reducing the revenue demand, the farmers found the resurvey escalating their revenue obligation to the government. A perusal of the holdings and ryotwari settlement in Malabar would show that, in 1933-34, which was the worst famine-year for the district, the area of land assessed to make the revenue demand had increased by about 41 thousand acres over the Average for the previous two years. This happened in spite of the fact that, on the face of the deeply depressing prices and mounting indebtedness, a large number of farmers had to dispense with cultivation. During years of famine, if farmers cultivated a second crop in the same season to meet the dwindling subsistence sources, it should have been exempted from land revenue assessment, as provided under the Famine Code, 1883. But the authorities conveniently ignored the relevant provisions in the Code Rule. The second crop assessed in 1933-34 as a percentage of the total assessment was the highest in the four agricultural years until then, for which data are available. Even though in paper across-the-board reduction was granted in 1933-34, the total assessment in that year stood actually at 13 per cent higher than during the previous year. On record, however, it could be seen that the remission allowed was about 71 per cent more than the assessment for the preceding two years, though, in effect, the figures failed to corroborate this claim. As several miscellaneous additional demands were included in the assessment, the total demand for 1933-34 had registered an increase of 10 per cent over that of the last two years (Table-2.14).

In addition to the usual land revenue demand, the government imposed a cess on the assessed imposts. These figures are not available separately for Malabar district. The information for the presidency as a whole shows the break-ups of the imposts for permanently settled areas, whole *inam* villages, the *ryotwari* lands and miscellaneous

Table-2.14: Malabar - Holdings and Settlement of Ryotwari Revenue

(1931 to 1935)

	1931-32	*1932-33*	*1933-34*	*1934-35*
1. Total Land (Acres)	1633056	1655243	1684712	1687666
2. Assessment (Rs)	3794477	3924814	4352888	5356283
3. Second Crop (Rs)	49308	59976	69834	56823
4. Total assessment	3843785	3984790	4422722	5413106
5. Remissions (-)	187727	173015	307558	173300
6. Remainder	3656058	3811775	4115164	5239806
7. Miscellaneous (+)	171315	170392	170652	152817
8. Demand (grand total)	3827373	3982167	4285816	5392623

Source: Season and Crop Reports of Madras Presidency (various issues).

imposts (Table-2.15). While the cesses imposed on permanently settled areas and whole *inam* villages slightly declined from year to year, on *ryotwari* areas it was not only the highest of all imposts, accounting for 72-73 per cent of the total, but also had gone on increasing from year to year, including the worst famine year. That was the reason why, in Madras presidency, the additional cesses on land revenue had shown an increasing trend.

Table-2.15: Madras - Additional Cesses on Land Revenue

(Rs / lakh)

Cess on areas under	*1932-33*	*1933-34*	*1934-35*
1. Permanent Settlement	25.71	25.37	24.89
2. Whole Inam Villages	7.14	7.13	6.98
3. Ryotwari settlement	84.08	85.15	86.81
Total	**116.92**	**117.65**	**118.68**

Source: Season and Crops Reports of Madras Presidency (various issues).

Table-2.16: Madras - Coercive Processes in Revenue Collection

	1929-30	*1930-31*	*1931-32*	*1932-33*	*1933-34*
Demand notice	765749	1014321	972681	1174528	1499500
Attachment notice	49646	82873	89745	132310	192160
Sale notice	38036	57036	66889	82048	143344
Sale (defaulters)	4868	6795	10062	11244	14655
Total	**858299**	**1161025**	**1139377**	**1400130**	**1849659**

Source: Board of Revenue, Madras - Land Revenue and Settlement (various years).

For realising these excessive imposts, the district revenue officials applied the coercive tactics that Lytton used mercilessly during the famine of 1876-78 so that they could wipe out most of the arrears, no matter that process precipitated the miseries already being suffered from famine and famine-related epidemic diseases. Thus, during the fiscal year 1931-32, there was a decline in the number of demand notices issued to the defaulters but the notices indicating coercive processes started increasing from the next year and reached the highest of the preceding five years in 1933-34, the peak year of the famine in the district. The latter year was marked by the highest levels of demand notices, attachment notices, notices for sale and actual sales. It was in 1933-34 that percentage of attachment of all personal properties of the defaulting ryots also reached the maximum (Tables-2.16 & 2.17).

Table-2.17: Madras - percentage of Attachments to Demand Notices

Year	*Personal property*	*Real property*	*Total*
1931-32	11.12	2.97	14.09
1932-33	10.17	3.11	13.28
1933-34	12.95	5.93	18.88
1934-35	6.86	4.21	11.07

Epidemics and Mortalities

At the peak of the 'slump famine' of the early 1930s, the north Malabar found some of its seasonal epidemics escalating and spreading everywhere, taking many more lives than usual. This region was generally under attacks of a number of contagious diseases because of its nearness to the sea and the humid weather that persisted most of the year. Cholera, dysentery and diarrhoea, smallpox, plague, fevers and certain respiratory diseases were common in this area. When famine intensified, deaths from some of these epidemics, mainly pneumonia, tuberculosis, dysentery and diarrhoea took the lead in killing the underfed population. These mortalities were more pronounced in the municipality limits of Cannanore. In Calicut, it was plague that devastated the entire area while in southern parts of Malabar, cholera flared up.[42]

There were several causes for the sharp rise in epidemics and mortalities during this famine. In the entire district, facilities for medical treatment were extremely insufficient. For example, in north Malabar, which had experienced the worst form of famine diseases and deaths, according the official report, there were only three hospitals, which were all situated within Cannanore municipality: one civil hospital, one military station hospital, and a private institution.[43] The affected people had to travel all along from other parts of the region to these hospitals for treatment. Quite often, the patients died on the way. This was not the case of north Malabar alone. Moreover, as the official reports indicated, the number of deaths reported was just a tip of the iceberg. The actual deaths might be several times more. Apart from the insufficiency of medical facilities, the government did not fill the vacancies of medical personnel in the existing hospitals. The post of the Registrar of Births and Deaths was lying vacant for many years. The reason given was the government's 'financial depression.'[44] The Sanitary Inspector, with the assistance of two peons, was directed to register the vital statistics of the region. But they could not carry out the job as their regular workload had itself gone up due to the ongoing famine.

A gazette notification issued by the Presidency of Madras in June 1933 declared that the Malabar Collector should notify by 'tom-tom' and by publication in the district gazette the names of places or areas in his district which were infected by plague or any other contagious diseases. The notification also directed the Collector to close down the markets in the infected areas; evacuate people from such areas by invoking the relevant provisions of the Epidemic Disease Act, 1897; acquire the concerned buildings under attack of plague or other epidemic diseases under the Land Acquisition Act, 1894; and compulsorily isolate the infected persons away from the people in specially constructed tents.[45] In 1933, this instruction was very strictly implemented by the district Collector. The people fearing the trauma and the pathetic manner in which the isolated patients were to die in the absence of proper medicine, food and water, concealed the disease infected persons as well as deaths from such diseases. That was why even official sources were reluctant to reveal the number of people died of epidemics in the 1933 famine.

This apart, the district administration had tried to prevent the epidemics through vaccination. It asked the local people that everyone should undergo vaccination against all contagious diseases. While declaring so, however, there were no proper facilities nor did the administration appoint any trained staff to do the job. As usual it entrusted the sweepers and peons attached to the sanitary inspectors in the municipalities to make house-to-house visits and vaccinate every resident in the areas likely to be infected by the epidemics. The people refused to undergo vaccination by these untrained and illiterate staff, knowing well that the refusal was an offence punishable by imprisonment.

D. The Famine of 1943

The fourth episode of famine was narrated, as we noted in the introductory chapter, by Jawaharlal Nehru in his *Discovery of India* that in the year 1943 a ghastly, staggering, and horrible famine had taken place not only in the fertile and rice-rich Bengal province but also in Malabar, Bijapur and Orissa. Furthermore, Nehru stated that thousands of men, women and children died daily for want of food in these places. With the outbreak of the Second World War, a major boom sparked off in the Indian economy and the food prices shot up beyond the purchasing power of the people. For the first two years, the British administration did not feel the necessity to intervene in the market to control the prices. Undivided India, with Burma in the same continent, was a surplus producer of foodgrains, mainly rice, and the government was able to import Burmese rice to make up for any shortage in any part of the country. In January 1942, Japan air-raided Rangoon, the capital of Burma (later renamed as Yangon and Myanmar, respectively) and disrupted free imports of rice to India. This led to further increase in the prices of foodgrains. The index number of wholesale prices of rice in 1939 at 100 rose persistently to reach 218 and that of wheat at 233 in 1942.[46]

The inflationary upsurge in prices was further strengthened by the spurt in public expenditure towards war financing on the Government of India account as well as on the account of the Allied Powers. The war expenditure of the Indian government was met by the issue of currency notes, as the dollars paid by the U.S. for this purpose were retained by Britain in what was called the 'Empire Dollar Pool' and an equivalent value of pound sterling was credited to the account of the Reserve Bank of India. It was with the backing of these dollars that the latter issued currency notes (Dutta 1978). This led to a substantial increase in British administration's deficit financing in India from a very nominal amount of Rs 4 crore in 1939-40 to Rs 438 crore in 1942-43.[47]

Moreover, there was a rapid rise in the strength of Indian army, which went up from a mere 1.93 lakh at the start of the Second World War in 1939 to 25.7 lakh in 1945, when the Second World War ended. This necessitated increasing diversion of a part of the food available within the economy for the requirement of the defence personnel. Faced with the closure of the Burmese source of imports and the difficulty to source from elsewhere due to disruptions caused by the war, the government started procuring and stocking whatever foodgrain was domestically available. It was also the time when the administration declared to introduce statutory rationing in major cities like Calcutta. The speculators complicated the situation. They hoarded whatever quantities were left in the open market after public procurement (See, Ghosh 1959).

With the relentless rise in prices of essential consumption goods, the British administration feared that if preventive actions were not initiated to hold the price line, there might be additional domestic troubles against its continuance in India. Therefore, it decided to initiate certain price control measures, the main features of which were the following: First, since agriculture was constitutionally a provincial or state subject, the central government convened frequent 'price control conferences' with the provinces and states, and issued 'Foodgrain Control Orders' with their concurrence. The Orders fixed: (i) a ceiling price, above which the grain price should not go up; and (ii) a floor price, below which the producers' price of the grain should also not fall. The responsibility to implement the Order was imposed on the provinces and states. Second, the central government assumed the right to start a monopoly procurement scheme, according to which the foodgrain growers had to surrender the entire surplus with them to the authorities at a price announced just before harvests. Third, this was to be supplemented by a levy on traders, who were required to part with a portion of the supplies passing through the secondary wholesale market. Fourth, in order to facilitate these programmes, the central government also imposed a ban on exports. Fifth, as a justification for these decisions, the government announced that the native population would not suffer from the compulsory procurement and the shortage of foodgrains that it might result, as it was going to introduce rationing at fairly subsidised issue prices (see Knight 1957).[48]

At the operational level, none of these programmes worked as expected. Instead, the flourishing black-market in foodgrains continued unabated. Surplus farmers and traders in foodgrains hoarded their stocks rather than surrendering the levy portion to the public procurement agencies or selling in the open market so that prices soared to unreachable heights for the common man. Studies indicated that, during this period, speculation in foodgrains was more attractive than cotton trading in Bombay. Some of the speculators, who lost in the futures trading in cotton, took up to foodgrains trade in rural countryside and made up their losses (Pavlov, 1978). The traditionally food deficit areas, like Malabar, were the first to face starvation and famine. It was also Malabar that faced the worst indifference of the British administration in tackling epidemics that sprung up from malnutrition and the resultant physical debilities. The local people themselves came up to give some succour to the affected people. A recent study published by a village panchayat in north Malabar gives a number of examples of how the peoples' collectives could overcome the rigours of 1943 famine. These people formed co-operative societies and conducted rationing at affordably low prices and also arranged to sell the agricultural produces of the peasant farmers at reasonable minimum prices. They formed groups in different areas to help the people suffering from cholera as the government was not doing anything to control the epidemics devastating the whole of Malabar. Even though there were attempts to take up community farming in some parts of the district, uneven rainfall and the difficulty that it caused for taking up timely sowings defeated the attempt (Mohandas, 2009).

Monsoons and Food Production

It would appear from the archival records that, historically, every famine in Malabar preceded a peculiar seasonal pattern. Contrary to the usual experience of the south-west monsoon arriving in the district on the 1st of June, two-three years before the 1943 famine, the monsoon arrived on the West Coast invariably a few days in advance. And by the 1st of June, the rain turned excessively heavy so that there were floods in most parts of Malabar. The rainfall was irregular and scanty in a few of the areas where drought-like conditions prevailed. These affected timely sowings. It is well known that even during better monsoon-years, which facilitated more than normal harvests, availability of foodgrains from own production in Malabar were insufficient to meet the local requirement. When the harvests were poor, what could happen is easy to imagine.

To clarify, the year 1940 saw a relatively normal monsoon and an excellent harvest in Malabar. The next year was characterised by irregular and uneven rains. The south-west monsoon arrived in the last week of May and by early June it turned into cyclonic storm and created widespread destruction, particularly in the southern parts of Calicut. Sowing was affected not only in Malabar but also the entire West Coast region and many other agriculturally important areas in the presidency. Again, in 1942, despite the south-west monsoon being normal, the subsequent north-east monsoon was a complete failure. From October that year, when late sowings were to take place, the rainfall being inadequate and ill-timed, the farmers could not take up cultivation. However, according to meteorological accounts, the south-west monsoon in 1943 was normal to above-average in the district and the north-east monsoon, which arrived in time, gave abundant rains and compensated the deficiency of the previous monsoons to a large extent. The area under food crops were above average for wet-farming, though the area under dry-farming was slightly lower.

Table-2.18 presents the consolidated position of the crops in both the seasons. In 1943-44, the area under rice crop, which gives the principal cereal of Malabar, was more than 4 per cent higher than the normal area under the crop. That year's production of rice was about 8 per cent higher than normal. The combined area of other cereals produced in Malabar, viz. jowar, bajra and ragi, in 1943-44, was higher by 25 per cent, and their total production, 26 per cent higher than normal. However, compared to the average local requirement, the total production of cereals in Malabar in

1943-44 was estimated to be almost 42 per cent lower. This meant that even when the harvest is more than normal, Malabar had to depend on other regions, or on imports, to meet its total consumption requirement.[49]

Now, consider the position in Madras presidency. The compilation by George Blyn, presented in our Table-2.19, reveals the following: After achieving an impressive level of production in 1940, the rice harvest declined in the next two years. Taking 1940 as the base year, in 1941, the output of rice declined by less than 5 per cent while the total cereals (i.e. foodgrains minus pulses), the decline was more than 26 per cent. In 1942, the decline in rice production was almost 10 per cent while the production of total cereals slipped by about 12 per cent. In 1943, the production of foodgrains recorded an impressive increase over the previous year, though it was slightly lower when we compare with the 1940 base year. What is significant to note here is that though the overall production in Madras presidency, including Malabar, declined very steeply in 1941 and 1942, there was no devastating famine in both these years. However, in 1943, the outputs of cereals, though slightly lower than in 1940, was impressively above the level reached in 1942, as is evident from an increase of 5.4 per cent recorded by all cereals and 5.8 per cent by rice, the staple cereal of the region (Blyn, 1966).

From our discussion so far, the causes of 1943 famine in Malabar were clearly discernible since January 1942, when the availability of Burmese rice was stopped. The people of Malabar, who used to go to the neighbouring Mysore state to bring rice on such occasions, could not do so because of the war-time disruptions. To compound the agony, government adopted aggressive compulsory procurements of foodgrains even from perennial deficit areas of Malabar, on the strength of the consensus reached in various 'price control conferences'. It was the most opportune time for the speculators. Finding that the prices were going up in the market and that the rationing system adopted even in the city areas was ineffective in providing enough food or in controlling the prices, speculators indulged in hoarding their stocks to push up the prices further. And the British administration kept its eyes closed on the unprecedented inflationary rice in prices, as the super-normal profit that the speculative traders pocketed was a convenient source for it to get enough subscriptions for the 'war bonds' issued at that time. A sizeable segment of the population, which was already suffering from destitution on account of non-availability of works in agriculture or elsewhere in Malabar, was pushed into hunger and famine, and succumbed to death. It was about this predicament that Jawaharlal Nehru wrote, as we quoted earlier: "men and women and little children die in their thousands daily for lack of food."

Prices and Cost of Living

The prices of foodgrains had been firming up in the Madras presidency, including Malabar, since mid-June 1941. By December 1942, these prices, measured by their index number for the week-ending August 1939 as 100, rose by about 46 per cent within a period of six months from June 1942.

Table 2.18: Food Production in Malabar, 1943-44

	Rice	*Millets*
Area (acre)		
Normal	854000	20680
Actual	889533	25883
Difference	+35533	+5203
Production (tons)		
Normal	328300	5650
Actual	353890	7130
Difference	(+) 25590	(+) 1480
Required	614000	7000
Difference	(-) 260110	(-) 130

Source: Foodgrains in Madras State (Govt. of Madras, 1951).

Table-2.19: Production of Cereals in Madras Presidency

(in '000 tons)

	Year	*Rice*	*Jowar*	*Bajra*	*Ragi*	*Total*
	1938	4504	1276	644	778	7202
	1939	4876	1398	704	832	7810
	1940	5552	1338	714	920	8524
	1941	5283	1223	641	896	8043
	1942	5002	1105	607	809	7523
	1943	5294	1157	639	843	7933
	1944	5433	1209	606	801	8049
	1945	4602	912	493	621	6628
percentage						
1941/1940		-4.8	-8.6	-10.2	-2.6	-5.6
1942/1940		-9.9	-17.4	-15.0	-12.1	-11.7
1943/1940		-4.6	-13.5	-10.5	-8.4	-6.9
1943/1942		5.8	4.7	5.3	4.2	5.4

Source: Estimated from George Blyn (1966), op.cit.

It shot up further by another 14 per cent in the next June 1943. In other words, the foodgrains price index (1939=100) estimated at 199 in end–December 1940 became 236 at the end of June 1943 (Table-2.20). Compared to the prices of foodgrains, the prices of commercial crops moved rather sluggishly below the prevailing level of foodgrains prices. This indicated that a section of the farmers, whose foodgrains purchasing power was predicated on the prices received from selling their commercial crops, could not access the same quantity of grain from the market as they did before. To put it differently, the price that the producers of commercial crops obtained being less than the corresponding price of foodgrains, their 'entitlement to food' suffered a setback.

The last two columns in Table-2.20 show the cost of living index at Madras and Calicut centres during the war-years. It is well-known that cost of living index is a proxy for the food purchasing power of urban workers, landless labourers, and peasant farmers who depend on the market for a part, or whole, of their food. These figures tell that, compared to Madras, the cost of living index in Calicut remained excessively high throughout the period from August 1939 to December 1943 for which published data are available. This indicates that the impact of famine was harsher in Malabar (which is represented by Calicut in Table-2.20) than in other areas of the presidency.

The inflationary upsurge of food prices during the Second World War was not a specific experience of any regions in the British India such as Malabar alone. In the absence of large-scale food imports due to disruptions caused by the war, Great Britain also had faced food shortage and inflationary rise in prices during this period. But we shall see in Chapter-6 that, in the midst of the war, British government had introduced a universal rationing with controlled prices for cereals, fruits, sugar, cheese and fats and also fixed the prices and quantity of meals served in hotels and restaurants consciously calculated to save the entire population of Great Britain from hunger and malnutrition. It was true that the British administration in India had also declared a war-time rationing, which however was confined to industrial centres and major cities like Calcutta. Interestingly, during this period, the Madras presidency had announced a statutory rationing in Malabar in respect of rice, ragi and samai. The quantity fixed was the highest of 1.06 lb for Palghat, the lowest of 1.02 lb for Cochin and 1.03 lb for Kozhikode, Cannanore and Tellicherry. But the release of the ration quota of rice was subject to the condition that the card-holders lifted some wheat and the admissible quantity of ragi. This was in spite of the fact that in Madras presidency there was no rationing in wheat, as it was not a commonly consumed staple cereal in this part of the country. Furthermore, the declared rationing system had not come into operation during 1943 and the first half of 1944, when the famine was the most gruelling. Instead, it was introduced only with effect from 9 August 1944, when the famine in Malabar had almost subsided.[50]

Table-2.20: Prices and Cost of Living Indices

Price Index (Madras)			*Cost of living index*		
Half year Ending	*Food-grains*	*Commer - Products*	*Period*	*Madras*	*Calicut*
Dec-40	119	96	Aug-39	98	103
Jun-41	122	95	Jan-42	117	129
Dec-41	140	114	Dec-42	158	180
Jun-42	142	123	Oct-43	184	222
Dec-42	207	187	Dec-43	189	228
Jun-43	236	229			

Note: (i) Price index is at week-ending 21st August 1939 = 100; and, (ii) Cost of living index is at agricultural year 1938-39 = 100.

Source: Chapter XIV, Report of Civil Supplies Department, Madras 1943.

Land Revenue Demand

The British administration's policy of raising the land revenue year-after-year continued recklessly during the Second World War. This was one reason for the intensification of the plight of the people who were reeling under the onslaught of epidemics and famines in Malabar. It may be recalled that, during the 1933 famine, the Madras government had declared that the land assessment and revenue collection would be strictly in line with the provisions of the 1883 Famine Code. Nonetheless, at the implementation stage, the revenue officials gave scant regard to the proclamation. During the famine of 1943, the government did not even make such a declaration, not to say about any reprieve that it was pleased to offer the peasants who were undergoing a major famine. The revenue settlement on the *ryotwari* lands in Malabar during the first half of 1940s will reveal how the officials treated the Code Rules (Table-2.21):

The area of land assessed for revenue demand went on increasing from 1940-41 through 1945-46 even though in 1941-42 and 1942-43 sowings were disrupted in several areas of Malabar due to adverse weather conditions. During the peak famine year of 1943-44, the government had in fact allowed remission of assessment made during the previous year. But the remission was lower by more than 38 per cent of the remission granted in 1940-41, which was crop-wise a better year. Furthermore, there was a marked increase in the miscellaneous imposts of land revenue in 1943-44 which, compared to 1940-41, was 36 per cent higher. Had the government limited the miscellaneous imposts at least to the level of 1940-41, the total land revenue demand from Malabar for 1943-44 could have come to Rs 45.4 lakh, a figure which was still higher than that for 1940-41. On the other hand, the total assessment, less remission plus miscellaneous imposts reported for 1943-44 was Rs 46.7 lakh.

Table-2.21: Malabar - Revenue Settlement under Ryotwari Lands

	1940-41	*1941-42*	*1942-43*	*1943-44*	*1944-45*	*1945-46*
Land (acres)						
Dry	1142032	1146300	1150103	1152860	1157214	1160467
Wet	562305	562984	563318	563650	563801	563486
Assessment (Rs)						
Dry	2124575	2129803	2135440	2139256	2143258	2150007
Wet	2263482	2265787	2266267	2267278	2268227	2267541
Total						
Land area (acres)	1704337	1709284	1713424	1716510	1721015	1723953
Assessment (Rs)	4387557	4395590	4401707	4406534	4411485	4417548
(-) Remission allowed	10083	120045	8847	6237	6956	5914
(+) Miscellaneous	148509	176195	166934	201900	172093	171734
Total demand	4352006	4510084	4651511	4667143	4576622	4583368

In the past, such large revenue demands were realised by the British rulers from the impoverished farmers in famine years by applying ruthless methods like putting the defaulters behind bars, attachment of their belongings (including lands), sale of attached properties at lower than their extant market prices so that the ryots could never come out from their indebtedness to the government. During 1943-44 also the British administration employed coercive tactics to collect the arrears of land revenue from farmers. However, the data presented in Table-2.22 and table-2.23 would suggest that the intensity of the coercive processes adopted this time was rather less rigorous than during the previous decades. Compared to 1940-41, the number of coercive demand notices issued for the collection of revenue arrears, actual attachments and sales through public auctions were sizeably lower. A closer look at the available evidences would say that this had nothing to do with any lenience on the part of the British rulers.

A reduction in the coercive processes adopted to collect revenue arrears during this period was attributable primarily to the Government of India Act, 1935, which replaced the existing diarchy with a responsible

Table-2.22: Malabar - Coercive Processes Adopted for Revenue Collection

	1940-41	*1941-42*	*1942-43*	*1943-44*
Demand notices	1209528	1053095	849750	298255
Attachments	83620	73647	36653	30317
Sale notices	60987	57006	30689	9143
Sale (defaulters)	9895	8160	4223	1283

Table-2.23: Malabar - percentage of Attachments to Demand Notices

Year	*Personal property*	*Real property*	*Total*
1940-41	5.94	1.81	7.75
1941-42	6.25	1.79	8.04
1942-43	4.36	1.02	5.38
1943-44	5.58	1.11	6.66

Source: Board of Revenue, Madras - Land Revenue and Settlement Reports.

government in all the departments of administration under an All India Federation. As the elected representatives being mostly local leaders, there were restrictions against unnecessary harassment of ryots. This was an unexpected outcome of the Act. Some pro-British authors and officials argued that, if the federal system according to the Government of India Act failed to take off as envisaged because it was conceived as a "paper federation." In fact, the real intention of the Act was later clarified by the then Viceroy, Linlithgow: "After all we framed the constitution of 1935 because we thought it the best way to hold India to the Empire."[51] On the contrary, the elections conducted as stipulated in the Act disappointed the British rulers as it gave an overwhelming majority for the Congress candidates in all provinces. Their ministers curbed the undue powers wielded by the police. They also passed agrarian legislations dealing with the tenancy rights, security of tenure, rent reduction and relief, and extended protection to all the peasant-debtors. These legislations were responsible for a decline in the coercive processes during the famine (Chandra 2009). Nonetheless, there were still several cases where the relief measures extended to the cultivators by the Congress ministers were overturned by the British rulers with the help of the non-Indian judges in higher courts and non-Indian bureaucrats at district levels. In this context, it would be instructive to quote three such instances from the archival sources: First, in January 1943, the High Court of Madras heard a case filed by a farmer under Section 36 of the Madras Revenue Recovery Act, 1864 against the revenue authorities of Malabar auctioning out his land measuring 15 acres and 75 cents for a sum of Rs 300 to recover the land revenue arrears amounting to 20 rupees and 14 *annas*, despite the land was valued at Rs 20,000 as per the existing market price. While agreeing with the contention of the appellant, the High Court averred that even though the manner in which the sale was executed by the revenue authorities was not in terms of the provisions of the Revenue Recovery Act, "the matter was not that serious for this court to interfere."

Second, the Madras High Court handed down a decree in April 1943 in favour of a *janmi* who filed a petition to recover from his tenant the land revenue payable to the government even though, according to the Malabar

Tenancy Act, 1929, which came into force in 1930, the payment was actually to be made by the appellant. The Act had stipulated that the *janmi* should bear "all renewal fees and arrears of *michavaram* or rent" in future. After the Act came into force, in 1931, a resettlement was made presumably to raise the land revenue in Malabar. The *janmi* argued that the tenant has to bear the charge as the tenancy agreement was made in 1893 by the present tenant's head of the family and, therefore, the provisions of the new Act was not applicable to him. The High Court gave the verdict in favour of the *janmi* stating that the Malabar Tenancy Act was not applicable to a tenancy agreement signed by the parties before the Act came into force.

Third, the Collector of Malabar had been indiscriminately imprisoning every cultivator who failed to pay the land revenue, before their properties, including land and other assets, were put on auction. This power was wielded by the Collector in terms of the provisions incorporated in the Madras Revenue Recovery Act. He had thus put behind the bar a cultivator who failed to pay a small portion of the revenue demand for 1943-44 and initiated action to attach and sell his belongings. The cultivator filed a case against the harsh action of the Collector and requested the High Court to issue an order to release him from jail and to stop the processes initiated to sell his belongings. The High Court, after hearing both sides, decreed that there was nothing wrong in what the Collector had done.[52]

Crime Records

The law and order department of the presidency used to give a chapter in the Annual Administration Report on the working of the department, including the district-wise crimes recorded during the year under review. A perusal of the data released in the 1943 report would show that most of the crimes recorded in police registers in respect of Malabar were not of very serious nature (Table-2.24). Of the different types of crimes reported, it was theft and the receivers of stolen properties who dominated the list. The number of depredators who were brought under surveillance was also relatively large because, once they were released from the jail they repeated the 'crime' probably with the intention of going back to the jail where they could get their food.

We noted that, during the famine of 1918, Malabar and many other districts in the presidency witnessed large-scale food-riots. Such incidents were rarely reported during the 1943 famine. This was probably because the famine took place during the midst of the Second World War when the police and army were in strict vigil. In 1943, Malabar and other parts of the Madras presidency were under surveillance of the specially recruited Armed Reserve Police, Special Emergency Force, Village Police, and Civic

Guards. There was hardly any space for collective attacks on food stocks hoarded by private traders for indulging in speculation, or on stocks held by official agencies for feeding the army personnel. The nature of 'crimes' therefore shifted from collective food riots to single-individual based dacoity, robbery, house-breaking, cattle-theft and certain ordinary thefts of paddy, banana, coconut, jack-fruit etc.

From 1940 to 1943, the number of persons imprisoned for the types of 'crimes' mentioned above showed a tremendous increase of more than 50 per cent and convicts among them by around 45 per cent (Table-2.25). Another important factor about the prisoners of these famine-crimes was their health. Most of the prisoners at the time of their arrests were reported to be physically weak due to hunger and malnutrition and attacks of famine-related epidemic diseases. Between 1940 and 1943, on average, 245 prisoners had fallen sick every day and as many as 243 of them died in their prison cells.[53] It is clear from these figures that poverty and famines had pushed them to commit the reported petty 'crimes'.

Table-2.24: Famine Crimes in Malabar, 1942 – 44

	1942	*1943*	*1944*
1. No. of known depredators, receivers of stolen properties	10534	11089	12623
2. No. of depredators brought under surveillance	6756	8097	9296
3. Cases in which enhanced punishment given	2466	3042	2613
4. Brought before magistrates under security sections	2248	3225	4010
5. No. of those committed cognisable crimes	3492	4572	3883
6. No. of criminals caught and reported to police	3356	4428	3801
7. No. of cases categorised as grave crimes	2748	3152	3193

The age-wise composition of the convicts would show that the persons of every age-group had been indulging in petty crimes and that the number of such offenders increased with their age up to 22-30, after which it slowly declined. In the peak famine period of 1943-44, the average age-groups of persons who took to petty crimes increased to 22-40, constituting to around 70 per cent of the total convicts. The other points emerging from the data compiled and presented in Table-2.26 are the following:

Table-2.25: Malabar: Prisoners and Deaths in Prisons

	1940	*1941*	*1942*	*1943*	*1944*
1. Prisoners	15903	18786	20970	24331	21012
2. Under trials	3679	3860	4885	5745	4863
3. Civil prisoners	89	95	95	52	51
4. Security prisoners	19	149	236	886	331
5. Convicts	12134	14682	15698	17554	15683
6. Sick (avg per day)	164	197	251	323	266
7. Death (avg per day)	128	168	198	354	313

Table-2.26: Malabar: Age-wise Distribution of Convicts

	1943	*1944*
Under 16 years old	27	15
16 - 18	1310	1140
19 - 21	3883	3140
22 - 30	22982	19361
31 - 40	15276	13038
41 – 60	9902	8165
Above 60 years old	1113	1077

Source: Madras Administration Report, 1944-45. (Part II), pages 60, 61, 65, 66, & 80.

Table-2.27: Malabar - Year-wise and Epidemics-wise Mortalities, 1941 to 1950

Year	*Cholera*	*Smallpox*	*Plague*	*Fevers*	*Dysentery Diarrhoea*	*Respiratory Diseases*	*Total*
1941	1	326	0	18403	9364	8899	36993
1942	82	57	1	17816	8976	8145	35077
1943	28432	418	84	19419	11067	8816	68236
1944	107	898	70	19833	8027	8588	37523
1945	6	1226	21	16596	4912	7633	30394
1946	5	821	24	13717	4191	7113	25871
1947	1	85	34	12762	4677	7729	25288
1948	74	41	7	10977	4120	8088	23307
1949	53	75	0	9595	3313	7574	20610
1950	53	390	1	13047	6117	8306	27914

Source: Census Handbook, 1951: Malabar (Government Press, Madras, 1953).

(1) Even elderly people above 60 years of age had indulged in petty crimes due to the rigours of famine. (2) The juvenile convicts were relatively small in numbers. This was because, according to police accounts of these

crimes included in the official report for 1944-45, the number of juvenile offenders had been steadily increasing during the war years. In the year 1943-44, these offences reached the highest level and both boys and girls were involved in the category of crimes classified as 'petty offences'. These petty offences suddenly came down when the famine conditions receded, employment started picking up and the food supply as well as the food purchasing power became by and large normal.

Epidemics and Mortalities

By the middle of 1943, a number of epidemics, which were a constant menace in Malabar during wet-seasons, started proliferating in the entire length and breadth of the district. The most common among them were malaria and other fevers, respiratory ailments like tuberculosis as well as dysentery and diarrhoea. Along with these diseases, some other chronic epidemics, particularly cholera, smallpox and plague, which had more or less disappeared from Malabar, returned with increased ferocity. Official notes prepared at the district headquarters, being preserved in the regional archives at Kozhikode[54] indicate that, by the middle of January 1943, plague appeared first in Tellicherry and, by March, spread to the entire district. Next month, cholera erupted from Calicut and spread to the whole of Malabar. Though, by the third week of August 1943, this epidemic almost subsided, it reappeared in Calicut and Palghat by the beginning of January 1944 and, by the next month, engulfed the entire district. Malaria was another significant famine-led epidemic, which was seen all over the district in the beginning of 1943 but subsided by the end of the year, except in Wayanad where it continued until March next year.

Lack of sanitation, non-availability of protected drinking water, and poor environmental hygiene made this region the abode of epidemics. The immediate aggravation of these epidemics was attributed to the general poverty among people, heavy south-west monsoon, and the massive rise in the prices of foodgrains stimulated by deficit financing to meet the war expenses. As we noted earlier, 1943 was not a bad harvest-year. The available foodgrains, especially rice was increasingly diverted even from deficit areas like Malabar to the defence personnel, fearing that India's eastern border might be attacked by Japan, which in the previous year had conquered Burma. Though Japan did not attack India, using this to create a fear psychosis, British rulers intensified the procurement operation. It also declared that, once procured, there would be equitable distribution, especially of rice, to all households at subsidised rates through a system of rationing, as was introduced at that time in Britain. The assured rationing came up, despite partially in certain urban centres like Calcutta, where large number of Europeans lived, but not in chronically deficit areas including Malabar. Instead, it led to increase in food prices by further strengthening speculative hoarding by private traders. The people who found it extremely difficult to access food in the face of incessant upward pressure on prices became easy victims of various diseases.

Although the administration reports of the Madras presidency had references to the widespread epidemics and mortalities in 1943, no reasonable information on the number of attacks and deaths were given out in these reports. However, the 1951 census report, which gives district-level information, has the most authentic time-series data on epidemic-wise mortalities in Malabar from 1941 to 1950 (Table-2.27). These figures show that there was a sharp increase in mortalities due to epidemic diseases in 1943, estimated at 95 per cent higher than in the preceding year. Epidemic-wise, the highest proportion of the loss of lives was recorded in 1943 by cholera in Malabar at 42 per cent of the total deaths. This was followed by 28.5 per cent from fevers, 16.2 per cent from diarrhoea and dysentery, and about 13 per cent from respiratory aliments. Deaths due to smallpox and plague were insignificant. The fevers, mainly malaria, continued for another year and subsided only from the beginning of 1945, whereas the scourges from all other epidemics seemed to have abated at the end of 1943 itself, or latest by the middle of next year.

A significant development of this period was that the attack of cholera shook the entire district and attracted the attention of the print media, officialdom and philanthropists from even outside the presidency. The department of public health under the presidency of Madras, in an inspection report dealing with the widespread epidemics in Malabar stated that the attack of cholera had started from the second week of January 1943 in Palghat and Alathur ranges and, by March, the pandemic spread to the Ponnani range. After receding slightly in the month of April, it again cropped up in these areas and spread to Tirur, Chowghat Calicut, Quilandy, Tellicherry, Taliparamba, Cannanore, and South Canara.[55]

Among the newspapers published from the presidency, the *Hindu* and *Indian Express* reported cholera cases almost everyday in June and July, when the epidemic claimed the largest number of lives. *The Hindu* had a column, 'Cholera in Malabar', in which most of the days during these two months it reported the number of fresh cholera attacks and deaths in new areas of the district. On 1 July, the newspaper reported that 'at present there is not a single taluk in Malabar which is free from the epidemic'. It also stated that within the Calicut municipality, which was terribly affected by the disease, on average, more than fifty deaths were being reported every day.

On 26 July 1943, the Madras edition of the *Indian Express*, in its editorial, 'Stricken Kerala' wrote: "From sporadic attacks, the disease (cholera) seems to have assumed devastating epidemical proportions. The daily toll of deaths runs to several scores......Heart-rending stories of persons dying in the open and whole families being exterminated have become quite common. That the percentage of deaths to attacks remains as high as 85 to 90 which speak volumes for the low vitality and resistance power of the poor victims." The editorial highlighted the acute food situation being the basic cause of the malady and pleaded that coordinated action by all concerned be initiated to provide food and shelter for the sufferers. The editorial further noted: "We appeal to the generous public, both in the city and outside, to extend a helping hand to the famished and stricken people of Kerala."

There was regular official briefing to the press about the condition of epidemics and deaths in Malabar. But these briefings were silent about what role the administration played in mitigating the on-going crisis. The government went on repeating the reasons why the epidemic was spreading in the district as follows: (i) the beggars strolling on the streets were the main carriers of the disease; (ii) the chlorination of drinking water was not effective as the wells from which people drew water were overflowing because of heavy rains. These briefings also claimed that the administration was "trying to find out ways and means to check the spread of the epidemic in Malabar." One of the 'ways and means' that it adopted was to forcefully prevent beggars from entering the municipal limit, with an amendment effected to the District Police Act, incorporating provisions similar to those of the Madras Police Act that prohibited beggars moving from one part of a district to another. The second solution that it designed was a massive vaccination drive. In spite of these drives why cholera attacks and deaths could not be controlled to any noticeable extent remained unanswered in these briefings.[56]

Contrary to the lukewarm attitude of the government, several philanthropists and charitable organisations came forward to fight the cholera menace in Malabar. The *All Kerala Grama Seva Sangham* established relief camps in different parts of the district and extended medical and nursing services to the infected persons. When the disease flared up as a pandemic, the *Sangham* formed a Cholera Relief Committee and made an appeal to the public for generous contributions either through Mr. M.K Raju, the then Editor of *Mathrubhumi* (the popular Malayalam daily) or directly to the Secretary of the *Sangham*. Another relief committee set up by the local philanthropists pooled their resources together and opened cholera relief centres in and around Calicut municipality. It also sent a request to the Editor of *the Hindu* to put a special column requesting individuals and charitable organisations for contributions towards cholera relief works in Malabar. This prompted Malayalees living in Bombay, together with Bombay-based coconut traders in Malabar to collect and forward funds for the cholera-relief-works in the district. The Malayalees Club of Madras also opened a Malabar Cholera Relief Fund, collected donations and forwarded to the *All Kerala Grama Seva Sangham*. While the relief works by private charities were thus going on, the officials effectively used the newly enacted District Police Act and indiscriminately scared away the beggars and destitutes from the city limits.[57] By end-July 1943, the scourge of cholera started receding, with the reported daily deaths in the municipality coming down from an average of fifty to less than thirty.

To conclude: as against what the British administrators and several economic historians argued, the lessons that this survey, spanning for over two centuries, are the following:[58] First, even those who claimed that Malabar could not have famines had agreed that the district used to face frequent attacks of various fatal and not-so-fatal epidemics at every climatic change. But they conveniently ignored that, in a poverty ridden region, deficiency diseases spreading in the form of pandemics should invariably end up in famines. However, their assertion was based on two reasons: (i) historically, the West Coast region in general and Malabar in particular had sumptuous monsoons, facilitating to produce enough food so that the people in the area could easily withstand starvation; and (ii) in the closing decades of the colonial rule, the British rulers had initiated several developmental activities, including import substituting industrialisation. These were supposed to create enough employment opportunities and wipe out poverty and famine. Our survey in this chapter showed that both these arguments were untenable. Nonetheless, in Malabar, even when harvests were normal, the output was insufficient to meet the internal demand of the district. As regards employment and purchasing power, it is true that during the inter-war period, the colony had witnessed the development of certain import-substituting industries. However, as some authors pointed out, these industries benefited England more; it scarcely increased unskilled employment to the extent of improving the standard of living in the colony (see Ghosh, 1995).

The second lesson of this survey is that a combination of several factors had caused repeated famines and large-scale mortalities in Malabar. Of these, the most important were: thoughtless public policies like the *ryotwari* land revenue and the monetisation of transactions that destroyed the social network existing for centuries to withstand any food scarcity in the villages;

excessive morbidity and mortalities among women, children and old-aged people due to adverse intra-family distribution of food even during years of better harvests; a host of water-borne and air-borne epidemics afflicting diet-deficient people at the turn of every season; rising prices of everything edible and declining prices of everything non-edible that affected exchange entitlement to food for non-food producers; restrictions during wars on movement of food and other items through rails, roads and waterways; speculation and hoarding; insufficiency of investments in health-care, food production and infrastructures. Had the colonial rulers practised at least what they professed, Malabar could have escaped from these famines?

Notes

1. See, Report of the Indian Famine Commission 1880, Part-III, para-20.
2. Camouflaging uneasy developments under one's administrative jurisdiction seems to be an age-old practice, not only of bureaucrats but also of political leadership in authority. For example, Jean Dreze and Amartya Sen write that Chandragupta Maurya, the fourth century ruler of India had boasted to impress the royal visitors from Greece that famine was completely absent in his Empire. Conversely, Kautilya, the official economic and political advisor to Chandragupta Maurya had made extensive suggestions on how to deal with famines. It is unbelievable that an official advisor, who is otherwise busy with his work-load, would have advised solutions to problems which did not exist (Dreze and Sen, 1989).
3. See, the *Imperial Gazetteer of India*, Volume III, 1907; pp. 477 – 483.
4. For instance, Seavoy (1986) placed the estimated deaths during the famine of 1876-78 at 6.1 million, Roy (1909) at 7 million, Maharatna (1996) at 8.2 million, and Digby (1901) at 10.3 million.
5. As quoted in Chandra (2009), op.cit.
6. Estimated from the information given in the report of Indian Famine Commission, 1880 on occupied area of land, cultivated area, the *ryotwari* land revenue remitted, net-demand and total collection in Madras presidency during the famine years from 1875-76 to 1879-80.
7. This is the justification given in the land revenue report (1877-78) of Madras Government, for the increase in the revenue collection during the 1876-77 financial year.
8. These lengthy quotations were taken by the Indian Famine Commission, 1880 from the Parliamentary Papers (Parliamentary Blue Book, Vol. II, p. 39.)
9. A bunch of hand-written notes and parts of its printed version obtained from the then Malabar Collector William Logan's office, are available in the Regional Archives of Kozhikode (Kerala).
10. This is contrary to Logan's statement in *Malabar Manual* that there was no record of any famine in Malabar after the 1727 famine.
11. See Imperial Gazetteer of India, Volume III, Chapter X, p. 479.
12. For this view, see Bhatia (1967), McAlpin (1979), Dyson (1980), Klein (1984), Stein (1997), James (2000), Attwood (2005), and Roy (2006). McAlpin had further argued that since the internal movement of grain was predicated on the

responses to the highest price in a region, the low-income people have to starve further. Realising this, according to these authors, the British rulers in India had, in addition to expanding railroads, guaranteed a subsistence level of living through a set of famine relief policies. Bhatia (1967), James (2000), and Stein (2006) also argued that the British policy of commercialisation of agriculture was another reason for the sharp reduction in the risk of famine in the first half of the twentieth century. Our disagreement with this view will be reflected in subsequent chapters where these points come up for discussion.

13. Report of the Administration of the Madras Presidency for the 1918-19, printed and published by the Superintendent of Government Press, Madras, 1920.
14. The types of pests and insects that swept throughout the district in 1918-19 were given out as 'poller beetle' on pepper, 'hepsa' and 'caterpillars' on paddy, stem weevil on cotton, un-named insects on coconut trees, 'brown bast' on rubber plantation, and bleeding disease on palms. It also stated that pests and insects had not spared ragi and sorghum. See, Report of the Administration of the Madras Presidency for the Year 1918-19 (Chapter-IV: Production and Distribution).
15. *Ibid*, p. 56.
16. The report of the President, Malabar District Board for 1917 and 1918, to the Acting Secretary to the Government of Madras Presidency.
17. Report of the Health Department, Madras Presidency, for 1918.
18. Census of India 1921, Vol XII, Madras (Part-I), printed and published by the Superintendent of Census Operations, Madras, 1922.
19. The Malabar Sub-Collector's note No. 1414 M, dated 15 September 1918 included in the Health Department report of Madras Presidency for 1918-19.
20. The report of the President, Malabar District Board for 1918-1919, submitted to the Acting Secretary to the Government of Madras.
21. *Ibid.*
22. See the report of the Survey, Settlement and Land Record Department incorporated in the Madras Administration Report, 1918-19, printed and published by the Superintendent, Government Press, Madras, 1920.
23. See para-181(a) and (b) of Famine Code 1883, adopted by Madras Presidency; printed and published by the Superintendent, Government Press, Madras, 1905.
24. Reported in the Madras Board of Revenue 'Discussion Paper' prepared after the famine of 1918-19 was over.
25. *The Hindu* (editorial), "*The Food Problem*", 5 September 1918, quoted in Ram (1995), op.cit.
26. It appeared that, in spite of widespread criticisms in *the Hindu* and other news papers like *Indian Express*, *Mathrubhumi* etc. the senior administrators continued in Ootacamund. On July 17, 1919, when the famine started subsiding, A.Y.G Campbell, the Acting Secretary to Government issued a Press Communiqué: "It is well known that owing to the war and the unfavourable season during faslis 1327 and 1328 a serious situation has been created in India by reason of the reduction in the stocks of food-supplies that has resulted. The Government of India have taken steps to conserve the existing stocks and to increase the supplies

by stopping exports from India except under license to certain countries with a considerable Indian population and by arranging for imports from other countries, while measures have been taken to see that the best use is made of the deficient rolling-stock on railways by controlling movements of goods by rail. Arrangements have also been made for the import of rice into India proper from Burma at controlled rates" (Supplement to Malabar District Gazette, 1920, published with the caption, "*Increase of Food Supplies*").

27. See the Season and Crops Report for the Madras Presidency for Fasli 1334 (1924-25).
28. The Reuter report date-lined Delhi with the caption, "*Unabated Flood in Malabar*", July 27, 1924 (net resource, accessed on 18-03-2014).
29. See, Season and Crop Report for Fasli 1334 (1924-25) of Madras Presidency.
30. *Ibid.*
31. *Ibid.*
32. These are taken from the file notings of the district headquarters as are available at the Regional Archives at Kozhikode (See files R.D. No. 6527/24 and B-1/9834).
33. See Season and Crop Report for Fasli 1334 (1924), op.cit.
34. Report of the Administration of Madras Presidency for the year 1924-25.
35. I am grateful to Professor M.G. S. Narayanan, former Chairman, ICHR for drawing my attention to this.
36. See (*a*) "Season and Crop Report of the Madras Presidency for the Agricultural Year 1932-33", Board of Revenue, Land Revenue and Settlement (Government Press, Madras, 1933); and (*b*) "Season and Crop Report of the Madras Presidency for the Agricultural Year 1933-34", Board of Revenue, Land Revenue and Settlement (Government Press, Madras, 1935).
37. Season and Crop Report of the Madras Presidency for 1933-34, op.cit.
38. *Ibid.*
39. *Ibid.*
40. *Ibid.*
41. See, the document, Local Self Government Department - Cochin: "Cholera – Final Report", 1935.
42. "Public Health Administration Report of the Cannanore Municipality for the Year 1933-34", Appendix-A.
43. *Ibid.*, p.(iii).
44. Gazette Notification G.O. No. 1307, P.H; Fort St. George, June 15, 1933.
45. See, Report of the Foodgrain Policy Committee, Chaired by Theodore Gregory (Delhi, 1943).
46. See, Report of the Currency and Finance, 1945-46, (Bombay: Reserve Bank of India).
47. Also see the Theodore Gregory Committee report mentioned at f.n (36).
48. See (i) Report of the Settlement of Land Revenue of the Madras Presidency for 1941-42; (ii) Board of Revenue, Madras: Report on the Settlement of Land Revenue for 1943-44; and (iii) Madras in 1943: Outline of the Administration (all the three printed by the Superintendent, Government Press, Madras)

49. Taken from "*Statistics–Foodgrains in Madras State: Production, Procurement, Allotments, Imports, Offtake, Prices*", published by Superintendent, Government Press, Madras, 1951.

50. Quoted in Bridge (1986) and reproduced by Bandyopadhyay (2004) and Sarkar (1983).

51. These three cases were, respectively: (i) Madras High Court: Krishnan Atiyoti and Others vs Province of Madras (17 December 1943); (ii) Madras High Court: Sankunni Variar and others vs Thavazhi Karanavar and Manager (April 12, 1943); and (iii) Supreme Court of India: Collector of Malabar vs Ebrahim Haji and Others. The third case related to the decision of the Collector in 1943-44 but the court decree came in 1954 (website materials downloaded on 25 October 2012).

52. These are simple averages of upper and lower ranges of 165–325 and 130–355 prisoners who died daily in jail.

53. Madras Administration Report, 1944-45 (Part II), Chapter V, pp. 97-98.

54. These notes are available at the Regional Archives, Kozhikode under B. Nos. 19 and 20 of the Madras Records of Education and Public Health Department.

55. "Cholera Inspections in Malabar", prepared by Assistant Director of Public Health (Epidemics), dated 28th June 1943 at Camp: Palghat (copy available in Regional Archives, Kozhikode).

56. *The Hindu*, Madras date-lined July 25 from Calicut with the caption "Peak of Epidemic Reached".

57. These are taken from various reports that appeared in the Madras additions of the Hindu and Indian Express in July 1943. These newspaper cuttings are available in Regional Archives, Kozhikode.

58. These are not however Malabar-specific features but applicable to famines anywhere in the world. (See, Cormac O' Grada (2009).

Chapter 3

Food Availability Crisis and Famines

3.1 The Concepts

Almost all academic studies since Adam Smith's *Wealth of Nations* (1776) and until Amartya Sen published his path-breaking work *Poverty and Famines* in 1981, as well as some of the official reports released by the British rulers had associated famines in the third world colonies, especially in India, with crop-failures caused by droughts or floods and the resultant decline in the availability of food, even though other factors contributing to famine also had come up in the discussions (about which later). While reviewing the food-based arguments of famine, Sen christened it as 'food availability decline', or a FAD approach to the study of famine (it may be remembered that the dictionary meaning of 'fad' is craze, or idiosyncrasy). A section of the British administrators and academicians interpreted FAD as arising from what is called the 'Malthusian imbalance', or a situation in which population increased at geometric progression and food production in arithmetic progression so that there was always a persistent shortage in *per capita* food availability. The solution that they suggested to solve this problem was the people themselves consciously limit their family size in such a way that the imbalance between population and food supply automatically disappeared, so that the question of frequent famines ceased to be a thing of the past (see Roy, 2006). Another somewhat short-term view, though closely connected with this argument, was that famine broke out in a region on account of a sudden decline in the harvested food output. However, the term 'food availability' is a larger concept than what 'food output' conveys. The former is the same thing as the term 'supply' implies in text-book economics. In official literature, 'supply' or 'availability' of food is made up of three components: (i) the size of the current food output, (ii) 'carry-over stocks' from previous harvests, and (iii) 'net imports'. Before discussing the FAD approach to famine, it would be appropriate to bring in the meaning of these three components of food availability.

Current output

This is the volume of food output from the harvest available for consumption in a given year. As we discussed in the introductory chapter, India raises three crops in a year. Roughly, the harvesting of the crops and their consumption pattern are assumed in the following sequence: Let us denote 1943 as the 'current year'. Then, most of the *winter crops* reaped during December-February of 1942 would be available for consumption in the next three months of the 'current year'. Similarly, the *autumn crops* harvested during August-October of 1943 would also be fully available for consumption in the same 'current year'. The *spring crops* are sown at the fag end of 1943 and harvested early in 1944 and hence not available in 1943 for consumption. In other words, when we denote the 'current output', it comprises most of the *winter* harvests of the preceding year and the entire *autumn* harvests of the same year but not the *spring* harvests.

The winter crops, generally known as *kharif* crops in India (with local variations, for example, *kanni* crops in Malabar) provide the largest number of food items. Cereals like paddy, jowar, bajra, maize and ragi; pulses like tur, moong and urad; edible oilseeds like groundnut, soyabean, sunflower seed, sesamum and nigerseed; and the industrial raw material, particularly cotton, are grown during the *kharif* season. The main *kharif* cereal crop, viz. paddy, requires some time for drying up after harvest and, then, for hulling and milling. At least three months are required for this process of drying and dehusking paddy into rice and reach the market for consumers to buy. It is well-known that rice is the principal cereal for the people in southern and eastern regions. The main *autumn* crops, known generally as *rabi* crops in India (or *makaram* crops in Malabar) also consist of some rice. The other major cereals of this season are wheat and barley; pulses like gram and lentil; and edible oilseeds, mainly mustard and safflower seeds. The cultivation of *rabi* crops depends on irrigation or on moisture retained in the soil from the previous rainfall. Failure of the monsoon affects water for the replenishment of irrigation network as well as moisture retention in the soil for the next crops, thereby increasing the possibility of a decline in the relevant 'current' food output.[1]

Carry-over Stocks

The second component of 'food availability' is the 'carry-over stock' or the surplus of production over consumption carried forward from the previous harvest. The carry-over stock is, statistically, an elusive quantity. Though difficult to judge with whom or in which area the carry-over stock lies, it has a lot to do in tackling the food shortage arising from the 'current' harvest. Common sense would suggest that the areas blessed with timely, adequate and properly distributed rainfall, coupled with better fertility of soil, will produce sufficient food to meet the current needs as also to 'carry-over' a part of the quantity for the next season. However, the density of population in such highly fertile areas will also be relatively high. If famine occurs after a few seasons of scanty rainfall, it is unlikely to have a carry-over stock even in such otherwise surplus producing regions. On the other hand, in moderately food producing regions with low density of population, at least certain classes among them might hold carry-over stocks for use in times of general food availability decline.

This is easy to understand if we consider the class status and production condition in agriculture.[2] It is a well-known fact that capitalist farmers, who are equipped with enough land and non-land resources, cultivate with hired labour, purchased inputs and advanced farming methods. They are in a position to generate enough surpluses from cultivation. After selling a part of the surplus in the market, they will be left with enough stocks to 'carry-over' for the next season. If the region is famine-prone, they will be careful to maintain sufficient carry-over stocks for the subsistence of their family as well as for making a profit during periods when scarcity of availability pushes up market prices.

Similarly, landlords who lease-out land and receive their share of the produce are likely to hold back a part of it for consumption in times of famines or other food crises. This is also true of the rural money lenders who appropriate in kind the loan given to farmers on the eve of sowing. Their age-old practice was to advance loans, on condition that the borrower returned a pre-specified quantity of the produce, equivalent to the loan and the interest estimated at the highest pre-harvest price anticipated to prevail by the end of the season. Another class of farmers, known as 'middle peasants' whose production over good and bad seasons, on average, is just enough to meet their family consumption, may not be left with any stock to 'carry-over' for use in times of food availability crises. Others who cannot keep any stock for future use are understandably the agricultural labourers, rural artisans like carpenters, blacksmiths, masons etc., and the traditional weavers in rural areas, though they may be getting their payments partly or fully in foodgrains (Gadgil, 1924).

The role of 'carry-over stock' in preventing, or the absence of it in accentuating, famine is generally being explained as follows: Famines occur primarily because of bad harvests from irregular and scanty rainfall for two or three years, wiping out the entire carry-over stocks from previous harvests. While explaining the famine of 1876-78 that struck several areas in India, and devastated British Malabar, D.R. Gadgil had noted that the rainfall in these areas had failed continuously for some years before the actual famine took place. The people in the affected regions consumed whatever stocks they had. When the food scarcity continued, they consumed the seeds kept for sowing in the next season. Then they ate what is known as 'famine food', including cattle forages. In the initial phase of the famine, wage earners and rural artisans were the most emaciated from hunger and malnutrition, and they died in large numbers. When famine persisted, even the relatively better off among the population in the affected areas perished. The recovery from such famines took longer duration of time than expected owing to the absence of seeds, which were already eaten up, and the death of drought animals, whose forages like oilcakes were consumed by their masters, and the absence of male members in farm families, as they had either died or emigrated in search of employment, resulting in the dearth of inputs and labour for cultivation (Gadgil, 1924).

The view that the absence of reserved stocks from the preceding harvests was the main reason for exacerbating famines in India had several adherents. Even the Famine Inquiry Commission of 1945 had assigned the lack of carry-over stock to have an important role in precipitating the Bengal famine. The Commission stated in its report that the Bengal famine resulted from "a shortage in the stock of old rice carried forward from 1942 to 1943." One of its members, however, was not fully convinced about this argument. He pointed out that, sensing the emerging market situation, whatever little stocks of crop available in 1943 might have been held back by the big farmers and traders for speculative purposes. As these stocks did not immediately come to the market when the crops failed, it would be a mistake to rely on 'surplus stocks' accumulated from previous years to ward off famine.[3]

Net Imports

The third component of 'food availability' is the 'net import', which is derived as the difference between 'exports' out of and 'imports' into a given territory. Official documents categorise two types of 'net imports'. One arises from inland movements of foodgrains across states through rail and river, i.e. the difference between the quantity transported out of a state-border called 'export' and the quantity moved into the state from other parts of the same country, called 'import'. The second type of 'net import' is estimated as the difference between gross imports into and gross exports out of the national border. These quantities are available from the records of the port authorities. If the volume of import from abroad is higher than the volume of export out of the country, we say, the 'net import' is positive, and vice versa. The 'net import', together with 'current output' and 'carry-over stock', adjusted for the existing population, is the index of the 'food availability'. If it is lower than the normal requirement of the people, we say there is FAD or a 'food availability decline'. This is a condition arising primarily from a persistent decline in harvest, which wipes out the carry-over stocks. It could also happen if net-imports decline. The situation becomes grim when all these appear together.

3.2 FAD Approach to Famine

The so called FAD approach as an explanation of how famine breaks out is apparently very simple. The European social scientists in general and British colonial rulers in particular used to dump tropical countries, mainly India, as naturally unhealthy and disease-prone. Being entirely dependent on monsoons for cultivation, these countries, according to them, could not avoid recurrent failure of rains leading to crop losses and decline in the availability of food items originating in agriculture. In extreme situations, this deepens from malnourishment to debilitation, fatigue, morbidity, and to famine, famine-related epidemics and large scale mortalities. The best example of this could be seen in the report of the Famine Inquiry Commission 1945, which investigated the 1943 Bengal famine. In the backdrop of the 1942 cyclone, torrential rains, flooding and fungus diseases to crops, worsened by the Second World War and the stoppage of Burmese rice imports, the Commission stated that the Bengal famine of 1943 was caused by "the serious shortage of rice available for consumption in Bengal as compared with the total supply normally available."[4]

The definitions of famine that Sen (1981) quotes from different authors, before putting forward his argument, also emphasise decline in food availability as its essential cause. For example, according to Masefield (1963), "any satisfactory definition of famine must provide that the food shortage is either widespread or extreme if not both, and that degree of extremity is best measured by human mortality by starvation." Johnson (1973) defined famine as arising from "an extreme and protracted shortage of food resulting in widespread and persistent hunger, evidenced by loss of body weight and emaciation and increase in the death rate caused either by starvation or disease resulting from the weakened condition of the population." In the words of Mayer (1975), famine can be defined as a "severe shortage of food accompanied by a significant increase in the local or regional death rates." A similar definition, though Sen did not quote but is equally emphatic on FAD as the basic cause of famine, is that of McAlpin (1979): "We can think of periods when harvests are low as periods of *dearth*; and when these periods of dearth result in high mortality, we can say that a *famine* has occurred."

Some researchers have argued that FAD approach to famine, though apparently simple and overtly harmless, was part of an 'imperialist project' in conquered territories of the third world countries (see Satya, 2011). This 'project', according to them, envisaged the flow of wealth from the colonies to Great Britain, by the use of a policy guided by the influential *laissez-faire* ideology of the classical political economy. It was Adam Smith, the most notable proponent of this view, who argued that the state intervention in the market, even during acute human miseries like famines, was against the system of natural liberty. Any government that follows the ideology of *laissez-faire* should perform only three duties: "first, the duty of protecting the society from the violence and invasion of other independent societies; secondly, the duty of protecting, as far as possible, every member of the society from the injustice or oppression of every other member of it, or the duty of establishing an exact administration of justice; and thirdly, the duty of erecting and maintaining certain public works and certain public institutions." Adam Smith further noted that the performance of these duties presupposes certain expenses, which should essentially be met by collecting taxes from the citizens who would benefit from these duties (Smith, 1776). The British administration in India was sanctimonious in pursuing this last advice without fail, i.e. the collection of taxes from the subject-people, though much more than needed to meet the expenditure incurred on the public works beneficial to them was extracted.

When the Malthusian theory of population was incorporated into the FAD approach to elaborate the cause of famine, the hidden 'imperialist project' came out in the open. What Malthus had presented was "a constant tendency in all animated life to increase beyond the nourishment prepared for it", or "to increase beyond the means of subsistence." This was a general tendency everywhere, not in third world countries alone. Explaining further, Malthus argued that the "population when unchecked, goes on doubling itself every twenty-five years, or increase in a geometrical ratio." But "considering the present average state of the earth, the means of subsistence, under circumstances most favourable to human industry, could not possibly be made to increase faster than in an arithmetic ratio" (Malthus, 1878).

Malthus clarified later that when population outstrips food supply the prices would go up. If food prices show the symptom of a rising tendency, the speculators would further push up the prices and worsen the sufferings of particularly the poor. Subsequently, he argued that the system of 'parish allowance' being doled out, rather than solving the problem of price-rise and hunger would only exacerbate the tendency of the rising prices to further firm up. Because of this tendency, according to Malthus, the 'parish allowance' would maintain the market demand for food at a higher level so that the price would refuse to come down. "This price, however", stated

Malthus, "has been most essentially and powerfully affected by the ability that has been given to the labouring poor, by means of parish allowances, of continuing to purchase wheat notwithstanding its extraordinary rise" (Malthus, 1880: 16). Nowhere had Malthus stated that his theory was meant for the third world countries like India alone (Sen, 1981: 175).

Nonetheless, using this theory, some of the western scholars argued that famine broke out in third world countries, especially in India, as a natural check to excessive multiplication of population. The positive side of the famine, according to them, was that it brought down the level of population to the available level of food stuffs and provided a reprieve to the imperialist government from incurring 'unreasonable' famine-relief expenses (see, Caldwell, 1988). The way in which the theory of 'Malthusian-imbalance' was used to explain the cause of famine would also reveal, explicitly in some respects and implicitly in some others, the European cultural bias against the people of the third world colonies. The most explicit form of cultural bias exhibited in India was a sort of racial segregation that they adopted while preparing their settlements: (a) in the trading centres, called 'factories' that the EIC set up in different port centres, the 'white' people lived ostentatiously in palatial buildings, separating the 'natives' by new roads and malls; (b) they kept large number of servants in their houses to exhibit their colonial feudal status; and (c) they used to organise social clubs exclusively for the 'whites' where Indians were not permitted to enter, except in their capacity as servants dressed up as Maharajas (Dasgupta, 2003).

The social and physical separation between Indians and British nationals working in India could also be seen in their explanation of the attack of recurring famines during the colonial period. For example, some of the British social scientists argued that the civilisation of Western Europe does not and will not permit its population to increase beyond any economically advantageous optimum level. On the other hand, in India, it was 'the animal instinct predominating over foresight and enterprise' that increased the size of population faster than the increase in food production. The pre-historic practice in India of early marriages, and the decision of the British administration to abolish female infanticide and widow-burning in the funeral pyre of the husband, further instilled the fire for uncontrolled explosion of population. Rather than anything else, it was the explosion of population far above the minimum requirement of food to feed them that, according to some of the British social scientists, dragged India into repeated famines during the late nineteenth century (see Loveday, 1914).

At the operational level, the most harmful effect of this academic view originated from the British bureaucrats. Almost all officials of the Indian

Civil Service appointed in the nineteenth-century being trained in England, it was not unnatural that they were influenced by the popular opinions prevailing there. The theory of Malthusian-imbalance as the cause of famines in colonial India was one such view that these bureaucrats held firmly with them, and influenced the formulation of the British famine policy in India. We have noted in the introductory chapter as to how an Indian-born civil servant appointed as Collector in the eastern region and entrusted with the stewardship for implementing famine prevention activities, refused to supply gratuitous food to the starving people during the 1943 famine, even though it was arranged by the government in terms of the Famine Code of 1883, and therefore a part of his duty. The Malthusian theory of population reinterpreted as 'Malthusian-imbalance' as the prime cause of famine was the intellectual basis of these bureaucrats, who took a negative approach in this respect (Ambirajan, 1976).

The blatant cultural bias inherent in the Malthusian-imbalance ideology of famine will be clear if we compare that position with what Gunnar Myrdal argued in his celebrated *Asian Drama*: "In Western Europe population showed a tendency to increase beginning in the eighteenth century or earlier, whereas in South Asia (mainly in India) a similar trend appeared around the beginning of the nineteenth century." Furthermore, according to Myrdal, "in Western Europe opportunities for gainful employment began to rise at about the same time that the population began to grow" so that this tendency was reckoned as an optimum growth. It was the increasing employment opportunities in the West that protected people from the danger of starvation and famines. Notwithstanding the fact that the level of fertility in Europe and India was by and large similar, it was the lack of economic development and improved sanitation facilities that pushed the latter into repeated famines (Myrdal, 1968).

Apart from Myrdal, who was a Swedish economist and sociologist, there were in England itself isolated voices in the late nineteenth century that put the causes of Indian famines in an entirely different perspective. The most influential among these voices was that of Florence Nightingale (1820–1910), the celebrated British nurse, statistician and a prolific writer. She was born in Florence (Italy) into a very rich, upper-class, and highly influential British parents. At a very young age, Nightingale decided to enter the nursing profession against the stout disapproval of her mother and elder sister, both of whom wanted her to abide by their traditional family custom of becoming a wife and mother at the young age. With the strong support from her father, she defied their opposition, went to study nursing and became famous all over the world, after her pioneering service in tending the wounded soldiers during the Crimean War (1853–56). This service also earned her the nickname, 'The Lady with the Lamp', which was derived from a phrase in a report published in *The Times* that extolled her for her soothing care of the injured and mutilated soldiers in the Crimean War (Gill, 2005).

Another commendable service that Nightingale did was her relentless crusade for improving the healthcare and famine-relief programmes in India. When the British authorities were insensitive to her pleadings, she wrote extensively about these tragic conditions in the rural countryside with a view to educate British citizens who, she thought, could put pressure on their government in initiating appropriate measures. These crusades were instrumental in changing the attitude of the imperialist administration on Indian famines. Nonetheless, these writings seldom find mention in the otherwise vast and comprehensive literature on famines in India. What follows is a brief summary of her views on British India's recurring famines, epidemics and mortalities.

3.3 A Different Voice: Florence Nightingale

Not long after Nightingale returned to England on the conclusion of the Crimean War, the British India witnessed the historic 1857 revolt. She made a request through Lady Canning, wife of the then Governor General, Charles Canning, her willingness to travel to India and attend to the victims of the revolt: "should you think it possible for me to be of the smallest use, I would come out, at twenty-four hours' notice, to serve in any capacity 'in my line of business' that you would direct" (see Vallee, 2006). The British administration however did not feel the need for her services. This was also the time when she was intermittently bedridden with a variant of spondylitis and depression. Still she continued with her interest in India's poor public health services and recurring famines. Taking help of an impressive network of highly placed collaborators, including social workers and a few powerful British administrators, she made a comprehensive statistical study of sanitation in Indian rural life and lobbied for the introduction of improved medical care and public health services in the colony, about which we will discuss in Chapter-5. The objective of this sub-section is to see her views on Indian famines during the colonial rule.

The causes of Indian famines that Nightingale detected from her research were diametrically opposite to what the British administrators and social scientists had made out. She was emphatic on the fact that famines repeating in India were not due to the failure of crops arising from any sudden bout of droughts. Her studies on India, in fact, were taken up in the midst of the worst famine of 1876-78 that spread to several parts of British India and wreaked an unprecedented havoc in Malabar. At the peak of the famine in 1877, Nightingale argued that, apart from the drought, the real causes of that famine rested much deeper beneath the surface: "The land in India is not specifically subject to famine; the cultivators of soil are industrious; the native races compare favourably with other races in capacity to take themselves." She put the onus of the recurring famines in India squarely on the British rulers. Citing the grave injustice of large-scale export of food to England, to the British war theatres, and elsewhere at the time of the raging famine in the colony, she protested: "Londoners are in effect eating India's bread." And she went on: "It seems an anomaly with her famines on hand India is able to supply food for other parts of the world" (see Vallee, 2007). In her numerous published papers and letters addressed to the ruling formations, she reiterated that, rather than ascribing to the decline in food availability, the real reasons for famines in India should be seen in the British policy that infringed on the ability of the people to access their day-to-day necessities of life. Such infringements traversed in many directions.

To clarify, for centuries, salt was produced by native Indian citizens through solar evaporation of sea-water. Those living away from coastal areas got it on payment of an extremely meagre price. The British government enacted a Salt Act in 1802 and took away this age-old right of the people to produce and use salt. The Act made production and sale of salt the inalienable monopoly of the government. It debarred private individuals from producing salt as they did earlier. In case they had already taken license and manufactured salt, the Act provided that the entire quantity that they produced so far should be surrendered to the government. Moreover, it was made compulsory to buy salt only from the depots set up by the government in different parts within the British territory. Violation of the Act was treated as a criminal offence. Using this provision of the Act, several people in different parts of the Indian colony were arrested, fined and even imprisoned.

In addition to prohibiting its production by private individuals, the government levied heavy taxes on salt. As a result, it became costlier than even foodgrains. The writers on famines in British India could not realise the physiological consequences of depriving salt and its link with famine. It was Nightingale who pointed out for the first time (decades before Gandhiji's 'Salt March' in 1930) that salt is one of the most essential nutritional factors for human body and that its deprivation to the colonial population by the British was one major cause that led to famines. In one of her writings, she stated that "the salt in India which costs 12 shillings has a tax of £ 7 per ton. This virtually debars ordinary people from using salt, restricts the preservation of food, and absolutely forbids native manufacturers."[5]

Taking specific cases of some of the famine-districts, Nightingale pointed out that in those districts people had great suffering for water, though there was, in fact, no scarcity of water. "Plenty of water in these districts means irrigation, cheap water-transport, improved methods of cultivation, and forest plantation." Referring to the famine of 1876-78, she said: "had we given them water, they could have brought food from wherever it was available, as also ship their own produces over the world and become the richest instead of the poorest of the colonies.....in that case, there was no need for the government to spend on feeding them" as the British administration was morally bound to do in times of famines and epidemic diseases (see Vallee, 2007).

Nightingale was indignant about the activities of the indigenous money lenders who were instrumental in precipitating famines in the colony. She stated that a class of rich men, who established themselves all over the country as money lenders, advanced loan to the cultivator against his forthcoming crop, or to buy oxen or seed, charging him anywhere from 50 to 100 per cent interest. "This he can't repay when his crops are gathered, or, if he does pay it, he has nothing left for his family, and must again borrow on his next crop. As unpaid interest becomes principal in the next year with a higher rate of interest, thereby increasing the debt burden, the cultivator is compelled to sell his land." Nightingale pointed out that the British Indian law was such that "if the debtor has nothing to pay, the money lender has authority to sell the man himself, his land, and every thing he possesses, even the honour of his wife and daughter." This has been going on all over India and the government took no action to check such shocking human right violations. The dispossession of assets by the money lenders had intensified famines. Commenting on the government's negative attitude in preventing famines, she stated: "Here is ship-wreck, utter, disastrous, of some, not hundreds, but millions of souls; it is ship-wreck which is repeated every year. No hand is stretched out to save. It is a ship-wreck which will be repeated, more disastrous, more complete, if that be possible, every year." She was terse in demanding that, "if the money lenders, who in most cases are not natives, are not arrested and stopped their land grabbing spree, a large part of the people (in India) will be reduced to chattel slavery."

Being a pioneer in virtual presentation of complicated statistical data in graphics, like pie-chart, or polar area diagram, Nightingale's writings on health and famines in India were phenomenally objective in nature.[6] British rulers and some of the social scientists who supported the imperialist famine policy could not challenge her views on epidemics and famines in India as these were based on solid facts that she gathered through various sources (Cohen, 1984). Nonetheless, the credit for disproving the FAD approach to famines with robust empirical data and a new theory of famine goes to Amartya Sen, long after Nightingale's works. In the following section, we will examine some of Professor Sen's country-studies, which showed that though the FAD approach to famine is not altogether irrelevant and even when it appears right in the outbreak of a famine, this does not provide any guidance about the character of the famine Professor Sen, by himself and in collaboration with Jean Dreze, had examined famines in a number of countries and regions within countries to see whether the FAD approach as the conventional explanation of famine is in any way tenable[7]. Sen's own case studies given in *Poverty and Famines,* being more fundamental to his argument, the findings of these studies are briefly outlined below.

3.4 Empirical Proof: Amartya Sen

The first case study in *Poverty and Famine*s relates to the Bengal famine of 1943 that resulted in an excess mortality of more than 3 million people. Before Sen's study, famine was generally perceived as FAD famine, though there were authors, as we noted earlier, like Florence Nightingale, Gunnar Myrdal etc. who contested this proposition. Still the report of the Famine Inquiry Commission of 1945 and the periodic submissions made to the Viceroy by the commissioners and district officers in Bengal also had held the view that Bengal famine was caused by a decline in the availability of food (Sen 1981). However, Professor Sen's survey proved that the available data on food availability in Bengal for 1943 could not support such a contention. As we noted in Chapter-1, in 1943, the food supply was only 5 per cent lower than the average for the preceding five-years but it was 13 per cent higher than in 1941. While in 1941 there was no famine in Bengal, in 1943, there was an extremely calamitous famine and large-scale mortalities. He attributed this to a wild upsurge in the prices of foodgrains, particularly of rice, the main cereal of the region. The agricultural labourers constituted the largest segment of the population affected by famine in Bengal. They faced a decline in employment, and a sticky wage, so that there was a dramatic deterioration in the index of the ratio of the exchange rate of money-wages to food prices, from 100 estimated for 1940 to 34 in 1943. There was similar or even deeper plunge in the exchange entitlement of other occupational groups in Bengal, for example, those engaged in weaving, making bamboo-umbrellas, livestock-rearing, hair-cuts, fishing, and so on.

The second case study narrates the two famines in Ethiopia: one in the north-east province of Wollo during 1972-73 and the other in the southern province of Harerghe during 1973-74. Both these were years of droughts in Ethiopia and the main victims of starvation and famine-deaths during these years were pastoral communities. The official figures released by the Ethiopian Ministry of Agriculture showed that, in 1972-74, there was no abnormal reduction in the output of food produced in the country. The harvest was, in fact 'above normal' in 14 per cent of the total districts in Ethiopia, 'normal' in another 65 per cent, and only the remaining 21 per cent reported 'below normal' production. Large quantities of foodgrains from the famine affected areas were shifted to the Ethiopian capital of Addis Ababa, and to Asmera. Nonetheless, the food prices did not increase substantially. On the other hand, conversion of large stretches of grazing lands in the country for the cultivation of commercial crops, mainly by foreign monopolies, had led to substantial loss of livestock, more so during droughts. Consequently, the exchange rate between the prices of animal products and that of grain deteriorated so steeply that the livestock-dependent people sunk into starvation and famine. The delay in reaching relief to the affected sections further worsened the tragedy.

The third case study relates to the Sahel belt of Africa, comprising Mauritania, Senegal, Mali, Upper Volta, Niger, and Chad. In these places famine broke out when there was a drought, as in the case of the Wollo and Harerghe in Ethiopia. But the difference was that, unlike in Ethiopia, the *per capita* food production in the Sahelian countries had actually declined in 1973 when the region's famine reached its peak. In that sense, even though the decline in food output was not very substantial, the FAD view of famine could appear plausible. However, quoting figures from the *FAO Production Yearbook 1976*, Sen noted that while the food output had declined in most of the Sahelian countries, on average, the estimated average *per capita* food availability had actually gone up. On the other hand, there was a decline in the production of cash crops. The livestock also perished in large numbers. Using these facts, Sen argued that, the 1973 Sahelian famine could be attributed, not to the FAD view but to the collapse of entitlement arising from: (i) unequal distribution of food; (ii) decline in the output of cash crops, which its growers used to access food; and (iii) loss of livestock, resulting in the inability of the pastoral population to access food by exchanging animals or animal products.

Sen's last case study of the Bangladesh famine in 1974 had preceded (just as the cyclone and torrential rains occurred prior to Bengal famine) repeated floods from the Brahmaputra, causing severe damages to *aus* and *aman* rice crops, which together formed more than 80 per cent of that country's rice production. Nonetheless, referring to Alamgir (1980), Sen argued that "it wasn't a FAD famine" because, in 1974, the overall production and per capita availability of foodgrains had actually increased.

What dragged the country into famine was the rumour of a decline in *aus* and *aman* crops, firming up prices and strengthening speculative withdrawals of foodgrains from the market. Though the cash-constrained Bangladesh government could manage to import some grain from abroad, the stoppage of food-aid by America as a punishment for Bangladesh's trade-relation with Cuba, made the condition worse. An analysis of the occupational distribution of destitutes, who were fed with gratuitous supply of food in *langarkhana*s showed that as high as 45 per cent of them were labourers who lost their employment due to floods. The next highest group of destitutes comprised farmers, estimated almost at 39 per cent, who lost their crops in floods. Using these evidences, Sen concluded emphatically that "the FAD view provides no explanation of the Bangladesh famine.....a better understanding of the famine can be found through the entitlement approach."

3.5 Amartya Sen Criticised

In all these case studies, Sen showed that more than FAD, there were other stronger causes, which dragged people of the third world countries into disastrous famines. He argued that these causes, including FAD, could be taken together in another concept called 'failure of exchange entitlement' (FEE), which is capable of explaining famine better. This new insight, while exhilarating to many, has disappointed a few. Both these positions continue to adorn the pages of journals even after more than three decades of the publication of *Poverty and Famines*. The former group considers it as 'our new understanding of the famines' while the latter group continues its unrelenting criticisms against Sen's FEE thesis. One of the most vigorous criticisms came from Peter Bowbrick who, after publishing his initial reactions in *Food Policy*, the journal of International Food Policy Research Institute (IFPRI) has been sprucing up these criticisms and uploading on his own website.[8] Though the debates between Bowbrick and Sen have since turned out to be acrimonious and, as Colin Blackman, the editor of *Food Policy* noted, "the tone of this whole debate has left much to be desired – and detracted from the issue,"[9] there are certain fundamental points in their debate that cannot be ignored while considering the FAD view of famine. We will, therefore, pick up some of the major points of arguments between Bowbrick and Sen to have a deeper view of how famine occurs. To begin with, let us consider Bowbrick's arguments:

To Bowbrick, Sen has attacked a strawman, called FAD, to justify his own FEE theory of famine, producing a large amount of evidence from Bengal famine of 1943. This new theory of famine is untenable, argued Bowbrick, both because of analytical errors and because it is factually inaccurate, basically because Sen's production figures are not only just untenable but also wrong. It will take only a few minutes with a computer to show that Sen's theory cannot be correct. Anybody will know that, physically, it is impossible for one group to eat so much that most of the population goes hungry and millions of people starve. Assuming that fifty thousand defense service personnel were additionally recruited from Bengal in 1943, Bowbrick calculated the per capita food availability for that year in calorie/ounce terms for different classes of population in the presidency and asks: How many ounces of rice would have been eaten by these defense personnel? To what extent this could bring down the consumption of rice by five million people of Bengal below their normal requirement?

According to Bowbrick, Sen was able to reject the FAD view of famine because of an erroneous method that he adopted to calculate the food availability. For example, in one of his key tables, entitled 'Food Availability in Bengal, 1938-1943' given in *Poverty and Famines*, Sen assumed that, during the peak famine period of 1943, there was zero carry-over stock in Bengal. In the absence of carry-over stock, the concept of food availability consisted of only production and imports. Bowbrick argued that all available evidences conflicted with the assumption of zero carry-over.

The second flaw in Sen's FAD analysis, argued Bowbrick, is that he considers the demand-side of famine when he states that, in any famine, the people who die are those who cannot afford to buy food. This was in fact the view of the English classical economists since Adam Smith, who proposed *inter alia* food handouts and public works that created effective demand for tackling famines. This remedy, when applied in many of the famines, including in India, had proved disastrous. Of late, economists have started arguing that, along with demand supply-side also should be considered to have a better understanding of famines. But while analyzing the causes of famine, Sen rejected its supply-side effects.[10]

A third criticism that Bowbrick raised is that, in *Poverty and Famines* and in many of his other writings, Sen has argued that "most famines are not caused by sudden declines in food availability due to droughts, floods etc. On the contrary, they happen when there is plenty of food available, but one part of the population suddenly eats a lot more than normal, because of a war-time boom, or inflation, for instance. As a result, there is less food available for the rest of the population, so the poor starve."

While responding to Bowbrick's argument of wrong production figures used to reject the FAD view of famine, Sen stated that "in discussing the causation of the Bengal famine of 1943, I had used *all* the available production statistics, without exception, including the 'unadjusted' and 'adjusted' figures of output (and current supply) presented by the official Famine Inquiry Commission. It was clear on that basis that the food output per capita was *higher* in the year of the famine, viz. 1943, than in 1941, when there was no famine." Regarding the possible errors in the official statistics, particularly the tendency of the reporting agencies to over-estimate bad years and under-estimate good years, Sen argued that "this will apply *both* to 1941 and 1943, so that my point, which was concerned with the relative picture of 1943 vis-à-vis 1941, is not affected" (Sen, 1987).

On Bowbrick's argument relating to carryover stock, Sen clarified that "not only did I not make any such statement, nor any such assumption. I had in fact made extensive use of moving averages over two-year and three-year periods respectively to take note of the possible variations of carryover from year to year.......My point was not that there was 'zero carryover', but that we cannot just arbitrarily make those assumptions about carryover variations that would be needed for the validity of FAD and then, on the basis of those dreamed up assumptions, assert that FAD is okay after all" (Sen 1986).

The argument of Sen committing the 'folly' that the Classical Economists did, considering demand-side and ignoring supply-side of famine might have probably arisen from his empirical analysis of Bengal famine by dividing the period into two phases, *viz.* Phase-I, the period immediately preceding the famine, i.e. January 1939 to January 1943, and Phase-II, the severe phase of the famine, from January 1943 and subsided in May 1943. In Phase-I, Sen found that food supply was exceptionally high. Still, there was a sharp increase in the prices of rice, caused by a general inflationary pressure exerted on the economy, mainly due to the government's deficit-financed war-expenditures. In Phase-II, Sen stated, "the demand forces were reinforced by the 'indifferent' winter crop and by vigorous speculation and panic hoarding." That is, in Phase-II, it was the combined effects of both demand and supply factors that made the famine very disastrous.[11]

If Sen has argued, as Bowbrick explained, that famine does not break out when there is a sudden decline in food availability, but when there is plenty of food available because one part of the population suddenly eats a lot more than normal, he will be guilty of not only distorting statistics but also making a mockery of the fundamental economic theory. Anybody who has gone through *Poverty and Famines* even cursorily will recognise that, this was not the way Sen made out his argument; such a characterisation is, to use the words of Sen, 'misdescription' and 'distortion (Sen 1987).

There are authors who feel that the criticism of Bowbrick cannot be rejected outright. For example, David Allen emphasised that "Bowbrick's attitude is fundamentally correct." Many readers of *Poverty and Famines*, not only Bowbrick alone, have come away feeling that Professor Sen virtually ruled out FAD effects of famine. That is the tone of the book. In this context, Allen felt that Sen should have at least accommodated "the distinctly, but of course not completely, FAD Irish famine of the 1840s, as well as some of the pre-1943 famines in the Indian sub-continent – the latter coming from the evident stimulus to re-read that major study by B.M Bhatia – the Soviet famine and possibly some of the pre-1939 Chinese experience in which there were FAD elements" (Allen 1986).

This argument may appear to hold some merit. However, while "re-reading" B.M Bhatia, the 'stimulus' that we get is not exactly what Allen stated. In the preface to his book, Bhatia had stated that in olden times, famine could be safely attributed to a decline in food availability arising from the lack of means of transport, and the absence of any well-established channels of trade. Under those conditions, whenever local crops failed in a region, people of that region could not look to other parts of the country, much less abroad, to make up for the deficiency in production. On the contrary, modern developments in industry, trade and transport have radically changed the causes of famine. From the food availability decline it was transformed into the problem of poverty that led to lack of purchasing power. An abrupt and sharp rise in food prices made food inaccessible to the poor, who suffered starvation and, in extreme cases, famine and unnatural mortalities (Bhatia 1963).[12]

Another critic who questioned Sen was Omkar Goswami of the Indian Statistical Institute. Using the same data-set that the Famine Inquiry Commission used, and adopted by Sen for 1941 and 1943, Goswami showed that the food availability in Bengal in 1943 was worse than in 1941. "It implies that", to quote Goswami, "one can no longer summarily reject FAD as an explanatory hypothesis." To make this conclusion, he bases his estimates on the following assumptions: First, in March 1943, Japanese army captured Rangoon and, thereby, imports of Burmese rice to Bengal were cut off. Second, there were entirely no carry-over stocks from 1942 harvests because of the tidal waves and crop diseases that resulted in a sharp decline in production. Goswami further criticised Sen for arguing that the worst Bengal famine of 1943 was essentially 'man-made'. Citing the 1942 tidal waves, crop diseases and harvest losses accompanying an unprecedented flare-up in market prices of rice in 1943, when there were large influxes of beggars in every upcountry town in Bengal and unusually excess mortalities, he claimed that the 1943 Bengal famine had 'all important ingredients of nature-made famine'.

What is significant to note here is that both Sen and Goswami have used the same data-set for their analysis. In the absence of certain crucial variables, mainly 'carry-over stocks', they had to base their estimates of food availability on a few assumptions. Using certain sets of assumptions, Sen found from his calculation that, in 1943, the food supply was only 5 per cent lower than the preceding five-year average. Compared to 1941, the food supply was 13 per cent higher. While in 1941 there was no famine in Bengal, in 1943, there were widespread famine and famine-related deaths. From these results, Sen argued that instead of FAD, the 1943 Bengal famine could be ascribed to other causes. Applying another set of assumptions, Goswami's calculation showed that the FAD in 1943 was sharper than in 1941. Any student of statistics will know that whenever assumptions are changed, statistical results will also change. To say that assumptions of Statistician-X are superior to the assumptions of Statistician-Y and therefore the findings of the former should be accepted and not those of the latter is to ignore this fundamental reality.

The most recent criticism of Sen came from Madhusree Mukherjee, a former editor of *Scientific American* and the author of the well known book on Bengal famine, 'Churchill's Secret Wars'. Quoting from the Nanavati Papers (the unpublished transcript of the secret hearings conducted by the Famine Commission set up in the backdrop of the 1943 Bengal Famine) she argued that Sen could reject the FAD view of famine as he used the manipulated rice production figures for Bengal She argued that, the estimates of *aman* crop production, as per the data given by the Food Department of Bengal, had recorded a steep fall in 1943. On the basis of this, when the presidency of Bengal sent a request for immediate supply of wheat and stoppage of procurement of rice to overcome the shortage situation that led to the ongoing calamitous famine, the Government of India at Delhi, presumably at the instance of the Secretary of State, replied that "we do not believe it and you have to get it out of your head that Bengal is deficit. You have got to preach that there is sufficiency in Bengal." When the administration of the presidency of Bengal stuck to the advice received from the above, the Famine Commission had to go by a via media, which was not completely against the official view but, at the same time, not fully out of line with the reality. Thus, the Famine Commission estimated a rice output figure for Bengal which was slightly lower in 1943 than the preceding year. Using this figure, the Commission stated that the decline in production was not significantly lower for the government to initiate advance preparations to prevent famine. According to Mukherjee, it was this figure that Sen uncritically used to prove his point (Mukherjee, 2014).

In this context, two points are important to note here. First, we have already seen above that Sen has not blindly used any single figure to arrive at the food availability for Bengal in 1943 vis-à-vis 1941, as Mukherjee argued. Apart from scrutinising various sources of data, Sen in fact applied a 'correction factor', which was higher than that the Commission used to arrive at the availability of food in Bengal. Secondly, a point that all the critics of Sen, without exception, have conveniently ignored is that his rejection of the FAD approach to famine is not based on the case study of 1943 Bengal famine alone. There are three more case studies in *Poverty and Famines*, viz, the famines of Ethiopia, Sahel belt of Africa, and of Bangladesh. With reference to all these case studies, what Sen argued was that, even when the FAD view appears plausible in the case of some famines, it does not provide any guidance about their character, whereas the FEE approach gives a better insight. There can have differences of opinion about this view. But that does not justify exaggerating or distorting what Professor Sen said. While presenting his theory, he has in fact stated that the winter crop in Bengal was 'insufficient' and that it had led to 'speculative withdrawal and panic purchases'. Coupled with the sudden withdrawal of price control, there was an upsurge in the market prices of rice, without a matching movement in wages so that there was an entitlement failure to the mass of workers that led to their famine. As prices of other commodities and services used for accessing food failed to rise in line with that of rice, there were similar entitlement failures of other occupational groups also.

Taking all the factors into consideration, a very recent study attempts to place Sen's thesis on an entirely new perspective: "what mattered more were the movements in the food prices or changes of income level in real terms, which pushed down the exchange entitlement of the affected people and shrunk their entitlement set. Sen, in a sense, rescued famines from a climate-population framework and lent their much needed ingredients of political economy" (Das 2008). Yet another point that the critics failed to appreciate was that challenging the FAD view of famine is not just an arithmetic exercise. By doing so, Sen could correct the cultural bias of the western scholars and the British rulers in India who continued to insist that, in third world countries – especially in India – famines broke out repeatedly because of the 'animal instinct' of their people to procreate much beyond the food production capacity of these countries could justify, thereby creating a 'Malthusian imbalance'.

3.6 A Long-term View

The concept of FAD could still stand, without diluting the FEE theory, had Professor Sen considered the impact of long-term decline in food availability in his framework of analysis in a little more detail. He was perfectly aware of this. For instance, while responding to Bowbrick, he had stated that his concept of FAD 'refers to a decline of food supply *over time*' (emphasis in the original) and that Bowbrick has been persistently confusing 'availability decline *over time*' and 'supply inadequacy and shortage *at a point of time*' (emphasis added) as the same thing (see Sen 1986; 1987). Secondly, in the discussion on 'the time contrast' of famine, Professor Sen states: "it is important to make clear distinctions between three different issues: (1) *lowness of the typical level* of consumption; (2) *declining trend* of food consumption; and (3) *sudden collapse* of the level of food consumption. Famine is chiefly a problem of the third kind, and while it can – obviously – be helped by the first two features, it often does not work that way" (Sen, 1981: 41).

That might be the reason why in the four case studies incorporated in *Poverty and Famines* Professor Sen limited the period of analysis to two or three years, when there was a weather-induced change in food production, though not sufficient enough to cause a famine. In a significant contribution, quite independent of the then ongoing FAD vs FEE debates on famine, Professor Utsa Patnaik contended that such a very short period as Sen took for analysis is too insufficient to explain the gravity of famines. She argued that long term economic and social forces, unrelated to weather, could set the stage for the development of 'pre-famine conditions' in rural countryside, even though famine might not thereby become inevitable. Ignoring this in the discussions on famine would be a grave error (U. Patnaik 2000).

Her estimates, using the data compiled by Blyn (1966), showed that, between 1901 and 1941, the per-head foodgrains output registered a negative growth of 29 per cent in British India. During the same period, the decline in the foodgrains output growth was (-) 30 per cent in Madras and (-) 38 per cent in Greater Bengal, i.e. Bengal, (including today's Bangladesh) Bihar and Orissa. The annual rate of decline in per capita production was the highest, estimated at 1.40 per cent in Madras, while it was 1.18 per cent in Greater Bengal and 1.14 per cent in British India as a whole (Table-3.1). From the same data base, she showed elsewhere that, in

Table 3.1: Decline in per head foodgrains output by regions, British India, 1901 – 1941

Region	*Period of change*	*Total % Change*	*Annual rate of change*
British India	1901-1941	-29	-1.14
Greater Bengal	1901-1941	-38	-1.18
Madras	1916-1941	-30	-1.40
Bombay-Sind	1916-1941	-26	-1.21
United Provinces	1921-1941	-34	-1.36
Central Provinces	1921-1941	-19	-1.05
Greater Punjab	1921-1941	-18	-1.00

Source: G Blyn (1966), reproduced from U. Patnaik (2000).

Table 3.2: Crop Production Trend in British India

	Index of annual crop output			*Per capita output*	
	Food	*Com. Crop*	*Total*	*Food crops*	*All crops*
1893/94 to 1895-96	100	100	100	100	100
1896/97 to 1905/06	96	105	98	95	97
1906/07 to 1915/16	99	126	104	91	97
1916/17 to 1925/26	98	142	106	90	98
1926/27 to 1935/36	94	171	108	78	90
1936/37 to 1945/46	93	185	110	68	80

Source: Thorner (1955), "Long-term trends in output in India", in Kuznets et all (Eds): Economic Growth: Brazil, India and Japan (Duke University).

absolute terms also, the five yearly averages of per-head food availability had steeply declined from 199 kg in 1897-1902 to 148.5 kg in 1939-44 and further down in 1945-46 to 136.8 kg (see U. Patnaik, 2001; 2007a; 2007b). She attributed this steep secular decline in foodgrains production *inter alia* to the following two major factors, which are inter-connected and not independent of each other: (i) the propagation of the 'free trade' ideology in the colonised third world countries by the British rulers that it was essentially beneficial for everyone who participated in it; and (ii) the commercialisation of agriculture.

The influential 'free trade' ideology prevailing in Britain since the latter half of the eighteenth century, as originally propounded by Adam Smith and later refined by David Ricardo, fooled the people in the third world colonies to believe that there was a 'comparative advantage' in the free trade policy followed by Britain. In this environment, if India could specialise in the production of agro-based industrial raw-materials and exchange with low-priced but qualitatively superior manufactured goods, it would be mutually beneficial for both the countries. But what actually happened, U. Patnaik argued, was not the assured 'mutual benefit' but a process of deindustrialisation, i.e., destruction of traditional manufactures and occupational structure in the colony, thereby cornering the dependants on these industries for their livelihood to move to the primary and tertiary sectors. The 'free trade' ideology thus enabled Britain to export its unemployment to the colony (U. Patnaik, 2007).

The second consequence of free trade that she noted, namely, commercialisation of agriculture, was equally or more pernicious for the colonial economies in exacerbating the rigours of famines. During the colonial period, lured by the persuasive propagation that commercialisation of farming would bring them prosperity, the farmers in India shifted their cultivation from subsistence crops to exportable commercial crops like cotton, jute, sugarcane, indigo, tobacco, condiments and spices as well as wheat, which had a very high import-demand in England. The stimulus for the shifts from food crops to commercial crops came from two other developments: (a) outbreak of the American Civil War that blocked the internal movement of cotton to the U.S. ports for exports to England and the latter's readiness to fill this gap by imports of Indian cotton; and (b) opening up of Suez Canal that reduced the distance and, therefore, the freight charges for the exports of bulk-goods from India to Europe. A third factor that persuaded the cultivators to adopt commercialisation of agriculture arose from economic compulsions brought to bear on the farming community by the combined effect of high land-revenue demand and indebtedness. After meeting these payments, even partially, the cultivators found that there was nothing left for subsistence. Expecting that production of exportable crops would fetch better price, they converted their lands from food crops to commercial crops.

This is eminently reflected in the trends in production of food and commercial crops. While the former registered a steep fall, the latter exhibited a sharp uptrend. This will be evident from the long-term crop production trend estimated by Thorner (1955) for the period from 1893-94 to 1945-46 in British India. Taking the average output for the years between 1893-94 and 1895-96 as 100, Thorner showed that, the index of annual food output declined to an average of 93 for 1936-37 to 1945-46. The index of commercial crops output, on the other hand, increased from 100 to 185 during the same period (Table-3.2). The estimates of Utsa Patnaik from Blyn's data, referred above, were more revealing. She found that in the half a century preceding independence, exportable commercial crops had registered a growth rate of over ten times higher than that of the domestically consumed foodgrains.

Contrary to what the Indian data revealed, it was the conventional wisdom in economics that such shifts in cultivation from food crops to commercial crops and the resultant high growth of production in agriculture would invariably contribute to overall economic development and removal of poverty and famines. Simon Kuznets had for the first time cogently plotted this link as follows: When commercialisation takes place in a big way, as a sector, agriculture makes a significant contribution to economic growth by: "(1) purchasing some production items from other sectors at home or abroad; and (2) selling some of its product, not only to pay for the purchase listed above but also to purchase consumer goods from other sectors or from abroad, or to dispose of the product in any way other than consumption within the sector. In all these ways, agriculture makes it feasible for other sectors to emerge and grow and for international flows to develop; just as these other sectors and the international flows make it feasible for the agricultural sector to operate more efficiently as a producing unit and use its products more effectively as a consuming unit" (Kuznets, 1965).

Unlike the Kuznets thesis, the historical evidences available in British India prove that an imperialist government could divert 'the international flows' from trade to its own advantage. The export earnings of Indian cash crops, in fact, increased more than the farmers could get from the cultivation of food crops. However, these earnings, instead of flowing back to the colony, were retained in Great Britain towards what was called 'home charges', defeating both the attractive proposition behind commercialisation. Thus, (a) it failed to contribute for the expansion of income and purchasing power of cultivators; and (b) it could also not increase capital formation in agriculture or industry. Whatever little that some of the farmers of exportable cash crops might have got, if at all, came to a halt all of a sudden, keeping them and their livelihood in peril, on account of the following: As soon as the American Civil War ended, exports of the U.S. long-staple cotton to England resumed with the result that, though Indian raw cotton was cheaper than American cotton, it was discarded on account of being short-staple in quality. Further, with the progress of Industrial Revolution, textile manufacturers in Europe started using synthetic fibres in place of raw cotton. This led to the stoppage of whatever demand for Indian natural fibre had here and there in Europe. Several social scientists, who studied the colonial history of India, and particularly Bipan Chandra, had narrated how these developments resulted into poverty and frequent famines in different parts of British India (see Chandra, 2009).

With the stoppage of exports of raw cotton and other cash crops to Europe, and particularly to England, there was a sudden decline in the income and purchasing power of these cultivators. As the unexported quantities had to be dumped back into the domestic market, their prices plunged in the home market. The condition became still worse when, in the second half of the nineteenth century, Europe witnessed a general shift in the consumption of coffee to relatively low-priced tea. Consequent decline in demand for coffee severely affected its cultivation and affected the livelihood of the producers in areas like Wayanad in Malabar.

When Lord Ripon declared his decision to expand the railway network in India, (as we noted elsewhere) he had boasted that the basic purpose of the programme was famine-prevention by quickly arranging movement of food from surplus centres to famine-prone deficit areas. Citing this attractive proposition, the British authorities declared the construction of certain newly proposed railway tracts as 'famine lines' and met the costs from the famine-insurance funds. But once these lines became operational, instead of bringing food to deficit and starvation stricken areas, the railways encouraged transporting away whatever quantity was available in these areas. The speculators even used railway yards, in connivance with the railway employees, to hoard the foodgrains and push up prices. At the same time, British industrialists used these railway lines to penetrate their price-wise cheaper but technologically advanced goods into interior areas, ruining India's labour-intensive handicraft industries. The worst affected were the cotton weaving and spinning units, followed by silk and woollen textiles and, then, iron, pottery, glass, metal, shipping, gun, oil-pressing, paper, tanning and dyeing industries.

The EIC forced the Indian craftsmen to sell their goods below the current market price and work for them as labourers at lower than the prevailing wage. As the gradual decay of traditional industries was not accompanied by growth of modern industries, those who lost livelihood in traditional industries could not find any alternative employment in urban areas. The only choice for them was to over-crowd into the already stagnated and decelerating agriculture sector for employment and food. The resultant excess labour supplies further pushed down the farm wages. As the income elasticity of demand for food is relatively high, the additional demand for foodgrains from the urban population migrated to rural areas pushed up the prices much above the wages could afford to buy, creating what Utsa Patnaik called a 'pre-famine condition'. If this was compounded by an aberration in monsoon leading to crop-failure, a full blown famine became inevitable. That was why several regions in India, including Malabar, simultaneously, witnessed more intensive and frequent famines especially after EIC passed on the reins of administration to the British Crown.

From this, it is obvious that famine culminated from a combination of adversities imposed on the underprivileged sections by the carefully designed imperialist policies. This chapter showed how the policies of the British administration in India led to the long-term decline in food production and the perpetual 'pre-famine condition' so that a sudden harvest failure could worsen the food availability, push up prices to levels unaffordable to the people at large and plunge them into disastrous famine. Ignoring these factors and analysing famine with reference to FAD in isolation was the product of an era characterised by lack of, or undeveloped, transport and communication system. In this condition, food shortages arising from crop failures in a region could not be made up by arranging from other surplus areas. Wherever transport and communication facilities were developed, FAD should not have dragged an entire community into famine, in case the state was vigilant. Our own survey of the five episodes of famine in British Malabar in the preceding chapter showed that, while famines of 1876-78, 1918 and 1924 had resulted predominantly from FAD, those of 1933 and 1943 occurred when food harvests in the district were normal to above normal. In all the five cases however the purchasing power of the masses to access food was handicapped by other more important factors even where FAD was discernible. This is also what Sen's case-studies of the four twentieth century famines of Bengal, Ethiopia, Sahel belt of Africa, and Bangladesh revealed.

Still, even some of the well-meaning researchers continued to use FAD as an analytical tool for explaining famine. It was when the induction of a distorted 'Malthusian-imbalance' theory as an additional explanation of famines in third world colonies that the real intention behind the FAD approach became clearer. We noted in this chapter how Florence Nightingale, the celebrated British nurse and author, forcefully and untiringly argued with empirically unchallengeable evidences that the famines haunting the British Indian colony was the result of wrong imperialist policies. In recent times, noted economic historians like B.M. Bhatia and Hari Shankar Srivastava who studied the Indian famines of the imperialist period had also pointed out that, more than FAD, there were other causes behind the famines in different parts of the country. The latter, in particular, had listed a number of factors and argued that the combined effect of all these were instrumental in escalating famines and excess mortalities in India. Srivastava classified these causes into three major categories, namely, (i) administrative and political, (ii) economic, and (iii) socio-cultural. The administrative and political causes included the existence of an ostensible gulf between the rulers and the ruled; the expansionary wars fought by the British against local rulers; the disruption of free movements of food from surplus to deficit areas; and the indifferent and dishonest attitudes of the bureaucracy in implementing famine relief measures. The economic causes of famine, according to Srivastava, were extortionate and excessive collection of various taxes; destruction of domestic industries to create markets for British goods; and compulsory procurement of food, even from deficit areas, for exports or for feeding the rising number of defence personnel.

An immediate question that arises here is why, after Sen refuted the FAD view of famines, a barrage of writings started coming up, while the other authors who held similar views long before the publication of *Poverty and Famines* were casually quoted, if at all, but not given credit that Sen received? To us, there are at least three reasons for this: First, while refuting the FAD approach, Sen elevated the study of famine from climate-induced natural causes to the level of political economy in the tradition of classical economics. Second, in conjunction with the rejection of FAD thesis, Sen also rejected the 'Malthusian imbalance' argument of famine. By doing so, he rescued the third world colonies from the cultural and racial biases inherent in this argument. Third, while rejecting the FAD view, Sen also developed an alternate FEE theory, which is more powerful and applicable to any famine anywhere in the world.

Notes

1. The information on cropping pattern and seasonality in general has been taken from *Hand Book of Agriculture* brought out by the Indian Council of Agricultural Research, New Delhi (1961); the book *Rice in Kerala* by Sahadevan, P.C, 1966.
2. For a better and more cogent categorisation of the peasantry into different economic classes, see U. Patnaik (1975; 1976); op.cit.
3. Quoted from the report of the Famine Inquiry Commission, 1945 in Sen (1981), Chapter 6, "The Great Bengal Famine"; pp. 52 – 85. See also Bhatia (1967), in an extended chapter added to his original work published in 1963.
4. See Sen (1981), op.cit.
5. The Settlement Report of Malabar for Fasli 1286 (1876-77) indicates two points in this regard: First, salt had to be brought from outside to meet the requirement in Malabar. But in1876-77, one of the worst famine years of Malabar, there was a sharp decline in the supply of salt. Secondly, the price fixed for salt by the government was Rs 38-6-4 per garce. Adding the salt tax, the price shot up to Rs 255-14-4 per garce.
6. Although pie-chart as a visual presentation of complicated numerical data was first introduced in statistics by William Playfair in 1801, it was Nightingale who used this technique quite effectively in her writings on public health. In recognition of her contributions, in 1859, she was selected to the Royal Statistical Society of England and later as an Honorary Member of the American Statistical Association.
7. For this, in addition to what is being presented in this section, see Dreze and Sen (1989), op.cit.
8. See, Bowbrick (1986 & 1987) and his website *http://www.bowbrick.org.uk*
9. See the letter dated 30 July 1986 from Colin R. Blackman, Editor of *Food Policy* to Peter Bowbrick, and published in the same issue of the journal.
10. It is not Bowbrick alone who argued that Sen's thesis considers only demand side of the problem. See Devereux (2011), and for a counter see Osmani (1989).
11. There is a confusion in certain quarters that what Amartya Sen has done is to discredit the supply-side views of famines. For how supply side is incorporated by Sen, see Osmani (1995).
12. See, preface to Bhatia (1963), *op.cit.*

Chapter 4

Famines and British Land Revenue Policy

4.1 The Genesis

A number of economic historians had asserted that repeated famines in Indian sub-continent during the British period were caused not often by bad harvests but by the imposition of heavy land revenues and the oppressive manner in which these were collected. Even when crops were normal, the forceful collection of excessive land revenue left nothing for subsistence with a sizeable section of farmers for whom the only way out was to undergo starvation and, in extreme cases, slip into famine, famine-related epidemics and unnatural deaths.[1] The British political sway over India began when the EIC's forces under the leadership of Colonel Clive[2] deposed Siraj-ud-Daulah, the Nawab of Bengal in 1757 over the Battle of Plassey and installed Mir Jafar, a leading man of the Nawab's court. It secured the right to land revenue collection, or *diwani* in Bihar, Bengal and Orissa from Shah Alam II, the titular head of the Mughal kingdom, after the 1764 Battle of Buxar (in Bihar). Thereafter, the British mastery over eastern India became complete and paved the way for gradual extension of its administrative power to the whole of India (Chandra, 2009). While introducing the land revenue policy in different parts of its dominion in India from time to time, the EIC had repeatedly stated that it was only systematising what, before their advent, the local rulers followed. In this chapter we will see that, contrary to this assertion, in practice, the British policy was instrumental in destroying the socio-economic fabrics of the rural countryside and stagnating, if not destroying, India's agrarian system so that famine became a recurring feature.

When it received the *diwani*, the EIC was confronting a major problem of how to raise the revenue for meeting its own administrative expenses in the presidency of Bengal and, at the same time, fulfil other obligations entrusted upon it by the Court of Directors of the EIC, viz. financing the unending wars with the native rulers as also of bridging the revenue deficits in the presidencies of Madras and Bombay. Agriculture being the main economic activity in India, land was the principal source of revenue. The EIC's attention therefore focussed more on raising funds from land tax than through trade, which was the original objective of a group of London merchants who formed themselves into a joint stock company and obtained in 1600 a royal charter from Queen Elizabeth-I.

The land revenue collection, being a new function, the EIC had to first of all solve *inter alia* three issues: First, *on whom* to impose the land revenue, i.e. should it be on each cultivator directly, or on a group of cultivators, or on an intermediary between the cultivators and the government? Secondly, *how to collect* the land revenue, i.e. through intermediaries, or through its own officials? Thirdly, *how to create a common land-law* that could clearly establish uniform rights on land between the state, revenue collectors and cultivators? While determining these aspects, the EIC wanted to see that right conditions had been created to: (i) ensure security of revenue-flow without disruption; (ii) stimulate agriculture and make landed property a commodity with an exchange value; and (iii) provide a surplus in revenue collection for investment in England, after meeting all the internal needs noted earlier (Kumar, 1983; Chaudhuri, 1983). In this perspective, the first attempt of the EIC was to dovetail the existing Mughal system of revenue collection that existed in eastern India before the *diwani* was handed over to it.

The Mughal System

By the time the EIC became a ruling power, there were several types of land revenue administration systems in different parts of India. In the vast areas under the Mughal rulers, a *zamindari* system had prevailed, extending from northern India to some of the districts in Madras. The landlord was answerable for the payment of revenue to the state in the North-Western Province but in Bombay it was any of the local land officers, known as Deshpande, Deshmukh, Desai, or Patel, who were managing the system in terms of the rights conferred on them by the authorities and passed on from generation to generation (Baden-Powel, 1894). The institutional arrangement for land revenue administration that the EIC inherited in the presidency of Bengal was devised and operationalised as early as the sixteenth century by Akbar, who was particular in fixing the land revenue only after conducting a thorough survey of all villages under his suzerainty. From those surveys, an average of the gross produce for nineteen years (presumably to even out good and bad crop-cycles) was estimated to use as the basis of determining the rate of land revenue, which was generally one-third of the average produce. If the crops were not divisible, their estimated average market price formed the basis of calculation. The emperor then left it optional for the assessees to pay the revenue either in cash or in kind as they wished. The revenue paying estates were known as *jagirs* and those authorised to collect the land revenue for the emperor as *jagirdars*, who came from the locally powerful *rajas* and the large landlord classes. Once they were chosen for the job, they became automatically incorporated in the Mughal bureaucracy and continued in that capacity so far as they regularly paid the *peshkash*, or a fixed land rent, to the emperor. In the land tenure literature these *jagirdars* were known as 'intermediary zamindars'.

Below the intermediary zamindars, there was a stratum of 'primary zamindars' or the *malguzari* as they were known in local language (Hasan, 1969). These zamindars collected the land revenue from cultivators and passed on to the higher level, i.e. to intermediary zamindars for onward transmission to the government. In return, primary zamindars received a *mankar*, or revenue-free land, from the emperor. They also received ten per cent of the total collection as service charge. The land revenue administration that Akbar and his successors adopted was essentially a three-tier system: At the lowest tier, there were the actual cultivators who paid a pre-determined portion of their produce as land revenue. At the middle tier, the intermediaries, known by different names in different parts of the Mughal kingdom, (but were commonly called '*zamindar*' by the rulers) got the right to collect the land revenue from cultivators. At the topmost tier was the state, which wielded the power to decide the tax collection right and award it to the middle tier (Baden-Powell, 1894; Roy, 2006).

Over time, this system however could not work as successfully as it was originally designed. During the reign of the emperor Bahadur Shah, this practice became almost entirely faltered. The zamindars, both primary and intermediary, turned against the emperor, quite often with the support of cultivators because of the increasing oppression they faced at his hands. The emperor retaliated against the revolt with the introduction of a new system of *ijaradari*, or revenue farming, under which wealthy bankers and merchant magnates were granted the right to collect land revenue from cultivators in each designated place. The revenue farmers, in turn, assumed police-power and coerced the cultivators to part with more than what the emperor prescribed. The excess collection, along with the commission received, were used by the revenue farmers to enrich themselves while the peasants became increasingly impoverished (Bandyopadhyay, 2004; Stein, 2001).

Pre-1793 EIC System

When the EIC received the *diwani*, its first effort was to fix the legal owners of the land. In 1769, the EIC divided the *parganas* into 'lots' and auctioned each of them for a given amount of revenue to be paid to it. The rent was negotiated, not fixed as was done during the regime of Akbar. According to the method adopted by the EIC, anybody who received a part of the *pargana* in the auction for payment of a fixed rent was treated as the owner of that land. The auction sale was for such a huge amount of revenue, which was beyond the reach of the ordinary peasants who cultivated the land for ages. This resulted in the dispossession of the land by the actual tiller of the soil. Those who became the owners were old money-lenders or traders. These 'owners', called zamindars, became a new aristocracy with the right to pass on the revenue burden on the poor ryots. The land revenue imposed on the ryots was so heavy that they abandoned cultivation and joined the 'reserve army' of agricultural labourers. Thinking that the growing misery of the rural population was due to frequent auction and revision of the land revenue, the EIC decided to lengthen the period of lease under the auction system. But that did not bring about the desired result (Bandyopadhyay, 1993).

The EIC did not have administrators with the knowledge of local customs, practices and conditions of cultivation to make assessment of revenue demands. Nonetheless, to see that the assessees were not put to untold miseries owing to unethical practices followed by the new zamindars, it entrusted the British officials with the duty to collect the land revenue. These officials were widely known to be equally, if not more, corrupt. As expected, they extracted as much as they could from the cultivators and pocketed without remitting in the government treasury. Compounded by this, in 1770, a devastating famine broke out in Bengal and Bihar, taking away the lives of more than one-third of the population and reducing the land under cultivation to almost one-third of the normal (Chaudhuri, 1983). Knowing well that the impact of the famine had become unusually severe due to the unreasonably high land revenue extraction, the then Governor-General, Warren Hastings, introduced a five-yearly assessment of land revenue and its collection was entrusted with 'tax farmers', who received a free hand to determine how much to collect from the tenants. This arrangement was made "without any demarcation of boundaries, without any survey of land, without any attempt to value the land in detail or to record rights" (Baden-Powel, 1894). Though Hastings had appointed British officials as supervisors to oversee the revenue collection by the 'tax farmers', the new system, contrary to expectations, also flopped on account of *inter alia* the following: In between the five-yearly assessments, the tax-farmers absconded with whatever they could extract from the tenants. This could have been prevented by the supervisors appointed by the government. But the official supervisors, in stead of overseeing the activities of the 'tax farmers', engaged in cornering the foodgrains available in the market and indulging in speculation for profiteering (Bhalla, 2007).

In order to meet this situation, the British Parliament passed a Regulating Act for India in 1773 and directed Warren Hastings to implement its provisions. Using this opportunity, Hastings first withdrew all feudal powers exercised by zamindars, including their judicial and police powers. At the same time, he ordered to imprison those zamindars who failed to make timely remittance of the land revenue they collected. The estates of the defaulting zamindars were confiscated and 'farmed out', as was done earlier by Bahadur Shah. Every year the defaulting zamindari estates were auctioned to new 'tax farmers' who, on winning the auction, revised the land rent upward. This made the revenue assessment virtually an annual affair, instead of the declared five-yearly revision. The condition of the cultivators, who were already impoverished during Bahadur Shah's time, became worse under Warren Hastings. Those who could not meet the EIC's rising demand for revenue had to abandon cultivation. Consequently, within a few years of Hastings' administrative stewardship, almost a third of the presidency of Bengal remained uncultivated (Baden-Powel, 1894; P. Sen, 1937; Stein, 2001).

When Cornwallis took over as Governor-General from Warren Hastings, there were several complaints against the latter in both England and India. One of the complaints was that the land revenue policy devised and implemented by Hastings had ruined the agriculture sector and impoverished the agriculture-dependent population, namely, owner-cultivators, tenant-farmers, artisans and agricultural labourer. Along with this, the EIC's trade suffered severe setbacks because of a steep decline in the production of silk and cotton, two of the major items of export from India (Bandyopadhyay, 2004). Another complaint was that the EIC under Warren Hastings had unjustly deprived the rights on land of the *rajas*, *zamindar*s, *polygar*s and, *talukdar*s. (This was however a criticism aired by some of the British historians based on their wrong notion that the Indian zamindars were similar to the European feudal landlords).

Having regard to these criticisms, one of the first decisions that Cornwallis took was to stop the practice of passing the proprietary rights on land from zamindars to merchant-money-lenders on the grounds of non-payment of land revenue in time. He introduced, on the advice of the Court of Directors of the EIC, a decennial system of revenue settlement in 1790 and, as it was found working satisfactorily, in 1793, declared a Permanent Settlement for the Bengal presidency, a system, according to some authors, was similar to the zamindari system of the Mughal rulers in its baseline revenue policy (Brown, 1994; Peers, 2006). Within another six decades, the EIC adopted two new land revenue systems in other parts of the country, viz. *mahalwari* and *ryotwari*. There were thus three land tenure systems for revenue collection in India during the British rule: (i) the landlord estate or the *zamindari* system, (ii) the village estate or *mahalwari* system, and (iii) the system of separate holdings or *ryotwari* (Baden-Powel, 1894).

4.2 Post-1793 Systems

It is significant to note here that, though apparently different, the objective of all the three systems for the EIC was in practice the same, viz. maximisation of revenue collection. Whenever any change is effected to the land tenure and land revenue systems that traditionally existed, it would immediately reflect in the social fabric of the rural countryside and, therefore, in the economic conditions of the agrarian society as a whole. Furthermore, it had an over-riding influence in precipitating famines in the rural countryside of India during the British era, as R. C. Dutt had repeatedly emphasised in his *Open Letters to Lord Curzon* as well as the other writings on Indian economy.

The Zamindari

The Permanent Settlement, or the zamindari system of land revenue, which was initially introduced in Bengal, was extended to most of northern India (except Avadh and Agra), Bihar, most of Orissa, Rajasthan (except Jaipur and Jodhpur), and parts of Madras presidency, aggregating to about 57 per cent of the total area under cultivation in British India (Bhattacharya, 1983; Bhalla, 2007). The difference between the zamindari system during the Mughal period and in British India was that while the Mughals collected the land revenue *through* zamindars, the British rulers collected it *from* zamindars. Thus the zamindars, who were just collectors of revenue for the state during the Mughal period, became proprietors of land under the British rule. They also got the right to determine the terms and conditions for authorising a plot of land to any cultivator according to whims. During the Mughal rule the actual cultivators were the owners of the land they cultivated. But during the British rule, they were reduced to the status of tenants working at the mercy of zamindars for a share of the output that the former produced on the land. It is also argued in some quarters that the Mughals collected only 'economic rent' i.e. the gross output less cost of cultivation plus labour charges. Though the British rulers stated that their imposts were on the net output, in fact, they had used coercive methods to collect the revenue. Moreover, while the EIC insisted that the land revenue should be paid in cash, the zamindars, who collected rent from the cultivators on behalf of the EIC, insisted that the payment should be made in kind. This enabled the zamindars to corner from the tenants a larger cash-equivalent output immediately after the harvests when the farm-gate prices were the lowest and to sell during the off-season when the prices peaked. The zamindars, thus, got a larger profit than that the EIC allowed them as the revenue collection charge (see Bandyopadhyay, 1993).

While commenting on the Permanent Settlement System in one of his well-known letters to Lord Curzon, Dutt (1900) had lauded its far-reaching beneficial effects not only to agricultural sector but also to the entire economy on four counts: (1) By placing a limit on the demand for land revenue payable to the government, Cornwallis could effectively prevent zamindars from making excessive collection from the cultivators. This made "cultivators of Bengal more prosperous, more resourceful, and better able to help themselves in years of bad harvest than the cultivators in any other part of India." (2) "The limitation of state-demand has fostered agricultural enterprise, extended cultivation, and led to the accumulation of some capital in the hands of private proprietors." The capital so accumulated was used by them in "fostering trade and industries, in supporting schools, dispensaries, and charitable institutions", in constructing "irrigation tanks and wells" and above all in "supporting poorer classes in seasons of distress and famine." (3) The capital generated under the Permanent Settlement was not concentrated in the hands of a few zamindars. Instead, it was distributed among those who could take up infrastructural and industrial development. (4) By promulgating Permanent Settlement, Cornwallis could enlist loyalty of the people of Bengal, especially of the zamindars, to the British rule in times of uprisings against its continuance in India.[3]

Dutt had claimed that the Permanent Settlement was the best piece of law that protected the cultivating class more than any other law enacted by the British in India. As we shall see later, this view was not without merit, if we compare it with the practice followed under the other systems, particularly the *ryotwari* system in southern India. However, to believe that zamindari system of land revenue was without any blemish in both the concept and practice might not be entirely valid. The expectation of the EIC, when it transferred the proprietary right on land from the actual cultivators to zamindars, was that the latter would become an instrument of revenue-generation for the government; protect the rural lives of the peasantry; preserve the local customs; and put an end to the corrupt practices that the EIC's own officials indulged in while collecting the land revenue from cultivators. In practice, none of these fructified fully; and neither the EIC nor the British Crown that took over the reigns from the EIC made any attempt to correct the situation. As Habib (2000) argued, Permanent Settlement was promulgated at a critical time when the unrelenting pressure on the zamindars to collect maximum revenue from '*diwani* lands' created a crisis in Bengal. Even then the British rulers went on claiming that there was scope for increasing land revenue further in India.

At the time of promulgating the Permanent Settlement, the British administration had anticipated that the newly created class of landlords would initiate modern farming practices and regenerate the already sagging agriculture sector. Instead, the zamindars moved out of the villages for living a luxurious life far away in towns. For the collection of land revenue, these zamindars appointed in the rural areas a hierarchy of intermediaries who, in turn, went on extracting excessive payments from the tenants. To clarify, even though the Permanent Settlement System was considered as a policy of "assessment for ever", the rate fixed in 1793 was around 20 per cent higher than what was fixed in 1757, the year in which Siraj-ud-Daulah surrendered Bengal to the EIC. In fact, by 1793, when Permanent Settlement was promulgated, the revenue actually paid by the cultivators recorded double the level prevailed in 1757 and, by 1872, the revenue demand reached another seven-fold increase. When the EIC realised that they had already reached the limit to raise the land rent, they used other methods to raise the collection. One such method was to use arbitrary short standards of measurement, which automatically inflated the recorded area under cultivation and therefore the assessment of rent. The second method was to impose various kinds of *awabs*, or cesses, for which there was no official sanction. Sheer physical coercion was yet another method. The combined effect of these unfair practices increasingly enfeebled the tenant farmers, both physically and economically so that when a famine struck they were the earliest to be under its fatal spell (Sarkar, 1983).

While introducing the Permanent Settlement, the British administration had given an assurance to the tenants that their interest would be protected by the enactment of appropriate laws. This assurance took more than 90 years to fulfil with the passage of the Bengal Tenancy Act of 1885, which declared that adequate protection would be ensured to the cultivators. The Act also provided for conducting regular inquiries to be sure that the rents realised by the Bengal zamindars were fair and moderate. Nonetheless, since the rent was collected in cash, the zamindars raised the rent on the pretext that there was an increase in the market prices of the produce. This became more rampant during famine years when market prices shot up. The Bengal Tenancy Act had required the revenue courts to accept the price data compiled by the district authorities as valid evidence to support zamindars in raising the land revenue. This provision thus nullified the protection clause available in the Act (Sarkar, 1983). In other words, while the new system was understandably beneficial to the zamindars and agriculture, it was patently unfair to the tenant farmers

Between 1793 and 1885, what the British rulers had actually done was to promulgate certain regulations that facilitated forced-collection of rent from tenant farmers. One such regulation was titled the *Haptam* or Regulation VII, which was declared in 1799 by Governor-General Richard Wellesley (1798–1805). The *Haptam* gave the zamindars absolute powers to forfeit the crops, cattle and other belongings of the defaulting tenants. It also gave them the authority to imprison, without reference to the court of law, the tenants who failed to pay the rent in time as demanded by the zamindars. Though a subsequent regulation, known as *Pancham* or Regulation-V of 1812, took away the power of the zamindars to arrest defaulting tenants, simultaneously, it allowed them to expel the tenants from the leased land and create fresh tenancies. The provisions of Regulation-V led to the multiplication of tenures and sub-tenures on the one hand and dispossession of the livelihood sources of the tenant farmers, on the other. Whenever a new tenure was created by expelling the existing tenant, a heavy fee was to be paid by the new tenant to the superior landlord of the village. This was an additional burden on the tenant farmer. In short, despite the zamindari or the Permanent Settlement system provided for the rent once fixed to remain unchanged, in actual practice, it went on increasing year after year. In addition, there were other imposts over and above the rent that the tenant was called up on to pay. For meeting these payments, the cultivators had to depend on the trader-money-lenders, who unscrupulously imposed exorbitant interest rates on loans and further impoverished the farm families.

Thus, the rural impoverishment of Bengal under the British rule, as Chaudhuri (1983) noted, was caused by the adverse consequences of the implementation of the Permanent Settlement: (i) the high pitch land revenue demand, (ii) relative inflexibility in the imposition and collection of revenue, (iii) establishment of private property and free transferability of land, (iv) proliferation of a class of 'parasitic' landlords, (iv) increasing burden of rent leading to mounting indebtedness and, (v) large-scale land alienation of the peasant classes. All these led the rural villagers in Bengal to perpetual poverty. In the event of a crop failure in any season, even if not very major, it could immediately push these poor villagers into famine. However, it was claimed by Chaudhuri that over time this had slowly dissipated so that the zamindari system by itself did not drag the peasants of Bengal to famines as other systems, mainly the *ryotwari* land revenue had done. (See Chapter-7 for detail).

The Mahalwari

In the early nineteenth century, when the EIC annexed the territories under the rule of Mughals and Marathas, they found in some of those areas a peculiar system of ownership and management of land. According to this system, land holdings in a village or a group of villages, known as a *mahal* or estate, was owned and operated by the entire people within the area. The assessment of cultivated land and the settlement of revenue and other imposts were therefore fixed for the estate as a whole. The individual's share out of the total revenue payable to the government was determined in proportion to the land holding that he possessed. All these activities were managed by the head of the village, known as Patil. In order to help him carry out the work, he had an assistant, called Chaugulla and a clerk, known as Kulkarni. According to R.C. Dutt, Patils were the most important functionaries in the villages. They held their position as awarded by Mughal rulers. These individuals were customarily treated as zamindars but were called *lambardars* or village headman in local language (Dutt, 1904). This practice was later legalised by Lord Wellesley with the incorporation of a provision in the *Haptam* or Regulation VII, which was originally enacted for the collection of revenue in zamindari areas of eastern India.

The *Haptam* regulation, as extended to the *mahalwari* areas, provided for a detailed field-to-field survey for revenue settlement and to make the settlement with the village community or with a *lambardar*. Furthermore, if the estate was held by a single owner, the land revenue would be 80 per cent of the estimated rental value. In case of common tenancies in the village, the state demand was 95 per cent of the rental value. Two points are important to note here: (i) *mahalwari* system did not totally wipe out the zamindari system; and (ii) the heavy zamindari revenue-burden that came into existence in eastern India, therefore, crept legally into the *mahalwari* system (Bandyopadhyay, 2004).

It was the collective ownership and collective payment of land revenue that came to be known as *mahalwari* system. Within a period of twenty years between 1820 and 1840, this system was extended to Punjab, Haryana, parts of Madhya Pradesh and Orissa, and the princely states of Avadh and Agra in Uttar Pradesh. In terms of area under cultivation, *mahalwari* system however existed only in a relatively limited tract, accounting for about 5 per cent of the total British India (Bhalla, 2007; Chandra, 2009; Roy, 2006). In due course, the rate of land revenue under this system became too heavy for the cultivators to shoulder, so that many of them failed in their payment to the government and the system broke down within a few years. During William Bentinck's term as Governor-General (1828–1835), a thorough review of the working of the *mahalwari* system was carried out under the provisions of the *Haptam* or Regulation VII. On being revealed from the review that it was highly burdensome to the cultivators, in 1833, Bentinck issued a revised order according to which the land revenue was reduced from the existing 95 per cent to 66 per cent of the rental value. The period of settlement also was fixed at 30 years. When Dalhousie took over as Governor-General (1848-1856), he found that even this 66 per cent was too heavy. He reduced it to 50 per cent (by what was known as the Saharanpur Rule).

During the Mughal era, though the revenue settlement was made estate-by-estate, the land ownership was vested with each individual farmer within the estate. If a member of the village decided to discontinue cultivation, his land was transferred to the common pool and came under the collective ownership of all the villagers. Outsiders were not permitted to buy lands within the *mahalwari* village. Even the common land, including forest and grazing lands, was collectively owned by the village community. When the *mahalwari* areas were annexed by the EIC, this practice was discontinued so that the transfer of land to anybody within or outside the village became legally acceptable. This enabled the merchant-money-lenders, who were often from outside the village, to confiscate the lands mortgaged by the owners for borrowing money from them. With the reduction of the *mahalwari* land revenue to 50 per cent of the rental, the cultivators felt that they would be highly relieved from the land revenue payments and that, in future, their lands would not be alienated by money lenders. Nonetheless, the settlement officials in many *mahalwari* areas ignored the Saharanpur Rules and continued to collect at the higher rates fixed earlier (Chandra, 2009). The condition of the actual cultivators turned pathetic due to excess revenue demands, arrears of revenue, mounting debt burdens, and sale of properties of the peasants for which favourable decrees could be obtained very easily from civil courts. This system was therefore not different from that of the zamindari system in Bengal. Some authors have stated that the ire of the rural people that arose mainly from this oppressive system of land revenue was expressed in the revolt of 1857, so loudly and very violently (Metcalf, 1979).

The Ryotwari

In 1792, that is, a year before Permanent Settlement was declared for Bengal, Captain Alexander Read and one of his assistants, Thomas Munro (a lieutenant who later became the Governor of Madras) were asked by the Court of Directors of the EIC to prepare a suitable settlement for the Baramahal district (now Salem) in Madras presidency[4]. Accordingly, they worked out a plan, which involved, in the words of Baden-Powel, "the germs of the modern method of collecting revenue from each holding." This is what is called the "settlement without a middleman" or the *ryotwari* system. It presupposes "the state itself as the supreme landlord, and the individual peasants as landowners who obtained title by paying annual cash rent, or revenue assessment to the government" (Ludden, 1985). The ryotwari system was later extended from Salem to other districts annexed to the Madras presidency by the EIC in quick succession between 1792 and 1801 through "lapses, treaties or conquests" (Baden-Powel, 1894).

Read and Munro took almost seven years, living in the village, learning the local language and surveying all the lands minutely before arriving at a methodology to fix the rent. It is believed that the land rent that they arrived at for Salem district was lower than that Tipu Sultan fixed for Mysore. But greater exactness in accounting and less corruption meant that just as much as Tipu collected from the peasants accrued to the treasury of the EIC. At the same time there was a lot of relief to the cultivators who, until then, had to fork out relatively very high land rent without any assessment of what the land could pay. In that system, the revenue officials were given a 'target' to be attained in the revenue collection every year. In order to hit the target, they adopted ruthless coercion no matter the peasants were facing cholera, plague, drought or famine (Mason, 1985).

The Salem method of survey and settlement was found to be not only attractive to the government but also acceptable to peasants in comparison with the past practice. Therefore, the EIC decided to conduct, before the introduction of the *ryotwari* system, a detailed land survey in all villages in the presidency and give holding-wise 'survey numbers' in an attempt to easily identify the owner of each piece of land. For this purpose, the government appointed specially trained survey-staff, who prepared the village maps accompanied by a descriptive register of every holding. Once the survey number was given to a holding based on the details given in the descriptive register, it became a title-deed as well as the official confirmation of the ownership right of an individual to that holding. The dispute, if any, was settled by the Civil Court, independent of the government and the survey-staff, though the latter had to furnish the information recorded in the descriptive register to the court for scrutiny. The survey number and the ownership right, once confirmed, could not be altered except by formal proceedings arising from the death of the owner or any other reason that had necessitated internal sub-division and transfer (Baden-Powel, 1894).

The second stage in the process of revenue settlement under this system was to classify the cultivated lands in each village as 'dry' or rainfed and 'wet' or irrigated. These villages were again grouped into separate categories according to climate, situation, market facilities, proximity to the railway station or town, and according to the height of the village from the sea level as 'upland' and 'lowland'. The 'wet' villages were further categorised according to the source of water-use for cultivation from public or private irrigation. Once the grouping of villages was complete, the next stage was to work out the average gross-produce of each group of villages. The methods of calculation were mostly that followed since the time of Akbar in different parts of the country. The most popular method was the *plough rate*. There was always a certain number of ploughs required for tilling a given area of land. It was found easy to estimate a rough rate of produce per plough. The second method was the *soil rate*, that is, according to the generally perceived productivity of land in different areas. Then a certain quantity of output for each area was arrived at either arbitrarily or by bargain. The third method was called the *seed rate*, assuming that when 'so much' seed was sown 'so much' quantity of output would be produced (Logan, 1887).

After arriving at the gross output separately for dry and wet lands by applying the *plough rate*, *soil rate*, or *seed rate* in different areas, the value of the produce was calculated at the average market price for about 20 non-famine years. From this, the input costs and labour charges were deducted to work out the net-value of the produce. Fifty per cent of the net-value was fixed as the land rent payable to the government by the ryot. The principal foodgrain grown in the village, namely, rice, was taken as the basis of calculating gross and net values. In respect of holdings under cultivation of other food crops, such as small millets, ragi and horse-gram, the revenue demand was reckoned with reference to the approximate ratio of the price of the relevant crop to the estimated market price of paddy (Baden-Powel, 1894).

The assessment and collection of revenue under the *ryotwari* system was taken up in Madras presidency through a huge contingent of government appointed revenue officials. This entailed maintenance of a large number of civil servants under the district Collector, who was to supervise the land survey, issue title-deeds and make revenue demands to tens of thousands of cultivators. The additional administrative expenditure involved was extremely large as against the revenue collection charge under the Permanent Settlement system in Bengal (Stein, 2001). Therefore, there was a strong view among the British administrators, both in India and England, that instead of frittering away huge amounts as collection-expenses, it would be ideal to introduce the Bengal system in the other two presidencies. Another criticism against the proposal was that the systematic procedure that Munro devised for *ryotwari* settlement was only logically sound. In practice it would remain only in paper. At the implementation stage, the bureaucrats might make only guess-works, as otherwise such a comprehensive survey that Munro suggested would become time-consuming and tedious. A third criticism was that the revenue demand under the new system could be irrationally higher; its collection might require application of coercive tactics, which would lead to heart-burnings and widespread protests in the villages.

However, since Munro was insistent that his method was far superior and should be continued, nothing could be done for the time being. It was only after he left for London that this system could be replaced by the Permanent Settlement. And the revenue collection, instead of entrusting to the civil servants, was given to specially appointed tax farmers, in line with the Bengal model. Unfortunately, these tax collectors, unlike their counterparts in Bengal, followed arbitrary methods to determine the revenue. This soon led to massive protests in village after village. The Bengal model had therefore to be given up, except in areas where the native rulers were already implementing it in a systematic manner.

The discontinuation of the Bengal model of zamindari system, however, did not set the stage for automatic switching over to the *ryotwari* system. When the EIC took over various districts that constituted the Madras presidency, there were certain villages in Tanjore and Chingalpet where traces of co-sharing *mirasidar* families existed. In these villages, revenue collection through village headmen was considerably successful. The British rulers thought of trying this system, which was analogous to the *mahalwari* system, to replace the Permanent Settlement in the Madras presidency. Thus, followed the second experiment of extending the practice existed in the co-sharing villages of Tanjore and Chingalpet to the other villages in the presidency. Selected village-level headmen, called 'renters' were entrusted to collect the revenue and remit it to the government in time. What actually happened under the new system was that, using the supremacy that the government gave them, the 'renters' became virtual autocrats. Their irrational and coercive methods of assessment and collection of land rent disturbed the conventional farming practices as also the livelihood of the village people to the extent of creating a 'pre-famine' condition.

In this backdrop, the government had no other option but to do away with the *mahalwari* type experiment in Malabar and other parts of the presidency. The British Parliament's periodical review by a Select Committee of the House of Commons found that the revenue collection practices followed in India, and especially in the presidency of Madras, had become chaotic over time. For Madras, the Select Committee was uncompromisingly in favour of the methodology developed by Read and Munro. The British Parliament accepted the Committee's recommendation and decided to depute Munro to Madras as Governor for reintroducing his revenue collection system (Mason, 1985). As a prelude to this, the Court of Directors of the EIC ordered in a despatch that the *ryotwari* system, which was withdrawn from the southern presidency be brought back, except in areas where the *zamindari* system of land revenue was working well under the native rulers. One such area in the presidency where the zamindari system was successfully operating was Calicut in terms of a settlement entered into between the EIC and the Zamorin Raja, the local ruler. According to the agreement, 80 per cent of the total collection of the land revenue was to be submitted to the EIC and the remaining 20 per cent to be retained by the Zamorin as *malikhana* or perpetual pension for the service rendered to the British EIC against the onslaught of its European rivals in India. The agreement was initially for five years but continued after the expiry of the period of agreement (M.G.S., 2006). Except such areas as Zamorin's Calicut, the *ryotwari* system became prevalent in due course in major parts of today's Tamil Nadu, Andhra Pradesh, Karnataka, Kerala, Maharashtra, large areas of Madhya Pradesh and Assam, and the princely states of Jaipur and Jodhpur in Rajasthan. This system was the second major revenue collection practice under the EIC, covering nearly 38 per cent of the total area under cultivation in British India (see Bhalla, 2007).

4.3 Implementation

Thomas Munro was Governor of Madras presidency for five years during which period the *ryotwari* system worked very well to the satisfaction of the government as well as the peasants. The revenue collectors under this system, as Munro visualised were large number of locally recruited officials. Most of them were trained by him during his earlier stint in the presidency. These officials gave full backing to Munro for the re-introduction of *ryotwari* system so that it became the most successful revenue collection system in British India.

However, after Munro left Madras, the operation of the *ryotwari* system generated several harmful effects to the farm families more than the other two systems of revenue collection that the EIC adopted within its administrative limits. This was not unintended. A general manual of *ryotwari* assessment prepared and internally circulated for the use of the revenue officials had all the ingredients required to harm the cultivating households. The manual had prescribed that, for the purpose of doing away with the widely prevalent sub-division and fragmentation of *ryotwari* lands, the rate of assessment should be devised in such a way that it should, in effect, be inversely proportional to the size of holdings. That is, the smaller the holdings, higher the revenue demands so that, apart from controlling the splitting up of land, it would give the government 'a premium on small holdings'. Another suggestion in the manual related to the collection of revenue arrears. Taking into account the need for reducing the unnecessary delay in recouping the arrears of revenue collection, the manual suggested that the district Collector should permit the sale of the defaulter's land without waiting for the prior sanction of the Board of Revenue, or of the court of judicature. Lastly, in order to prevent any untoward things to happen, including an injunction from the court of law, all defaulters must be imprisoned, before being ousted from their land (Dykes, 1858).

Officially, this was just a draft guideline under circulation. Yet the district level authorities took it as a government directive for implementation, leading to a number of adverse consequences to the farm sector. The excessively high assessment and frequent revisions encouraged fraudulent practices and held back the farming system from productivity improvements. The situation became so bad that the cultivator had to quite often sell even his bullocks and other household-assets to meet the land revenue demands. As nothing was left with him after payment of the revenue, he had to depend on the merchant-money-lenders for the next season's cultivation as well as for subsistence requirements of his family. The practice followed by British rulers to confer the land right on anyone who was prepared to pay the revenue to the government in time led to large-scale land alienation and further deterioration of the economic conditions of the cultivators. These 'pauper ryots', who lost their land, had to lead a life of destitution, under-nourishment and starvation in several parts of the *ryotwari* areas. Though, in public, the government would not agree that it was the flawed land revenue system that led to persistent hunger and repeated famines in the late nineteenth century, in private, it seemed to have realised that there were serious deficiencies in the implementation of the *ryotwari* system. Thus, the EIC announced that it would conduct afresh a systematic land survey and correct all the distortions, as are being complained by the assessees, in case these were found true from the survey (Kumar, 1983).

As soon as the fresh survey report was received, the Madras presidency took up its major findings with the British government. After prolonged debates between Madras and London on these findings, finally in 1864, the government decided to revise the principles of fixing the land revenue. According to the revised system, the assessment of the previous year would be reviewed in the current year and, if felt necessary, fresh revisions would be carried out for remissions or additional imposts. A cursory survey of the Settlement Reports of the Madras Board of Revenue would show that, in addition to land revenue, each year's tax demand included: (i) additional assessment for the previous year; (ii) water tax; (iii) local fund cess; (iv) village-service cess; (v) salt tax; (vi) sea customs; (vii) land customs; and (viii) stamp and collection charges. These reports also reveal that remissions allowed in one year were withdrawn next year. In addition, penalties were imposed on farmers for 'offences' like: (a) cultivating the waste land or the home garden without prior permission, and (b) leaving fallow of the title-deed holding land, even if it was done under unavoidable circumstances like flood or drought.

Though the new survey was conducted to ascertain why the ryots had faced disenchantments with the system and to correct them to their satisfaction. But, in effect, it created more harm than good to the peasantry. Instead of correcting the defects, the survey was interested more in identifying new methods to bring in larger and larger areas under the revenue net. It also devised methods to enhance the gross revenue from season to season. In 1864, when the new rates were announced on the basis of the fresh survey, it was found to be 26 per cent higher than the existing rates. As Dutt (1900) pointed out in his letter to Lord Curzon (who was the Governor-General and Viceroy of India from 1899 to 1905), in 1857, the Madras Board of Revenue had recognised the right of the cultivator "to retain his land in perpetuity without any increase of assessment." But the announcement made in 1864 gave the administration absolute powers to revise the revenue upward by any means. The government declared that, by virtue of the findings of the new land survey, as approved by the Secretary of State in charge of India, it wielded the right to revise the assessment and enhance the revenue demand on any ground as and when it thought tenable. "Thus", Dutt wrote to Curzon, "so far as the Madras cultivators are concerned, there can be little doubt that the rights previously assured to them have in effect been withdrawn, and the pledges previously given to them have in effect been violated. And at the present time the Madras cultivator, instead of holding his land in perpetuity without any increase of assessment, is subject to enhancement at each recurring settlement, and has been reduced to a state of poverty and indebtedness which makes him an easy prey to famines in years of bad harvests."[5].

Malabar Model

When the EIC took control of Malabar from Tipu Sultan, it had a rather complicated land tenure and revenue collection system. The traditional practice in Malabar was for the native rulers to grant "hereditary right on land" to certain class of people. This right was called *janmam* right and the person who got it, the *janmi*. As the *janmam* right was hereditary, such land could be freely bought and sold by those who received it. The *janmi* appointed supervisors, called *kaanakkaar*, who leased lands to tenants for cultivation against the payment of a rent, called *paattam*. During the rule of Hyder Ali and Tipu Sultan, many of the *janmis* in Malabar had to flee from their villages to escape from the terror unleashed by the ruthless officials. Therefore, the EIC had to make the settlement in most cases with *kaanakkaar*, not with *janmis*. Though its declared decision was to continue with the Mysore system of land revenue assessment and to use the same administrative machinery for revenue collection, there was constant turmoil in the district because of the unruly manner in which it was implemented by the Bombay presidency to which, as stated earlier, Malabar was originally attached (Logan, 1887; Panikkar, 1978).

Initially, in Malabar, the Bombay presidency started with a system of annual revenue settlements. Then, it was changed to a five-yearly settlement. Whenever the *raja*s, on whom the revenue was imposed, failed to pay the revenue in time, their lands were confiscated by the presidency. The affected *raja*s rose in revolt against this draconian practice and it was then that Malabar was transferred in the year 1800 to the presidency of Madras (Bandyopadhyay, 1993). A year after affiliating with Madras, Major Macleod was appointed the Principal Collector of Malabar district. In 1803, Macleod decided to revise the land revenue and the rates at which the assessed revenue was to be distributed among the stake holders, viz. the government, *janmi*, *kaanakkaar* and the ryot. The declared basis of determining the produce to arriving at the revenue on land and its rates of distribution among the stake holders was the same as that Tipu followed, viz. to roughly estimate the quantity of seed sown in a given field and the traditionally known output-multiple, which ranged from six to ten times of the quantity of seeds sown in different parts of the district, depending on the quality and productivity of land. Using this rough method, Macleod worked out the holding-wise quantity of gross and net produce of the 'principal grain-field', i.e. the field in which paddy was cultivated. The output for every other food-crop was estimated assuming certain relative ratios of yield between paddy and the other crop in question. Estimates were made separately for wet-land and dry-land as their yields could not be same.

In respect of garden lands, the practice was to court the fruit-bearing trees, make a guess about the likely number of fruits on each type of trees, and arrive at an approximate value of gross produce to determine the shares of different stake holders. "A garden, therefore, came to be known as a garden of so many coconuts, areca, or jack trees, and of so many pepper-vines" (Logan, 1887). Before EIC took over, there was a fourth category of land in Malabar, called "miscellaneous land" for which revenue was assessed separately. The method that the Mysore rulers followed was to work out the gross produce, convert it into money-value and then determine the land revenue. The EIC also followed the same method and the estimated net-produce was assigned to different parties as follows: (i) for wet lands, one-third to the cultivator, two-fifths to the government, and four-fifths to the *janmi* or *kaanakkaar*; (ii) for garden lands, one-third to the government, one-third to either *janmi* or *kaanakkaar*, as the case may be and the remaining to the cultivator; and (iii) for miscellaneous lands, three-fifths to the cultivator, one-fifth to the government, and one-fifth to the *janmi* or *kaanakkaar* ((Logan, 1887).[6]

This was the Malabar version of the *ryotwari* system, which, unlike the zamindari or mahalwari systems, became a 'settlement without middleman'. The difference between the Malabar model of *ryotwari* system and that in other regions under the EIC rested in the method of sharing the estimated produce. While, in the former, the produce was shared among the government, the *janmi* (or the *kaanakkaar*) and the tenant, in the latter, the sharing was between the government and the ryot. Another significant aspect of the Malabar model was that it did not represent, as generally perceived, a continuation of the practice followed by Tipu Sultan. Despite the external similarities, in effect, the EIC's method was far from fair. As we quoted elsewhere from Logan, the officials fabricated the accounts, inflated the produce, assessed the value of the produce that did not exist, imposed the revenue demand on wrong people, and exacted it ruthlessly. As soon as the new *ryotwari* system was implemented, a rebellion broke out in the district. Unable to face the situation, Major Macleod submitted his resignation and handed over his charge to Justice Rickards of the principal court at Mahe. When Justice Rickards assumed charge, the first step that he took was to cancel his predecessor's revised assessment and go back to the practice that the district followed during its attachment with the Bombay presidency.

However, the next Principal Collector of Malabar decided not to summarily discard the Macleod-method. He directed the revenue officials to impose one-fourth of Macleod's increased assessment to the existing revenue demand in each field. He also ordered that they should charge an additional 15 per cent of the impost from each ryot towards the expenses involved in revenue collection. Frequent hikes and unethical practices in the assessment and collection that the EIC adopted in Malabar created widespread heart-burnings as had happened when the district was with the Bombay presidency. In 1881, therefore, the government appointed William Logan as a Special Commissioner to inquire into the working of the land tenure and tenant-rights in the district. Logan submitted his report in 1882, containing graphic accounts of a number of unfair practices going on in Malabar. We have already brought out some of these unfair practices in the foregoing. There are at least three more important points worth noting in Logan's report:

First, the EIC had declared that the land revenue was fixed on the net-produce of grain-fields and that the netting formula was exactly as Hyder

Ali and Tipu Sultan had adopted in Mysore. However, while netting, the EIC officials had left out certain items that the Mysore rulers included in the calculation of the net-value on which the revenue was fixed. The excluded items comprised bullock charges, threshing expenses, storage charges, and costs of transportation of inputs into and outputs out of the village. They also excluded the payments actually made by ryots in the process of cultivation to carpenters, blacksmiths and other rural artisans. According to Logan, when the Mysore rulers had estimated the net-produce for assessment, as much as 20 per cent of the gross output produced in each field had remained within the village. This 'farm retention' in kind was a major source of insurance against food deficiency and famine. The EIC forfeited this source of subsistence that the people could fall back on bad times.

Second, while determining the rate of distribution of the produce among the stake holders, the EIC treated the *janmi* and the *kanakkaar* as the same entity and only one share was set apart, thereby reducing the quantity that customarily the landlord and the land-supervisor received. In times of food crises the *janmi*s had enough stocks of grain with them to meet their own subsistence and to help the labourers attached with them for at least partly overcoming the scarcity situation. The reduced share of the produce that the EIC fixed for the *janmis* restricted their ability to extend a helping hand to the poor, especially during periods of destitution and famines.

Third, the purpose of switching over to the *ryotwari* system was to eliminate frauds and maximise revenue collection. But this system also was beset with problems. The officials of the EIC who were entrusted to collect the revenue were interested more in advancing their own social status by getting rich through any means. Within a short period they proved themselves to be shrewd manipulators who pocketed most of the revenue collected from the farmers (see also Stein, 1969). Thus, the Malabar model of *ryotwari* system led to rising payment defaults and pushed the ryots into penury. The EIC mercilessly evicted the defaulters from their land. There was a steady rise in evictions of the peasants from land in Malabar. Between the two quinquennia of 1862-66 and 1877-80, the increase was 144 per cent in the annualised eviction suits filed against the ryots, 341 per cent in the number of persons against whom higher rent was decreed by the court of law, and 342 per cent in the number of persons against whom actual eviction-decrees were obtained. These figures would also show that, compared to normal times, evictions were much more during years of famine.

While presenting these figures, Logan had stated that his estimates were only 'suggestive' and that there was possibility for the actual number of evictions to be larger than the figures he presented. Logan had also pointed out that the evictions were not preceded by taking a decree from the court of law or that these were due to defaults of revenue payments alone. The other reasons for which evictions were made, according to Logan, included: (a) ancestral lands; (b) demand by *janmi* for return of the land; (c) the trees on the land given to the tenants started fruit-bearing; (d) non-payment of renewal fees; (e) refusal of the tenant to cut the trees by the *janmi*; (f) for refusing to give up the *janmam* title to other lands; and (g) for submitting petitions of complaint to the authorities; and so on.[7]

The *ryotwari* land revenue was revised upward every year, using clever tactics that required no prior official announcement. Quite often, the land under cultivation was over-estimated by the revenue authorities, in spite of the annual administration report of the presidency stating that ryots could not take up cultivation in parts or the whole of their areas either because of the drought or delayed monsoons. The Famine Code of 1883 as adopted by the presidency of Madras had a provision to suspend the revenue collection and to remit the collected revenue in times of scarcity or famine. It further specified that "prompt inquiries as to the necessity for the grant of remissions should be instituted, and it should be remembered that reasonable remissions are from the point of view of relief."[9] In the detailed statements prepared every year by the Madras Board of Revenue would indicate that remissions had been granted for: (a) "withered crops", (b) the second crop cultivated in the past but not undertaken during the year of assessment, (c) reduction in the normal area under cultivation of the ryot that was transferred for other purposes, including land acquired by the government for public purposes, and (d) *inam* and religious lands. However, there is no proof from the available land revenue statistics for Malabar that, despite announcing these remissions, it had given genuine relief to the ryots from their burden of revenue payments to the government.

It is interesting to note that, simultaneously with the announcement of remissions, the revenue authorities made several additional "miscellaneous revenue demands", such as: (i) land cultivated for which *putta* was not officially granted; (ii) earnings made by ryots from production and transactions of honey, wax, brick-kilns etc; (iii) cultivation of jungle lands, dry lands and backyards of the residences without prior permission; (iv) quit-rent on bungalows and gardens; (v) fees for licences; and (vi) penalties on unstamped and insufficiently stamped papers; and so on.[9] The value of such items taken together in all cases was observed to be far above the value of remissions allowed. In addition to these imposts, arrears pending and penal interest imposed thereon were also added in the 'current' year's land revenue demand. These imposts, in several cases, were larger in famine-years than during normal times. Secondly, the net revenue demand, after allowing for remissions and adding the miscellaneous imposts remained higher than the initial imposts. Thirdly, when arrears payable by the ryot were also added, the total revenue demand became extremely burdensome so that he had no other way but to leave the land uncultivated. However, this did not give any respite to the ryot, because a penalty was

Table 4.1: Ryotwari Land Revenue Assessment in Malabar

(1874-75 to 1945-46)

Year	*Area assessed (acres)*	*Total revenue demand (in rupees)*		
		Initial Assessment	*– remission (+) miscel. imposts*	*+ arrears previous years*
1874-75	786912	1791464	1824767	4035615
1875-76	786989	1795222	1828167	3647136
1876-77	796947	1806501	1833221	3306029
1877-78	800864	1803835	1836469	3061614
1916-17	1288165	3303841	3584713	3873637
1917-18	1294850	3310117	3559061	3874557
1918-19	1303493	3316795	3565102	3893759
1919-20	1314491	3326573	3573424	3904612
1931-32	1633056	3794477	3827373	4214814
1932-33	1655243	3924814	3982167	4500917
1933-34	1684712	4352888	4485816	4884019
1934-35	1687666	4356288	4968178	5205688
1935-36	1689229	4357330	4998289	5414396
1940-41	1704337	4444143	4583243	5047397
1941-42	1709284	4453934	4510084	5146891
1942-43	1713424	4464173	4651511	5248346
1943-44	1716510	4474680	4667143	5349801
1944-45	1721015	4476883	5087815	5445708
1945-46	1723953	4479694	5508486	5541614

Source: Report on the Settlement of the Land Revenue of the Districts in the Madras Presidency; Superintendent of Publication, Madras (various years)

then imposed on uncultivated land at the rate of six annas per acre. Later, there were occasions when the net demand for the current year plus arrears of the previous year had registered a decline over the preceding year. This indicated not any leniency in assessment but a reduction in the arrears of the previous years because of the ruthless coercive tactics that the revenue authorities adopted in the methods of collection. The net result of the *ryotwari* land revenue system, as practised in Malabar after Thomas Munro left for England, was an ever increasing demand from the ryots, no matter the year of assessment in question faced a disastrous flood or cyclone and the cultivators had abandoned farming in those areas. As Table-4.1 shows, the area assessed for revenue demand does not decrease in any of the years, including the years of famine, though the general administration report of the presidency might have mentioned that 'in view of the adverse weather condition, timely sowing was disrupted'. There was a steady rise in revenue demand, including the years in which there were floods or droughts. This was more noticeable during the first half of the twentieth century. When remissions granted as per the Code rules were reduced, and the miscellaneous imposts and the arrears of the preceding years were added, the revenue demand for the 'current' year showed a substantial increase. As a result of this, the woes of the peasantry continued even after the famine was over.

4.4 Concluding Remarks

The three land tenure systems that the British administration identified in different regions of India and refined from time to time for their revenue collection programme, viz. the landlord estate based *zamindari*, the village estate based *mahalwari*, and the individual holdings based *ryotwari* systems, might appear clearly distinct from one another. Nevertheless, the objective of all the three systems being the same, viz. maximisation of revenue collection from the rural sector, it could be seen that the methods adopted to achieve this objective were also not different under the three systems. Compared to the pre-British era, the unethical practices followed by the British revenue officials led to widespread land alienation, indebtedness, penury and a state of pre-famine existence for the people in village after village. The plight of the peasantry became worse when the EIC (and subsequently the Crown rulers) legalised the ruthless practices that the officials followed for collecting the arrears of land revenue through the attachment of personal properties belonging to the ryots, such as household utensils, ornaments, cattle and cattle-sheds, in addition to the lands they cultivated. Similarly, the money-lenders could just file a suit in a court of law and take away the land and other personal properties of the ryot to recoup the unpaid credit and the exorbitant interest thereon. More unethical was the practice of fixing the sale value of the property under attachment at far below the existing market prices as also the value of pending arrears. At the same time, the revenue officials auctioned the attached properties at the extant open market price so that they could obtain at least the estimated value of arrears, if not more. Even while the government recouped more than the arrears outstanding, the ryots were perpetually in debt and bondage. Of late, under the zamindari system, despite the pre-famine existence caused by land revenue administration had by and large disappeared, the condition in the *ryotwari* areas, particularly in Malabar, continued to persistently deteriorate.

In *ryotwari* areas, there were other problems. For example, the Madras Legislative Council had passed a Bill (which was later extended to the Bombay presidency also) to levy water-rates on all lands within the wet-areas under cultivation, without allowing the farmers any option to accept or refuse water. The rate was as high as 15 per cent per unit in Madras presidency, while it was just 4 per cent in the highly irrigated areas of Punjab. The High Courts of Madras and Bombay rescinded the indiscriminate water-rates imposed by the government on all wet-lands, and decreed that water charges should be collected only from those farmers who applied for water from the public sector source of irrigation. The EIC immediately amended the Bill, to over-rule this order and to make water rates compulsory on all wet-lands, irrespective of whether or not the ryot had applied for and actually used water. It also debarred the jurisdiction of the civil courts and even High Courts in cases relating to water charges imposed by the district authorities (Dutt, 1900).

The distorted manner in which *ryotwari* system was implemented had led to the disintegration of socio-economic cohesion that existed for ages and enabled the rural population to collectively withstand odds like famines. Before the introduction of *ryotwari* system in Malabar, the rights of the landlords, called *janmam* rights, and the rights of the tenants were well defined, not by any written law but by unwritten customs that existed for centuries. This customarily determined landlord-tenant relationship was succinctly brought out for the first time by E.M.S. Namboodiripad in his dissenting note to the Report on Malabar Tenancy Reform. According to E.M.S., these customs were such that "the landlord in Malabar could not evict the tenant from the land he cultivated. He could also not arbitrarily increase the rent. However, the *janmi*s had evicted their tenants for non-payment of rent. They had also raised the rent but not above a certain customary rate. Rack-renting and arbitrary evictions were not in practice........The *janmi* was the agent of the Raja or Zamorin" and "he was the head of a social system based on feudal relationship which regulated not only the economic but also social, political and cultural life......The right to the property that the *janmi* or the *kaanakkaar* wielded had, along with it a corresponding obligation to society. He was the centre of a system around which the people of the locality gathered to regulate their social conduct.....The redivision of the country into revenue areas and paid-officers to look after their affairs placed the administration system on an entirely new footing and the *janmi* had no place in it" (E.M.S., 1937).

The 'obligation to society' that is mentioned here came to the fore in times of testing times in the villages, like a food scarcity and famine or even on ordinary times when some of the labourers dependent on the landlord were facing unusual economic stress. Thus, the *janmi* was simultaneously a guardian for the workers and peasants, who were looked after by him in times of distress and, though, at the same time, he was an exploiter of 'labour rent', just as the *corvee* system that existed in the pre-revolution Russia (see Lenin, 1899). With the introduction of the *ryotwari* system of revenue collection, the EIC not only debilitated the landlord from continuing with the role of a guardian to his attached labourers and peasants but also legalised the eviction of ryots from land and auctioning of the attached land. This was rare before the advent of the British rule.

As regards the eviction of ryots from land, the archival records indicate that, in Malabar, the revenue authorities had attached and auctioned land and other properties of the peasants to recoup the defaulted arrears of as low as *one rupee*. The method adopted was very simple. A gazette notification in identical language would be issued in respect of each holding for which arrears were pending, a sample of which is reproduced here: "It is hereby notified that the under-mentioned lands will be sold by public auction for arrears of land revenue under the provisions of the Madras Act-II of 1864, unless the defaulters or other persons acting on their behalf or claiming an interest in the land, tender the full amount of the arrears of revenue with interest and other charges before sunset on the day previous to that appointed for the sale."[10]

The woes of the farming community became worse year after year because, in addition to excessive imposts and evictions from land, the officials adopted corrupt practices in the assessment and collection of land revenue. This was brought out by Thomas Munro in one of his letters to the Governor-General. "We see every day Collectors who have lived above their salary amassing great fortunes in a very few years. The operation by which this is accomplished is very simple. When rents are paid in money, by giving Government a rent roll below the real one; and when in kind by diminishing the produce of the land or of the sales. It is vain to say that Collectors, being men of education and character, will not descend to such practices; the fact is against this conclusion."[11] Thus, while corruptions fattened the pockets of rent collectors, the losers were the government and, much more, the farmers and other agriculture dependent population whose conditions of life became bad in normal times and worse during famines.

The pre-famine existence of the rural people was further accentuated with the introduction of monetisation that accompanied the British administration's high-pitch revenue collection spree. Monetisation of rent payment was not entirely new to British India. Before the British administration introduced it in *ryotwari* areas, the zamindars in other parts of the colony used to demand land rent payable by the tenants in pre-fixed amounts of money in case the former anticipated a fall in farm prices. Along with the introduction of a common rupee-coin for the entire colony, replacing other coins locally used until then, the British administration issued a directive that, in future, all farmers should pay the land revenue in the new currency. This led to an overall deterioration of the already deteriorating livelihood of the people. The justification that the government offered for monetisation of transactions was that: (a) conversion of the age-old system, which was the product of the primitive era, into monetary transactions indicated the symbol of progress; and (b) it would increase the efficiency of farming. No doubt, the economic history of the world would tell that the invention of money marked the greatest advance in material civilisation. Nonetheless, in British India, instead of increasing the efficiency, it turned out to be the most painful and degrading experience for the farming community. A short digression from our main theme would clarify the point.

It is well-known that as a 'medium of exchange', money eliminates the disadvantages of the barter system; as a 'unit of account', it permits easier valuation and calculation; and as a 'store of value' it allows economic transactions, over time and across regions, without any ambiguity (Ferguson, 2008). The history of monetisation would show that this was not a smooth transition. For instance, when a metal currency was introduced at the beginning of the Greeco-Roman civilisation, there was a revolutionary change in the lives of the peasants who, until then, had been going through a hand-to-mouth existence. They used to carry their produce to the market and exchange for the goods they needed. Kind payment was also in use for all the services rendered in the pursuit of cultivation. Once the currency became the common mode of transaction, most of the service-providers to the peasants, like the rural artisans, refused to accept kind payment. In order to make the payments in money, the cultivators had to sell their produce in the market immediately after the harvest when the prices were the lowest. Moreover, they had to depend upon the middlemen to dispose off the produce, as they had no knowledge about the pricing mechanism taking place in the open market. These middlemen made a living out of the commission they received for their service. In this process, the Greeco-Roman farm families were alarmed to find that no margin was left as usual after converting the output into money for various payments. Their only source for survival was to borrow from the indigenous money lenders at exorbitantly higher rates of interest (Paul, 1918).

The condition of the British Indian peasant families was the same as that of the Greeco-Roman peasants after the introduction of the rupee coin and conversion of land revenue from kind payment to money payment. Several authors who dealt with this issue had argued that the actual intention behind the introduction of a common currency in British India was to ensure a fixed parity of rupee exchange rate with gold so that the prices realised for British exports to India did not fluctuate (Chaudhuri, 1983; Chandavarkar, 1983; Roy, 2006; Chandra, 2009). While the gold exchange rate remained stable, monetisation led to untold predicaments to the Indian economy as a whole. And the worst sufferers were the peasantry. For instance, when the new rupee coins were introduced throughout the Indian colony, the existing local coins were demonetised. This disturbed the exchange ratios in various transactions being carried out until then. Similarly, the insistence of the government that the land revenue should be paid in money forced the peasants to sell their entire harvested outputs in the market immediately after the harvest.

Along with this, all other payments, mainly wages to workers and artisans, had also to be changed to cash payments. As the ryots sold their produce immediately after harvests at relatively lower prices, wages paid to the labourers and rural artisans also decelerated over time. If a famine broke out, when market prices of food shot up, these classes of agriculture-dependent population found it difficult to buy enough food for their minimum subsistence. Had the kind payments continued as before, they could have, at least for a while, withstood the horrors of famine. The position of the ryots was still worse. Once the demands from the government and the money lenders were met, nothing might be left either for their subsistence or for taking up cultivation in the next season so that they had to again approach the money lenders. Thus, in stead of bringing prosperity, the monetisation of revenue payment pushed the ryots permanently under the grip of money lenders without freedom from impoverishment.

Before concluding, it would be educative to recall some of the 'moderate and practicable' suggestions that R.C. Dutt made in his *Open Letters to Lord Curzon* for ameliorating the living conditions in the rural countryside and, through that, putting a stop to recurring famines faced by the people in general and in the *ryotwari* regions in particular. These suggestions were such that they did not involve any basic change in the existing land systems that prevailed in different British Indian provinces. Dutt pointed out that, ever since Cornwallis made a Permanent Settlement of the land revenue with zamindars or landlords of Bengal, there was no famine in those tracts to cause serious loss of lives. This was because the rate of rent payable under the Permanent Settlement, once assessed, was 'fixed for ever'. As against this, in the *ryotwari* areas, where cultivators paid the land revenue directly to the government without a middleman in between, the assessments were revised at shorter intervals and, at each revision, the revenue payable went up inordinately above the produce that the land could afford. This was, according to Dutt, the primary reason for the *ryotwari* tracts to face repeated famines with shorter intervals and increased ferocities. However, while rejecting these suggestions, the British rulers justified the increased imposts on the grounds that: (a) the revenue from land in India had enough elasticity and that the Indian people possessed a lot of recuperative capacity; and (b) expenses on developmental activities and on wars waged within India were increasing public debts, which could be wiped out only through taxation (Dutt, 1900).

Dutt wrote to Curzon that famines might have been caused by "the failure of annual rains over which man has no control; but it is equally certain that their intensity and their disastrous effects can be to a great extent mitigated by moderating the land tax, by the construction of irrigation works, and by the reduction of the public debt"[12]. Some of the practicable solutions that Dutt suggested to achieve this objective included: (1) the rates of land revenue imposed in the *ryotwari* areas being so high to the extent of pushing the people into penury and recurring famines, should be brought down at least to the level prevailing in northern India; (2) the revenue settlement under *ryotwari* system be kept unchanged for a period of thirty years, as in the case of the Permanent Settlement; (3) imposition of any cess over and above the land revenue be discontinued, except for purposes directly beneficial to the land, and that such cesses should not exceed *one anna* per rupee; and (4) now that the railway development work was complete, the Famine Insurance Fund diverted for the purpose be spent for the construction of protective irrigation works "without the expectation of any direct return" and "that the cultivator be left the option of using the water when he requires it, and paying for it when he uses it."[13] None of these suggestions appealed the British administration nor did the latter make any attempt of its own to moderate the ever increasing revenue demand. Instead, as we showed from the ryotwari land revenue settlement reports, the government went on raising the land revenue year after year. Famines repeatedly taking place in Malabar when other regions in British India started feeling a respite from hunger and destitution cannot be disassociated from the unethical practices crept into the otherwise well meaning system of the *ryotwari* land revenue.

Notes

1. Dutt (1900; 1901) argued that the single most important cause of repeated famines that haunted British India was the flawed land revenue system. Prominent among others who held this view was Naoroji (1876).

2. Later in 1786, Clive returned to Bengal as Governor. During this period, he masterminded to depose the Nawab and to take full administrative authority, including the direct revenue collection right in Bengal (Chandra, 2009), op.cit.
3. See *Gazetteer of India*, Vol.II: History and Culture. New Delhi: Government of India, Publication Division, 1973.
4. See "Fourth Letter to Lord Curzon: Bengal", in Dutt (1900), op.cit.
5. In fact, Alexander Read had already started revenue collection directly from each cultivator in Baramahal (Salem) district on an experimental basis. Later, Thomas Munro argued that it would be far better to vest proprietary rights on land "in the hands of forty to fifty thousand small proprietors than four or five hundred great ones" and collect revenue from them directly.
6. See "Second Letter to Lord Curzon: Madras", dated 20 February 1900, Dutt (1900), op.cit.
7. There seems to be an arithmetic confusion in the apportionment of the produce among different stake holders. According to Dharma Kumar, after the introduction of *ryotwari* system in Malabar since 1805, the apportionment of the produce estimated on a wet land was: one-third of the gross produce to the cultivator; out of the remaining, 60 per cent to the government and 40 per cent to either the *kaanakkaar* or the *janmi*. There was no separate allocation for both the parties, due to which there was a decline in the farm retention ratio in the village (Kumar, 1983).
8. These details are compiled from the Settlement Reports of Madras Presidency for the late nineteenth and early twentieth centuries. A careful perusal of these reports would show that many such items were included under "miscellaneous charges" every year to increase the revenue demand.
9. The Famine Code 1883, as adopted with locally needed changed by the Madras presidency.
10. Malabar Gazette 1934-35, notification of October 1934 gives a large number of holdings advertised for auction in all the talukas of Malabar. In many cases the amount of arrears was too paltry that it did not call for confiscation of large areas of land and put on auction. For instance, in Ponnani taluk, the highest amount of arrears of all the declared auctions was 8 rupees and 4 annas and the land attached for that amount was 1.37 acres. In the same taluk, for an arrear of 4 annas, 0.06 acre of land was confiscated and auctioned off.
11. See Madras Gazette 1934-35, op.cit.
12. Munro's letter to the government dated 31 January 1795 (quoted in Dutt, 1904)' op.cit.
13. Dutt had argued that, in Great Britain all attempts were made since the Crimean War to reduce public debt to the extent possible. But in India the public debt rather than getting reduced was being pushed up to extract as much revenue as possible for the imperialist expansion (Dutt, 1900).

Chapter 5

Epidemics and Famine Mortalities

5.1 General Observations

Any discussion on famines will be incomplete without reference to epidemics and mortalities that accompany and create severe human miseries. We have already brought out in Chapter-2 the famine-related epidemics that devastated several parts of Malabar since the inception of the EIC as a trading organisation. The objective of this chapter is to consider some of the wider issues connected with this problem, which could not be highlighted there, as the context of discussion was limited. In addition to the factual materials culled out and presented earlier, conflicting views exist about the manner in which the British rulers dealt with epidemics-related human miseries in the colony. While examining some of these views, it is also pertinent to consider how certain major epidemics, which had once disappeared of their own, erupted unawares during the time of famine in regions like Malabar and caused excessively enormous mortalities. This is in contrast with the advanced areas in Great Britain and other West-European countries, which almost completely wiped out the scourge of all fatal and not-so-fatal epidemics by the beginning of nineteenth century, whereas in British India such contagious diseases began flaring up since then. It was a period when, on the one end, European medicine in the realm of scientific inquiry was increasingly becoming 'de-socialised' through patronised individual research and, on the other end, getting attracted to the field of what was called 'social medicine' addressed primarily to understand the social determinants of diseases and public health.

Some of the western scholars, who dealt with the plight of the people from frequent epidemics and mortalities in India under the British rule, placed its onus on Indian doors. According to them, the historians and other social scientists in India gave scant attention to this unparalleled human misery, probably assuming that disease was a problem to be addressed by medical science. Thus, in the beginning of the last millennium when one or two economic historians took interest in the study of famine, they disregarded its epidemic aspect.[1] This attitude was grossly in contrast with that of Europe and particularly North America, at least on two counts: First, the historians in those parts of the world were in the forefront in bringing into limelight even relatively milder attacks of contagious diseases in their countries during the late eighteenth and early nineteenth centuries leading to popular mobilisation so that their governments could not sit idle but initiate public health services on a priority basis. In the absence of such interest among the academic community and intellectuals in India, the imperialist administration disregarded the sufferings of the local population and went on with its policy of surplus extraction for empire building (Arnold 1986). Second, the fatal diseases had receded from large areas of the western world before recognising whether it was an epidemic or a pandemic, as the people could compel their local administrations to give utmost importance to environmental cleanliness. Thus, the European society could ward off malaria by keeping clean their drainages, adopting careful farming practices and maintaining abundance of cattle – all of which cumulatively reduced mosquito population and avoided the chances of human beings getting bitten (Rosenberg, 1966).

These scholars also blamed the indifference of Indian public in persuading the authorities for the inadequate provisions made by the British administration in healthcare services. They argued that the people in India were not interested in the promotion of public works and sanitation, as they were opposed to the unfamiliar western methods in this regard. Whatever public works and health services developed during the British period were fostered by the western officials working in India. Almost the whole range of municipal services was evolved in British India because of the pressure exerted by the imperial bureaucracy in the colony and not because of the desire expressed by the local people.[2]

To say that the British administration in India took least interest in the development of healthcare services because nobody campaigned for it was factually indefensible. We have seen earlier the extensive researches conducted by Florence Nightingale in collaboration with several investigators, most of them from India, on social, economic and political causes of famines and famine-related epidemics. Apart from writing extensively on these issues and getting published in England, America and India, she was also known to have campaigned for the reform of social medicines in the colony (Krause, 2005).[3] In a subsequent section, we will have more to say about Nightingale's contributions in this regard. What is significant to emphasise here is that it was not because of the lack of campaign but because of the preoccupation of the British administration with the programme of imperialist expansion that the healthcare and other social development issues in India took a back seat. Of course, the Indian scholars took interest in the study of famine *per se* only long after the country won independence from Britain. While investigating, however, they ignored that undernourishment is precipitated into famine by debilitating diseases and parasitic infections. The credit for taking up epidemics as an integral part of famine goes to Amartya Sen who, in his *Poverty and Famines*, not only conducted a very detailed analysis of the diseases that infected different classes of people during the 1943 famine in Bengal but also brought out the seasonal pattern and sequences in which these epidemics proliferated. Scrutinising closely, he observed that all epidemics had not appeared together but in different phases of the famine. To quote Professor Sen, "malaria and fevers, which are sometimes difficult to distinguish, were the biggest killers in the pre-famine days, followed at quite some distance by 'dysentery, diarrhoea and enteric groups of fevers', cholera, and smallpox in that order." He also established *inter alia* that unnatural mortalities from famine-related epidemics continued its devastation months after the famine subsided (Sen, 1981).

Another notable contribution on the attacks of epidemics in South Asia in general and in the Indian sub-continent in particular was that of Gunnar Myrdal, who attributed poor sanitation to the cause of several contagious diseases in the region. Myrdal noted that the British administration was indifferent in providing budgetary allocation for sanitation and healthcare programmes in the colony. The advisories issued by top officials in the Madras presidency would show that they had imposed the responsibility to keep the sewages and streets clean on the lower level staff in local administrations. Without fund, the employees failed to discharge this duty. Myrdal explained that as the environment was unclean, the people at large also could not keep themselves clean. The poor sanitation in British India was reflected in the food the country-men ate, houses they lived in, cloths they wore, unclean water they drank, their sewer system, and the human excreta lying scattered all over the ground. Combined with contacts of foreign nationals, consequent on conquests and colonisation, the local people were exposed to new diseases or more virulent agents of old diseases (Myrdal, 1968).

Unlike many other western scholars who attributed cleanliness as a European virtue, independent of other contributing factors, Myrdal cited widespread poverty of the people for unsanitary surroundings that caused repeated outbreaks of various epidemics in different parts of the British colonies. Although food often accounted for two-thirds to three-fourths or still more than the total private consumption expenditure in these countries, the actual food-intake of the relatively poor was so low that they suffered from "calorie insufficiency and still more from a deficient intake of some nutrients, specifically protein and several sorts of vitamins and minerals and the result", according to Myrdal, "is to expose masses of people to a number of deficiency diseases like anaemia." More striking in this regard was the poor nutritional intakes that resulted in Myrdal's words, 'a hidden hunger' and a state of general physical weakness, impairing people's immunity to resist diseases.[4]

The recent area-specific researches in India have found that the emergence and spread of epidemic diseases leading to an escalation of mortalities was the result of new settlement patterns aided by the 'modern' economic activities initiated by the colonial administration. For instance, urbanisation programmes taken up in the colony, instead of improving the living conditions of the native population, tended to contribute to the spread of certain fatal contagious diseases. Construction of railways and irrigation canals are the two examples being cited in this regard. Uneven grounds and hóles left unfilled on both sides of the railway-lines and on embankments of irrigation canals are swamped during rains. Together with the still-water in canals, these became breeding spots of mosquitoes, which carried epidemic diseases to the people living nearby. After the rainy season, rats proliferated particularly on the sides of the railway lines. These rats formed the main transporters of plague. Malaria was the other fatal disease that accompanied the otherwise well-intentioned developmental activities. Available evidences showed that, in the closing phase of the nineteenth and the first half of the twentieth centuries, it was malaria that accounted for more than two-thirds of all mortalities from epidemic diseases (Roy, 2006).

There are researchers who do not agree that the British era was characterised by any unusual increase in mortalities caused by epidemics and famines. Their argument is that the developmental activities, including urbanisation programmes and increased healthcare facilities provided by the British administration in India had actually resulted in a perceptible decline in famine-related mortalities. For example, McAlpin (1983a) explains how the British rule could wipe out famine, famine-led epidemics and mortalities in the following sequence: (i) the large transport and communication network developed by the British administration enabled to move grain quickly and cheaply from surplus regions to the regions of local scarcity; (ii) once the capacity was built to move the grain for famine prevention, the next step that the British administration initiated was to put money into the hands of the people to buy the grain by creating employment in construction sector and in labour intensive enterprises like cotton textile industries; and (iii) as quick movement of grain was made possible by the railways, the farmers could save money that otherwise they might have spent on construction of barns to stock their grain for longer period. This allowed them to shift part of their land from the cultivation of subsistence crops to high-value commercial crops. McAlpin argued that these positive aspects of British policy were not appreciated in India due to the absence of any meaningful study.

However, in the context of British Malabar, we have already seen that no discernible decline in famine or epidemics had taken place after new railway channels were constructed in the region. If anything, these had only aggravated the situation, as the available food was carried away for exports. Furthermore, authoritative analysis of Indian data had proved beyond doubt that there were too little public health services and sanitation arrangements worth the name under the British rule. In this context, Asok K. Mitra, who had served as a civil servant in British India, stated conclusively with reference to census figures that "the percentage of population with protected water supplies was no more than about 10 per cent in any major province; the population served by sewers was less than 5 per cent; and the great majority of people who lived in rural areas had no protected water supplies nor any sanitary form of waste disposal." His analysis also showed that there was no identifiable reduction in mortalities even during the closing years of the British rule in India. For example, according to Mitra, while registered deaths from smallpox exhibited a very insignificant decline in the beginning of the 1940s, it rebounded to over more than three times of the estimated reduction by mid-1940s (Mitra, 1978).[5]

Before closing this section, it is essential to recall what we have already pointed out earlier: i.e. the link between famine and epidemics. In almost all studies, the link is drawn on the following line: When access to food comes down, for whatever reason, the people concerned are forced to consume 'famine food' viz. seeds kept for the next season's sowing, oil-cakes preserved for drought and milch animals, wild plants, tapioca, mango kernels, dead animals, etc. As most of these are deficient in essential nutrients, those who eat 'famine food' lose their natural ability to produce immunising agents in the body. In case the water they drink is contaminated, as it is generally noticed in areas where poorer people live, their vulnerability to epidemic diseases goes up further (Roy, 2006). If the victims are bread-winners, the food intake of all family members would suffer. Starvation that follows further precipitates the disease already infected. This is the stage at which newer epidemics also surface among physically weaker members, mainly the elderly individuals, children, and pregnant or lactating women in the family. From them, the diseases spread to the neighbours and in no time turn into pandemics.

A reverse of this link, which is rarely seen in the discussions, is some times witnessed in certain regions like Malabar: Unhygienic surroundings and swamps formed in rainy seasons provide breeding grounds for various contagious diseases. People who go out of their houses, especially children, catch these diseases and transmit to others, including the earning members. There is then a decline in the income and food consumption in the affected families. The accompanying starvation, dependence on 'famine food' and the resultant nutritional deficiency would facilitate other famine-related epidemics to creep in. Afterwards, the cycle of events will be the same as in the first case. As we noticed in Chapter-2, this happened in Malabar where heavy rains and swamps were common because of which epidemics and famines recurred and intensified. Authors like McAlpin do not seem to consider these two-way links between famine and epidemic diseases. For example, in a major study on famine in western India during the imperialist period, the author estimates excess mortalities separately on account of: (i) famine *per se*, (ii) plague, and (iii) influenza (McAlpin 1983b). Such desegregation does not seem tenable.

It has also to be recognised that all epidemics are not famine-diseases. Some of them, by their very nature of proliferation, would appear not to occur in times of famine. Nonetheless, such epidemics had in fact sprung up during famines and caused large-scale mortalities. British Malabar was more conspicuous in this respect. Another distinguishing characteristic of famine-diseases is that, like famine itself, these occur mostly during rainy seasons. If famine precedes a drought, the impact of the diseases might be relatively insignificant and the famine-mortalities rather less. If it coincides with heavy rains, there would be virulent attacks of these epidemics leading to exceptionally large-scale loss of lives (Dyson, 1991).

5.2 Epidemics in British India

In the introductory chapter we saw the studies made by various authors arguing that, compared to the pre-British era, the EIC period witnessed more famines, famine-led epidemics and excess mortalities and that, after the British Crown took over the Indian administration from the EIC, the number of famines and the severity of epidemic diseases and mortalities had further increased manifold. Going by this, the burden of proof falls more on those who hold the view that, in the imperialist era, there was a massive increase in epidemics along with the rising number and severity of famines in quicker succession. Major diseases noticed in different parts of the British India, including Malabar, were cholera, plague, smallpox, ague (malaria), yellow fever, respiratory infections (mainly pneumonia and tuberculosis), dysentery and diarrhoea, anaemia, leprosy, syphilis, elephantiasis, scabies, and dropsy (Logan, 1887). Just as these diseases were not all 'famine-related', they had not all originated in Malabar or in India. A few of these had developed and spread due to unsanitary, crowded and poverty-ridden conditions in the colony, and some others were 'imported' from abroad.

What happened to their trend over time can be ascertained only if concrete data are available. Though district-wise reports or Indian decennial census were published since 1872 giving information on total population, age-wise and sex-wise break-ups, and births and deaths, the data on mortalities due to epidemics are not available in these reports, except in the 1921 and 1951 census-reports. And, for Malabar, which is our focus of investigation, only the 1951 census gives separate annual time series data from 1941 to 1950 in terms of mortalities by epidemics. Despite the 1921 census report also giving similar information from 1911 to 1920, these are for the West Coast region as a whole, i.e. Malabar, Nilgiris, Anjengo, and South Canara. Since the disease-causing climatic conditions of these places are by and large homogeneous and distinct from the rest of south India (Kumar, 1983), we will use these figures in this chapter for a general understanding as to how various epidemics-related mortalities behaved during famines in the region.

The other sources of information are annual administration reports and the reports of land revenue settlement of the district administrations. These are not as comprehensive as the corresponding census data. Only some of the *talukas*, where epidemics were severe and the reimbursement of official expenditure had to be claimed from the headquarters of the district or presidency would find reflections in the administration reports. Similarly, the revenue settlement reports highlighted the details of diseases and deaths only if the concerned officials could not meet the target of revenue collection in a particular year, by way of an explanation that several assessees, bedridden with epidemic diseases, could not pay the land revenue. It was to get this 'justification' accepted by the higher-ups that they gave statistical details of the types of epidemics, the number of people infected, and the mortality out of infected persons. The veracity of these data was always in doubt because: (i) these were collected by village policemen and peons, and not by trained statistical enumerators; thy recorded the deaths only if there was time after their regular duty; (ii) if any of these policemen or peons became bed-ridden or died due to the attack of the on-going epidemics, the information from their areas of duty remained unreported until a new appointment was made; and (iii) the officials just cooked up the data to get their reimbursement bills passed.

Gadgil (1924) adopts a statistical technique to 'judge' the possible excess mortalities and decline in births caused by famines and famine-related epidemics on the basis of growth of population between census periods. According to this method, the decadal increase in population of British India between 1872 and 1921 was insignificant in relation to normal decadal changes during the three comparable census-periods, namely, 1872-1881, 1891-1901, and 1911-1921. These three periods encompass three famine-years of 1876-78, 1890-91, and 1918-19, respectively. Out of these, we have already discussed the first and third episodes in Chapter-2 as these were years of terrible famines in Malabar. A consolidated statement for 1872 to 1921 is given in Table-5.1:

Table-5.1: The Decadal Change in Population of India, 1872 - 1921 (in million)

Decade	*Change*
1872–81	3.0
1881–91	24.3
1891–01	4.1
1901–11	18.7
1911–21	3.7

Source: D.R. Gadgil (1924), op.cit, p.197.

Gadgil's disaggregated presidency-wise analysis showed that the decadal changes were extremely irregular from region to region. For instance, during 1872–81, while the total population in British India increased by 6.8 per cent, it increased by just 2.05 per cent in the Bombay presidency, but decreased by 1.35 per cent in the presidency of Madras and by 17.19 per cent in Mysore. From this, Gadgil came to the conclusion that the steep decline in the decadal population in two of the four regions he analysed indicated the impact of epidemics and famines, which, on the one hand, increased the death rates and, on the other hand, reduced the fecundity and birth rates.

The above inference would be equally applicable to any relatively smaller areas like a district. This is evident from Table-5.2, which shows the variations in population for a longer period of 50 years during 1891-1941 in Malabar. According to these figures, if epidemics and famine occurred in the beginning of the preceding decade, or just after the population census, the change in population in the succeeding census

Table-5.2: Variations in the Population of Malabar, 1891 – 1941

Year	*Persons*	*Males*	*Females*	*Variation over preceding census*		
				Persons	*Males*	*Females*
1891	2648172	1312282	1335890	...	...	...
1901	2795738	1381625	1414113	147566	69343	78223
1911	3015099	1482608	1532491	219361	100983	118387
1921	3098871	1510732	1588139	83772	28124	55648
1931	3533944	1716138	1817806	435073	205406	229667
1941	3929425	1901404	2028021	395481	185266	210215

Source: Census of India, 1941, Vol II, Madras - Tables by D.H. Elwin (Manager of Publications, Delhi, 1942)

(vis-à-vis the previous one) was not significantly lower than the expected normal change. This is because there was enough time between a famine and the next census year for an increase in births to compensate for the loss of lives during the famine. Variations in population in 1911, 1931 and 1941 over their respective preceding censuses for Malabar can be cited as examples. On the other hand, the 1921 census shows a steep decline in population. This can be attributed, in line with the reasoning given by Gadgil, to the major attack of epidemics that coincided with the 1918 famine, which was very close to the 1921 census period when the time was too short for additional births to compensate for the loss of population in the district. The historical experience all over the world is that birth rates would register a sudden increase as soon as the famine subsides because of the anxiety of the affected families to get replacement of the children lost, by a new set of births. In the above three cases that we cited in respect of Malabar, this is what appeared to have happened. During the intervening years, there were also no famine-deaths in the district (Gadgil, 1924; Stein, 2001; Roy, 2006). Another significant point to be noted here is that the extent of decline in population would depend on the types of epidemics accompanying a famine and the relative vigour with which they inflict mortalities vis-à-vis the availability of medical care. What follows is an attempt, in general, to consider some of the major famine-related epidemics and the mortalities that they could let loose.[6]

Cholera

It is an infectious disease caused by a water-borne bacterium. There is a belief among the medical profession as well as among the historians of social medicine that cholera originated in India, particularly in Bengal. It was first noticed during the Battle of Plassey in 1757 among Robert Clive's army-men encamped in overcrowded barracks under unhygienic conditions precipitated by contaminated water and insufficient food. Although the treatment available in the barracks was better than that available for the civilians, more than 60 per thousand cholera-afflicted army-men succumbed to the epidemic (Visaria and Visaria, 1983). Later, it again emerged in Bengal during 1817-19 and spread through the trade routes, devastating the entire eastern India. The disease was at that time locally known as '*jari mari*' or sudden sickness and '*kala mari*' or the disease that caused 'black death'. It is from these widely known local terminologies of the epidemic that the western scholars assumed India as the original home-land of cholera (Arnold, 1986).

This fatally terrific epidemic generally attacks small intestines. The common symptom of the disease is vomiting and diarrhoea. According to Kaper, Morris and Levine (1995) cholera, in its severe manifestation, is characterised by the passage of voluminous stools, like rice-water, that rapidly leads to dehydration. If no prompt and appropriate treatment initiated, death becomes certain, irrespective of whether the victim is an adult or a child. A distinctive feature of cholera is its tendency to appear in explosive outbreaks and its propensity to progressively affect many countries in multiple continents over the course of a number of years (Arnold, 1986).

A better and elaborate description of the disease was given by Arnold (1993) as follows: "Cholera struck suddenly and unpredictably. A person in apparently sound health at one moment might be seized the next by violent vomiting and uncontrollable purging. The massive loss of body fluids that followed produced some of cholera's most alarming symptoms – the agonising cramps, the cold, clamming surface of the skin, the deathly palla - which led rapidly to death, often within hours of the first seizure....the attack is so severe, it exhausts the vital energies so rapidly that the patient in six or eight hours loses his pulse at the wrist; his body is bedewed with a cold clammy sweat, the eyes, dull and heavy, are covered with a film, occasionally suffused blood and insensible to the stimulus of light, and in this stage of the disease he is often afflicted with deafness, the breathing becomes greatly affected, and is sometimes performed.....the death has been observed to ensue from 10 to 24 hours from the commencement of the attack".

Arnold further stated that "few diseases in nineteenth-century India appeared to be as violently destructive as epidemic cholera." The 1946 report of the Health Survey and Development Committee of the Government of India had given the total cholera deaths in British India between 1877 and 1916 at 2.9 million (Table-5.3). On the other hand, according to Arnold, "from such imperfect statistics as are available, it would appear that at least 15 million deaths occurred in British India alone between 1817 (the year in which cholera erupted as the century's major epidemic in Bengal) and 1865 (when mortality data began to be collected systematically for the first time). A further 23 million cholera deaths were recorded between 1865 and 1947, a figure likely to understate the full extent of the mortality." In the case of the presidencies of Madras and Bombay, Arnold stated that cholera coincided with famines when large number of poor people from villages migrated to urban areas begging for food. He also noted that cholera mortality was the highest in Madras presidency in the 1876–78 famine (Arnold, 1993).

Until the late 1820s, there were two misconceptions about cholera, when it was mainly concentrated in India. One was that this disease was the concern of the medical profession and not of the government or public men or social scientists. The other was that it was the disease of the poor and the under-nourished. This view originated mainly from the European observers who insisted that the slum-dwellers living in crowded huts, without even elementary sanitation, and their compulsion to drink unclean water from stagnant pools caused cholera among those people. The first misconception came to an end when, in the late 1830s, "this seemingly new and certainly appalling disease" appeared in Russia, Poland, Germany and some other advanced European countries. Then onwards, cholera came to be extensively discussed by the American and European historians so that, from the realm of medical profession it came out to the social scientists, politicians and public at large (see Arnold, 1986). The second misconception that it was essentially a disease of the poor could not sustain after the death in 1827 of Sir Thomas Munro, the Governor of Madras, reportedly from the cholera-epidemic and, in the words of Arnold (1986), this was "one reminder that there was no absolute immunity" however high and mighty the person is. Poverty was certainly a cause for cholera infection and proliferation. But there were also other causes. In the context of the nineteenth-century Europe, Rosenberg (1966) gives the following reason for excessive deaths from cholera.

When several Western and Eastern European countries were attacked by cholera in the beginning of the 1830s, the governments of Britain and France appointed two separate medical commissions to inquire into the causation of this dangerously fatal epidemic disease, which had no previous history in the western world. These commissions attributed moral degradation of the people as the fundamental cause of cholera-attacks and the consequent unavoidable mortality. Such a conclusion was based, not on any proof from the medical science but on the orthodox religious belief during those years in the West that the individuals who were likely to be infected by cholera, being sure of imminent death, indulged in whatever pleasure they could have before they died: excessive inebriation, overeating, and sexual excess that dissipated the vital energy of the individuals, both men and women, to withstand the attack of cholera. This helped cholera to easily attack those overindulgent individuals. Once a person was infected by this disease, his body became defenceless. The general public in the West therefore concluded that, apart from the individual's moral transgression, "the national failings in morality" also added to the cause of this unknown misery.

It took sometime for the European medical profession to disprove the centuries-old beliefs in the western hemisphere and to establish the superiority of pathological tests for identifying and treating the fatal diseases like cholera. This was not very difficult for them as the nineteenth century Europe was far ahead of the third world colonies in education and prosperity. Equipped with intellectual and economic capital, the medical profession could win the confidence of the people and vanquish cholera much easily. On the contrary, the countries like India under the British rule, with illiteracy, superstition and acute dearth of capital to invest in health care, had to suffer more and more loss of lives from cholera and such contagious diseases (Rosenberg, 1966).

In British India, cholera and famine occurred together and devastated several parts of the country, particularly during the second half of the nineteenth-century. Arnold (1986) gives several reasons for the attack of cholera in India: religious congregations, immersion of pilgrims in sacred tanks and rivers, sipping of river-water as a ritual of purification, and the pilgrims carrying the cholera-infected water as 'holy' water to relatives and friends. He further noted that pilgrimage centres like Haridwar and Allahabad in Uttar Pradesh; Puri in Orissa; Nasik and Pandharpur in Maharashtra; Tirupati in Andhra Pradesh; and Kanchipuram in Tamil Nadu were the epicentres of this disease. Even though in times of epidemic-diseases the British administration tried to prevent such religious congregations, these were stoutly resisted by the pilgrims, stating that it was an affront on their religious belief.

Another source of cholera pandemic was the troop maintained by the colonial rulers, particularly the locally recruited army-men, who were kept in unsanitary and crowded conditions of barracks and encampments. Arnold believed that these army men were the principal agencies through which cholera disseminated throughout British India. While they were on movement from one camp to another, they spread the disease to the locals on their way. When they visited their homes, they transmitted it to the family members before leaving back to the barracks.

Table-5.3: Cholera Mortality in British India (Quinquennial Averages), 1877 - 1916

Years	*Mortality*	*Years*	*Mortality*
1877-81	288,949	1897-01	383,294
1882-86	286,105	1902-06	367,160
1887-91	400,934	1907-11	397,127
1892-96	443,890	1912-16	328,593

Source: Report of the Health Survey and Development Committee, 1946; Vol.1. (Reproduced from Arnold, 1993, op.cit).

Table-5.4: Plague Mortality in British India, 1897–1930

Year	*Mortality ('000)*	*Rate (per '000)*	*Year*	*Mortality ('000)*	*Rate (per '000)*	*Year*	*Mortality ('000)*	*Rate (per '000)*
1897	48	0.2	1909	145	0.6	1921	69	0.3
1898	89	0.5	1910	413	1.8	1922	77	0.3
1899	102	0.5	1911	735	3.1	1923	229	1.0
1900	74	0.3	1912	263	1.1	1924	361	1.5
1901	236	1.1	1913	198	0.8	1925	117	0.5
1902	453	2.0	1914	266	1.1	1926	139	0.6
1903	702	3.1	1915	380	1.6	1927	304	1.3
1904	906	4.1	1916	205	0.9	1928	121	0.5
1905	941	4.2	1917	437	1.8	1929	72	0.3
1906	300	1.3	1918	440	1.9	1930	24	0.1
1907	1166	5.2	1919	74	0.3			
1908	113	0.5	1920	99	0.4			

Source: Ira Klein (1988), op.cit.

Cholera had also spread through the unhygienic drinking water contaminated with infected human faeces. In British India, according to Arnold, one of the principal means by which the disease spread through open tanks and water courses, which served the ordinary people as drinking water and for washing, bathing and other preliminaries. Malabar was a classic case of night-soil lying scattered everywhere, facilitating the attack of cholera and many other infectious diseases.

Being a water-borne disease, it was believed that dry conditions were inimical to the survival of cholera bacillus and would develop and attack only during rainy seasons. Later it was realised that when dearth and drought drove villagers to go to common wells, reservoirs, tanks and stagnant pools for drinking, bathing and other purposes, these quickly became contaminated by cholera and attacked the users. From this it became clear that cholera has no specific season to attack and kill.

Plague

This was the second most important famine-time-killer, which is a contagious bacterial-disease characterised by fever and delirium and the most feared and deadliest of maladies that afflicted British India. Black rats, and fleas living on rats, are the transmitters of plague. Fleas suck blood from plague-infected rats and pass on the bacilli to all living creatures around, including human beings. The bacilli first enter the skin of the person and travel to other organs. After an inhibition period of three to seven days, the infected person shows flu-like symptoms characterised by chills, body-aches, vomiting and nausea. Clinically, three types of plague epidemic have been identified: (i) the *bubonic*, or glandular plague, which is the most common type of plague all over the world in terms of the number of people being attacked and the extent of mortalities; (ii) the *septicaemic* plague that occurs when infection spreads directly through the blood stream and is regarded as an explosive form of bubonic plague; and (iii) the *pneumonic* plague, which is more virulent than the other two forms of plague and transmits from an infected person to another without the involvement of rats or fleas. It was bubonic plague that appeared first in various urban centres of British India at the closing years of the nineteenth century. By the beginning of the twentieth century, it attacked even many rural areas (Orent, 2004; Klein, 1988).

In India, the earliest plague-attack was recorded in the year 1895 when it conquered most parts of Calcutta city (Seal, 1960). The second massive plague-outbreak appeared in 1896 throughout the city of Bombay. Quoting two official records of the imperialist period, Klein (1988)[7] showed that, between 1897 and 1930, the total deaths from plague in India accounted for about 10.3 million. With the addition of death tolls in the two earlier plague attacks in Calcutta and Bombay, some authors projected the total mortality from plague in British India to over 12 million (Table-5.4). Of all the countries in the world, it was India that faced the worst scourge of plague in terms of deaths and social dislocations. This pandemic was terribly frightening as it induced not only large-scale fatalities but also disrupted the ordinary life. Therefore, during the worst phase of plague, people were reported to have evacuated their homes and camped in open fields. As a result of this, by the time it subsided, many urban houses were seen empty (Seal, 1960).

Ira Klein, who made a major study of the plague epidemic in British India stated that the massive plague-deaths during the latter half of the nineteenth century were reminiscent of the fourteenth-century *black deaths* in Europe "where human immunities were low, where economic relapse promoted malnutrition, where re-urbanisation left large market towns sinking in their own refuse, where black rats were domiciled densely with people,....where plague followed major trade routes once it reached the continent."[8] Compared to other European countries, Great Britain was the worst affected by *black deaths*. But all these countries were able to protect from this deadly pandemic because of the improved nutrition, sanitation, displacement of black rats, housing and other social advancements. Thus, deaths due to plague in North and South Americas and Europe between 1894 (when plague reappeared with its devastating strength) and 1938 (when it receded from all over the world) constituted just 0.2 per cent of the estimated world plague-deaths. During this period, the mortality from plague in India was estimated at 95 per cent of the total deaths due to plague all over the world. The other major sufferers of plague-attacks from the closing years of the nineteenth century to the first half of the twentieth century were China and Taiwan, and Indonesia in the Asian continent. But the mortality caused by plague in these countries was just two per cent of the total. Deaths from plague reported in Africa were still lower, barely one per cent (Table-5.5).[9]

The British Indian health officials believed that in Europe where cool climate continues for six to eight months helps the plague bacilli to survive and proliferate whereas India's warm temperature was relatively unfavourable for plague attacks. However, there were other reasons why plague became one of the most dreaded epidemics in British India. First, poverty, under-nourishment, low immunities and lack of sanitation played a major role in the conflagration of plague. Second, the modernisation programmes, particularly expansion of railways and urbanisation were the other causes for its continued devastation. Along with these developmental activities, the British administration in India failed to plug the loopholes in these works that enabled rodents to live and multiply.

Table-5.5: World Plague Mortality, 1894-1938 (in '000s)

Area	*Deaths*
India	12500
China and Taiwan	250
Indonesia	214
Madagascar	32
Africa	120
N. America	1
S. America	24
Europe	1
Rest of World	10

Source: L.F. Hirst (1953), reproduced in Ira Klein (1988).

Table-5.6 (a): Deaths by Epidemics in West Coast, 1911-1920

Year	*total*	*male*	*female*	*% female*
1911	54057	27363	26694	49.4
1912	65789	34342	31447	47.8
1913	56906	29182	27724	48.7
1914	53449	27077	26372	49.3
1915	41099	20915	20184	49.1
1916	44210	22497	21713	49.1
1917	51199	25990	25209	49.2
1918	93018	45153	47865	51.5
1919	112624	54611	58013	51.5
1920	53050	26468	26582	50.1

Source: Census of India 1921, Vol XII, Madras (Part-I) Superintendent of Census Operations, Madras, 1922.

Table-5.6 (b): Epidemic-wise Deaths in West Coast

Year	*Cholera*	*Smallpox*	*Malaria*	*Dys& diar*	*Plague*	*Total*
1911	1147	3366	37045	12124	375	54057
1912	3212	984	43357	17780	456	65789
1913	4702	660	35454	15713	377	56906
1914	1175	945	36448	14735	146	53449
1915	686	540	29769	9901	203	41099
1916	63	1064	32505	10360	218	44210
1917	888	2940	34708	12299	364	51199
1918	5652	5842	68699	12477	348	93018
1919	23458	7174	58829	23036	127	112624
1920	898	1287	39525	11270	70	53050
% of :						
Total	6.7	4.0	66.6	22.3	0.4	100
1918-19	14.2	6.3	62.0	17.3	0.2	100

Source: As at Table-5.6 (a) above.

Going by the fact that the European cool climate was highly favourable for plague, the wet seasons of Malabar was also responsible for large number of deaths from plague in the district. Plague-attacks increased sharply in areas where people and rats lived together, such as Indian huts and grain-barns as well as godowns stacking grains in city areas, which were nesting places of rodents. In British Malabar, Calicut municipality was such a congested urban centre with wholesale grain godowns, and Palghat,

Table-5.7 (a): Deaths by all Epidemics in Malabar

(1941-50)

Year	*Total Deaths*	*Deaths by epidemics*	*Of column (3)* *Male*	*Female*
(1)	*(2)*	*(3)*	*(4)*	*(5)*
1941	86592	36993	19577	17416
1942	82173	35077	18688	16389
1943	124787	68236	31287	36949
1944	90674	37523	19483	18040
1945	74108	30394	15912	14482
1946	66523	25871	13652	12219
1947	66661	25288	13329	11959
1948	65422	23307	12059	11248
1949	60517	20610	10594	10016
1950	73832	27914	14154	13760

Source: 1951 Census Hand Book: Malabar District, (Government Press, Madras; 1953).

Table-5.7 (b): Epidemic-wise Deaths Reported in Malabar, 1941–50

Year	*Cholera*	*Smallpox*	*Fevers*	*Dys& diar*	*Respira*	*Plague*	*Total*
1941	1	326	18403	9364	8899	0	36993
1942	82	57	17816	8976	8145	1	35077
1943	28432	418	19419	11067	8816	84	68236
1944	107	898	19833	8027	8588	70	37523
1945	6	1226	16596	4912	7633	21	30394
1946	5	821	13717	4191	7113	24	25871
1947	1	85	12762	4677	7729	34	25288
1948	74	41	10977	4120	8088	7	23307
1949	53	75	9595	3313	7574	0	20610
1950	53	390	13047	6117	8306	1	27914
% to total	8.7	1.3	45.9	19.6	24.4	0.1	100.0
% of 1943	41.7	0.6	28.5	16.2	12.9	0.1	100.0

Source: As at Table-5.7 (a) above.

a major rice producing area. These were known to be abodes of rodents. The other major areas where rat proliferated and communicated the contagion were: (i) the Himalayan foothills from where it spread to Punjab, Uttar Pradesh and Bihar, though it was rather mild in thinly populated areas like Himachal Pradesh; (ii) the Vindhya hills and its surrounding central Indian region; and (iii) the Western Ghats in Southern India, including Malabar. There are certain seasonal patterns in the incidence and peaking of plague epidemic. A significant empirical study showed that it was during the autumn and spring seasons that plague infections went up in most parts of India. In Madras presidency, according to the study, the incidence of plague slowly appears between May and July and, then, develops into its virulent form during August-September, or December-January (Seal, 1960).

There was a belief that, unlike most of the epidemic-diseases associated with famines, the fatally dangerous plague could not be found during food crises. This belief stemmed from the fact that famine was associated with FAD, whereas the rodent population and plague attacks increased during years of bumper grain harvests. From a comparative account of the indices of food output, worked out from Blyn (1966), and plague attacks available in official health statistics, Ira Klein, an authority on epidemics in India, found that between 1899 and 1918 the attacks of plague was observed to have substantially increased whenever there was a bumper harvest of foodgrains (Klein, 1988).

Fevers

Even though cholera and plague were the two major famine-related epidemics that killed unusually large number of people throughout the world, including several parts of India, during the late nineteenth and early twentieth centuries, the available data would indicate that, in terms of mortalities, these were not that significant in British Malabar. Only in times of famines did Malabar witness massive attacks of cholera, killing substantially large number of people. For instance, during 1911-20, the death tolls from cholera in the Western Ghats region (including Malabar) were estimated at 6.7 per cent of the total deaths from major epidemic diseases whereas it went up to 14.2 per cent during the famine of 1918-19. Similarly, during 1941-50, the death tolls estimated at 8.7 per cent of the total deaths by all epidemics shot up to 41.7 per cent of the total in the 1943 famine. Compared to these figures, deaths registered from plague were relatively insignificant in the district (see Tables-5.6 and 5.7). As against these, the epidemics that killed thousands of victims in Malabar were various types of fevers, dysentery and diarrhoea, and respiratory diseases.

The fevers had a constant presence in Malabar during the 'pre-antibiotic era' when medical profession was yet to identify their variants, causes, and treatments. With the advancement in science, a number of fever-types are now dissected. The fatal characteristics of a few among them are also brought under control. It is now known that all the fevers are infectious and comes out with continuous or intermittent high body-temperature, such as common fever, pneumonia, typhoid, kala-azar, septicaemia etc. Some fevers are transmitted by mosquitoes, for example, yellow fever, dengue, influenza, and malaria. Some are spread through water contaminated with faeces of infected persons. Typhoid is an example. Infants, young children, and elderly people with chronic asthma and diabetes are the first to catch these diseases. If left untreated, these spread to others in the family and neighbourhood. In the nineteenth and early twentieth centuries, influenza and malaria were the two major epidemic diseases that devastated Malabar, especially during famines.

Influenza was first identified as a fatal disease during the First World War. Known as 'Spanish flu', this usually deadly pandemic was noticed in the barracks where soldiers were accommodated. Close troops-quarters and massive troop movements in connection with the war facilitated to hasten the spread of the epidemic. As the immune system of the army men was weakened by insufficient food and over-exertion, their susceptibility to flu increased. It spread from the army men to all over the world. Outside the army also, the victims of 'Spanish flu' were healthy young adults. However, in its emergence later as influenza, the victims were predominantly children, the elderly, or those who were otherwise weakened by malnutrition. Undernourished pregnant women, hailing from poor families, were the other group that became extremely susceptible to influenza. The fatality from influenza was very large mainly due to non-availability of appropriate treatments leading to development of complications like haemorrhages that result in bleeding of nose and intestine (Barry, 2004; Potter, 2006).

Malaria was another major killer-fever. This mosquito-borne infectious disease was widely prevalent in all tropical and subtropical regions characterised by high rainfall combined with hot weather. Warm temperature, high humidity and existence of stagnant waters created by rains provided suitable environment for the breeding of mosquitoes, the bites of which led to intermittent and, on occasions, continuous fever. Malabar, with its ideal climatic and environmental conditions for mosquitoes, was always gripped by malaria and, in times of famines, it took away a sizable number of lives. Similarly, the Bengal presidency, which was considered as pleasant and salubrious for wealthy British officials working in India to retreat for rest, was also a hunting ground of malaria. Studies in Bengal had linked malarial fever with prosperous development of agriculture. The poor persons with weakened physical conditions, while working in the fields, became easily vulnerable to the contagion.

The causes and proliferation of malaria were identified with canal construction in advanced agricultural regions. In this context we had earlier referred to the findings of Elizabeth Whitcombe from her research in Doab region that the development of canal irrigation had, on the one hand, resulted in over-cropping, salination, destruction of wells and, on the other hand, obstructions caused by canal embankments led to water-logging with fungus formation. The alarming proportion of malarial fever was a continuous cause of large-scale deaths in North Western Provinces, Punjab and some of the districts of Madras presidency. The declared objective of building roads and railways by the British was ostensibly to minimise famines arising from monsoon-failures that led to a decline in food availability in some centres by facilitating quicker transport of food from other areas. While this objective could not be served with the improvements in the net-works of railways and roadways, they helped proliferation of malarial fever and widespread human mortalities. In the late nineteenth-century, when there was an outburst of malaria-related deaths in Bengal presidency, the government appointed a committee of inquiry, which found that railway lines and roads created swamping on their sides and stimulated mosquito breeding and spread of malaria (Visaria and Visaria, 1983).

In Malabar, the death rates due to fevers, mainly malaria, accounted for around two-thirds of all deaths due to famine-related epidemics in the early part of the twentieth-century. In the 1940s, all fevers taken together accounted for 46 per cent of total mortalities from epidemic diseases. However, in 1943, when the famine broke out in Malabar, the percentage of mortality from fevers declined to about 29 per cent because, in that year, cholera took as large as 42 per cent of the total mortalities. If we consider the entire period from 1941 to 1950, except 1943, only 382 deaths were recorded in Malabar due to cholera epidemic, whereas it registered as high as 28814 deaths in the 1943 famine in the district. Leaving apart the cholera deaths in 1943, the fevers were the largest killers in Malabar.

Respiratory Diseases

Like other epidemics that killed excessively large number of people during famines, respiratory infections are another set of diseases that are very common during rainy season and accelerate the intensity of mortalities if famine strikes at that time. Arrival of the monsoon is the time when the relatively undernourished should fall ill, as the ability of the immune system of such people becomes too weak to fight sudden decline in atmospheric temperature, rise in humidity, and wetting from heavy rains. Considering these factors, Malabar is climate-wise extremely congenial for respiratory ailments to sustain and flare up at appropriate times. Starting from common cold, bronchitis and sinusitis, which are debilitating but not fatal, the respiratory diseases culminate to more serious problems like asthma that erupts with wheezing, coughing, chest tightness and shortness of breath, obstructing the airflow and leading to the death of the victim. It is the most common obstructive lung disease that flares up in the cold and humid conditions, as also due to allergy for pollen that fills the air during the flowering season (Yawn, 2008). If the wet-weather during which this ailment intensifies is associated with famine, it leads to further complications and kills many more.

Other respiratory tract infections, which are more ferocious and can turn fatal if left untreated in the early stages, are pneumonia, diphtheria, tuberculosis, lung cancer etc. Among them pneumonia and tuberculosis were prevalent among wider sections of the poor for long and are still prevalent in the backward areas of third world countries. Pneumonia was a leading cause of mortality in British Malabar and still continues to be a widely noticed respiratory ailment among the very young, the clinically ill, and among the very old. So was tuberculosis, which was known in the West as 'consumption' and 'white plague'. In the primary stage of the disease, it infected more children than adults. Then it spread to others through frequent exposure to the victims. At this stage, poor appetites, loss of weight and fever are the symptoms. When the body defence of the victim is lowered through malnourishment, tuberculosis enters the most dangerous secondary stage to develop into pulmonary and broncho-pneumonic tuberculosis and kills the victim (William, 1997).

In Malabar, because of the damp environment, tuberculosis and its higher stages of attacks used to kill larger sections of the poor every year. As this disease is generally seen among the malnourished people living in overcrowded areas, it is known as the disease arising from poverty. Unlike the other famine-related epidemics and mortalities about which we discussed in the foregoing, we do not have any data on deaths in Malabar by respiratory diseases for the earlier years. The census data for 1951 for the first time gave the most comprehensive details of certain famine-related killer-diseases. Of which, the respiratory diseases represented mortality-wise the second most important epidemics in Malabar.

Dysentery and Diarrhoea

After fevers, the next significant cause of deaths in Malabar, as well as in most of the British colonies of third world countries during the late nineteenth and early twentieth centuries was by dysentery and diarrhoea. According to the World Health Organisation (WHO), diarrhoea is a case of loose bowel movement caused by bacterial, viral or parasitic infection through contaminated food or water, or amoebiasis. The main victims were people living in crowded conditions with poor hygiene and lack of sanitary arrangements. In such environment, generally, faeces of an infected person pass on to others through the water they use for multiple purposes. In the nineteenth-century, diarrhoeal infection was believed to have killed more soldiers than wars killed them. Among civilian population, those who became weak due to malnutrition are more susceptible to this infection. Diarrhoea is also regarded as one of the main causes of infant mortality in third world countries, not only during but also after the colonial period. The diarrhoea-spreading micro-organism that enters a victim's body creates inflammation of the intestinal-wall and causes abdominal pain, fever, nausea and vomiting. The continuous loss of fluid and minerals from the body of the victim through bowel movement leads to dehydration, which, if not prevented by oral rehydration therapy, death is certain. During the British imperialist era, diarrhoea caused massive deaths in India because of the non-availability of treatments.

If the inflammatory disorder of the intestine resulting in severe diarrhoea is accompanied by visible blood, as per the WHO description, it is called dysentery. Though clinically distinct, both dysentery and diarrhoea are referred as the same ailment in common parlance. Citing these epidemics in Malabar, William Logan, who used a single term for the two diseases, stated that "dysentery is a very common disease.....I have not seen this problem so common with the rich. But the poor suffer fearfully from it, and generally the acute variety. The season for it is June, July and August, and the cause is climate. The hot and dry months of April and May are succeeded by the very wet June and July. The houses of poor are mere huts, thus exposing the inhabitants to damp and cold. Children suffer terribly from this. Dysentery is often the result of malaria and it first affects liver. It may be sometimes due to eating bad fish" (Logan, 1887).

Recent researches conducted on famine-related diseases like dysentery and diarrhoea have brought out certain unconventional knowledge about these afflictions. While it is not denied that these ailments generally attack the relatively poor and malnourished, the researchers point out that even the rich and the powerful cannot escape from them (see Chapter-1). Medical science has now established that, generally, the possibility of dysentery and diarrhoea would increase with the patients suffering from tuberculosis and cholera. Furthermore, these diseases had killed hundreds of thousands of army men during the American Civil War, the Second World War, Vietnam War and many other wars in history. Their life in barracks and in prisons as POWs (Prisoners of War) was so pathetic that they could not escape from these ailments (Marr, 1970). And so was the situation in British Malabar, particularly in matters of health care and sanitation. Massive deaths that resulted from diarrhoea and dysentery were due to the indifference of the British administration in improving the medical facilities and sanitary conditions in Malabar.

It is believed that a rising trend in diarrhoea and dysentery is the first symptom of an imminent famine, as these are associated with the sudden decline in food intake. Therefore, the causes of sporadic deaths that take place prior to the peaking of a famine was commonly called 'famine diarrhoea' in several places in India (Sen, 1981:203). In Malabar, however, dysentery and diarrhoea were perennial problems of the poorer segments of population, who were generally malnourished and lived in unhygienic conditions. Nonetheless, the data on the number of people afflicted and died of diarrhoea and dysentery during the early British period are not available. The census data available for the first time between 1911 and 1920 relate to the West Coast region as a whole, and not separately for Malabar. From these figures, it is seen that these were the third largest killers in normal times during the earlier part of the twentieth century in West Coast. The severity of these epidemics shot up in the famine of 1918-19 and proved to be one of the most calamitous killer-diseases in the region. For the 1940s we have separate data on epidemic-wise mortalities in Malabar district. These figures indicate that, in normal times, dysentery and diarrhoea constituted the third largest cause of deaths in Malabar, the first and second being fevers and respiratory diseases. During the 1943 famine, Malabar witnessed a tremendous flare up of deaths from cholera so that, despite an increase in the absolute number of mortalities due to dysentery and diarrhoea, their relative position in total deaths took the third position in the district. However, it was dysentery and diarrhoea that attacked the famished people, facilitating other more fatal epidemics to infect the affected people.

5.3 Nightingale's Views

We have already discussed in Chapter-3 about the comprehensive surveys conducted by Florence Nightingale and her persuasive writings on the causes of famines in different parts of India during the colonial period. She linked the various types of epidemics to poor sanitation and lack of public health services in British India for debilitating the victims and their families from earning their livelihood so that they were pushed into disastrous famines. In this section, we will briefly narrate her views on famine, epidemics and related mortalities in India during the latter part of the nineteenth century that no other writer, to our knowledge, had presented as cogently as she did. With the experience she gained from her services in Crimean War and the 'charity patients of the hospitals' in which she worked, Nightingale started investigation on the health status of

British India's army-men and later extended the findings to the civilian population. In several of her writings she incisively dissected the reasons why epidemic diseases repeatedly erupted in the Indian sub-continent during the colonial period. Nightingale insisted that the poor health-conditions of the army-men were due to their unhealthy life styles like indulging in 'over-drinking, over-eating and sedentary habits'. The liver diseases noticed in a large number of army personnel arose from this callous life style. To make matters worse, their barracks and the amenities made available there were extremely pathetic. Being overcrowded, any epidemic that one of the army-men contacted conveyed immediately to all others in the barrack and to the civilian population, when they visited their families.

The army hospitals established near the barracks had only single wards, without proper ventilation, not to speak of other minimum conveniences that the patients admitted in hospitals were generally expected to have. Even the para-medical staff required to attend to them were insufficient. Worst of all, there was no arrangements for helpers from family or friends to visit and assist the patients. Those who were admitted in the army-hospitals, not insignificant in number at a time, had to themselves cook their food, thereby polluting the hospital environment and affecting further the already poor sanitary condition.

Nightingale repeatedly emphasised that unless sanitation and health of the general population were not simultaneously taken care of, it would be impossible for the army men to remain healthy. Just as they conveyed the diseases caught from the barracks to the civilians, the latter transferred their contagious diseases to the former. She called the attention of the authorities on a number of times to the fact that "native houses in Indian villages were filthy and native towns, proverbially unhealthy." Citing the conditions of the three British presidency head quarters, which were expected to be maintained better than other cities, Nightingale once wrote: "Bombay has water supply but no drainage, Calcutta has drainage but no water, and Madras has neither" (see Vallee, 2007).

She could also successfully put pressure on the British government for setting up a Royal Commission in 1859 to inquire into the general sanitary state of the Indian army. The Commission's chairman, Sidney Herbert, being a friend of Nightingale, sought her help in the preparation of the report. Accordingly, she drafted a questionnaire to collect the needed information, analysed the returns received from the respondents, and did much of the final writing of the report. As the British government refused to make the report public, she privately got it printed and circulated to the Queen, cabinet ministers and members of the India Council that oversaw from England the working of the colonial administration in India.

Her recommendations, as incorporated in the report *inter alia* included: (1) If the sanitation and other living conditions of the army-men have to be improved, it should start with similar arrangements for the civilian population. (2) The government should organise a campaign to inculcate healthy habits among the civilians. (3) The public hospitals of both defence and civilian population should be immediately renovated and enlarged. The practice in these hospitals of patients themselves cooking their food inside the ward should be discontinued. (4) For the successful implementation of these recommendations, it is essential to establish institutions of local self-government at municipal levels and the day-to-day administration of overall environmental sanitation and health care should be brought under their responsibilities. These institutions have to take care of not only the sanitation and hygiene within their areas of jurisdiction but also effectively prevent the recurring epidemics and famines in rural India.

Starting her research on the hygienic condition of the Indian army, Nightingale extended her interest in health, poverty, malnutrition and famine of the entire population in the country. With her untiring campaigns, including massive writings in the British, American and Anglo-Indian[10] news papers, Nightingale could successfully persuade the colonial government to create, for the first time, a sanitary department under the British administration. Though she had never visited India at any time in her life, as she was mostly bed-ridden after coming back from the Crimean War, with the continued research that she drafted through investigators for over four decades, she became an authority on India's sanitary conditions, causes of repeated famines, and many other influences that affected normal life of the native people, such as the land tenure system, flawed land assessment and revenue collection methods, and women's education (Currey and Hugo, 1984; Gourlay, 2003; Vallee, 2006).

5.4 Colonial Hegemony

Contrary to the writings based on direct field level information by Nightingale and a few other Indian nationalist writers, some of the recent contributions on the healthcare system during the imperialist era, even while apparently critical in tone, were cunningly pro-British in intention. For instance, David Arnold's interesting work, *Colonising the Body*, which is otherwise an excellent in-depth analysis of the British administration's response to epidemics and mortalities in India during the nineteenth and early twentieth centuries, would bear testimony to this. Despite being ambivalent on some of the controversial issues on the imperialist healthcare system, his emphasis was that western medical practice in dealing with various fatally contagious diseases, which, if coincided with famines, had flared up exponentially and snatched away millions of lives in India essentially because of the hegemonic manner in which it was attempted to be implemented in the colony, though the British rulers were rather weak in using hegemony as an administrative weapon (Arnold, 1993). Before taking up his arguments, it is necessary to understand the meaning of 'hegemony' that Arnold had in mind while dealing with the British Indian healthcare system, as the term is used differently in different contexts by different authors.

In common parlance, the word 'hegemony' implies 'a sphere of dominance'. The term became popular in the writings on political science where it is expressed in the sense of the ruling class dominance over the subordinate social classes. In the nineteenth-century imperialist political history, 'hegemony' conveyed the idea of authoritarian power meant to establish European suzerainty in Asia, Africa and Latin America. Initially, the Europeans exercised military power for the purpose, like all imperialist conquerors. Once the right to rule an alien territory was achieved, in the second phase of day-to-day administration, they abolished the military power and followed a new kind of authority over the subjects. Examples of the first phase of this process can be seen in the conquests of Louis XIV and Napoleon Bonaparte to build French 'hegemony' in the continental Europe. The first and the second processes together were eminently evident in India when the British conquered various local kingdoms with its mighty army and then discarded the military power to continue the imperialist 'hegemony' by creating a fear psychosis among the colonial people who, despite unwillingly, accepted the will of their masters (Howson and Smith, 2008).

The difficulty to comprehend the meaning of the term 'hegemony' arises from its use in two apparently same but implicitly opposite senses: one, to mean 'domination' as Mao Zedong used while speaking about 'hegemonism'; and two, to mean 'leadership' as Lenin used to convey that it is acquired with what is called 'collective consent'. Mao Zedong spoke about 'hegemonism' to indicate a kind of domination by one country over another, but not to establish imperialism. Lenin, on the other hand, used the word 'hegemony' to mean political leadership being endorsed by the consent of an alliance of workers and peasantry. However, the term owes its present day use in politics and sociology to Antonio Gramsci (1891-1937), the man who helped to establish the Italian Communist Party in 1921 and converted it into a mass movement. He was arrested in 1926 and sentenced to more than twenty years of imprisonment. During the jail-years, Gramsci wrote more than thirty notes, each containing several concepts relating to a particular debate or historical reference. These were smuggled out from the jail and, long afterward, parts of it published in 1971 with the title *Selections from the Prison Notebooks*, which contain an elaborate version of the concept of 'hegemony'. According to Gramsci, hegemony or domination of a state over its subjects, to be successful, must rest on the active consent of various socio-economic groups among the subjects.

While clarifying the meaning of hegemony in the application of allopathic medicines in British India, David Arnold quotes from Gramsci's prison writings: "the spontaneous consent given by the great masses of the population to the general direction imposed on social life by the dominant fundamental group; this consent is 'historically' caused by the prestige (and consequent confidence) which the dominant group enjoys because of its position and function in the world of production" (Gramsci, 1971). Arnold elaborates the implications of the concept of hegemony as unfolded from the words of Gramsci and applies in the healthcare system that existed in India during the British period as follows: By 'spontaneous consent' what Gramsci meant was nothing but the 'coercive' imposition of the imperialist will on the hapless masses. Though the masses of people could not accept the unilateral imposition of the ruling class will, they, being helpless, meekly extended their 'consent'. However, despite ostensibly giving 'consent', the colonial people resisted to accept any of these dictates, wherever that was possible. Such a resistance arose from the embedded belief of the native people in the superiority of exorcist practices in curing epidemics. That was why the British rulers, despite attempting to overcome these prejudices and treating the fatally dangerous epidemics in the Indian colony, failed in the attempt as their hegemony was relatively weak.

Similarly, Arnold stated that, for Gramsci, 'coercion' need not necessarily be in the form of direct use of force by the state apparatus. It can also be in the form of the state absenting from its basic responsibility to citizens when they want it the most. In times of epidemics and famines what the people want is the state support in providing medical care and low-priced or free food supply. The state failure on these two fronts, in the Gramscian concept, is nothing but coercion and the 'hegemony' in this context becomes a shrewdly calculated exercise of control over the masses for exploitation. On the other hand, coercion could be the direct imposition of the will of the ruling class by the use of force. In this latter sense, Arnold states that, "the colonial rule has often been depicted....as a coercive domain, founded on conquest, governed by greed, and sustained by the strength of its army and police, its courts and jails." However, distancing from this view, Arnold sides with the opposite view that British colonialism did not have much capacity to regulate or transform indigenous society in line with what the imperialist rulers wanted because, to Arnold, the British hegemony in India was "weak, alien, ill-informed, and often blunderingly ineffectual and hence an improbable candidate for Gramscian hegemony" (Arnold, 1993:243).

Arnold's argument is not only self-contradictory but also factually untenable, at least in the context of sanitation and healthcare in British India. The 'hegemony' that the British imperialism unleashed in different parts of the Indian colony in this respect was unquestionably analogous to the Gramscian concept of hegemony. However, it was imposed only in areas where the British could perpetuate its economic imperialism, and not indiscriminately on everything and everywhere. Wherever applied, the 'hegemony' did not exhibit any weakness; it was extremely powerful and, in most cases, ruthless so that the subjects, though unwilling, had to submissively accept it for the fear of repression that could otherwise follow. One of the most important examples in this regard is the British public health programme. The size of the population requiring medical and health care services being very large and the likely cost stupendous, the British rulers used extremely harsh form of hegemony to dispense with it. To put it in other words, wherever, in its reckoning, a large revenue outgo was involved in providing a healthcare system, the British administration carefully avoided it by giving some excuse. In such cases 'hegemony' came out as an instrument to impose 'parsimony' so that the colonial administration could divert as much as possible for its imperialist expansion. That is to say, hegemony and parsimony were two sides of the same coin. The archival records and some of the recent writings on epidemics and mortalities in British India would reveal that, at least in the following four concrete cases, the British hegemony of the Gramscian perspective was unmistakable: (i) the policy of anti-contagious vaccination; (ii) evacuation of disease-infected persons from their families and neighbourhood to isolated quarantines; (iii) women's medical and maternity treatments; and (iv) suppression of indigenous medical and health-care practices for the propagation of allopathic medicines.

Vaccination

We have noted earlier that there were several regions in India where the development of certain fatal contagious diseases like smallpox, cholera, plague etc. coincided with the rainy season. For dealing with these pandemics, the government in 1897 enacted an Epidemic Diseases Act. This legislation was amended from time to time and notified in the gazettes, declaring whichever places were bought under its purview at any given period. One such amendment to the Act was regularly brought out for compulsory vaccination against fatal diseases. And the language in all such notifications were similar: "Whereas the Governor acting with Ministers is hereby pleased to declare that certain parts of the Presidency of (Madras) are visited by and other parts are threatened with an outbreak of the dangerous disease known as (plague); and whereas the ordinary provisions of the law for the time being in force in the said Presidency are insufficient to prevent the outbreak of such disease or the spread thereof. Therefore, in exercise of the power conferred by rule-2 of the rules declaring vaccination compulsory is hereby enforced."

With the above introduction, the notification used to authorise the district Collector of the selected area to directly supervise the vaccination programme being undertaken by the District or the Municipal Health Officer. It needs no mention that vaccination as a preventive technique against contagious diseases was unknown in the prevailing indigenous medical system in India. Being an entirely new medical practice, when the British administration introduced it in the colony, there was serious apprehensions about the purport of the practice. For a smooth functioning of the programme, the administration should have first educated the ignorant local people about its advantages. Instead, the British health officials imposed it coercively on them with the cheapest possible way. Quite often the people entrusted with the duty were illiterate municipal sweepers and coolies, who were not even given training on how to vaccinate.

Despite the district administration repeatedly deciding in the periodic meetings of its officials to arrange training for the vaccinators, each time it went on postponing the programme citing one reason or the other. Even as late as 1943, when Malabar district was attacked by a number of fatally infectious diseases and the people died in large numbers every day, the Director of Public Health decided that "the suggestion regarding training of Class-II vaccinators is kept in abeyance pending the publication of results in the recent Sanitary Inspector's examination." The administration continued with compulsory vaccination, ever since the Act was passed, with the help of unqualified vaccinators, primarily because they were not to be paid any extra salary as the qualified vaccinators were to be given. Arnold himself states that native people resented vaccination not because of their opposition to it but because of the cruelty involved in the method of vaccination. According to Arnold, there were severe criticisms in the local administration councils against the unqualified vaccinators who, in the name of vaccination, "were making scratches six inches long on children's arms" so that "the cries of these infants were a most horrible sight." Some members of the council, stated Arnold, while defending the vaccination programme in general, condemned the employment of unqualified vaccinators who made scratches on the arms which appeared like 'ploughed fields'.

Quarantine Policy

The second case in which the Gramscian type of hegemony appeared in its most disconcerting form was the quarantine rules framed under the Native Passenger Ships Act, 1870 and the Epidemic Diseases Act, 1879. These rules distinguished between two types of quarantining: (i) maritime quarantining, and (ii) the quarantining of epidemics-infected local people. The maritime quarantine rule stipulated that all travellers coming in ships from foreign countries, which were reportedly affected by any epidemic disease, should be quarantined at the Indian ports for a minimum period of fifteen days and until a qualified doctor certified that the person in question was completely free from the disease. This rule also insisted that the pilgrims going abroad from India should be subjected to strict medical check up at Indian ports to be sure that they were not carrying any contagious disease with them. These rules were stiffly objected by the ship owners on the ground that: (a) since the quarantine facility was not made by the government but had to be provided by the ship owners, it involved an extra cost for them, and (b) the time taken for medical check up at the port was too long that, in the process, they had to undergo substantial business loss. When the objections mounted, the British administration decided that the maritime rule would be applicable only during May-August, known as 'cholera months'.

When the shipping companies and the chamber of commerce objected to 'such a long period of four months' of medical check up and quarantine policy, government once again diluted the provision. Accordingly, it was announced that Port Officers of Calcutta, Bombay and Madras would inspect the ships coming from infected ports, and only those who were suspected of carrying infectious diseases were to be detained in quarantines. However, as the inspection by port officers was not acceptable to European countries, it was decided to set up Medical Boards in Calcutta and Bombay, the two major ports of India, for the determination of whether travellers coming from abroad were infected and, if so, whether the infection called for quarantining. As this was also objected by the business community, finally, the maritime quarantine was withdrawn fully, giving out two alibi: (i) the government was dispensing with the rules requiring maritime quarantine 'in the interest of public order'; (ii) in India, there was no immigration issue, and the government had nothing to gain from imposing quarantine rules against the foreign nationals coming to this country; and (iii) the volume of trade was much greater in Bombay and Calcutta which make restrictions of any kind, including maritime quarantine, as these were both impracticable and economically undesirable (Harrison, 19920).

The other type of quarantine, more coercively imposed, related to the rules framed under the Epidemic Diseases Act. According to the Act, the buildings in which epidemics affected people resided were to be fully evacuated and the infected persons separated from their families and neighbourhood to isolated tents set up far away so that the disease could not spread to other people. The Act also provided that the infected persons, who were evacuated, should be given accommodation "within reasonable distance with adequate and suitable shelter and necessary water-supply." While doing so, it directed the District Collector concerned to "satisfy himself that such shelter and water-supply have been provided by *private agency*" (emphasis added) and not with public funds.[1] At the same time, there was no provision for arranging medicines to the infected patients, whether or not quarantined, and whether the medicine was sourced from government funds or through private agencies. The native population resented this inhuman quarantine policy, though without raising their voice. The usual practice of the natives was not to reveal certain diseases to the officials, fearing repression that might follow. (This was one of the many reasons why, in British India, famine mortalities remained under-reported).

The most inhuman part of the quarantine policy in British India was that the isolated patients could not get enough food and drinking water in the tents situated at uninhabited areas, as the local administration quite often failed to arrange these from private charities. The only hope for the patients quarantined was their family. However, if it happened during the height of a famine, the family source also dried up. For treatment of the quarantined patients, the families had to rely on the traditional local remedies, knowing fully well that, when the diseases reached the last stage of severity, these were not as effective as western medicines. The people also adopted exorcist practices, with beating of drums and blowing of locally made bugles, to scare away the evil spirit, which they believed had brought the disease. Ultimately, the quarantined patients died for want of food, water and proper medical treatment.

Women's Healthcare

The third case of Gramscian hegemony that we can clearly discern in British India was in the sphere of women's healthcare, child delivery and maternal treatment. European countries had given a pride of place for all aspects of women's healthcare ever since allopathic medicines started progressing on a purely scientific basis. In colonial India, on the other hand, women's health received scant attention from the imperialist rulers.

The hospitals set up by the government were primarily meant for the limited purpose of treating British defence personnel and the Europeans, particularly the British officials and their family members living in India. These hospitals, situated mostly in cantonments, were pre-occupied with the treatment of their "epidemic diseases, communicable diseases in cantonments, civil lines, and plantations, the diseases that threatened European lives, military manpower, and male productive labour." The defence personnel, who were recruited from among the native population, despite being the major military manpower in the colony, did not receive the same treatment in these hospitals, not to speak of their wives and other Indian women at large (see Arnold, 1993).

In later years, however, a few dispensaries (not full-fledged hospitals) were opened in British India. These were too insufficient to meet the needs of the civilian healthcare. The extent of scarcity of allopathic medical facilities in the colony could be judged from the fact that, by the beginning of the twentieth-century, there was, on average, just one dispensary within every 330 square miles, catering to more than one lakh people. Moreover, these dispensaries were primarily male-oriented. Only generalist male doctors, mostly of British origin, got appointments. These doctors insisted that they alone would attend women in labour, arguing that female doctors were not capable of doing such arduous jobs like attending to gynaecological duties. (The actual fact behind this argument was that, if female doctors were appointed, they might lose a covetous source of extra income). The native people, both men and women, resented the male doctors' presence at women in labour for child delivery and making deeper physical check-up of women during the post-natal period. There were demands for appointment of female doctors for such services. British civil surgeons working in Indian hospitals and dispensaries stoutly resisted the demand, arguing that women were capable of working only as paramedical staff to assist male doctors.

There were other reasons for the women from Indian families to spurn the services of government dispensaries even if the treatments did not require too much body-touch for diagnosis, namely, respiratory diseases, malaria, cholera, dysentery and diarrhoea, ulcers, skin diseases, rheumatism, and attacks of worms. The dispensaries run by the government were asylums for almost entirely of 'the mendicant classes' belonging to beggars, pilgrims and criminals, "the very dregs of the society." They came to these dispensaries to seek a home, food and shelter. Secondly, the police regularly brought prostitutes apprehended from streets to these dispensaries for the treatment of venereal diseases. Their presence offended women patients from respectable households, not only of 'high status' but also from among the poor, and they stoutly resisted to take treatments offered in these dispensaries. The only recourse for them was to approach the traditional Indian midwives, called *dais*, who used 'barbaric' and often dangerous techniques to conduct child delivery. In most of these cases, both child and mother died at the time of delivery (Arnold, 1993).

Indigenous Medicines

The fourth case of hegemony was reflected in the British attitude towards indigenous medical practices in India. During the imperialist period, India had three widely popular systems of medicines, which existed side by side with one another, catering to the needs of people according to their beliefs and convictions in the efficacy of the system: (i) *ayurveda*, sourced from age-old Sanskrit texts by certain elites in the social hierarchy and patronised by the wealthy for their healthcare; gradually it became popular with all classes of people; (ii) *siddha* medicine, which originated from ancient Tamil scriptures, was practiced by every section among of the people, particularly belonging to the lower rung of the society; and (iii) *unani*, based on the teachings of the Greek physician, Hippocrates, and the Roman physician, Galen, was developed later into an elaborate medical system by the Arab and Persian physicians; it was since adopted and even now practiced by *hakims* of northern India. All the three originated centuries ago and expanded qualitatively over time through the experience acquired from experimentations on the patients by the practitioners. They passed on their knowledge to selected family members from generation to generation. The most notable common feature of these medical systems was that, while treating the ailment, rejuvenation of the body of the individual under treatment also received attention. These treatments were generally clubbed with black magic or exorcism to scare away evil spirits, which they believed had brought the ailment into the human body. Clubbing exorcism with medical treatment was more common with *siddha* than with *ayurveda*, essentially wherever subaltern sections constituted the main patrons.

In British Malabar, *Ayurveda* was the most popular and perhaps the only medical practice widely prevalent since the pre-colonial period. Along with *ayurveda*, another indigenous health promotion practice that prevailed in Malabar was *Kalarippayattu*, a combination of ayurvedic treatments and physical training in the art of combats. It was (and is even now) practised on an arena (*kalari*) bedecked with weaponry, such as swords, shields, daggers, spears, and a variety of wooden staffs and stickers. Its origin could be traced to the Chera-Chola period and afterwards re-emerged more powerfully during the British era in Tellicherry as a reaction against the colonial rule. At this stage, men, women and children had practised this health-promoting physical training-cum-art of fighting (see McDonald

2007; Weiss 2009; and Ganesan 2010)[12]. Anticipating that it could be a threat to law and order as well as to the British rule, all *kalari*s in Malabar were legally banned by the colonial administration (McDonald, 2007).

As against *Kalarippayattu*, which was ruthlessly suppressed, the attitude of the colonial rulers towards indigenous medical practices was somewhat different. Initially, the EIC used to encourage its officials to go for local medicines rather than preferring for the costly allopathic drugs to be imported from abroad, understandably because the burden of medical expenses to be reimbursed to the officials by the administration on indigenous medicines was lower than on imported allopathic medicines. Subsequently, however, the money-centred approach that favoured the indigenous medicines was replaced by the imperialist interest in promoting western medicine as the only universal healthcare system in the entire third world colonies. At the same time, the colonial administration was conscious of the fact that suppression of the age-old systems of indigenous medical practices like *ayurveda* for establishing *allopathy* in its place might not be very easy. Therefore, it devised a multi-pronged strategy. To begin with, it decided to project 'modern allopathy against primitive *ayurveda*' among the English-educated natives. For this purpose, it drafted western medical practitioners and pliable Indians to write pro-allopathic articles in respected journals like Indian Medical Gazette, Journal of Ayurveda and Hindu System of Medicine, and British Medical Journal.[13] On getting the unique opportunity to publish in well-known journals, these writers competed with one another to propagate that the indigenous medicines were not only inferior to allopathic drugs but also unscientific, degenerate and superstitious. They asserted through their writings that the government should not spend public money to foster indigenous medical practices like *ayurveda* in India as that would be a waste (Varier, 2002; Weiss, 2007; Ganesan, 2010).

These writers further argued that the rapid progress and spread of western medicine had already made claims to superiority of indigenous medicines rather anachronistic and self-deceptive. For the native population, therefore, the choice should be between scientific progress and the Indian backwardness immersed in obsolete absurdities and metaphysical rut. One pro-British Indian writer, who was associated with the public health service of the Madras presidency, contented that "the method of patient research into the causation, treatment and control of diseases pursued by western medicine must remain the sheet anchor for man in his fight against ill-health....the Indian systems represent a stage of arrested development, while the western medicine is dynamic with all the life of a growing organism."[14] The indigenous medical systems were, apart from being practised by unqualified quacks in conjunction with exorcism, undependable for certain crucial aspects of healthcare. The illiterate quacks were ignorant about the newly emerging diseases associated with economic progress. Moreover, for ages they unpardonably neglected surgery, which no medical practice could afford to ignore, but they left it for 'local barbers' to perform.[15]

While addressing the educated sections in the colony, the British rulers wanted to administratively and statutorily repress *ayurveda*, the most preferred indigenous medical system prevalent at that time. As a first step in this direction, the government issued a notification suspending the *ayurveda* course in Calcutta Medical College. This was objected by the *ayurvedic* practitioners throughout the country. In 1907 they formed a resistance group, known as the All India Ayurvedic Congress. After two years, they floated the Madras Ayurvedic College as a full fledged institution in the private sector.

To hoodwink these attempts, the British administration enacted, in 1914, the Madras Medical Registration Act, which stipulated that only those who registered under the Act could undertake public practice of *ayurveda*, even if they were qualified from the private sector ayurvedic college at Madras. When all round protests surged against this declaration, the government established the Indian Medical School in 1924 to teach *ayurveda* in the public sector. The graduates passing out from this institution were accorded A-class status under the Act, whereas those who graduated from the prestigious Madras Ayurvedic College in the private sector as well as the traditional ayurvedic practitioners without any institutional training were granted B-class status.

In short, at a time when famine-related epidemics and unnatural mortalities were mounting in the colony, the government, in stead of encouraging the available healthcare facilities, pitted the allopathic doctors against ayurvedic practitioners, and one set of ayurvedic practitioners against another set of ayurvedic practitioners. In the process, the epidemic diseases started flaring up, rather than subsiding, in areas like Malabar. These killer-diseases were not Malabar specific nor did they confine to British India or third world colonies ruled by western powers but had also sprung up and spread in several parts of Europe. The developed countries among them, including Great Britain, could effectively bring them under control by waging concerted battles at more than one front: (i) increasing public investments in sanitation, drinking water supplies, and modern medical research; (ii) at the beginning stages of the outbreak of any epidemic, social scientists in these countries used to write extensively in popular print-media about the dangers that these could unleash on human beings unless the government took prompt action; (iii) use of a sort of *monopsony* power to purchase anti-epidemic medicines in bulk for treatments in the state-run hospitals, so that it could drive down drug prices in the open market to affordable levels for all; and (iv) a marked shift from the 'de-socialised' medical research to the realm of 'social medicines', with the result that, in times of widespread pandemics, people could use these medicines without difficulties. The combined effects of all these developments were the virtual disappearance of most of the epidemics from the developed western world, including Britain, in the beginning of the nineteenth-century.

In the third world colonies, the attitude of the British rulers was entirely different. As far as India was concerned, it gave one excuse or the other and desisted from spending on sanitation, supply of safe drinking water, control of food prices to remove 'hidden hunger' and related deficiency diseases, or establishment of hospitals and dispensaries to treat widespread epidemics in the colony. Whenever demands for such development programmes came up, the government made several excuses: (a) the native people by nature being unclean, there was no point in spending on environmental sanitation; (b) when the available hospitals and dispensaries were not used by the people who believed more in exorcism than in English medicines, additional investments in medical care was meaningless; and (c) even otherwise, resources available with the government were too meagre to maintain treatment facilities for so vast a population as in India. This attitude, however, was not India-specific. Observers who closely watched the conditions of the third world colonies ruled by England had noted that the wrong imperialist policy was fundamentally responsible for the spread of several virulent epidemics in these colonies. Their perceptions of epidemic diseases that sprang up in third world countries from time to time were "biased, false and delusional" (Watts, 1997).

The real reasons for this rested elsewhere. In fact, the tax revenue collected from the colony was more than enough to maintain environmental sanitation and medical facilities needed for the native population, after meeting the administrative expenses. Every additional expense incurred in the colony meant a *pro tanto* slow down in the imperialist expansion. Therefore, to achieve its paramount objective, the colonial rulers imposed, as we explained earlier, a combination of hegemony-cum-parsimony. Before concluding this chapter, we will take two specific examples to clarify the point further: one from Arnold (1993), and the other from the archival records of British Malabar.

According to Arnold, the declared stand of the British administration about the establishment of hospitals, involving heavy capital investment and long-term recurring over-head costs, was that it would consider the same in case the requisite funds came from public subscriptions and individual philanthropy, just as the practice followed in England. Taking this as an official promise, the residents of Calcutta, both British and Indian, mooted a proposal to set up a 'fever hospital'. They collected Rs 52,000 from the public for the purpose and submitted along with an application to the presidency. All of a sudden, there was a change in the attitude of the government. George Eden, the First Earl of Auckland, known as Lord Auckland was the Governor-General of India (1836-1849) at that time. On receiving the proposal, he constituted a committee to elicit the public opinion. The committee, after conducting a survey, reported that the so-called prejudice of the natives against western medicines and hospitals that the officials used to thump up was an exaggeration. The residents of Calcutta were unanimously in favour of the proposed 'fever hospital'. They were of the view that the hospital, apart from facilitating the treatment of patients suffering from frequent fevers in Calcutta and the neighbouring areas, could act as an urban improvement scheme. Auckland warmly welcomed the proposal but regretted that he could not approve it as a sizable chunk of the construction-cost and future maintenance and recurring expenses might fall on his 'resource-poor' and 'fund-starved' government (Arnold, 1993).

The second example, taken from the archival records, relates to the municipalities of Palghat and Calicut, the two urban centres of Malabar, where the night-soil lying scattered on the ground and polluting the atmosphere created a perennial problem of spreading epidemic diseases. There were two night-soil depots in Palghat and three incinerators in Calicut but not enough scavengers and carts. In view of the public nuisance, the two municipal councils decided to appoint a few more scavengers and procure some additional carts for the removal night-soil. They also proposed three methods for the final disposal of the filth: (i) fill the night-soil in the incinerator, burn down with saw-dust and sell the ash as manure to needy farmers; (ii) if saw-dust was not available, since it was used by locals as fuel for cooking food, they would use an emulsion of carbolic acid and kerosene oil; and (iii) adopt a trench system for the its disposal. The head quarters of Madras presidency found all these proposals unacceptable. The two municipalities were informed that: (a) appointment of additional scavengers and purchase of more carts could not be approved due to revenue constraints; (b) of the three alternatives suggested for the disposal of filth, the first two were too costly to implement; and (c) because of the lack of space in the urban areas of these municipalities, the third alternative was also unworkable. Thus, the filthy, unhealthy condition that existed in the municipalities of Palghat and Calicut continued as such. The people had no escape from the repeated proliferation of contagious diseases but to succumb to unnatural mortalities.

Notes

1. See for example Dutt (1901), Bhatia (1963), and Srivastava (1968)
2. This view is attributed to Hugh Tinker and quoted in Arnold (1993), op.cit. p. 245.
3. Krause has also stated that, in addition to Nightingale, there was another physician, William Farr who collaborated with her for twenty years in this task. He calls both of them together as 'two giants of the Victorian age'.
4. Myrdal (1968), op.cit, Volume III, Chapter 30: *Health* (pp. 1553 – 1620).
5. These figures were quoted by McAlpin (1983) from Mitra (1978), probably to context his claim.
6. The general attitude in the nineteenth-century Europe appeared to be like this. Remember the Colombian Nobel Laureate of 1982, Gabriel Garcia Marquez's well-known novel *Love in the Time of Cholera.*
7. The official documents cited are (i) Report of the Indian Sanitary Commissioner, 1897-1918; and (ii) Report of the Commissioner for Public Health, 1919-30.
8. See, Klein (1988), Part-II, page 734.
9. These figures were quoted by Klein (1988) from Hirst (1953), op.cit.
10. Her writings on these issues appeared in the Anglo-Indian publications, particularly in the *Statesman* of Calcutta to see that these received the attention in India and England. Some of these writings had been compiled and brought out by Priyaranjan Sen (1937), op.cit.
11. These were amended by a notification issued by the Madras Government in 1933 to extend the relevant provision for compulsory evacuation of the epidemics-infected areas. See, Notification: Fort St. George, June 6, 1933 (G.O.No. 1253, P.H) reproduced in Supplement to the Malabar District Gazette, 1933.
12. There were legendary heroes and female warriors who excelled in this martial art such as Thatcholi Othenan, Aromal Chekavar, and Unniyarcha, who are remembered in north Malabar even today.
13. For a large number of writings in these journals, see Ganesan (2010), op.cit.
14. See Ganesan (2010), op.cit for the view as also the quotation given in this paragraph.
15. While commenting on this, David Arnold states that surgery does not constitute an integral part of the treatments under the indigenous systems like Ayurveda, Siddha or Unani. However, as and when facilities for surgery became available in British India, these practitioners had in fact referred their patients to, or patients themselves had approached, the English doctors, for "setting broken bones, excising tumours and cancerous growths, amputating diseased or crushed limbs, removing cataracts, or dealing with ophthalmic cases". Still, Arnold agreed that there might have been cases of local people approaching the indigenous practitioners, not because of their beliefs in those practices but because of the lack of enough hospitals and dispensaries needed for such services (Arnold, 1993).

PART-II

Chapter 6

Entitlement Approach to Famines: Some Comments

6.1 The Meaning

In his *Poverty and Famines* Amartya Sen refuted with empirical evidences, the 'food availability decline', or FAD as an insufficient explanatory variable in the study of famine. He substantiated his arguments with reference to four case studies of the widely quoted famines of the twentieth-century in Africa and South Asia, which we summarised in Chapter-3 for ready reference of the readers[1]. Sen argued that famine may be due to "some people not *having* enough food to eat" but not because "there *being* not enough food to eat." Even when there is enough food to eat there may be some areas in which people do not have enough food to eat so that a famine might erupt. But that is only one of the many reasons. There can be other reasons for famines, which the FAD approach is incapable to explain. Furthermore, devastating famines had occurred when FAD was nowhere in sight. According to Sen, in a free market economy, it is the "failure of exchange entitlement" or FEE that drags a person into starvation and, in extreme cases, into famine (Sen, 1981).

While elaborating the concept of FEE, Sen cautioned that the term 'entitlement' as he used to explain famine is essentially 'descriptive' in nature and, therefore, should not be confused with the term that Robert Nozick used in his well-known 'entitlement theory of justice'. The treatment of the term in Nozick is 'prescriptive' or 'normative' in nature whereas, for him, it is not (Sen, 1981; 1995). To clarify, assume that there is a private ownership market economy. In such an economy, the basic unit of analysis, viz. a representative individual (who represents the entire classes of people like, say, a firm in the industry under perfect competition) faces four different forms of entitlement relations: trade-based entitlement, production-based entitlement, own-labour based entitlement, and inheritance and transfer based entitlement. Taking in the limited sense of a person's entitlement to food we can translate this respectively as buying food, producing food, working for food, and food being given by others (say, by state, relatives, or charity). For the purpose of explaining how famines take place, Sen applies these entitlement relations to three conceptual categories: (i) the *endowment* bundle, (ii) *entitlement* bundle, and (iii) exchange entitlement mapping, or *E-mapping*, for short.

The *endowment* bundle is a combination of all resources, both tangible (land, equipment, seeds, livestock, and so on) and intangible (knowledge, skill, labour-power, citizenship in a country etc), which are available to an individual in an economy through certain rules of legitimacy. The rules may be either formally sanctioned by the state, or bequeathed to the individual in accordance with established social norms, for example, kinship-based inheritance. Taken together, Sen calls them as 'legal entitlement'. The endowment, or ownership, bundle will vary with the type of economic system in which the person lives: socialist, capitalist or feudal. In general we can say that the *endowment* bundle of a peasant consists of his land, equipment, seeds, livestock, labour power etc; that of a labourer, the labour power; of a fisherman, his fishing equipment, labour power, and fishing skill; of an old person or an unemployed individual, his 'citizenship of the country' in which he was born and brought up, so that he deserves certain rights derived from the citizenship.

The *entitlement* bundle is a set of all possible goods and services an individual can obtain against the resources available in his *endowment* bundle. That is why Sen likes to call it 'exchange entitlement' bundle and not simply 'entitlement' bundle. A peasant uses his resources to produce the food he needs, or for the cultivation of commercial crops, which he can exchange for the food he needs; a labourer uses his 'labour power' with which he buys his food; a share-cropper leases-in a plot of land, undertakes cultivation, and the share of the produce that he retains after payment to the landlord is his entitlement; or a fisherman uses his endowment (viz. fishing equipment, labour-power and skill) to catch fish and then exchanges it for the cereal he requires. In other words, a person *exchanges* his *endowment bundle* with the *entitlement bundle* in the form of production, exchange, or transfer.

E-mapping is the function that specifies the set of alternative commodities, including food that a person can command in a market economy with his endowment bundle. That is, *E-mapping* indicates the rate at which the endowment can be converted into entitlement. Considered in traditional economic theory, this means that, in a market economy a person exchanges his endowment bundle at given relative prices for any commodity bundle costing no less, no more. So far as the endowment bundle and the entitlement bundle are in market-clearing equil brium, according to Sen, there will be no starvation and famine. Translated nto the traditional micro-economic theory, we can further simplify this: at the point of intersection of the demand and supply curves, where the market for food that a person requires is in equilibrium, he will not face any starvation or famine. It follows from this that famine occurs when this equilibrium is upset and an unfavourable entitlement relation ensues. In simple term, it means that famines are caused by what is called FEE, or the failure of exchange entitlement.

The FEE occurs in many ways. For example, the person may be having the ownership bundle but the exchange entitlement may not contain any feasible bundle, including food. Similarly, even when the total food supply remains unchanged (that is, FAD is not in sight), a group may face worsening of exchange entitlement and fall into starvation while another group can get hold of the food that is there. This has been explored in *Poverty and Famines* by "going from economic phenomena into social, political and legal issues" (Sen, 1981). The FEE also occurs with a decl ne in employment and wages. That is, if a person's employment possibilit es are affected or his wages fall behind prices of essential items of consumption, the result is FEE and, therefore, starvation and famine. It does not mean that Sen considers FAD approach to famine altogether irrelevant. His argument is that even in cases where a famine is accompanied by a reduction in the per head food availability, the causal mechanism precipitating starvation into famine has to bring in many variables other than food availability. In view of this, Sen states that "the FAD approach gives little clue to the causal mechanism of starvation…Whatever may be the oracular of the FAD view it is certainly Delphic in its reticence" (Sen, 1981). What is significant to note here is that wherever the FAD approach becomes inadequate to explain a famine, Sen proved that the FEE approach would emerge as an eminent framework for its analysis in a free market economy (Osmani, 1995).

Entitlement Theory: Nozick vs Sen

Before Amartya Sen introduced the theory of entitlement to explain famines that engulfed at different times in different parts of the third world countries like India during the last millennium, it was Robert Nozick who developed and applied the concept of entitlement in political philosophy. Sen had indicated more than one occasion that the treatment of the entitlement approach by him and Nozick are not simi ar. The former is 'descriptive' in nature, following the methodology of 'positive economics' in the great tradition of classical economics, that is, a pure value-free description of the causes and effects of famines, supported by strong empirical evidences to substantiate what he described. On the other hand, Nozick's entitlement theory focuses on what 'ought to be' the political role of state-policy under a given situation, and therefore is essentially 'prescriptive' in nature. Recognising this fundamental methodological difference is essential to have a clear perspective of Sen's entitlement approach in the analysis of famine.

Nozick begins his theory, in *Anarchy, State and Utopia*, which was published in 1974 with the statement that in a world which is wholly 'just', a person who acquires a 'holding' (any property) is rightly *entitled* to that holding. If the person acquires the 'holding' through voluntary exchange, then also it is his *entitlement*, provided he has not broken the generally accepted principles of justice in doing so. It is not necessary that every member in the society would follow such unwritten though respectable principles while acquiring a property. "Some people may steal from others, or defraud them, or enslave them, seizing their product and preventing them from living as they choose" (Nozick, 1974: 152). This is unjust and inevitably requires rectification. It is here that the need for a 'minimal state' arises. The minimal state is like a 'night-watchman', whose duty is to just protect all its citizens against violence, theft, fraud and any other violation of justice.

The minimal duty of the 'night-watchman state' also involves compensating those who have been disadvantaged on account of the violation of their rights by others. The extent of compensation to each individual, according to Nozick, should be limited to raising him to his original position on an indifference curve from where he has been unjustly pushed down through violation of the principles of acquisition and transfer of properties by others. The 'night-watchman state' should not go beyond this minimal duty. The rest of what he requires as a citizen should be left to the rational individual behaviour that would strengthen private property in a free market economy, as it would otherwise be, according to Nozick, incompatible with liberty.

We have seen that, like Nozick's theory of entitlement, Sen's theory of 'exchange entitlement' is also envisioned to operate within a private ownership market economy. Just as Nozick does not approve an individual acquiring his entitlement by breaking the generally accepted principles of justice, Sen also disapproves the use of extra legal means, when he states that, "while entitlement relations concentrate on rights within the given legal structure in that society, some transfers involve violations of these rights, such as looting or brigandage. When such extra-entitlement transfers are important, the entitlement approach to famines will be defective. On the other hand, most recent famines seem to have taken place in societies with 'law and order', without anything 'illegal' about the processes leading to starvation" (Sen, 1981:49). In other words, food riots, thefts and other crimes which Sen called 'looting and brigandage', the inevitable concomitance of famines that we observed in Chapter-2, are outside the purview of his theory of entitlement.

Even though Sen does not totally rule out the state intervention or 'public action' in combating famines, he believes in the open market to do the job more effectively than the state on two grounds: First, "the reach and role of the market transactions has substantially expanded in recent time" and "added new economic opportunities and new ways of achieving prosperity." The crucial need of speedy intervention for famine prevention is now possible through the institution of free market, for example, "the operation of private trade stimulated by cash support to famine victims." Second, though the state may be having an important role to play in combating hunger, "many famines in the world have actually arisen from and been sustained by inflexible government policies: the Soviet famines of the 1930s and the Kampuchean famines of the late 1970s are obvious examples" (see Dreze and Sen, 1989).

Nozick and Sen are not only great believers in the efficiency of the free market in protecting the entitlement of each individual but they also apply the same economic tool of analysis to substantiate their points. Economic conditions of the people at any point of time, according to both of them, can be read with reference to an indifference map. While Nozick explicitly uses the indifference map as a criterion for the state to compensate individuals whose rights have been violated by others and pushed them down from their original position, Sen implicitly indicates it with reference to the concept of *e-mapping*, which is defined as a combination of entitlement bundles that an individual can obtain in the market from the endowment bundle he possesses. These combinations taken together are nothing but an indifference map.

However, there is a fundamental difference between the two: While Nozick imposes a 'moral' duty on the state to protect and compensate the entitlement-loss of individuals whose rights are violated by others, Sen simply 'describes' the failure of exchange entitlement in a free market economy that causes famine. Even when Sen observes certain explicit failures on the part of the state in precipitating famine, as he observed in the Bengal famine of 1943, what he does is just to describe the phenomenon without expressing any moral element of indignation. His methodology is to use the objective information based on hard facts and to apply theoretical insights in the tradition of the classical economists.

It would appear at the same time that Nozick and Sen do not apply what is known as the 'Hume's Guillotine', i.e. a watertight logical distinction between positive and normative methodologies in the treatment of their respective concepts of entitlement[2]. For example, Nozick assumes the existence of a free market economy, which consists of a number of 'competitive clubs' of individuals with voluntary entry and exit. Concurrently he gives a role to the state, even if it is 'minimal', to intervene whenever the entitlement of an individual is violated (see Buchanan, 1975). Sen's entitlement theory also assumes to operate in a private ownership market economy. However, the Bengal famine of 1943, as presented in *Poverty and Famines*, occurred at a time when there was hardly any free market. The British administration had been actively intervening in the foodgrains market for procurement, stocking, exports and distribution between the civilians and the defence personnel. To cite a case in point, during the Second World War (1939-45), when the prices of food were skyrocketing on the face of a runaway inflation, the government attempted to bring them under control by fixing the upper and lower limits to the fluctuations in the market prices. It is one thing that neither the upper limit nor the lower limit fixed for the market prices of foodgrains worked as declared, yet another thing that such a policy was in existence (see Raghavan, 1985). At least in this backdrop, we should have expected a value judgment incorporated in the FEE theory of famines.

Nevertheless, Professor Sen is emphatic that his treatment is not at all 'prescriptive'. His position in this respect is that if a human misery like famine is approached in terms of value-judgment, it would primarily become a subjective exercise, "unleashing one's personal morals on the statistics of deprivation." According to Professor Sen, "to describe a prevailing prescription is an act of description, not prescription." This will become clear if we carefully read the way he describes the famines that occurred in different parts of the world. Many famines of the nineteenth and twentieth centuries had gone worse not because of any decline in food availability but because of exports of available food from the affected areas. Professor Sen cites the Irish famine of 1840s, the famine in the Hunan province of China in the early twentieth-century, the Wollo famine and the Bangladesh famine of 1970s being worsened as the available food was exported even in the face of domestic distress. He *just explains* these famines in the tradition of positive economics: "Indeed, in many famines complaints have been heard that, while famine was raging, food was being exported from the famine-stricken countries or regions." Similarly, about the Bengal famine, which became one of the worst human miseries of the last century because of the insensitivity of the British administration in distributing the available food to the people in distress, he states that, "in the Bengal famine of 1943 the people who died in front of well-stocked food shops protected by the state were denied food because of lack of legal entitlement, and not because their entitlements were violated" (Sen, 1981).

6.2 Some Critiques

In recent memory, after J.M. Keynes's *General Theory of Employment, Interest and Money*, no other work has evoked such a barrage of critiques and counter-critiques as Amartya Sen's *Poverty and Famines* generated, especially on the FAD vs FEE approach to famines. The writings on Sen's study of famine is so vast that some commentators have stated that just as Adam Smith is associated with the phrase 'invisible hand' and Joseph Schumpeter with 'creative destructions', Amartya Sen is associated with the subject of 'famine', albeit his several other notable basic contributions in economics and other branches of social science, because he has completely changed how economists until then thought about famine (Massing, 2003). However, while debating on this collective catastrophe by different authors in the context of Sen's *Poverty and Famines*, the concept of famine itself has deflected away from his original focus. Some of the comments by the critics runs like this: (i) famine is not a sudden development, but an intensification of the normal economic process; (ii) excess mortality is not a prerequisite for famine; (iii) deaths during famines are related more to epidemics than to hunger and malnutrition; and (iv) mass starvation is only one indicator of famine while there are others like fertility and fecundity decline, economic destitution, breakdown of community network, and distress migration. What is more intriguing is that the interpretation has deflected to the extent of saying that FAD and FEE are nothing but same, i.e. when there is a decline in food availability and many people lose the ability to access food, or their 'entitlement' to food, both the views of famine become remarkably similar (see Mukherjee, 2014). Nonetheless, the centre of all debates remains on Sen's assertion that famines are triggered less by FAD but more by FEE (see Devereux, 2000).

Apart from these 'deflections', the entitlement approach has been subjected extensively to critiques and counter-critiques. Some authors have classified these as: (a) favourable assessments, (b) less favourable reassessments, (c) critiques, (d) refutation, and (e) outright dismissal as a theoretical failure (see, Osmani, 1995; Devereux 2000; 2001). It appears that there is no end to strident criticisms of the FEE theory of famine. For instance, Fine (2004) argues that the entitlement approach is individualistic in methodology whereas famine is a collective human misery. While this is what Sen also postulated and therefore unexceptionable, Fine further argues that Sen's analytics are not food-specific or specific to starvation and famine alone; it can be equally applicable to the rich and their luxurious consumption. Some of these points have already been highlighted in Chapter-3 in the backdrop of the FAD approach to famine. Here we will selectively consider a few other major critiques which are directly associated with the FEE theory or with the host of other issues coming up in the book as a whole.

The earliest major review of *Poverty and Famines* that appeared in India was that of Ashok Mitra, whose comments, no doubt, might be harsh though not 'antagonistic' as some writers have accused (see Osmani ,1995; Devereux, 2001). There are important arguments in Mitra's review that cannot be sidelined. The basic causes of famine, which is the terminal point of poverty are, according to Mitra: (i) a failure of output and the absence of any worthwhile mechanism for equitable distribution of whatever has been produced; (ii) even when there is no shortfall in production, or the shortfall is marginal, the poor starve and, often, starve to death because: (a) they are short of purchasing power to acquire food; and (b) the food prices shoot up while the purchasing power of the poor to buy food does not correspondingly rise, with the result that the terms-of-trade between wage-labour and wage-goods turn against the former. It is the outcome of this process that leads, in extreme cases, to famines. Even when the decline in output is not discernible, famines can happen.

Mitra compliments Sen for his 'forte for detailed empirical research'. In this context, he further states that "despite clinical rigour in which the book describes the famines" in Bengal and other selected countries, "it is difficult to dispel the impression that basic data from countries are put to use as raw material for rarefied research in the milieu of the rich." To support this contention, Mitra states that "the monograph is careful not to relate the problem of poverty and famines to the phenomenon of asset and income inequalities" (Mitra, 1982).

The second major critique of the book came from Utsa Patnaik. We have already noted her argument that Professor Sen's thesis of famines occurring not due to FAD but due to FEE is 'in itself perfectly correct' and that fixing the causation of famines on decline in the exchange entitlements 'is a very necessary antidote to neo-Malthusian naiveté' (see U. Patnaik, 1991). The irrational and anti-developing-country stance that the West held had sustained the FAD view of famine for a long time. Introduction of a more reasonable and powerful FEE theory in its place has in fact elevated the discussions on famines since the publication of *Poverty and Famines* to an intellectually higher pedestal. At the same time, while defending this new approach to the analysis of famines, she disagrees with the definition of food availability that Sen applied, which we have already discussed in Chapter-3.

Her expression, 'neo-Malthusian naiveté' seems to require some elaboration. The entrenched belief in England among the administrators and a section of the academic community was that famines in developing countries in general and in India in particular resulted from the 'Malthusian imbalance', created by their population increasing at geometric progression as against food production increasing at arithmetic progression. Following this belief, the British administration in India stuck to the view that famine was a natural check on population and that famine relief operation was a waste of wealth (Caldwell, 1988). Likewise, some of the British economists argued that the civilisation of Western Europe does not and will not permit its population to increase beyond any economically advantageous optimum level. As against this, in India, the population tended to multiply out of 'the animal instinct predominating over foresight and enterprise'. Early marriages among Indians, coupled with the British government's decision to abolish 'widow burning' and female infanticide further strengthened the tendency for population-explosion, especially since the second half of the nineteenth century (see Loveday, 1914).

One point of her disagreement is that, in all the case studies, Sen considers a short period of two to three years to show that food production and availability in these countries did not decline, and if at all, the decline was too small to explain the intensity of those famines. In this context, Patnaik states: "In order to monitor and identify what might be termed a 'pre-famine conjuncture' with the objective of intervention to avert actual outbreak of famine, it is quite essential to track long-run trends in food production and availability per head, which in most underdeveloped countries have been profoundly affected by the commercialisation of agriculture and by resource transfers......However much we may reject – quite correctly – short-run weather-induced output decline as the 'explanation' of famine, we may underestimate at our peril the long-run trends of declining food production at the cost of increasing commercial crop production, or the monetisation of food production itself, which has physically reduced availability for the rural poor" (U. Patnaik, 1991).

This happened because, according to her, the British era had witnessed a growing trend towards shifting the area under food crops to commercial crops and the commercialisation of certain foodgrains consumed by local people to meet the growing metropolitan demands It would be a grave error, she argued, to ignore the consequent long-term decline in per capita food availability, which continues even today. Quoting from several authoritative sources, she showed that from around 200 kg per head in the triennium ending 1918, the per capita food production in British India collapsed to 150 kg at the time of independence. Adjusting for net imports, the decline in food availability for Greater Bengal (Bengal, Bihar and Orissa), which witnessed in 1943 one of the most disastrous famines, saw a 38 per cent fall. Compared to this, the commercialisation programme was so strong that the total non-foodgrains production expanded at an annual trend rate of growth of 0.11 to 1.31 per cent. During the same period, real per capita national income remained stagnant around Rs 260, estimated at 1948-49 prices. Even if we assume that, during these years, the income distribution remained unchanged, given zero change in real income per head means a steep pushing down of substantial sections of rural population below subsistence levels. She has asserted in several of her studies that this was not the experience of India alone but of all British colonies (see, U. Patnaik, 2000).

Another point of her disagreement with Sen related to the lumping together of highly unequal social classes under a common concept of 'endowment' in order to compare with 'exchange entitlement' vis-à-vis his e-mapping. Only a disaggregated analysis can identify the extent of 'famishment' being suffered by different rural classes[3]. In order to prove this point, she presents a 'highly stylised categorisation' of the rural population and the manner in which deflation of farm harvest prices and inflation of secondary market prices may be expected to affect different categories of population: (a) the *landlords*, who do not participate in manual labour at all but commanding substantial land and other assets, which they lease out to tenant-farmers and share a part of the produce; (b) *rich peasants*, participating in manual labour but with excess land and other resources, permitting them to rely mainly on non-family labour for cultivation to obtain a surplus; (c) *middle peasants*, who are well-to-do sections among the self-employed peasants, meeting ends normally and employing hired labour to a minor extent; (d) *small peasants*, the less viable section of the self-employed peasants, unable to make ends meet from their cultivation always and occasionally working for others as well; (e) *poor peasants* with even less land and livestock than small peasants, obliged to work for others as hired workers or petty tenants to a small extent and obtain the necessary income; and (f) *landless labourers*, entirely dependent on working for others, notably the landlords and rich peasants. She further clarified the distributional impact that emerged while looking at these class categories separately rather than all of them in a single group: "The point is that the different classes of the rural population (defined by their differing command over means of production and over assets generally, and their associated pattern of labour use) are affected in quite different ways by a given trend, say, in the prices of necessities, even when they might have the same occupation" (U.Patnaik, 1991).

The third criticism of the entitlement theory came from Amrita Rangasami, who argued that there are two weaknesses in the FEE theory of famine. One is that Sen has treated famine as an 'episode', 'an aberration in the economic history of the region or country' leaving out long-term processes that culminate suddenly into a calamitous famine. Such an approach, she stated, might be sufficient to get to know the famine at its terminal point but not its recurrence over time (Rangasami, 1985). It is significant to note here that this point was also raised by many other critics, particularly Muqtada (1981), Arnold (1988), and U. Patnaik (1991). Commenting on this criticism, Osmani (1995) points out that "for his immediate purpose it was not necessary for Sen to look deeply into history. His immediate purpose, it will be recalled, was to demonstrate the power of entitlement approach over the FAD approach."

Rangasami's other criticism is that there is nothing new in Sen's entitlement theory of famines. The Famine Code of 1883 promulgated by the British administration in India had already articulated this theory, though not using the same terminology. According to Rangasami, Sen has only 'baptized' various types of tenures described in the Famine Code as 'endowment'; people's economic rights in land dealt with in Famine Code are what Sen has called 'entitlement'. The Famine Code not only described the 'entitlement mapping' but also the tensions that underlie the asymmetric exchange relations between 'endowment' and 'entitlement'. She claimed that, what Amartya Sen has done was to 'juxtapose' these ideas into 'endowment', 'entitlement' and 'exchange entitlement mapping'. This is a wild criticism. It is as good as saying that Karl Marx's *Das Capital* is a juxtaposed version of Adam Smith's *Wealth of Nations* and Ricardo's *Principles of Political Economy*.

The fourth and the last critique of entitlement approach that we will consider here is that of Devereux, who brings together most other criticisms of the entitlement approach to famine in his review of Sen's *Poverty and Famines*. Devereux argued that, despite the term 'entitlement' sounds 'normative' in implication, Sen has reduced it to a descriptive analysis without going for any value judgement whatsoever. In this context, he states that "there is something odd – at best uncomfortable, at worst "defective"– "with an analytical approach that appropriates a normative term like entitlement and strips it of all ethical connotations" (Devereux, 2001). His other disagreement with the entitlement theory is highlighted by referring to Edkins (1996): In Sen's framework, people who become destitutes by famine would appear not entitled to food but instead entitled to starvation.

When Sen dispenses with normative aspect of famine what he has actually rejected is the right to food that any person commands from the state where he is born and lives as a citizen.

6.3 Role of the State

Though Amartya Sen articulates his FEE theory of famine in the milieu of a private ownership market economy, he does not altogether reject or disregard the role of the state in combating famine, as some critics have argued. However, the state's function in dealing with hunger and malnutrition in his analysis, as appearing in *Poverty and Famines*, is rather minimal. For such a role to arise for the state, according to Sen, two conditions are necessary: One, a person's entitlement, which is based on his own-labour, own-production and exchange or trade in the market, should fail to fetch him subsistence. Two, the person should not possess inheritance-based entitlement to food. Whenever these options are all exhausted, the state has to take the responsibility, in terms of the entitlement theory, to protect the citizenship-right of the person, which entails, among other things, freedom from hunger.

Later, in another authoritative work by Amartya Sen (in collaboration with Jean Dreze) surveyed the famines of a large number of countries in Asia, Africa and Latin America, and concluded that famine cannot be seen in isolated individual terms. Their investigation revealed that the positive involvement of the state in the management of food supply is often more effective in removing deprivation than leaving it to private trade. The role of the state in eradicating hunger and destitution, thus, comes to the central stage with a more emphatic focus, as against *Poverty and Famines* envisages a subsidiary role, that itself only after all other options in the private ownership market economy are exhausted. The terminology that they use now is not 'role of the state' but a more comprehensive expression, 'public action'. According to the authors, "by public action we mean not merely the activities of the state, but also social actions taken by members of the public – both collaborative (through civic cooperation) and 'adversarial' (through social criticism and political opposition). The state does, of course, have a major role to play in eradicating famines and in eliminating persistent deprivation, and the various aspects of this role we have tried to discuss fairly extensively in the light of general reasoning and empirical evidence" (Dreze and Sen, 1989).[4]

It is interesting to note that the types of states that they picked up for analysis included: (i) the well-known 'interventionist' states like China, Costa Rica, Jamaica, and Sri Lanka; (ii) the proclaimed market-oriented economies, such as Hong Kong, Singapore and South Korea;[5] (iii) a number of countries which successfully prevented famines through state intervention, though politically they were widely varied as Burkina Faso, Cape Verde, Kenya, Lesotho, Mali, Mauritania, Niger, Tanzania, Uganda, Zimbabwe, Botswana and even to some extent Chad and Ethiopia. From these countries they selected specific cases of Cape Verde, Kenya, Zimbabwe, and Botswana which had been experiencing grim episodes of repeated droughts and famines but could effectively avert those miseries through direct state support.[6]

Dreze and Sen further divided these politically and economically heterogeneous states into two broad categories: (i) those which adopted specially focused policies that increasingly expanded the state support for social and economic development; and (ii) those which pursued growth-centered policies that brought about 'unaimed opulence' on the assumption that economic growth in any way would 'trickle down' and raise the wellbeing of all. It was found that the first set of states could improve the living conditions and prevent hunger and deprivation much easily. The morbidity pattern of the people in these countries underwent radical transformations so that there was considerable decline in the infectious and parasitic diseases. Consequently, their life expectancy at birth also went up to the level achieved in western countries, particularly Great Britain and Germany. On the other hand, the second set of selected states, which were numerically larger in number, showed their policies leading to extremely sluggish improvement in the quality of life. Furthermore, there was no visible improvement in the life expectancy of the people. Even though they could achieve high macro-economic growth, that growth could not control simultaneous increase in undernutrition and morbidity among larger sections of the population.

Regarding the first set of states, which could eradicate famines once and for all, the authors stated that this was not achieved via economic growth. In fact the rates of growth of the Gross Domestic Product (GDP) of these countries were far less than those of the second set of countries. These states also exhibited great diversity in their political and economic regimes. Following are some of the notable lessons that the authors would like to draw for the information of the policy makers who want to pursue developmental efforts for the fight against hunger and famine.

First of all, the state-support to prevent or mitigate famines could be in the form of providing both direct and indirect social security. The direct social support that the state can provide to the victims of famine includes supply of free food and provision of cash with which they can access food from the market. It may also include the provision of unemployment insurance, free health services and basic education. The indirect social security that all forms of states (capitalist, socialist or mixed economies) offers to prevent famine are: (a) the creation of conditions for overall economic growth, and (b) planning a growth strategy that enables widespread participation of the population (called these days as 'inclusive growth'). These are means by which a rise in the economic welfare of the people gets assured. In elaboration, the authors state that the protection of food entitlements by the state encompasses gratuitous feeding, food distribution at subsidised rate, public works, cash doles, price control, tax relief, crop insurance, support to prices of livestock (which act as entitlement to food) from falling below certain critical minimum levels, etc.

All these successful regimes did not belong to the so called *dirigiste* states which, on becoming independent in the first half of the twentieth century, vowed to create a 'socialist pattern of society' by the adoption of the former Soviet-type economic planning. The achievement of the states was recorded during the closing phase of the twentieth century when the 'retreat of the state' from direct developmental activities or poverty alleviation programmes was a new global shibboleth. Even during this historical turning point, the study by Dreze and Sen showed that public action has not abdicated its role in combating endemic deprivation. This was equally true in the case of some of the proclaimed market economies.

It is a well-known fact that, in recent times, all big and small events taking place in any corner of the world is brought to the information of the public by the mainstream media. However, when governments attempt to direct their policies, and succeed in the prevention of hunger and malnutrition, it is unlikely that the media would even casually mention them in their reports. To cite an example, referring to the widespread African famine of 1983-85, there were many "worthwhile but under-reported successes in famine prevention in Africa, most of them involving large-scale government intervention." Carried away by the ongoing market fundamentalism, the mainstream media conveniently ignored or underplayed these achievements. Therefore, the people outside these countries failed to know about these success stories (Dreze and Sen, 1989).

Indigenous State vs Imperialist State

But there is a difference. Dreze and Sen were citing the positive involvement of the indigenously formed sovereign states in eliminating persistent deprivation and prevention of famines in their respective countries. Among the most successful four countries in their case studies, Kenya became independent in 1963 and has since been ruled by the government formed by an elected parliament. The island nation of Cape Verde, after getting independence in 1975, has been under the rule of a single-party with a socialist orientation. Zimbabwe has a limited multiparty-party democracy since 1980, when it became free from colonial rule. Botswana is another nation with a highly democratic political system[7]. These governments might be functioning mainly to protect their class interests and, in the process, holding down and exploiting the rest of the society in some other ways. Nonetheless, these regimes, irrespective of whether they are democratically elected or not, were aware that they had to meet certain minimum popular expectations, if not for anything else, for their own continuance in power. History gives several examples, including from the very recent past, of how the regimes which were not responsive to the minimum needs, especially freedom from hunger, of the people had to pack off from power either through bloodshed or through ballots. What we have observed in the four case studies cited by Dreze and Sen are examples of the governments established, after becoming independent from foreign powers, their own governments and directly intervened to eradicate famines. Along with that, they also got the legitimacy to pursue their own class domination without interruption.

Britain: A Classic Case

On the other hand, what we are considering here is the role of a foreign imperialist power, viz., Great Britain, in dealing with the miseries wreaked by repeated famines in different parts of India, including mostly unreported floods and famines in Malabar, during the colonial era. In fact, Britain did not have a uniform socio-economic policy for itself and for others. A closer consideration would reveal that it had apparently three strands of policy approaches: one for Great Britain; the second for its federating units, i.e. Scotland and Ireland; and the third for its colonial empires erected in Asia, Africa and Latin America. In the first case, the British government was more pro-active in protecting its citizens from poverty and hunger and in maintaining certain decent level of living in line with its economic development, irrespective of whether historically the country followed a laissez-faire policy or a policy of welfare state. In the second case, Britain wanted a homogeneous society in United Kingdom. Therefore, it was always eager to get an opportunity for 'ethnic cleaning', particularly in Ireland and Scotland. Whenever a collective human misery like famine struck in these federating units, Great Britain consciously permitted it to escalate and take away as many lives as possible. In the last case, as Britain had established the third world colonies by the use of force with imperialist motives and continued to annex more and more territories by force, it could not be expected to have any empathy for the sufferings of the people in these colonies.

An understanding of these three different policy approaches is essential to recognise, in our view, how Malabar suffered the most from some of the famines it encountered during the British Crown-rule. Let us consider the history of anti-poverty and social welfare policy measures adopted by England for the people within Great Britain (i.e. barring its federating units of Scotland and Ireland). These policy measures took shape in three fairly broad phases: (i) from the closing decade of the seventeenth century to the First World War; (ii) during the inter-war period; (iii) from the Second World War and after.

(i) Seventeenth Century to the First World War

Students of European economic history should be aware that, since the Glorious Revolution of 1688, when a union of parliamentarians overthrew James II, the then King of Ireland, Britain had been in fact moving on to the direction of a liberal society and building an economy based on "low government expenditure, low taxation, and minimum state activity" (see Stewart, 1967). During these years, the British government used to declare that, being an open economy, market should take care of the people's welfare. Despite such repeated pronouncements, it was extremely careful not to push the people of Great Britain into sufferings from poverty and malnutrition. Side by side with the 'free market' policies, the government continued to declare several social welfare measures, which some authors have characterised as a classic case of 'welfare before welfare state' (Gladstone, 1999). However, these measures were implemented with extreme care, without disturbing the functioning of the free-market. As a leading global power at that time, Britain not only experimented with mercantilism, free-trade and laissez-faire systems but also succeeded in persuading other countries in Europe to follow in these steps. For this purpose, it entered into separate free-trade agreements with each of the developed European countries so that they could mutually dispense with tariffs and other barriers to trade. By that time, as England was industrially far ahead of other countries in Europe, the actual beneficiary of these agreements was effectively the British economy. As against this, to conduct free trade with its vast colonial empire, there was no need for entering into any formal agreement. Its right to trade with the colonies arose from the right that it wrested from the colonies to govern by the use of the imperialist might.

In the mercantilist era, especially in the eighteenth-century, the British attempt was to ensure all-round welfare for the domestic economy through free international trade and the operation of a free-market system within the country. Thus, Britain encouraged its merchants to carry on the overseas trade, which resulted in huge inflow of gold into the country. Maintenance of the stability of the inflow of wealth into Britain was accepted by the government as its responsibility. For this purpose Britain adopted Gold Standard through which the exchange rate between Pound Sterling and the currencies of the trading countries was fixed without undue fluctuations. In return for facilitating the merchant community for their highly profitable international trade, the government claimed a share of the inflow in terms of taxes and duties. The huge revenue that it obtained through the imposition of import and export duties in this way was put to use mainly for two purposes, namely, (a) to strengthen the Royal Navy, which was instrumental in capturing and building British colonies in North America; the most lucrative sugar plantation islands of Trinidad and Tobago, Bahamas, Barbados, Jamaica, and Bermuda; and the third world countries like India; and (b) to import large quantities of food at cheaper rates from abroad and dump into the domestic market so that it could ensure all-round social welfare and economic prosperity without compromising the declared free-market policy. Though, subsequently, Britain lost its most prosperous colony of North America at the American War of Independence (1775-1783), this did not seriously affect the British economy because the loss could be made up through the vastly expanded overseas-trade with the European countries (see Floud and McCloskey, 1994).

The indirect prosperity that the free-market provided to the masses through a carefully designed trade and fiscal policy mix was further strengthened by the British government directly extending a number of welfare services for the protection and security of workers and other citizens, particularly women, children and old-aged people. Initially, these welfare services were entrusted for implementation to the local administrations. Over time, the public demand for the declared welfare services started multiplying and the local administrations found it difficult to meet the rising demand from their limited sources of funds. Therefore, the central government itself took over the implementation of these welfare programmes even while declaring that Britain was a laissez-faire state. This double-speak prompted some of the recent writers to remark that the 'administrative laissez-faire' that Britain implemented was nothing but 'ameliorative state intervention'. It may be noted here that while the leftists in England praised these attempts as a correct step in the promotion of 'welfare state', those who stood for the free-market welcomed it as a stabilisation measure necessary for the smooth functioning of the laissez-faire economy. The support of the latter continued, even when the government went on increasing the number of legislations to deal with the growing problems created by the expansion of private industry and trade (see Winch, 1969; Harris, 1992).

Considering the next historical phase, i.e., the nineteenth and early twentieth centuries, the British economy was the most eventful, compared to any other period before and after: (i) it abandoned mercantilism and in its place embraced laissez-faire; (ii) the shift from the 'enclosure movement' and agrarian revolution to Industrial Revolution, though began much earlier, reached its zenith in the nineteenth-century; and (iii) there was an explosive increase in employment both in the manufacturing and shop-floor establishments. In the backdrop of these developments, even when laissez-faire was holding sway, the Parliament of United Kingdom enacted a series of Factory Acts between 1802 and 1896 to regulate the working conditions of various types of industrial workers, to set uniform standards in the appointment and working-hours of children and women, and to prohibit employment of children below certain age in organised industries and shop-floors. Thus, the closing years of the nineteenth-century witnessed rising demands in England for working-class houses and educational institutions, old-age pension, health-care, school-meals, and for nationalisation of railways and cheap railway fares. The government conceded most of these demands by the early twentieth-century. The anti-poverty-cum-social-welfare measures put in place during this period included: (a) the introduction of school-meals in 1906, (b) compulsory medical check-ups in schools in 1907, and (c) old-age pension and unemployment insurance in 1911 (Whiteside, 1984). To be fair, some authors argued that in the last few decades before the First World War, Britain had actually retreated from the policy of undiluted laissez-faire, recognising that no government could ignore the need for social welfare reforms if it wanted to progress (Smales, 1975). However, what we notice here is that this recognition had always existed since the closing phase of the fifteenth century.

During the era of the Tudors and Stuarts, famines were viewed not only as natural economic disasters but also as arising from political indifference. To begin with, the British Crown tried to control the abuse of weights and measures used by unethical private traders. However, the traders fiercely objected the move on the grounds that by the introduction of uniformity throughout England, the Central Government was attempting to usurp the rights of the local administration. In support of the argument of the private traders, the British Parliament passed a legislation which made it impossible for the Crown to bring about any uniform system. Nonetheless, in years of grain shortages, the Centre stoutly over-ruled the objections of the traders and issued detailed instructions to the local magistrates to see that private dealers had not overstocked or over-priced. Specific measures were spelt out by the Central Government as to how food prices should be controlled. By this time, just as the official orders, the follow-up measures were systematically drawn up and implemented.

These policy interventions facilitated to wipe out famine and famine-related epidemics from Britain. Several authors had noted that it was not because of better weather, or any marked improvement in agricultural technology but because of the positive involvement and focussed pol cy of the British government that eliminated malnutrition and famine in their homeland (see Fogel, 1992)

(ii) Inter-War Period

The next phase of the British economic history, falling in the inter-war period, witnessed free-trade giving way to protectionism, and the state becoming more involved in public investment, technolog cal innovations, and more equitable distribution of income and wealth. A noticeable trend after the First World War was a fundamental transformation in the objective of commodity production basically away from the needs of international trade towards predominantly the needs of British domestic market. Despite the war arresting the external trade and the growth of real national income, some estimates showed that "the people (in Great Britain) ate twice as much milk, fish, vegetables and fruits; spent twice as much on cloths and fuel, and nearly three times as much on entertainment, and nearly four times as much on household furnishing and equipment" (Abrams, 1946).

This period also witnessed an enormous increase in British public expenditure partly because of the repayment of huge finances involved in the First World War and partly because of the continuance of its extensive social welfare expenses. Immediately after the First World War, the budget deficits of the exchequer shot up as, by then, he was overburdened with the obligations for: (i) repayment of war-loans with interest thereon; (ii) pension-payment to disabled ex-servicemen and war-widows; (iii) the fulfilment of war-time pledges given to the army-men that the government would build 'houses for heroes'; (iv) unprecedented increase in unemployment benefits; (v) institutional care for a range of infectious diseases; and (vi) financing of national health insurance schemes for the sick and the elderly. As taxes, which were already high, could not be raised further, there was no way to bridge the gap in the rising revenue demands over public expenditure other than by incurring budget deficits.[8] To make matters worse, public investment and therefore domestic employment nose-dived. Furthermore, the Great Depression that originated in the United States in the early 1930s started spreading out and terribly engulfing the British economy along with other non-socialist economies of the world.

To find a solution to the serious challenges facing the economy, the then Labour Government decided to set up a committee under the chairmanship of Sir George May. The report of the committee *inter alia* recommended a drastic cut in the existing unemployment benefits and high salary of the public servants. It appeared that England was again becoming, as at the time of Ricardo and Malthus, an "experimental laboratory for economic theory" (Screpanti and Zamagni, 2005). The report was widely criticised. Keynes described it as "the most foolish document I have ever had the misfortune to read."[9] The government, therefore, refused to accept the report. Keynes had been calling for stepping up of public investment (instead of waiting for the private capitalists to take the responsibility) and building houses, harbours, rails and roads that could create more and more employment for the idle capital and unemployed workers in the country. This remedy, which was fruitfully applied in the U.S. by President Roosevelt through the New Deal and got rid of the problems unleashed by the Great Depression also found no acceptance not only to the political class running the government but also to a large section of the intelligentsia in the country, necessarily because they feared that such a policy would convert England into Stalin's Russia or Hitler's Germany (Stewart, 1967).

(iii) Second World War and After

In the absence of fresh public investments, the market could not stave off the British economy from the continued stagnation and rising unemployment. It was only when the Second World War broke out and the Great Britain transformed itself from an imperialist super-power to a member of the Commonwealth, from a debtor to creditor nation that its economists, civil servants, politicians, businessmen and trade union leaders started appreciating the significance of what Keynes had advocated to deal with the depression (Winch, 1969). The strategy adopted by the Axis Powers (mainly Germany) from the beginning of the war was to sink the ships carrying food and ammunition to Britain, which had to import at that time almost 70 per cent of its total requirements of cereals, fruits, sugar, fats, cheese and meat from abroad. Faced with these challenges, two major developments took place in the welfare policy of England in the midst of the Second World War.

One was the acceptance by the British government of the recommendations contained in the report of an inter-departmental committee on social insurance and allied services, an influential document, popularly known as the Beveridge Report. It had two parts: the majority report and the minority report. The latter identified 'five giant evils' that an economy could suffer from, namely, squalor, want, ignorance, idleness, and disease. This part of the report recommended as the duty of the state to address these evils through social welfare reforms. Considering that this had general acceptance with various departments within the British government, the minority report was placed before a specially constituted

Royal Commission, which accepted the recommendations and cleared for implementation. Thus, the government declared that it was adopting the report and, from the first half of the 1940s, Britain became officially a welfare state.

The other was the introduction of universal rationing. Faced with the disruptions for imports and a bad harvest in 1942, the government instituted a system of rationing according to which each person got a 'ration book' containing coupons to purchase prescribed quantities of different items of food at a chosen ration shop. In addition to the general rates applicable for all households, there was special ration, consisting of more fruits for children and pregnant women. Along with this, the government also fixed the prices of meals served in British hotels and restaurants. The purpose was to restrict richer families from extravagantly eating out the limited food available in the country at that time, and to save its entire population from hunger and malnutrition (Dreze and Sen, 1989; Zweiniger-Bargiolowska, 2002). These measures were instrumental in saving the British economy from the inflationary heat that the other participants in the Second World War in general and Britain's third world colonies like India in particular had to face.

Irish Famine

Now, take the case of Scotland and Ireland. These federating units of the United Kingdom were frequently in the grip of famines. The most harrowing among them was the Great Potato Famine of 1840s. This catastrophe was called 'potato famine' as it was the result of the failure of potato crop caused by a hitherto unfamiliar fungus, popularly known as 'potato blight'. After attacking several north European countries, the potato blight spread to Ireland and the highlands of Scotland. A very recent study by a group of European scholars, and edited by Vanhaute, Paping and O'Grada of the Dublin University, finds that the impact of 'potato blight' was extremely calamitous in Ireland, followed by Scotland. The former was the largest producer of potato, with its one-third of the arable land under potato cultivation. Ireland was also the highest consumer of potato in the whole of Europe, estimated at a per capita daily consumption of 2.1 kg in normal years. The potato consumption in Scotland was the next highest. The production of potato in Ireland after declining to (-) 30 per cent in 1845, dipped further to (-) 80 per cent in the next year. The decline was (-) 88 per cent in Scotland. Together with this, in 1846, there was a poor harvest of wheat and rye throughout much of Europe. The outputs of these crops recorded the steepest decline of (-) 33 per cent in Ireland, creating an extremely serious food availability situation (Vanhaute, at al, 2006).

The 'potato famine' killed about one million people, or one-eighth of the total population in Ireland, making this the largest human disaster recorded in Europe in the nineteenth century. Most of the victims were the rural poor. Scotland also suffered but not as severely as Ireland. With the massive rise in the famine-mortality, there was also a serious decline in fertility, which fell back by a third, resulting in about 0.5 million averted conceptions. Furthermore, this was the classic case of a famine-driven mass exodus in which one million people of Ireland migrated to North America and Australia. What was appalling was that the British emigration authorities issued mass clearances with unprecedented speed to all those who applied to go abroad, without insisting on rules. The government also gave liberal transportation assistance to whichever country that the applicants wanted to migrate. It is believed that the famine mortality, fertility decline, and mass migration of 1840s had spurred population decline for more than a century. It is also argued in some quarters that the misery wreaked by the Great Potato Famine in Ireland might not have been so disastrous, had the government of United Kingdom followed the same policy that it adopted for the people in other parts of the country. Instead, it failed to provide access to other sources of food in the absence of potato available within the affected area. Rather than doing so, "substantial amounts of wheat were shipped from famine-affected Ireland... to more prosperous England" (Dreze and Sen, 1989), arguing that the poorer sections in Ireland, whose staple food being potato, might not be able to access the high-priced wheat.

The famine recurred in Ireland even earlier than the calamitous 'potato famine' essentially because of the unkind attitude of the British government towards the sufferings of those people. Referring the Dublin-based newspaper reports, the historian Michel Beaud stated: "Famines were especially deadly in Ireland. About this, there is a general opinion: An epidemic rages here among the people. The sick people who are brought to the hospital get well as soon as they are fed. Their sickness then is hunger. One need not be a wizard to guess that they are cured up on eating." About the 'attitude' of the British government towards the misery wreaked on the people of Ireland and Scotland by famines, Beaud further stated rather cryptically: "barbarous indifference, hard egotism on one hand, and nameless misery, on the other" (Beaud, 1983).

This 'barbarous indifference' of Great Britain towards the Irish potato famine of 1840s would be evident from the fact that Queen Victoria donates a miserly sum of £5 towards famine-relief. Immediately after that she makes a state visit to Ireland during which an immensely huge sum of £5000 was spent from the public fund to host a banquet in her honour. There are historians who argue that the potato famine provided the most convenient opportunity for the British government to commit genocide in Ireland with the implicit and calculated intention of ethnic cleaning. These historians further assert that, otherwise, "had a similar crisis occurred in England instead of Ireland then the government's response would have been very different" (Kenealy and Alasney, 1995).

This was put in another way by George Nathaniel Curzon (popularly known as Lord Curzon, who subsequently became the Viceroy of India during 1899-1905) in his campaign for the 1886 election to the House of Commons. In one of the speeches, he first criticised his own Liberal Prime Minister's *Home Rule Bill* as "the latest attack on the integrity of the Empire; the consequent drain of capital from Ireland would drive many of her own sons in exile from the soil, and draft them as competitors into the already overcrowded labour market of England."[10]

Imperialist State and Famines

The indifference of Britain in not taking effective measures to eradicate the catastrophe of famines that stalked Ireland might be influenced, as we noted earlier, by its hidden desire for 'ethnic cleaning' There was no such a hidden agenda in India for the British Empire to be indifferent in dealing with famines that erupted from time to time. On the contrary, the announcement of the Famine Code of 1883 would indicate that the empire was really 'concerned' about the recurring famines and the accompanying human miseries in the colony. There were also occasions when it had selectively implemented certain provisions in the Famine Code. However, a closer look at what they did would reveal that these were mere palliatives having no much financial implications. Wherever the implementation was expected to involve substantial financial outgo from the treasury, the government had either shifted the responsibility to the local rulers or simply refused to take any ameliorative actions, arguing that, under the system of laissez-faire, it was the market, not the government, to take care of them.

Thus, the British Empire in India remained steadfast in not implementing relevant guidelines of the Famine Code in case it involved heavy public expenditure because the basic objective of conquering and maintaining the vast Indian colony, as also all other colonies in the third world, was the same as the basic objective of imperialism, i.e. "capital accumulation on a world-scale in the era of monopoly capitalism" (Bottomore, 1983). This accumulation process had a dual characteristic. According to Eric Hobsbawm, imperialism flourished in "an era of unparalleled peace in the western world, which engendered an era of equally unparalleled world wars. It was an era of, in spite of appearances, growing social stability within the zone of developed industrial economies, which provided the small bodies of men who, with almost contemptuous ease, could conquer and rule over vast empires" (Hobsbawm, 1987). Students of political economy would know that the features and under-currents of imperialism take diverse forms. We do not intend to delve deep into all these aspects. Our objective here is to briefly explain just two of its dominant characteristics, which in our view are relevant to understand why the imperialist Britain, despite proclaiming otherwise, showed less enthusiasm in initiating appropriate measures to prevent repeated famines that devastated several parts of India during its rule.

The first and the most significant among them was the inter-imperialist rivalry. Prabhat Patnaik, who has written extensively about imperialism and its many facets, writes about the reasons for the rivalry between the western imperialist countries, as follows: "Competition between rival monopoly combines, each trying to increase its strength and undermine its rivals, directly takes the form of a striving for 'economic territory' as actual or potential sources of raw-material, as spheres for profitable deals, capital exports and commodity markets" (Patnaik, 1986). The history of India is replete with examples of such rivalries at different levels among European powers for the enhancement of their 'economic territories'. Ever since Vasco-da-Gama discovered for the first time a sea-route and reached somewhere near the shore of Calicut in Malabar in 1498, the Portuguese, the Dutch, the French and the British established their maritime power in the Arabian Sea primarily to engage in profitable trade, mainly in spices. Their first attempt was to subordinate and then ruin the Indian merchants who were the suppliers of exportable goods to Europe. They could do so with ease as the Indian merchants were financially too weak to advance credit needed to the domestic producers as the European traders had done. Their next attempt was to subordinate the artisans by forfeiting their share in trade (Bagchi, 2002).

After ruining the livelihood sources of Indian merchants and artisans, the British rulers did everything possible to establish their monopoly over the Indian trade. The British EIC had actually come armed with the notion that only by the use of force could they instil fear among the local rulers, easily conquer their territories and establish sovereignty in India. While other European companies had only a few insignificant areas of settlement, the British EIC started from the very beginning in right earnest to conduct trading activities on the one hand and conquer more and more Indian territories on the other. We have seen earlier that beginning with the setting up of export processing units or warehouses (called 'factories') at all strategic port centres, the British EIC conquered and colonised several areas in India.[11] It was in this process of trading and colonisation that the inter-imperialist rivalry started. Though other European traders did not openly state so, the British EIC was more explicit in this regard. The Court of Directors of EIC in England ordered the Governor-General of Madras to "establish such a policy of civil and military power and create and secure such a large revenue to maintain both as may be the foundation of a large, well-grounded, secure English dominion in India for all time to come."[12]

Ultimately, the British force succeeded in defeating the other European powers as well as the local rulers in India and in establishing their domination all over the country, except a few very small spots like Goa, Diu, Daman and Pondicherry. Compared to the vast stretch of 'economic territory' that the British Empire captured in India, these patches of lands were rather insignificant. In the meanwhile, the British rulers invested in major irrigation and railway networks, not with the surplus capital accumulated through the Industrial Revolution at home but with the revenue collected from within the colony. While taking up irrigation works, the declared objective of the colonial government was of course to increase agricultural productivity and prevent famines. In actual practice, however, the purpose of developing surface irrigation was to raise the volume of production for exports. Similarly, at the time of constructing extensive railway net-works, by diverting the budget allocation made for famine insurance and other social welfare measures, the government proclaimed that as and when railways were developed it would be able to prevent famine in any region as these railways could quickly transport food available from areas of surplus to the deficit regions.[13] What actually happened in fact was that, on the first sight of food shortage that signalled an impending famine in an area, speculators used the railways to transport away their stocks to other centres. Moreover, to quote Hobsbawm, "the tightening web of (rail) transport drew even the backward and previously marginal into the world economy, and created a new interest among the old centres of wealth and development in these remote areas. Indeed, now that they were accessible many of these regions seemed at first sight to be simply potential extensions of the developed world (mainly the imperialist Britain), extirpating or pushing back the native inhabitants" (Hobsbawm, 1987).

The second dominant feature of the British imperialism was oppression of the subjugated people in third world colonies and forcing them into impoverishment while continuing with the expansion of more and more 'economic territories' within these countries for imperialist aggrandisement. As Great Britain had already captured and established its colonial power in India, China, Africa, West Indies, Latin America, Canada and Australia even before the Industrial Revolution, it could carry out the 'oppression' that we indicated above in rather sophisticated ways: (i) supplying the technologically superior and relatively lower-priced industrial goods against qualitatively inferior and high-priced urban consumer goods produced in India with pre-capitalist technologies; and (ii) cajoling the local farmers to shift from food crops they had been cultivating for generations in the pursuit of subsistence towards export-oriented and, therefore, seemingly highly profitable commercial crops.

These developments, despite apparently attractive as a means to bring wealth and welfare in the pre-capitalist economies, were responsible for the existence of perpetual pre-famine conditions, especially in several parts of the Indian colony like Malabar. As we have elaborated elsewhere in this monograph, what the British did by exporting its technologically superior and price-wise cheaper industrial goods was to make inroads into India's traditional economy in an attempt to eliminate the pre-capitalist producers and create a permanent market for the huge surplus commodities produced in Britain since the Industrial Revolution. We have also seen that the period of *de javu* that the sudden increase in the exports of Indian commercial crops produced by shifting the areas under foodgrains had vanished soon after the American Civil War was over. Further, the exports of commercial crops from the Indian colony to Britain, instead of bringing prosperity, generated just the opposite effect (see P. Patnaik, 1972; 1973).

Thus, instead of diffusing development from the highly industrialised Great Britain to the backward colonies like India, the latter's imports of finished goods from the former and exports of agro-based industrial raw-material and food in exchange, in effect, led to a severe 'drain of surplus' through skilfully contrived mechanisms, most of which added fuel to the fire of famines. First, 'unequal exchange' in the trade relation between the advanced capitalist Britain and the underdeveloped Indian colony led to a 'one-way flow' of resources towards the former. Second, transfer of profits, interests and dividend for the British investments in railways, irrigation etc, albeit with Indian funds, was another source of the 'drain of surpluses' from the colony. Third, the agricultural economy of India during the British period being dominated by peasant production, the petty producers were exploited to the hilt by the colonial land revenue system on the one hand and by the trader-moneylender-landlord nexus with the support of imperialist rulers, on the other. Fourth, in the industrial sector, traditional small-scale production was decimated with the penetration of manufactured goods. It was when the machine-made cloths and yarn started flooding that the traditional urban spinning and weaving in India got wiped out. And, it was the main reason why the workers and artisans dependent on the traditional industries like spinning and weaving had fallen easy victims of famines (P. Patnaik, 1973; 2001; 2011)

It is important to note here that the 'drain of surplus' and the consequent poverty and the outbreak of famine about which Professor Patnaik spoke was not the legacy of British imperialism alone. Exploitation of the poor for aggrandisement of wealth had existed throughout the history of imperialism. For instance, the Roman Empire, one of the earliest and the largest in ancient history had enlarged its wealth and power through annexation of countries after countries covering the territorial holdings around Mediterranean Europe, Africa and Asia. Each war brought additional wealth and a mass of vanquished soldiers as slaves. Territorial conquests, which provided the bulk of the slaves, were the main source of the expansion of the Roman economy. According to some authors, not less than thirty five per cent of the population in the Roman Empire consisted of slaves, making it one of the largest slave societies in history (Bradley, 1994).

Slavery in the Roman Empire was, however, a complex institution. It comprised mainly of the 'home-grown' slaves and the 'war captives' or prisoners of war. The 'home-grown' slaves were not actually slaves as we generally understand the term today. They included various types of professionals like chefs, teachers, physicians as well as accountants, apart from those engaged in household services, agriculture, milling and mining. A sizable section among them had possessed small plots of land, which they used for the cultivation of subsistence crops. As and when the emperor declared war with any neighbouring country, these professionals from diverse fields were conscripted and forcefully paraded as warriors. Quite often these 'home grown' slaves had to leave their field before the harvest. On returning successfully after conquering the enemy country, they found their lives ruined as the crops and the lands they cultivated were robbed off by the patricians, the large land owners. Left with nothing to fall back upon, nor any house to live in, they roamed around the streets, begging for food. With the growing starvation, most of them fell sick with epidemic diseases and died on the roadside (Paul, 1918).

The other section of the slaves, viz. the 'war captives' were skilled and, at the time of their capture, relatively healthier. Had they been productively used, the Roman Empire could have created a robust economy. However, the emperors were known to be indifferent to invest in industrial expansion, as the ruling class could live a pompous life on large quantities of tributes, especially corn, taxes and tithes received from the colonies. This had serious consequences. The corn received as tributes and tithes being excessively large in quantity, the emperor ordered to dump the surplus portion in the home market. This inevitably depressed the market prices of the domestically produced corn and ruined the small farmers. Concurrently, the superior skills of the slaves belonging to the 'war captives' could have been fruitfully used for the lasting development of the imperial economy. In the absence of any investments, their skills remained wasted. They had to engage as menial workers such as domestic servants with paltry wages and live in semi-starvation (Paul, 1918).

As the slave population, which was the backbone of the economy, had to live in penury when the imperialist expansion continued to bring in more and more lands and wealth in the hands of the ruling class, there were frequent class struggles. Though these uprisings were quite often suppressed by force, side by side, the need arose for a constitutional arrangement that could safeguard the interests of all classes within the empire. The constitution that came up treated the emperor as the supreme power, assisted by a senate and the civil service. The senate was represented by various economic classes and their voting rights were determined according to the level of property that each of them possessed.[14] The constitution of the senate was such that the situation continued as before, without any reprieve to the poor from hunger, malnutrition and frequent famines. Thus, according to one of the many theories, the Roman Empire had to disintegrate as the imperial state failed to protect the lives of the proletarians and slaves, on whose labour the empire was built up and flourished (See Gibbon, 1776; Paul, 1918; Ferrill, 1986).

In the context of the British imperialism vis-à-vis its colonies, particularly India, Jayati Ghosh puts it cogently: "While in the early phase of colonial rule straightforward plunder and the exaction of tribute involved a drain of resources from the economy, by the late nineteenth century the state exchequer bore a substantial amount of 'Home Charges' which, along with other items of state expenditure, amounted to a unilateral transfer to Britain which further impoverished the country. For the first half of the twentieth century it was argued that while tariff protection did allow the emergence of some import-substituting industries in the inter-war period, this policy was still essentially directed towards serving the economic needs of Britain and the colonial state's industrial and credit policies actually were biased against domestic producers. Thus, in a variety of ways the state was seen to be the instrument of economic exploitation" (Ghosh, 1995).

6.4 Concluding Remarks

In an earlier chapter we noted why Amartya Sen rejected 'food availability decline' or FAD approach as an insufficient explanation of famine, though since Adam Smith postulated it in the analysis of famine in his *Wealth of Nations* (published in 1776), FAD was a major explanatory variable in the study of famine, though several others, mainly Florence Nightingale, R.C. Dutt, Gunnar Myrdal, B.M. Bhatia, Hari Sanker

Srivastava, Jean Dreze, etc. had contested such an approach to study famine. Even the Indian Famine Codes, introduced in the wake of a series of famines in the 1870s, defined famine by its early warning signals, namely, rising grain prices, increased migration, and increased crimes (see O'Grada, 2009; Dreze, 1995). The present chapter took up Sen's alternative theory of the 'failure of exchange entitlement' or FEE, which he postulated as a more comprehensive causal mechanism that precipitates famine. Sen visualises this theory to operate in a private ownership market economy. He does of course give a role for the state in the eradication of famine, though only after other options available through the markets are exhausted. Subsequent researches conducted by Sen (in collaboration with Jean Dreze) found that, instead of the 'free market', the 'state' was the most appropriate institutional arrangement for the prevention of famine. In their study, the focus of famine also shifted from what was treated as the precipitation of a single individual's hunger and malnutrition to collective human misery in a region or a country.

Their findings in this respect are unambiguous: In the closing years of the last millennium, when 'retreat of the state' emerged as the general trend in the economic policies all over the world, wherever the sovereign states of independent nations directly intervened, famines could be effectively eliminated. None of the specific cases studied by the authors to prove this point belonged to the well-known interventionist state. These states were either multiparty democracies or single party dictatorships Before becoming independent, each of these countries had a history of repeated bouts of famines. After independence, their governments involved themselves positively in managing the food supply so that famine became history in their countries.

Our own literature survey brought out in this chapter revealed that the same was the case with Great Britain throughout the imperialist era. For more than two and a half centuries, while practising mercantilism, laissez-faire and free trade, Britain imported large quantities of food from abroad at cheaper rates and dumped in the domestic market, enabling the masses to subsist at affordably lower prices. The positive involvement of the government of Great Britain in safeguarding its people from poverty and famines, even while preaching the free-market ideology, was particularly clear in the economic policies pursued by it during the nineteenth century through the first half of the twentieth century. In this period, Britain introduced all conceivable social security and welfare measures to protect each and every segment of the society in England from poverty and destitution. Similarly, in the midst of the Second World War, when imports of food from abroad were disrupted by enemy countries, Britain introduced strict universal rationing and stabilised prices of essential consumption goods so that the people of England, unlike those in many other countries, hardly experienced any general poverty or starvation.

The imperialist Britain failed to extend similar food and livelihood security to the masses in its own federating units of Ireland and Scotland, as also in its third world colonies, particularly India. In the latter, the imperialist aim being surplus extraction by hook or by crook, British rulers devised tactful policy instruments ostensibly beneficial to local people but, in essence, dragged them into hunger and destitution. This monograph has cited a number of such policy variables, which were instrumental in wreaking frequent famines: destruction of urban livelihood sources through deindustrialisation, disintegration of rural social networks, monetisation of the economy without giving sufficient time to the stake holders to cope with the new system, exorbitant land revenue demand and coercive manner in which it was collected, procurement and exports of foodgrains when the country was facing subsistence crisis, large scale conversion of lands under food crops for the cultivation of agro-based industrial raw materials, and so on.

In short, the crux of the argument in this chapter is that maintenance of exchange entitlement for the prevention of starvation and famine cannot be left to the invisible hands of the market. Being a collective human misery, only the state is in a position to safeguard the people from such calamities. For performing this critical function, it is not necessary that the state should actually be 'interventionist' in nature; it can even be an imperialist state, or a domestically formed sovereign state such as monarchy, oligarchy, democracy, or dictatorship. The state may actually perpetrate the economic interests of the dominant social class it represents. While doing so, however, if it fails to protect the interests of the other classes, recurring famines become inevitable is only one part of the history. The other side of the history is that, the very continuance of such a state in power becomes doubtful, as the experience all over the world would tell.

Notes

1. These case studies are, as appeared in Chapter-3, the Bengal famine of 1943, the Bangladesh famine of 1974 and the Ethiopian famines, and the famines in the Sahel belt of Mauritania, Senegal, Mali, Upper Volta, Niger, and Chad during 1969-74 (Sen 1981).
2. 'Hume's guillotine' of positive and normative methodologies assumes a watertight distinction in the analysis with the use of antonyms like 'is'/'ought'; facts/values; objective/subjective; descriptive/prescriptive; science / art; true/false; good/bad. David Hume, in his Treatise of Human Nature had pointed out that such a distinction is difficult to follow because "purely factual, descriptive statements by themselves can only entail or imply other factual, descriptive statements and

newer norms, ethical pronouncements, or prescription to do something" (See Blaug, 1980).

3. This argument has been countered by Osmani (1995:268) that "disaggregation is an essential feature of the entitlement approach" adopted by Amartya Sen.
4. See the preface to Dreze and Sen (1989), op.cit, p.vii.
5. Dreze and Sen (1989), op.cit. Chapter-13, p. 258.
6. *Ibid.* Chapter-5, p.71.
7. See Chapter 8, "Experiences and Lessons" of Dreze and Sen (1969), op.cit. pp. 122-158.
8. See Michael Stewart (1967), op.cit. Chapter 3.
9. *Ibid.*
10. See, Goradia (1993), op. cit., pp. 95-96.
11. Roy (2006) gives these annexations chronologically as Bengal and Bihar (1757), Carnatic (1765), Northern Sarkars (1766), Benares (1775), Dindigul, Malabar, Canara etc (1792-9), Ceded Districts (1801), Maratha territories (1803-18), North East and Burma (1825-42), Sind (1843), Satara (1848), Punjab (1849), Jhansi, Nagpur, and Hyderabad, i.e. Berar (1853), and Awadh (1856). By then 62 per cent of the Indian territory was annexed by Britain either by use of force or by threatening to use force.
12. Quoted in Michael Stewart (1967), op.cit. p. 64; also see Whiteside (1992).
13. It was during this period of railway expansion that the British administration set apart a 'famine insurance fund' for Malabar, despite declaring that Malabar was not susceptible to famine and that the Famine Code was not applicable to it. The purpose of keeping a 'famine insurance' now was understandably to divert it to the railway construction.
14. For determining the membership and voting rights in the senate, the whole population was divided into six classes, with a total number of 193 votes. The wealthiest class at the top got 98 votes, more than the vote-share of all other classes. This class controlled the political power, military, wealth, proletarians and the slaves. The other classes, divided according to their level of property were given membership and voting rights as follows: hierarchically the second class with 22 votes, the third class with 20 votes, the fourth class with 22 votes, the fifth class with 30 votes, and lass class belonging to the proletarians and slaves with just one vote (Paul, 1918).

Chapter 7

The 1943 Famines: Comparing Bengal and Malabar

7.1 The Dichotomy

A human misery in one part of the country is subjected to comprehensive analysis so that it receives world-wide attention, whereas a similar misery in another part of the same country during the same period is completely obliterated by researchers and hence fails to receive any limelight. These are the stories respectively of the 1943 famines in Bengal and Malabar. As we already stated at the beginning of this monograph, the present study has been influenced by a statement in Jawaharlal Nehru's *Discovery of India* that, in the devastating famine of 1943, along with Bengal, thousands of men, women and children had died daily in Malabar, Bijapur and Orissa for want of food. It is only legitimate therefore to probe why the 1943 famine in Bengal continues to evoke spine-chilling recollections even today while that of Malabar does not receive at least passing reference in the studies on south Indian economic history? A comparative account of the depths and magnitudes of these human miseries in these two regions is expected to shed light on this question. Before making such a comparison, however, we have to keep in mind some of the related basic facts.

It is well-known that, in British India, Bengal was the largest of the three presidencies, whereas Malabar constituted just a small ceded district in the southern presidency of Madras. Over time, the political geography of Bengal underwent several changes, adding different areas from the eastern part of the country and then separating certain parts into independent states presumably for administrative convenience. Though a few alterations had also been made in the geographical area of Malabar, these were rather insignificant. The presidency of Bengal was generally referred in official records as Greater Bengal, which comprised 'undivided Bengal', Bihar and Orissa. The former was later separated on religious basis as East Bengal and West Bengal. After independence, East Bengal became East Pakistan and now Bangladesh. In his *Poverty and Famines*, Amartya Sen demonstrates a political map of 'Bengal 1943', consisting of the 'undivided Bengal' under the British administration, leaving out Bihar and Orissa.[1] Geographically, 'Bengal 1943' or East and West Bengal accounted for 14 times larger than the Malabar district.[2]

Just as the physical size, the population of Bengal was also significantly larger. Taking the three presidencies under the British administration, Bengal reported the highest density of population (Kumar, 1983). The population density of Malabar was not less. However, in absolute terms, according to the Census of India 1941, 'undivided Bengal' had a population of 61.5 million, which increased to 66.9 million, as per the 1951 census. The corresponding census figures recorded for Malabar were, respectively, 3.9 million and 4.8 million. Interpolating these figures on a linear scale, we get the population during 1943, the year in which the famine peaked, at 4.1 million for Malabar and 62.5 million for Bengal. These figures would tell that the population of Bengal was 15 times higher than the population of Malabar.[3]

From the above, it goes without saying that the loss of lives in a massive calamity like the 1943 famine in Bengal should also have been massive in absolute terms. Some of the economic historians who studied the famines in India during the British period had stated that, in terms of the total number of people affected, Bengal famine of 1943 was an extremely cruel 'parting gift' of the British Empire at the instance of Winston Churchill, the then Prime Minister of England (about which we will have more to say after a while). If we can visualise another famine, mortality-wise more devastating than that of 1943, it also occurred in Bengal in 1770 and could be aptly called the 'inaugural gift' of the EIC, when it received the *diwani* or the tax collection right and the full-fledged administrative control over Bengal. As far as Malabar was concerned, however, a famine of the same intensity as it happened in Bengal could not engulf and eliminate the same number of lives, understandably because of the vast differences in their geographical areas and levels of population. In other words, absolute number of destitution, or mortalities, cannot be taken as appropriate yardstick to compare the intensity of famines that the people endured during 1943 in Bengal and Malabar.

Similarly, both regions are blessed with distinct natural endowments. In one region it could *ceteris paribus* be effective in mitigating, if not eliminating, hunger and famine while in the other region it could offer entitlement to food in normal times but not during famines. In the same way, a single state policy at the implementation stage could apparently encourage the rural economy to prosper in one region whereas it could repeatedly push the rural economy into famine in the other region. Such common and contrasting factors cannot be ignored while attempting to compare the calamitous 1943 famine in Bengal and Malabar. An overarching constraint that we confronted while attempting to prepare a comparative picture of this famine in the two regions was the non-availability of certain basic information. The most important among them were the following:

First, in any famine, even if it happens to a peace-loving and highly traditional people, the eruption of social disorganisation and, quite often, development of a situation of anarchy cannot be over-ruled. For instance, migration of bread-winning members of the family to far-flung places, leaving others at home; sale of children by parents and dumping of older members to mend for themselves; and petty-to-not-so-petty crimes are some of the most visible outcomes of famine. Even though there are casual references about such developments in the famine literature, as also in the official notes available in the archival sources, we could not lay hands on comprehensive data-based information for a detailed comparison of the position in Bengal and Malabar.

Second, some of the official data related to famine are known to be under-reports. Epidemics and famine-mortalities belong to this category. While dealing with the 1943 famine in Bengal, eminent scholars like Mahalanobis and Amartya Sen had applied ‘correction factors’ on the official figures for the purpose of visualising the enormity of the famine. In the case of Malabar, as nobody has until now bothered to look at recurring famines and related miseries, the question of analysing, not to speak of applying any ‘correction factors’, on the relevant archival data, does not arise. To make a comparison of mortalities, therefore, we have used the ‘uncorrected’ decennial census data for both Bengal and Malabar. Given these limitations, in what follows, we attempt to make a comparative account of the natural factors as well as man-made factors that propelled the 1943 famine in these two regions.

7.2 Soil and Crops

It is an undeniable fact that local production of food plays a major role in preventing hunger and malnutrition. It is also undeniable that the agronomic condition of the area, mainly the type of topography and soil, monsoons and rainfall are fundamental in food production. The Bengal region is endowed with three types of soil[4]: (i) old alluvial soil, (ii) red soil, and (iii) laterite soil. The old alluvial soil, which is full of clay, does not allow drainage of water from rainfall and, therefore, the land with this type of soil experiences water-logging and promotes accumulation of sodium and magnesium. These elements make the soil sterile. The old alluvial soil is generally seen in most parts of Murshidabad, Bankura, Burdwan and Midnapore. The second type of soil, i.e. the red soil, is concentrated in the hilly areas of Chhotanagpur plateau and, during rainy season, a sizable part of this soil used to erode mainly to Birbhum district. The third major type, namely, laterite soil, is interspersed between Damodar and Bhagirathi rivers. While the red soil is suitable for rice cultivation, the laterite soil is poor in lime and nitrogen, which are essential for the cultivation of field crops.

In the context of production of food and feed, Bengal exhibits certain peculiar features: First, the soils of eastern India in general and of Bengal in particular are known to possess saline and alkaline contents. These are *inter alia* the limiting factors in the choice of crops and levels of yield. The main cereal crop cultivated in Bengal is rice and, in a limited scale, minor cereals like jowar, bajra, maize, ragi and small millets are also grown. Among the pulses, Bengal grows mainly gram and tur. Second, the soils as well as the warm and humid climate of Bengal are highly suitable for jute, which is cultivated in plenty there. Third, Bengal also cultivates fodder crops, which are inferior in quality. The cattle fed with these fodders become easily susceptible to diseases. The consequence is well known. In times of famines, if cattle mortality also increases, the exchange entitlement of the owners of cattle to food is adversely affected. Fourth, the topography and the soils in Bengal are such that, during normal rains, vast stretches of the land under cultivation is water-logged, and during heavy rains floods ruin the crops. For Bengal, this proved to be a blessing in disguise. Water-logging and the salinity of water make Bengal highly congenial for the production of fresh water fish and fish-seeds. Fish is not only a significant item of food in Bengal but also a major source of entitlement to its staple food, the rice.

Compared to Bengal, as we noted in the introductory chapter, Malabar is endowed with three principal types of soil, viz. the laterite soil, coastal alluvial soil and non-coastal alluvial soil. The first two being sandy, it is easy for the rain-water to empty into the ocean or to filter into the underground. The non-coastal alluvial soil, seen on the river banks of Malabar, being filled with leaves and other sediments, is highly fertile. At the same time, as it does not allow water to flow out, there would be water-logging in times of normal rains and flooding during heavy rains. Both these destroy standing crops. In Bengal we found that the salinity of the soil and water-logging are fruitfully used for fresh-water fish farming. If famine strikes during rainy seasons, as it often does, fish becomes a major item of exchange entitlement to rice for the people of Bengal. However, while discussing the class basis of entitlement vis-à-vis rice during the 1943 Bengal famine, Amartya Sen felt that fishermen might have been one of the worst affected. There could be several reasons for this. For instance, in an extremely calamitous situation like famine, the mitigation of which is not in the hands of individuals, if the state takes a negative attitude as the British administration did, private traders could manipulate the market for their advantage. This was exactly what happened in rural areas of not only Bengal but all other famine-stricken areas in British India during 1943. Sen has further stated that, in Calcutta where there was price control and public distribution, famine was not felt except in the form of beggars surging from villages in search of food.

Unlike in Bengal, fresh water fish-farming is not a noticeable 'allied activity' under agriculture in Malabar. Therefore, fish cannot be considered as a significant item of exchange entitlement to rice in this region. On the other hand, coconut, which is a widely cultivated as a homestead plantation crop, is a major source of entitlement to rice. But there is a basic difference between fish-farming in Bengal and coconut cultivation in Malabar. For fish-farming, the rainy season is the most appropriate period. As coconut ripes every month, households use it to buy rice and other items of daily consumption in normal times. During rainy seasons, however, coconut takes almost three months to ripe and, if a famine strikes then, as it generally happens, it is of no use to its growers for the purchase of food.

As regards the production of rice, the principal food of both Malabar and Bengal, the latter cultivates three rice crops: (i) *aman* or winter crop, sown during May and June, and harvested between November and December; (ii) *aus* or autumn crop, sown around April and harvested in August and September; and (iii) *boro* or spring crop, planted in November and harvested in February and March. Winter or *aman* rice is by far the most important in Bengal, constituting, on a five-yearly average for 1939-43, almost 73 per cent of the total rice harvested, followed by autumn or *aus* rice with 24 per cent, and spring or *boro* rice with just 3 per cent of the total (Sen, 1981). Before the Second World War, Bengal was generally surplus in rice. An estimate given in the report of the Famine Enquiry Commission on Bengal (1945) shows that the average of rice production in Bengal for ten years from 1928 to 1937 was enough for 54 weeks' supply, even though there might be shortages in individual years.

As we noted in the introductory chapter, Malabar also had raised three rice crops, during those years: (a) the *viruppu* or autumn, the largest crop, sown in April-May and harvested in September-October; (b) *mundakan* or the winter crop, which is sown in September and October and harvested between December and January; and (c) *punja* or the summer crop, which is sown in December and January and harvested mostly in April. The first two crops, more prevalent in north Malabar, were also known respectively as *kanni* and *makaram* crops. We do not have time series data on the production of rice in Malabar to make a medium term trend rate of growth and compare with that of Bengal. However, it was well-known that, unlike in Bengal, even a higher than normal harvest of rice was not sufficient to meet the minimum requirement of the people in Malabar and that it happened due to the British policy of shifting large tracts of lands, including those under food crops, in Wayanad for the cultivation of export-oriented cash crops.

7.3 Food Availability

The conditions of production, availability and market prices of foodgrains that prevailed in India in general, and Bengal and Malabar in particular, during the immediately preceding years of the 1943 famines appeared to be by and large similar. In Bengal, the foodgrains production suffered a sharp setback in 1941 and it was followed in the next year by cyclone, tidal waves, storms and floods. Similarly, in 1943 also floods destroyed the crops in certain parts of Bengal. For instance, the Damodar flood in Burdwan in July 1943 aggravated the famine in that year.[5] The traffics had to be suspended on all roads and railways. The countryside was flooded to a depth of six-to-seven feet, inundating and destroying the crops in many villages. Nonetheless, estimates made by Amartya Sen showed that, the food availability of Bengal in 1943 was only 5 per cent less than the average for the preceding five years. Compared to 1941, the availability in 1943 was 13 per cent higher. Going by these figures, there ought to have been a famine in Bengal in 1941. Professor Sen noted that, while in 1941 there was no famine in Bengal, it was in 1943 that it witnessed one of the most disastrous famines of the twentieth century. In the same way, Malabar also faced natural disasters during the pre-famine period. Thus, in 1941, there erupted a severe cyclonic storm accompanied by flood, destroying field and commercial crops in several parts of Malabar. Next year, south-west monsoon was normal but the late sowing was disturbed as the north-east monsoon floundered. But in 1943, the peak year of famine, monsoons were normal. The area and production of rice were higher than during normal years. Still, the overall availability of rice in the district was about 46 per cent lower than the local requirement.

The relatively insignificant shortage in Bengal and the large gap in supply over demand in Malabar could have been bridged and the famine warded off, had early arrangements been made by the administration for bringing foodgrains from elsewhere. Within the country, Punjab was the major surplus producer. Compared to the previous years, the surplus quantity available in Punjab during 1943 was insufficient to serve the famine-struck areas in British India firstly, because the overall shortage was more than the available surplus; and secondly, a sizable part of the surplus had been diverted even before the famine peaked for the consumption of the rising number of army men recruited domestically to fight the Second World War. In such circumstances, private traders should have entered the market for speculative gains from whatever quantity they had with them. But they were not prepared to take out the grain hoarded by them and carry through rail, road, or waterways to the regions of shortage due to constant movements of troops to the southern and eastern theatres of war to protect the borders of British India from the anticipated attack of the Japanese army (Knight, 1954).

To make matters worse, the British administration was callous for long to invest in yield-raising foodgrains production, partly because of its preoccupation with surplus extraction from the colony for imperialist aggrandisement in whatever ways possible. Another reason for the indifference arose from the complacent attitude of the government arising from the fact that, food shortages in British India could easily be bridged by imports from Burma, the largest surplus producer of rice in the sub-continent. Before the Second World War, on average, around 15 per cent of the domestic requirement of rice in India was imported from Burma on government account. Unexpectedly, this source was closed as, in the midst of the Second World War, Japan suddenly directed the war to the eastern front and in December 1941 air-raided Burma. By early 1942, it captured Burma and positioned the army there due to which the entire high seas in the eastern block became unsafe for navigation. It was the stoppage of imports from Burma that intensified the 1943 famine in Bengal, Malabar and many other parts of the country (Mitra, 1953; Bailey and Harper, 2004).

Around this time, Great Britain also had a severe food crisis, leading to a sharp increase in the prices of all essential consumption goods. Despite its leadership position during the Second World War on the side of the Allied Forces, Britain had no difficulty to control the rising food prices and to prevent the possibility of a calamitous famine. The government introduced strict price controls and rationing in England. The prices and quantities to be served in private restaurants to families who wanted to eat outside were also brought under control[6]. The British rulers could have followed the same policy in India and saved millions of lives from shrinking supplies, rising prices and widespread hunger and malnutrition. Instead, it exhorted the people to store food stocks by themselves for at least two months of their consumption requirements. Using this as an opportunity, private traders cornered whatever quantity they could and hoarded for profiteering. This created an unprecedented increase in the prices of rice, worsening the already raging starvation and famine. The administration feared that, if it was permitted to continue, the ongoing anti-imperialist struggle building up in the colony might further escalate and that there was an urgent need to initiate palliative measures.

As a first step in this direction, the government appointed a Foodgrains Policy Committee under the chairmanship of Sir Theodore Gregory and asked it to suggest how the food problem in the country could be tackled once and for all. The Committee in its report recommended that the administration should initiate a Grow-More-Food campaign and, as a part of it, undertake the following: (a) encourage large-scale distribution of improved seeds; (b) promote the production of compost manure from night-soil and town-refuse; (c) assist industrialists to import plants and technical advice for the manufacture of ammonium nitrate; (d) use all energy for expeditious development of irrigation and drainage schemes; and (e) prevent the depletion of India's serviceable milch and drought animals[7]. The government accepted the recommendation in principle but it had no time to implement them in the thick of the Second World War, especially since British India was one of the theatres of war in its eastern border.

Nonetheless, on the face of the relentless increase in food prices and the rising antagonisms of the people against the continuance of the imperialist rule, the government had to pretend that it was doing something to save the people from starvation. Thus, it declared that, in view of the inability of the Central Commerce Department to deal with the management of food, in addition to its other pressing responsibilities, a newly created Central Food Department would take necessary steps to control the present food crisis and prepare a long-term plan for the stabilisation of supplies and prices of foodgrains. In this backdrop, the government directed the new Food Department to prepare a 'Basic Plan', giving reasonable indications about the likely surpluses and deficits in different provinces and manage the country's food through procurement, distribution, inter-province and inter-district grain movements as well as the fixation of wholesale and retail prices of foodgrains. Agriculture being constitutionally a state subject, the Food Department conducted a series of conferences with the local administrations and drew up the following measures to check the rising prices of foodgrains and maintain supplies without undue fluctuations: (i) a floor price; (ii) a ceiling price; (iii) ban on exports of foodgrains; (iv) compulsory procurement of cereals on government account; and (v) rationing in urban areas. In practice none of these measures worked as expected, except compulsory procurement, which further reduced the availability in the market and pushed up prices (Joseph, 1960). However, unlike other parts of the country, or rural Bengal, the people of Calcutta did not suffer much. The government had been releasing a part of the food stocks acquired through compulsory procurement to feed the people of Calcutta, especially the British businessmen, their employees, and the government staff. In addition, the Bengal Chamber of Commerce and other business chambers based in Calcutta arranged essential items of consumption for their employees. Railways, Port Trust, and Calcutta Corporation also covered their staff and families through programmes that, to an extent, guaranteed freedom from hunger (Sen, 1981). The same concern did not come from anywhere for the rural masses, which were, to use the words of Mukherjee (2010), 'left to the wolves', the private speculators. Large number of these starving people migrated from rural areas to Calcutta, begging for food and alms. There are harrowing accounts about these people, who travelled to beg for food; most of them collapsed by the road side, and even in front of the stock-piles of foodgrains that private traders hoarded in the city.

In the implementation of price control measures, Malabar was treated as a special case by the British administration. Considering the level of unprecedented starvation, starvation-led epidemics and large-scale loss of lives, the government declared that it would directly deal with famine prevention measures in the entire district. We have noticed in an earlier chapter that, on the eve of the food crisis of 1943, the government had announced a comprehensive rationing for both the urban and rural areas of Malabar. The announcement also included the monthly quantity to be issued per family-ration-card and the unit price for rice and other items being supplied at subsidised rates through the PDS. However, the actual rationing programme did not take off until the end of the Second World War and the devastating 1943 famine came almost to an end.

7.4 Churchill's Role

In Bengal and Malabar rural destitution was not uncommon during lean seasons. But by the beginning of 1943, it spread unusually far and wide. The prices of rice, the staple food of both these regions, had been shooting up from the month of March that year. Massive procurement of rice for the defence personnel and for supplies through ration shops in cities like Calcutta by the government, coupled with hoarding by private traders resulted in run-away rise in food prices. Between January and July 1943, a total quantity of 70,000 tonnes of rice, which could have kept alive 400,000 people in a full year, was exported for consumption in England though it was not a major rice eater (Mukherjee, 2010)[8]. When the mortalities mounted in all the famine-stricken areas in India, particularly Bengal, fervent pleas were made by the successive Viceroys, Archibald

Wavell and Linlithgow to the Prime Minister, Winston Churchill through the Secretary of State for India, Leopold Amery. Even the U.S President, Franklin D. Roosevelt requested Churchill to arrange food from elsewhere and save the lives of the people starving and dying in large numbers in British India. Being an inspiring leader of the Second World War, it was not difficult for Churchill to arrange a few shipments of foodgrains from abroad. Even a declaration of impending imports on government account was sufficient enough for the domestic speculators to release their hoarded stocks and moderate the market prices to some extent.

However, Churchill's advisor, Frederick Alexander Lindeman (officially known as Lord Cherwell), who was a firm believer in the Malthusian theory of population, could not agree. His recommendation to the Prime Minister was that sending more food to India, instead of controlling famine, would only worsen the situation as it would encourage them for breeding more. Churchill himself was known to be inimical to Indian people. He used to publicly declare Indians as "a beastly people with a beastly religion" who "bred like rabbits." When a telegram came to him from one of the viceroys for urgent dispatch of foodgrains to save the starving people from death, Churchill reportedly shot back: 'If people were dying due to scarcity of food and starvation, why Gandhi hadn't died yet?' (Mukherjee, 2010)

Apart from the requests of the American President offers came from others also for arranging the supply of food to control this devastating subsistence crisis in India. For instance, Netaji Subhash Chandra Bose, who was then somewhere in the far eastern part of South Asia, informed the British government that he would like to send a shipload of rice to India. Churchill straight away rejected the offer, as he apprehended that the ship could be used by Bose to carry weapons and fighters to wage war of independence against the British with the help of the Axis Powers. Offer also came from Australia and Canada, two partners on the side of the Allied Forces. They informed Churchill that they wanted to send their surplus wheat to India. It was at the peak of the famine in 1943 when thousands died daily on roads for want of food that these gestures came in. Churchill was adamant in preventing their attempts by all means. He ordered that any merchant-ship plying in the Indian Ocean be forcefully moved to the Atlantic. In case foodgrains were detected in the ship, the same be confiscated and transported to England for consumption of the British people.

Being partners in the Allied Forces, however, Churchill could not publicly spurn the offers from Canada and Australia. To be formally courteous, he expressed regret to both the countries stating that he could not accept their generous offers because: (i) Britain was facing extreme scarcity of ships even for the movement of ammunition and men to the war fronts. In this situation arranging ships to take delivery of wheat for India, though it was for a humanitarian purpose and extremely essential, was out of question. (ii) Even if some cargo ships were arranged somehow, it might not serve the intended purpose. The rice eaters in India, particularly of Bengal, would rather die instead of shifting their food habits from rice to wheat. Both these explanations, as per the information collected by Madhusree Mukherjee from the British archives, were factually incorrect. Churchill had in his command a number of extra ships after meeting the requirements of war. Some of the surplus ships at his command were at that time being used for the supply of white-bread to United Kingdom. The rest were kept aside for stockpiling the food procured from India and elsewhere in preparation for Britain's planned liberation of the Balkans as soon as the Second World War was over. As regards his arguments about the substitution of wheat for rice, it might be true in normal times when enough rice was available in the market at affordable price. It is a historical truth that during food scarcities and sky-rocketing prices, people ate whatever they got (Mukherjee, 2010).

Instead of providing basic food to the starving millions, Churchill adopted a 'denial policy' in and around the Indian colony through his officials, who forfeited food, boats, carts, motor vehicles, and even elephants from the owners, on the stated purpose of preventing Japanese army that might capture these items and use to attack the Indian sub-continent. Though such an attack never happened, applying the high handed 'denial policy', British administration seized whatever rice-stocks were held by private traders anywhere in the country. The British army also sunk, or captured, several private boats so that movement of foodgrains through rivers and sea became impossible (Bhatia, 1967)[9]. The scarcity of food and the accompanying hunger was felt more in the rural areas from where a large number of people crawled on to urban centres as beggars. Many of them died on the way. Those who survived went to houses and restaurants in urban areas, begging for starchy water in which rice was cooked. Lack of food and the resultant starvation was so acute that people, including little children, ate leaves and grass to fill their stomachs. When the condition became worse, parents dumped their hungry children into rivers and wells, and took their lives by throwing themselves in front of running trains. People without food for days were too weak to cremate their loved ones so that dogs and jackals feasted on piles of dead bodies. Quoting from the records kept in the British archives and interviewing the old people who were still alive and remembered the great ordeals they suffered during the Bengal famine, Mukherjee (2010) brings out several harrowing stories of the 1943 famine. She states that out of sheer helplessness, "mothers had turned into murderers, village belles into whores, fathers into traffickers of daughters." Those who escaped from the trauma were, according to her, the ones who migrated to the cities sufficiently early in search of jobs as well as the women who turned to prostitution and fed the members of their families (Mukherjee, 2010).

There were several reasons for Churchill to show his 'imperial brutality' of which the following two would appear more significant: (1) An unhappy feeling was haunting his mind that he had to preside over the liquidation of the British Empire in which India was the largest in terms of size and the source for resource-extraction. In retaliation to such a humiliation waiting for him, Churchill decided instead to preside over 'mass extermination' by forfeiting food to the people during the most depressing famine in recent history. (2) The 1943 famine had coincided not only with the Second World War in which Great Britain was the leading partner on the side of the Allied Forces but also with the massive civil disobedience and the 'Quit India' movement that Gandhiji had launched. It was his anger against Gandhiji, more than anything else that forced Churchill to mercilessly forfeit food supplies to the dying millions. This is reminiscent of the 'ethnic cleansing' that the British rulers adopted in Ireland during the 'potato famine' of 1840s, through 'barbarous indifference' in providing food and medical aid to the people reeling under starvation and fatal epidemics. Even wheat available in Ireland was carried away in ship-loads by the British rulers to other parts of England, giving justification that potato, not wheat, was the staple food of Irish people.

7.5 Land Revenue

If the negative attitude of Winston Churchill had worsened the food crisis and intensified the 1943 famine, it was the heavy land revenue demand and the oppressive manner in which it was collected that created general pre-famine conditions in British India during the past two centuries. In times of crop failures, rural employment dipped, prices rose to unaffordable levels and pushed the people into the grip of famines. As we noted in Chapter-4, Dutt (1900) in his *Open Letters to Lord Curzon* had established this fact beyond doubt. After the EIC received the *diwani* in Bengal from the Mughals and especially after the introduction of the Permanent Settlement in 1793, cultivators' rights on the lands they tilled were legally forfeited. Treating the Indian system on par with the practice in Europe, the British administration equated zamindars or the 'tax farmers' who collected revenue from the farmers on behalf of the government as virtual land owners. These zamindars, with their new-found rights on land, employed a number of unethical means on the tenants to increase the revenue collection, mainly: (i) arbitrary short standard of measurement to increase the cultivated area for assessment; (ii) imposition of various kinds of cesses over and above the land revenue, mostly without governmental authorisation; and (iii) sheer physical coercion to collect the arrears of revenue and to take away the cultivators' other assets in compensation for the outstanding payments. These unethical practices adopted ruthlessly in the collection of revenue impoverished the cultivators. Most of these cultivators, who had no other way to face the unbearably heavy land revenue demands made by the zamindars, discarded agriculture as their livelihood option and joined the reserve army of landless labourers. Whenever adverse weather conditions like floods or droughts affected agricultural activities, these people were the earliest to fall prey to the outbreak of famines.

However, in due course, the Permanent Settlement in Bengal appeared to have discarded the unethical and ruthless practices followed in the initial years. The widely read *Cambridge Economic History of India* has a long section, contributed by B. Chaudhuri, on the positive aspects of the Permanent Settlement in Bengal. Chaudhuri argues that firstly, the critics of British policy have only seen the rise in the revenue actually paid by cultivators. These critics, according to him, have "largely ignored the complex and the changing economic environment in which the increase had occurred – particularly the increase in the cultivation, its increased stability in some cases and the increase in peasants' resources in other ways – so that any increase in the peasants' rent had not been unfair to them and did not necessarily impoverish them." He elaborates it further: "Cultivation of cash crops, the increasing stability of agricultural prices, their upward movement in some cases and certain associated developments considerably improved the peasants' resources."

In Chaudhuri's perspective, the Permanent Settlement in Bengal was not a permanent or complete freeze on land revenue. Over the years, the revenue collection had in fact been coming down. In this context, he pointed out that the share of agricultural output in the land rent that the government received as land revenue was 90 per cent in 1793, the year in which the Governor-General Cornwallis introduced Permanent Settlement for Bengal. The receipt steeply declined to as low as 28 per cent by the end of the nineteenth-century and further to 18.5 per cent by 1940 when the Second World War was raging.[10] The implication of this is clear. The peasants who could increase the productivity of land, for which enough resources were left with them by the land revenue authorities in Bengal, could go on gaining from their physical labour. We can cite two concrete evidences in support of this argument. (1) Amartya Sen in his comprehensive analysis of the causes and consequences of the 1943 Bengal famine does not attribute any role to the Permanent Settlement in worsening the hunger and deprivation. (2) Dutt (1900), as we noted in Chapter-4, had in one of his letters to Lord Curzon agreed that the land revenue system that the EIC adopted in Bengal had actually benefited its agricultural sector by fostering farm enterprises and enabling the cultivating households to withstand stresses that their counterparts in other parts of the country had faced during harvest failures, whereas the same benefit had not accrued to the farming community in the *ryotwari* areas of Madras presidency. The pernicious impacts of *ryotwari* land revenue system on agriculture and the livelihood of the people would appear more pronounced in Malabar than in other parts of the Madras presidency.

When Malabar was separated from Bombay and attached to Madras presidency and, particularly after the *ryotwari* system of land revenue was introduced from 1805, it was hoped that the repeated turmoil that the cultivating households faced until then under the EIC rule might come to an end. In Bombay presidency, the ryots and landlords of Malabar had to confront very unruly systems of land revenue demand, which was marked by frequent changes in the method of assessment and hikes in the revenue imposts. Large land holders and the traditional *raja*s were evicted from their land indiscriminately when they failed to pay in time the excessively high revenue imposed on them. We have seen in Chapter-4 that, it was due to the revolt of the *raja*s that Malabar had to be shifted from Bombay to the Madras presidency. However, studies conducted with evidences from archival records show that, shifting of Malabar to the presidency of Madras and the introduction of the *ryotwari* system of land revenue, rather than ameliorating, had only worsened the woes of the ryots in the district (Kumar, 1983).

Though *ryotwari* was praised as a system without middlemen between the ryot and the government, and therefore free of corruption, officials who were deputed for the assessment and collection of revenue behaved worse than the manner in which 'middlemen' under *zamindari* or *mahalwari* systems behaved. These officials revised the land revenue upward every year; quite often they over-estimated the cultivated area, imposed other charges like cesses and salt-tax on the initial assessment and kept for themselves the excess collection without passing on to the government. In this context, Kumar (1983) states that in Malabar, "there were unrecorded depredations of revenue officials. The cultivator was left with pitifully little." During bad years, the government announced remissions of revenue, as provided under the Famine Code of 1883. In effect, these remissions were not reflected in the actual payments to be made by the ryots to the government. The officials, with the tacit approval of the higher-ups, nullified the succour provided by remissions through other means. Thus, when the revenue demand went on increasing year after year, if the ryots decided to dispense with farming out of helplessness and joined as wage labourers in others' fields, it proved more disastrous. The revenue officials imposed a penalty for not cultivating the land in their possession.

In addition to the excessively heavy land revenue, there were at least three other factors that strengthened famines in British Malabar with shorter intervals and increasing ferocity. One such factor was the change in the apportionment of farm output among different stake holders. Before the British rulers introduced the *ryotwari* system, the farm output in Malabar was divided among the ryot, the *janmi*, and *kaanakkaar*, and the government. After the introduction of the *ryotwari* system in the early nineteenth century, the British administration refused to treat *kaanakkaar* and *janmi* as separate entities and set apart only one share of output to either of them. This automatically increased the land revenue of the government while reducing the 'farm retention' of output, which was used by the *janmi* and *kaanakkaar* to partly distribute to their attached labourers and other poor villagers during starvation and famine. The second was the ruthless practice of indiscriminate attachment of lands of the defaulting ryots and assignment of ownership to anyone who was prepared to pay the land revenue in time. This practice greatly increased a class of 'pauper ryots' in Malabar. During famines, these relatively big farmers and their better-paid rural artisans also had fallen victims to hunger and malnutrition along with landless farmers and mendicants. That was why, in the case of Malabar, the victims of famine could not be seen taking a hierarchically upward sequence over time, as Adam Smith postulated, i.e. from the poorest in the first year, to the small peasants in the second year, and the middle class in the third year and so on. Conversely, it was the 'pauper ryots', belonging to the economically better-off middle-class, or above, who became victims of starvation and famine in the initial stage itself. Only subsequently had the food crisis came down to lower levels, mainly to the attached and landless labourers, through the process of what is called 'derived destitution'. The third factor was, as we have extensively discussed earlier, the coercive tactics adopted by the revenue officials to snatch away whatever quantity of grain came across their sight, irrespective whether the person concerned belonged to a land-owning small peasant, or an attached labour and no matter it was kept aside as next year's seed, or as subsistence for a part of the current season.[11]

7.6 Epidemics and Mortalities

The most harrowing aspect of famine is not starvation and destitution per se. Famine - a collective human misery - occurs when starvation is accompanied by widespread attacks of epidemic diseases and large-scale unnatural mortalities. Starvation emaciates the victims more than it kills whereas famine heightens the forces of mortality and kills the emaciated even more. In other words, it is when the starvation-phase of mortalities gives way to the epidemic-phase that famine-mortalities become frighteningly high. In his *Poverty and Famines*, Amartya Sen gives the sequences and intensities of epidemics and mortalities in three phases: He calls the first phase as starvation-phase, during which deaths are caused generally by diarrhoea and dysentery – the former is purely on account of starvation and the latter, mainly from eating uneatable objects, which are known in the literature as 'famine food'. If the area in question is poor in sanitation and environmental hygiene, and is devoid of protected drinking water, fatal epidemics come in one-by-one and exacerbate the death toll. This is the second and the most calamitous epidemic-phase of mortalities. According to Sen, in the 1943 famine in Bengal, the major epidemic diseases that contributed to excess mortalities were (in the descending order) malaria, cholera, dysentery, diarrhoea and the enteric group of fevers, the latter being a basket of diseases including influenza, measles, cerebro-spinal fever and kala-azar. The mortalities that accompany the starvation-phase, after intensifying in the second phase, do not retreat all of a sudden when famine subsides. Instead, in the third phase, death tolls continue further for a few months to a year or more, depending on the types of contagious diseases that infected the victims of starvation and destitution. To quote Sen: "starvation deaths (in Bengal) seemed to have peaked around September and October that year (1943). Cholera mortality reached its maximum in October and November. Malaria peaked in December, and continued in its elevated position through the next year and later. Smallpox reached its height in March and April 1944, and a greater height still one year later." (Sen, 1981: 203)

The phases through which starvation, famine and its retreat moved in Malabar were not perceptibly different from what we observed in Bengal, though the type of epidemics and the trends in mortalities caused by the epidemics in these phases might not be same in the two regions. So also was the speed with which they appeared, peaked and retreated. We have already explained earlier the epidemic-wise mortalities in Malabar through the preceding more than two centuries. We will now make a closer look at how these mortalities compare with those wreaked havocs in Bengal during the 1943 famine. While doing so, it is important to remember that, for Bengal, we have monthly data, adjusted upward for under-reporting by various authors who studied the subject whereas, for Malabar, our figures are taken directly from the population census without any adjustments for under-reporting. Given these limitations, our data reveal *inter alia* the following:

First, during the starvation phase of the 1943 famine, diarrhoea and dysentery had caused almost 7 per cent of the total deaths in Bengal while it was estimated at above 16 per cent in Malabar. This seems to indicate that the starvation phase was relatively longer in Malabar and the misery that it caused to its people, more severe than in Bengal. Fevers, including malaria, which occurred simultaneously with the initial starvation phase, were the largest famine-killers in Bengal. In Malabar also, fevers had taken away a sizable proportion of the famine-victims. What is significant to note here is that, in Bengal, the proportion of mortalities due to fevers accounted for 27 per cent of the total whereas the enteric group of fevers accounted for 28 per cent of the total famine mortalities in Malabar. Furthermore, unlike in Bengal, these were not the largest killers among the epidemics in the district.

Second, if malaria had caused the largest proportion of famine-deaths in Bengal during the epidemic phase, it was cholera that proved the largest killer in Malabar in terms of deaths per unit of population. This dangerous pandemic had almost completely disappeared from Malabar for a while. It came up all of a sudden and escalated in 1943, killing as high as 42 per cent of those who succumbed to all the epidemics in that year. Immediately after the famine, it again disappeared to insignificant level. As against this, the cholera mortality in Bengal was only around 9 per cent of the total famine mortalities during the 1943 famine.

We have seen in the foregoing that though mortalities by epidemics which started from the initial starvation-phase and intensified in the peak famine-phase did not subside along with the famine. This phenomenon was witnessed in both Bengal and Malabar. For example, in Bengal, deaths by malaria persisted after the famine was over for more than the next one year. Another epidemic, viz. smallpox, which was not very widespread in Bengal in the beginning of 1943, started flaring up in the latter part of the peak famine-year and continued until April 1944. Compared to this, in Malabar, deaths from fevers prolonged till the end of 1944 on an increasing scale. The smallpox, instead of raising its head in Malabar during the peak of the 1943 famine, came up and persisted in the next two years. From this, it would appear that the magnitude and depth of the attacks of epidemics and mortalities per unit of population were more severe in Malabar than in Bengal during the 1943 famine.

Registration Bias

Having analysed this much, a crucial question still remains: How many people had died in Bengal and Malabar during the 1943 famine? This is not an easy question to answer. In the context of Bengal, the Famine Inquiry

Commission 1945 had expressed its difficulty to accept the official mortality figures on the grounds that, in the whole of India, "even in normal times deaths are not fully recorded." The Commission attributed the following reasons for the undependability of these figures: The *chowkidars* or the village watchmen, who were generally illiterate and under-paid had to record deaths in addition to their other normal duties. They were therefore not very serious in this work. If famine coincided with a war, as happened in 1943, the *chowkidars* deserted their duty and went out in search of other works in better-paid and better-fed military or para military services. During their absence, whatever deaths occurred in the villages within their areas of duty remained unregistered. Some of the village-watchmen, who continued in their duty, died during famines. Their replacements took long delays and, in the interregnum, deaths were not registered by anyone else. Whenever famine preceded or coincided with floods, as in 1943, approach to the village office was disrupted so that the residents found it difficult to report the deaths in their families. Explaining these bottlenecks in the enumeration of death statistics, the Famine Inquiry Commission 1945 noted:

"The replacement of dead and vanished *chowkidars* was no easy matter and several weeks and months might elapse before successors could be found, during which deaths presumably went unrecorded. Further, in the height of the famine, thousands of people left their homes and wandered across the countryside in search of food. Many died by the roadside – witness the skulls and the bones which were to be seen there in the months following the famine. Deaths occurring in such circumstances would certainly not be recorded in the statistics of the Director of Public Health."[12]

As the Health Department figures were known to contain errors of registration in the direction of under-reports, authors who examined these figures used certain statistical assumptions and applied 'correction factors' on the official figures to arrive at the more likely level of famine mortality in Bengal. The Famine Inquiry Commission of 1945 revealed that the correction factor that it used was 40 per cent. On the contrary, Amartya Sen found that the actual correction factor that the Commission applied was, according to his calculation, 45 per cent and not 40 per cent. Applying this multiplier on a longer period beyond 1943, Sen arrived at the death toll in Bengal during the 1943 famine at 2.7 million to 3 million.[13]

The credibility of the mortality statistics reported for Malabar by the Madras presidency's Public Health Department would appear equally bad, if not worse. On occasions, while consolidating the report for the presidency headquarters, the district level officials themselves had stated that the mortality figures received from various *taluka*s were not necessarily reliable in their entirety. The reasons cited for the undependability of the figures were also by and large the same in Bengal and Malabar, namely, a downward bias. As nobody bothered to look at the repeated famines and the related epidemics and mortalities in British Malabar, we have no way to know the extent of under-reporting of famine-mortalities here. We are therefore forced to accept the unadjusted official mortality data for the district. To make the figures comparable, we have considered the unadjusted official data for Bengal also. According to Asok K. Mitra, who was the Superintendent of Census Operations and Joint Development Commissioner of Bengal, on the whole, 1,873,749 persons died in Bengal during the 1943 famine. In terms of deaths per unit of population, these figures worked out to 29.95 (rounded to 30) per every thousand persons. Compared to this, the total deaths in 1943 were recorded at 124,787 in Malabar, or 30.47 (rounded to 30.5) deaths per thousand persons. In other words, even though statistically the death tolls per unit of population in the 1943 famine in Malabar and Bengal were not strikingly different, it would appear that the intensity of human misery that Malabar suffered was a notch higher than in Bengal.

Gender Disparity

A significant aspect of famine anywhere in the world is the glaring gender disparity in human mortalities. This was equally the case of the 1943 famine in Bengal and Malabar. For Bengal, Amartya Sen adopted the following methodology to arrive at male-female mortalities per unit of population: (a) averages of the mortalities in 1941 and 1942 as the normal level mortality for each sex; (b) percentage of excess mortality over the estimated normal level, separately for both sexes in 1943; (c) average excess mortalities during the four-year period of 1943-46; and (d) district-wise differences in mortalities in normal times vs-a-vis the 1943 famine. From these figures, Sen worked out the excess mortality of men, women, children, and old people above 60 years of age in Bengal. His findings are the following: First, the average male-mortality in 1941-42, which represented normal years, accounted for 52 per cent of the total. Compared to this, the excess male-mortality in 1943, the year in which famine peaked, was 54 per cent. The four year average of excess male-mortality during 1943–46 was 52 per cent, a figure exactly the same as the normal level of male-mortality. From this, Sen argued that the male-mortality during the ten-year period under study was remarkably stable in Bengal. Secondly, the average normal female-mortality, reckoned for 1941-42, was 48 per cent of the total. During the peak famine year of 1943, female-mortality came down to 46 per cent, that is, 8 percentage points below the male-mortality estimated for Bengal. However, once again the female-mortality ratio moves up to the normal female mortality level of 48 per cent for 1943-46, indicating that both male and female mortalities in Bengal were remarkably stable during the 1940s but male-mortalities shot up in the peak of the 1943 famine.

In *Poverty and Famines*, Sen states that his findings agreed with most of the studies on the subject. For example, according to the Famine Commission of 1880, all the authoritative studies about the nineteenth century famines were unanimous that women succumbed to famine less easily than men. This was also the opinion of the Famine Inquiry Commission of 1945. Among the individual studies, Sen quotes the findings by Das (1949) that, during the 1943 famine in Bengal, "for every dead woman there were nearly two dead men." This was substantiated by Dreze and Sen in their subsequent study *Hunger and Public Action*: "women appear to have certain biological advantages over men in survival, and there is some evidence that these general advantages enhance the relative ability of women to cope with temporary distress situations vis-à-vis men" (Dreze and Sen, 1989). Conversely, the survey conducted by Mahalanobis et al (1946), showed that, during the 1943 Bengal famine, mortalities among women were larger than among men. Amartya Sen felt that this might have occurred due to sampling bias.

As regards Malabar, our estimates from census reports show that male-mortality during the 1943 famine was 45.9 per cent of the total. Compared to this, the female mortality accounted for 8.2 percentage points higher than male mortality. The extent of excess female mortality in Malabar was so sharp that, in 1943, it was 225 per cent higher than in 1942 (which was a normal year) whereas the male mortality increased by just 167 per cent over the same period. The larger female-mortality in Malabar and the larger male-mortality in Bengal during the peak of the 1943 famine call for an explanation. Though there are a number of studies on gender disparities in human mortalities, the causes attributed in these studies are more general. One such explanation given in some of these studies is that this happens because of the intra-family difference in the household food distribution, particularly when the family does not have enough food needed for equal distribution among all the members. A widely held view in this regard is that men take disproportionately larger share of household food at the expense of other members. In this situation, women and children get less than what men eat. According to this view, women themselves permit this pattern of skewed distribution of food in the family and invite malnutrition and morbidity due to which they are easily subjected to various deficiency diseases and unnatural deaths more than the male members. This becomes inevitable because, in the food-poor families, the distribution should be in favour of wage-earners and against those who are not working members in the household. Quite often, among conventional peasant societies and working class families, women eat last, the unserved residues or husbands' leftovers, which are insufficient to keep up minimum physical strength. Undernutrition leading to weaker physiological state and quicker than normal susceptibility to epidemic diseases also increases female mortalities. In households where intra-family differences in food sharing are knowingly or unknowingly unfavourable to women, their state of malnutrition and morbidity is higher, as a result of which their susceptibility to epidemics and unnatural mortalities is also higher.[14]

This condition faced by women was strengthened by other factors: (a) early age of marriage and the ensuing reproductive burden and burdens of household work; (b) lack of access to maternity centres and the dependence on illiterate local midwives who adopted crude methods for child delivery; (c) unwillingness of women from ordinary households to go for treatments available in limited government dispensaries overcrowded with beggars and street prostitutes; and (d) the practice of general unwillingness shown by women to reveal illness at the early stage of occurrence (Harriss, 1989). In this context, Bardhan (1974) finds that mortality rates are the highest in regions where health facilities and public health expenditure per capita are the lowest. In such areas, as British Malabar, female mortalities outstripping male mortalities during calamitous famines could not be over-ruled.

To sum up: given the limited availability of comparable information, this chapter has attempted to bring out certain broad similarities and contrasts in the dimensions and depths of human miseries that the 1943 famine inflicted on the people of Bengal and Malabar. The critical factors, the impacts of which were similar in both the regions included: (a) the failure or indifference of the colonial administration to anticipate the impending subsistence crisis and continuously engaging in compulsory procurement of foodgrains even from the relatively deficit areas; (b) difficulty to compensate the deficiency of domestic availability of rice through imports from Burma as it was captured by Japan; (c) hoarding of food stocks by speculators in connivance with officials; (d) ruthless 'food denial policy' adopted by Winston Churchill in retaliation against the independence movement launched under the leadership of Gandhiji; and (e) combined effects of the above factors resulting in the overshooting of food prices beyond the purchasing power of the common people.

The category of factors, the impacts of which were dissimilar in Bengal and Malabar during the 1943 famine included: First, the land revenue system ceased to be an aggravator of hunger and malnutrition in Bengal since the beginning of twentieth century, while, during the same period, it created perpetual pre-famine conditions in Malabar and pushed the people into famine whenever there was a slight symptom of food crisis. Second, as the intra-family food distribution was not generally adverse to women in Bengal before the Second World War as it was a surplus producer of rice, they survived more than their men folks during the 1943 famine. Malabar being deficit in food even during better harvest years, women in the district suffered perpetual morbidity because of adverse intra-family food distribution. Therefore, in Malabar, female mortalities in the 1943 famine were more than that of their male counterparts. Three, though the colonial rulers were notoriously indifferent in improving environmental sanitation and healthcare facilities, circumstantial evidences indicate that Malabar suffered more than Bengal in these respects. Lastly, the epidemic diseases that devastated both the regions were by and large same. Some of these diseases continued in both the regions even after the famine subsided – in Bengal, a few months and in Malabar several months after the famine subsided. It is true that, in absolute terms, the 1943 famine snatched away the largest number of human lives in Bengal but, in terms of mortalities per unit of population, the intensity of famine was more gruesome in Malabar.

Notes

1. See, Chapter-6, entitled 'The Great Bengal Famine' in *Poverty and Famines*, pp. 52-85.
2. Estimated from Census of India 1951, Vol.II: West Bengal and Sikkim – Part IA West Bengal.
3. *Ibid.*
4. See, *Handbook of Agriculture*, Indian Council of Agricultural Research, New Delhi, 1961 (reprint, 1997).
5. There is an elaborate note on that flood in Burdwan in the Census of India 1951, relating to West Bengal and Sikkim. See, its Vol.II, Part 1A, op.cit.
6. We have already brought out this in detail in the preceding chapter.
7. See, Report of the Foodgrain Policy Committee under the Chairmanship of Sir Theodore Gregory (Delhi, 1943).
8. This section heavily leans on a recently published and widely reviewed book written on the basis of the British archival records by Madhusree Mukherjee; see op.cit.
9. See Nanavati Papers referred earlier and Bhatia (1967), op. cit.
10. The Cambridge Economic History of India, Vol-II, pp. 86-176.
11. Quoted in Sen (1981:196), op.cit.
12. *Ibid.*
13. *Ibid.*
14. See, Wheeler, 1984; Esterik, 1985; and especially Harriss, 1989.

Chapter 8

A Postscript

We may now bring together some of the main findings of this investigation and wrap up. Famine is a collective human misery. Historically, the routes through which it originated and the process by which it escalated were not the same everywhere. The major episodes of famine that this monograph quoted on various occasions would prove the point: (i) most of the authors explained famine as extreme starvation, caused by natural factors like monsoon fluctuations or man-made factors like war, movement restrictions, speculation and hoarding, accompanied by attacks of epidemics and mortalities; (ii) in areas like Malabar, poor hygienic conditions coupled with heavy rains led to the development of a multitude of water-borne and air-borne diseases, which culminated into disastrous famines; (iii) Adam Smith postulated the South Asian famines as arising from food availability decline and spreading upward in a hierarchical manner, starting from the landless poor in the first year of the monsoon failure, followed by small farmers in the second year, and the middle level farmers in the next year, and so on; (iv) Amartya Sen found that famine could also spread from richer to the poorer classes through a process called 'derived destitution', that is to say, when the large farmers in a region undergo starvation and famine due to a serious crop failure, others dependent on them down the line would also become its victims; and (v) Gandhiji recorded a single flood in British Malabar plunging the entire population up to the middle-class and above into the horrors of famine.

Whatever be the routes through which and processes by which famine erupts, innumerable writings on the subject, especially after the publication in 1981 of *Poverty and Famines* by Amartya Sen, agree *inter alia* on one point: There cannot have a country in the world, either developing or developed, which has not experienced this misery at least once in its history. By the first half of the nineteenth-century, developed countries of the West could wipe out famines, famine-led epidemics and unnatural mortalities through concerted state action. The history of Great Britain provides the best example in this regard. Long before formally declaring as a 'welfare state' and pursuing not only free market economic policies by itself but also persuading other western countries to follow the same path, Britain was carefully building up on another front comprehensive social welfare measures for its own people. In fact, one of the implicit objectives of its imperialist ambition was to ensure that, economically, the British citizens stood above all others and in no way suffered from food shortages despite England, by virtue of its climate and soil, could not produce most of the items of food that they consumed. With this end in view, imperialist Britain went on extracting whatever food was available in its third world colonies and dumped into the home-market so that prices remained affordably low even for the poorest of the poor, while the colonial population lived a life of undernourishment and morbidity. No wonder, by the time famines disappeared in Great Britain, its third world colonies like India were increasingly reeling under famines with unprecedented ferocity.

British Malabar, which is our focus of investigation, was a special case. Colonial rulers including the best among the bureaucrats employed in the district had bluffed that, being blessed with unfailing monsoons and copious rains, Malabar produced abundance of food so that it remained impervious to famine. While claiming this, they conveniently ignored certain fundamental facts which should not have been unknown to them. As the district topographically slants from the Western Ghats to Arabian Sea and is endowed with porous or semi-porous soils, the rain-water received in rivers, rivulets and backwaters drained off the earth in no time. One or two bad monsoons in a row, which were not unusual in Malabar, created drought-like conditions and led to serious food availability crises and famines. Similarly, Malabar repeatedly experienced flash floods due to excess monsoons, destroying standing crops, washing off food stocks and other belongings of the people, and plunging the entire region into famines. After the British occupation, the district was increasingly handicapped in meeting its food demand even during years of better harvests, as large areas of the surplus producing Wayanad *taluk* were converted into plantation estates. William Logan, the well-known historiographer and administrator, who served the district for several years in different capacities, had stated in his *Malabar Manual* that: (i) this district was always on the brink of famine but it could not escalate into famine because of the timely intervention by the British government; and (ii) ever since the EIC took over the administration in India, there was no record of famines in the district.

Our survey has conclusively established that Logan's assertions, which his successors in the administration also echoed, were grotesque misrepresentation of facts. Malabar had experienced repeated famines during the British rule because of the indifference of the rulers in undertaking famine prevention activities. Whenever a famine broke out, the colonial rulers imposed merciless restrictions on private community kitchens and destitute feedings. For instance, in terms of Richard Temple's directive, charitable food distribution-centres were required to be set up far way from one another so that destitutes who received food at one centre could not reach another centre and fill their stomachs in full. In times of distress, the government invariably hiked taxes and duties so that richer sections in the society were incapacitated from conducting gratuitous kitchens. We have also noted that the devastating famine of 1876-78 took place in Malabar when Logan was serving as its Collector and that he himself had received under his official seal and dates several reports from taluk level officials about the raging epidemics and famines in different parts of the district. From the fact that the massive two-volume historiography was first published just eight years after the 1876-78 famine, his statement that after 1727 there was no record of any famine in Malabar cannot be considered as an oversight but a deliberate attempt to conceal the truth. As he concealed this fact, he had to also conceal the truth about the cattle mortality that accompanied the famine in Wayanad taluk, the major cattle rearing centre in the district.

Just as Logan argued about the nineteenth century, several economic historians stated in recent years that, in the first half of the twentieth century, there was no serious famine anywhere in British India, except the 1943 Bengal famine. The message implied in this statement was that, of late, the developmental works undertaken by the colonial rulers could effectively plug the possibilities of hunger and malnutrition. The evidences marshalled in this book unravel a different story. Between 1918 and 1943, there were four major famines of different magnitudes in Malabar district itself. Of these, one was globally transmitted; two had been experienced in several parts of British India; and only one originated and confined mostly to Malabar and neighbouring areas, making this argument vacuous. Given the general socio-economic conditions of British Malabar, which was extremely backward, there might have been other sporadic famines of varying magnitudes in different parts of the district. Since suppression of unhappy events seemed to be a common practice among the bureaucracy, such episodes might have hardly been reported. When archival records become one-sided history, these cannot be relied to sketch the events with relative accuracy. In the absence of other references, we were forced to fall back on these 'coloured' records for the preparation of this monograph.

8.2 Word vs Deed

Despite these limitations, our investigation into the archival records showed that the most important factor that led to repeated famines in British

Malabar (as also other parts of India) was the wide gap between the promises made by the colonial rulers and the manner in which those promises were implemented: For example, Lord Ripon had stated that famines would cease once and for all if extensive railway networks were constructed, connecting ports, cities and agricultural production centres because railways allowed movement of food quickly from surplus to famine-prone deficit areas. His grand design for Indian railways required large-scale investments, which he organised *inter alia* by diverting funds from the outlays set apart for social sector developments. At this juncture, the British administration's view that Malabar was impervious to famines took a reversal and it argued that the district was severely famine-prone. Accordingly, Ripon started allocating sizable 'famine insurance funds' in the annual budgets for the district and diverted the entire amount towards the construction of a few new railway lines on the contention that these were 'famine lines'.

The history of railways would show that by 1875 British Indian railways had become the fourth largest transport network in the world. Had the grand theory of Lord Ripon been materialised Malabar should not have experienced any serious famine. But 1876-78 witnessed a disastrous famine in Malabar. Thereafter famines repeated in quicker succession because, instead of using railways and feeder roads connecting them to bring in food from surplus to deficit areas, the British administration tacitly allowed private traders to carry away whatever food-stocks were available, either for exports or for indulging in speculation. The railway networks were also used to penetrate into Indian markets the qualitatively superior but price-wise cheaper industrial goods produced in Britain with modern machines under factory system. The increased inflow of these goods competed out the labour-intensive cottage and small-scale industries in India, compelling those who lost their livelihood in these industries for panic-migration to the overcrowded agriculture sector. The additional burden on rural demand from this section for the already shrinking food availability was one major reason for hunger and destitution dragging the entire villages into famine with a slight aberration in the monsoon. Thus, expanding the railway networks with much fanfare, instead of preventing, invited disastrous famines at progressively shorter intervals.

When the American Civil War blocked the internal movement of cotton and other agricultural commodities from that country to the port-centres for exports, the British industry was compelled to depend on the agriculturally large Indian sub-continent to fill up its raw material gap. For this purpose, the imperialist government cajoled the farmers in the colony to go in for commercialisation of agriculture, giving them the hope that their escape from perennial impoverishment to permanent prosperity rested in discarding the loss-making subsistence farming and embracing the cultivation of export-oriented cash crops. The temptation was so strong that farmers shifted their lands under foodgrains to cultivate cotton, indigo, jute, sugarcane, tobacco, condiments and spices, which could not be grown in the temperate western countries because of their peculiar soil-climate conditions. The cultivation of these crops, it is well-known, required additional costs. This came liberally from the trader-money-lenders but on the stipulation that the produce should be marketed only through them. To begin with, the promised 'prosperity' appeared very much in sight. The export demands for the Indian commercial crops, especially cotton and indigo, started increasing. The prices quoted for these goods in Britain were also far higher than what the peasants could expect at home from the cultivation of subsistence crops.

Soon the farming community realised that it was a chimera. The increased prices from exports hardly came back to them. A part of it was confiscated by the British government towards 'home charges', that is, the payment of salary, pension and other perquisites to the Secretary of State and his staff in charge of India. Another part was appropriated by the trader-money-lenders who advanced credit to the peasantry for cash crop cultivation. Thus, the economic condition of these farmers remained where it was before shifting to commercial crops. It deteriorated further with the cessation of the Civil War in America and the resumption of exports of the long-staple raw-cotton and an array of other agro-based industrial raw materials from the U.S. to England. The immediate impact was a veritable stoppage of Indian agricultural exports. Conversion of areas under subsistence-oriented food crops into the production of commercial crops for exports had already reduced the food availability in the country. When the export markets were closed, the unsold cash crops had to be dumped back on the domestic market. The resultant collapse of the prices of these crops and the steep decline in the entitlement of the growers to food aggravated the already rampant hunger and malnutrition. Whenever harvest failures occurred, even if minor, the agriculture dependent population plunged into disastrous famines.

We mentioned earlier about the rising penetration of British industrial goods into Indian markets and its adverse consequences to the domestic economy. The government, instead of ameliorating the predicament of the local economy, was anxious to see how, with the increase in trade, nominal exchange rate of export earnings of British private traders and thereby the flow of tariff revenue to the British exchequer did not fluctuate violently in terms of Pound Sterling. It was for this purpose that a rupee-coin was introduced in India, replacing other coins circulating in different parts of the country. This followed the introduction of a change in the mode of payment of land revenue to the government from kind to cash. While introducing the new system, the imperialist government claimed that monetisation was an index of progress and that henceforth India, which was until then regarded as a primitive economy, stood integrated into the prosperous world market of the western hemisphere.

What actually happened was not progress and prosperity but complete chaos in the existing system of accounting and transactions. Insistence of the government that the land revenue should be paid in cash forced the ryots to sell their produce in the market immediately after harvests when prices remained low. Apart from land revenue, all other payments, particularly to the agricultural labourers and rural artisans had to be converted from grain-wages to money-wages. Had the old system of grain-wages continued, the agriculture-dependent population could have withstood the horrors of repeated famines to an extent, if not in full. We have seen that, before monetisation, the food stocks available in the village came handy for mutual dependence among the people during periods of distress. Monetisation of the economy, rather than bringing prosperity, intensified the misery of the people so that whenever crop failures occurred and prices soared, famine became unavoidable. In the same way, during bumper harvests, as prices steeply declined, their conditions remained as they were during crop failures on account of monetisation.

8.3 Hegemony and Famines

In the second half of the nineteenth-century, when EIC was disbanded and the Indian administration became remote-controlled from Britain, we noticed famines repeating in the colony at shorter intervals. This was not accidental. At one stroke, imperialist rulers headquartered in England wanted to maximise revenue collection from within the colony, meet all its administrative expenses in India and in England, finance continuous annexation-wars against local kings and carry away the remaining funds gathered from the colony for augmenting prosperity at home. This strategy required, apart from devising ways and means of raising revenue, extreme parsimony in its utilisation within the colony. Though attractive as a proposition, it was not a cake-walk to achieve. Quite often the methods adopted by the colonial administration for this purpose was a kind of ruthless Gramscian type hegemony. Examples are plenty. The hegemony unleashed by the British administration appeared fiercer in Malabar than elsewhere in three spheres: (i) *ryotwari* system of land revenue collection; (ii) expenditures on socio-economic development; and (iii) popularisation of allopathic medicine.

Agriculture being the predominant economic activity, ever since the EIC received *diwani* in Bengal and until the British rulers left India in 1947, land was treated as their 'milch cow' for extracting the revenue they required, as other sectors of the economy were too underdeveloped to mobilise any appreciable resources. Despite declaring that they only 'adopted' the three land revenue systems existed in India before they came to power, in the assessment and collection, the British administration was more unethical. Among the three land tenures that the colonial rulers followed in India, the *ryotwari* being theoretically a system without middlemen between the state and the ryot, unlike the other two, was expected to be free of corruption and therefore favourable to the expansion of agriculture and maintenance of food security. Yet it turned out to be more exploitative than the *zamindari* and *mahalwari* systems. A compendium of facts marshalled from archival records and presented in Part-I of this monograph would show that British administration's revenue officials, who were entrusted with the job of assessment and collection, had to meet certain fixed targets every year. For this purpose, their political masters saddled them with police and judicial powers, which they used in every possible way to achieve not only the target given for revenue collection but also to pocket a sizable portion of what they collected.

During natural calamities and famines, there were regular announcements that, in terms of the 1883 Famine Code, the government would remit the revenue already collected and would dispense with further collection until the distress situation ended. However, these announcements remained on paper so that the overall revenue demand, instead of showing any reduction, went on increasing year after year, no matter there was a flood, a drought, or a famine. Naturally the ryots defaulted. Rules required the district Collector to first imprison the defaulters, and then attach and auction their properties to recoup the arrears. Quite often auction was made at lower than the prevailing market price of the attached property, and still below the arrears payable so that the ryots remained virtually indebted to the state for ever. If some of the affected ryots picked up courage and filed a lawsuit against the injustice, the decree came from the 'honourable court' that the grievance of the complainant was genuine but it was too small for the court to interfere. The only way out, then, for the ryots to escape from the ignominy of imprisonment, alienation of land and other assets was to approach the money-lenders who charged exorbitant rates of interest. These money-lenders were well-known to be extraordinarily generous in extending loans and advances for any purpose but, on failing to repay in time, created such a condition that the ryots had to surrender all their belongings, including land, bullocks, household utensils and even the honour of the women members in the family. The land revenue system under the British administration thus drove the agriculture dependent population into indebtedness, undernourishment, debilitation and famine.

Further, during the colonial era, several regions like Malabar in British India became breeding grounds of various epidemic diseases essentially because of heavy rains and poor sanitation arrangements. England before Industrial Revolution was not very different from this. While the British government almost entirely wiped out epidemics in its homeland through public investment in sanitation and medical care, it was extremely parsimonious in spending on such basic necessities in the colony. In Malabar, we have seen that the sanitation duty was entrusted by the presidency at one point of time to the lower level municipal employees who, in the absence of any allocation of funds, failed to carry out the job. The urban areas like the municipalities of Calicut and Palghat remained perennially filthy. Women's healthcare, which had a prime of place in England, was given least importance in India. The women in Malabar had to go to the multipurpose dispensaries for treatment of general ailments and to the generalist male doctors for child delivery. To prevent fatal contagious diseases, the administration asked its illiterate and untrained sweepers and peons to administer vaccination. Some of these diseases were imported through foreign visitors coming to India by passenger-ships. Even though there was a statutory rule for maritime-quarantine in respect of such passengers, the British administration did not implement it in order to oblige the private ship-owners from England who pleaded that the rule imposed extra costs on their business. The other statutory rule stipulated quarantining of epidemics-infected native people in isolated tents set up away from the inhabited areas, on condition that supply of water, food and medicines for the quarantined patients should be arranged by the district authorities through private charities. This rule was strictly implemented.

In quarantine cases, gratuitous helps hardly came by. The helpless relatives of the quarantined patients had no other way but to resort to black art and exorcism in the hope that such practices might scare away the evil spirits, which they believed, might have brought in the disease. For the British rulers, this provided a convenient excuse. They argued that there was no point in wasting scarce resources on sanitation and healthcare in the colony, as the native people did not believe in modern medicine and scientific way of living. At the same time, the imperialist government was keen to popularise allopathic medicine as a universal healthcare practice in the colony. Fulfilment of this objective demanded suppression of the existing indigenous medical and healthcare practices. On the receiving end were the two such age-old health care systems in Malabar: (i) the art of physical fitness and combat technique, called *Kalarippayattu*, which was practised generally by all men, women and children in the northern part of the district; and (ii) *ayurveda*, perhaps the only indigenous medical treatment and rejuvenation system in the district. Fearing that *Kalarippayattu* could be a threat to law and order, particularly in the backdrop of the rising independence movement, the government straight away put a ban on it.

For the suppression of *ayurveda*, the nature of hegemony that the imperialist Britain imposed was somewhat different and ostensibly sophisticated: (a) 'educating' the progressive sections in the society that *ayurveda* was a primitive and unscientific system of treatment, and (b) legally restricting public practices and sales of *ayurvedic* medicines. On the one side, British administration refused to set up enough government hospitals and dispensaries for allopathic medicines to treat fatal diseases and, on another side, repressed *ayurvedic* practices with the result that the native people, who had to otherwise live under unhygienic conditions in the absence of environmental sanitation and potable drinking water, repeatedly succumbed to epidemics and famines.

8.4 Theorising Famine

If 'hunger' is a personal travail, 'famine' is a collective human misery. While the former is invariably experienced by every individual sometimes in life, the latter is confronted by all big and small societies at least once in their existence. Innumerable studies on famines in various parts of the world by different authors approached the issue from any of the three perspectives: (i) food availability decline or FAD approach, with or without other factors; (ii) failure of exchange entitlement or FEE theory of famine; and (iii) state failure in dealing with the woes of the people that leads to, or exacerbates, famine. As these 'approaches' to identify the causal mechanisms underlying the state of famine involve logical reasoning, and not simply empirical narratives based on historical records, this monograph treats all of them as theories, though on purely technical grounds there may be hesitation for some to accept such a treatment.

While examining the food availability crisis and famines or what is called FAD approach to famine, we specifically noted that despite this being one of the earliest and widely known explanations of famine ever since Adam Smith postulated so in his *Wealth of Nations*, there were authors who asserted that, rather than FAD, other factors had been more prominent in escalating famines in third world countries, particularly India. As regards the FAD approach, it appeared innocently simple on the first sight. Later when a section of the western scholars and the British imperialist rulers, including the then Prime Minister Winston Churchill, linked it to a distorted form of Malthusian theory of population, the real intention behind the FAD approach became clear. In Chapter-3 we noted that: (i) at identical levels of economic development, the growth of population in Europe and the third world countries was not cognisably dissimilar; (ii) famine had taken place in third world colonies even when there was no FAD; (iii) the Malthusian-imbalance view itself arose from the 'racial bias' of the west towards the colonial people; and (iv) the British rulers went on repeating this view as an excuse to conceal their unwillingness to invest in sanitation and healthcare as also for improving the food productivity of land.

Another perspective of famine, known as the 'failure of exchange entitlement' or FEE theory, which Amartya Sen postulated relatively recently, has evoked fresh interests among researchers in the study of the subject. As we explained in Chapter-6, Sen attributes famine to a situation where the 'endowment bundle' of a person fails to fetch him his 'entitlement bundle'. In other words, according to FEE theory, famine occurs when a person's purchasing power is abysmally insufficient to buy his food and other essential items needed to sustain life. Making a clinical analysis based on unassailable empirical evidences, Sen argued that FAD is only one of the many factors leading to famine and that several famines of recent times could not be attributed to substantial decline in food availability. A distinguishing feature of the FEE theory is that it is visualised as an individual malady in a private ownership market economy and therefore should be ameliorated by the market.

Those who questioned the FAD approach, before Sen postulated the FEE theory of famine, had argued that, in British India, the most significant factors that escalated famines were: (a) lack of opportunity for gainful employment; (b) the Salt Act passed by the imperialist government, taking away the age-old right of the people to produce and consume salt as also to use it as a preservative of food; (c) large-scale exports of food; (d) excessive dependence on rainfall in the absence of irrigation facilities; (e) unethical practices in the land revenue demand; (f) free reign of trader-money-lenders in the rural country side; and (f) scarcity of potable drinking water, bad drainage system, poor sanitation, lack of health care facilities, etc. It is not difficult to recognise from these that, instead of the 'invisible hand' of the market, the 'visible hand' of the state could have prevented the flaring up of terrible famines in the colony. Sen does not altogether preclude, in *Poverty and Famines*, the role of the state in preventing hunger and destitution. But in his scheme, the state comes into the picture only when all other options for entitlement to food in the private ownership market economy are exhausted – these options being individual's own labour, own production, own skill, own equipment and even the inheritance-based entitlement.

However, in subsequent researches conducted by Sen in collaboration with Jean Dreze found that the state has not the last but the most primary responsibility in eradicating famine. They argued that, among the large number of twentieth-century famines, wherever the state positively involved in the direct management of food has proved far more effective in preventing hunger and malnutrition. The methods adopted by these states to eradicate famines included gratuitous feeding, subsidised distribution of foodgrains, public works, cash doles, direct price control, tax relief, crop insurance, and support to prices of commercial crops and livestock products from falling below certain critical levels. Interestingly, these pro-active states, which were successful in banishing famine, were not 'interventionist' as we understand the term. Instead, during the closing phase of the last millennium, most of these states were following open market policies and globalisation. Some of them were democratic states and others, dictatorships or oligarchies.

This may appear rather anachronistic. A cursory look at the origin and functions of the state would tell that there is nothing unusual about it. As we noted in Chapter-6, the state is historically a unique socio-political organisation that emerged along with the development of private property and accompanying struggles among contending classes for their due share in the national wealth. At that stage the role of the state appeared as a mediator among these economic classes and an apparatus that originated for maintaining peace and prosperity. In essence, however, from the very beginning, the state was an instrument – whatever the name by which it is called – to safeguard the interests of the dominant class it represented. Operationally, there was difficulty for such a policy to continue indefinitely. The more the state allowed the flow of income and wealth in favour of the economically dominant minority, the more became the incidence of poverty and famines among the majority outside the ruling class. Some of the regimes, which anticipated that the continuance of such a one-sided policy would endanger their own existence in power, initiated effective famine-prevention measures and eliminated hunger and destitution. The regimes which failed to do so invited recurrence of famines, as also the ire of the affected majority. History gives us a number of examples that, sooner or later, the latter category states were forced to pack off.

It is significant to note here that these cases relate to the indigenously formed sovereign states, whereas we are dealing in this monograph famines under an alien state – the British imperialism. Established by force and expanded through wars, its pre-eminent objective was to create more and more 'economic territories' with an eye on imperialist aggrandisement. Oppression of the subjugated people by means of a Gramscian form of hegemony was the method that it found feasible to defraud the available resources from the colony. British Malabar, the focus of our investigation, provides a typical example. Ever since this tiny region in the Western Coast was ceded by Tipu Sultan and brought under the Madras presidency as one of its administrative districts, the imperialist rulers and their high-profile bureaucrats used to loudly proclaim that, being a region blessed with sumptuous monsoons, Malabar could not have famines. Still, famines repeated in Malabar, not necessarily due to failure of monsoons and accompanying droughts but quite often due to excess rainfalls culminating into flash floods that washed away standing crops, carry-over stocks and other belongings of both under-privileged and privileged sections living in the affected area. On becoming indigent and infected by contagious diseases, they wandered around, emaciated and malnourished, and most of them died on the wayside.

Whenever such miseries occurred, the imperialist rulers declared a remission of land revenue, as provided under the 1883 Famine Code. However, these declarations remained, in effect, on paper. In the demand notice served on the peasants for revenue payment, the expected reduction due to the assured remission was nowhere in sight. Instead, the impost was found to be substantially higher than in normal years. We have noted that, in Malabar, the condition became worse as famine relief works were generally out of question. In case relief operations had to be initiated under inevitable circumstances, there were attempts to wipe out their beneficial effects by other means. One such example was the notorious Temple Wage and Temple Charity: i.e. to keep a register of physical weights of the beneficiaries on a weekly basis and to reduce the wage if the physical weight of the persons appointed for relief work remained unchanged. In case the person concerned was receiving gratuitous food a cut was to be effected in the quantity supplied. This was the general rule, even if the gratuitous food was distributed by private philanthropists.

Every monsoon in Malabar, whether normal or excessive, witnessed widespread debility diseases. Nonetheless, the British administration remained insensitive to invest in environmental sanitation and healthcare facilities. Public hospitals were conspicuous by their absence in several areas within the district. Coinciding with the suppression of indigenous medical practices, the predicament of the underprivileged sections in the district intensified. During the eighteenth and early nineteenth centuries, if similar developments occurred in the western world, the intellectuals, particularly the historians took up the issue for popular mobilisation, forcing the government in question to initiate ameliorative measures so that, by the mid-nineteenth century, epidemics and famines largely disappeared from today's developed west. As against this, the British rulers in India had a confrontationist attitude towards such problems, in case these were brought to the fore by the nationalist leaders associated with independence movement. In this backdrop, it was for the academic community to take up the travails of the people, just as their counterparts in Europe had done. Throughout the history of Malabar, the social scientists as a class seemed to have an 'imperialist indifference' towards the sufferings of the underprivileged sections in the society. This indifference continued, even when the famine was preceded by a flash flood and the people belonging to the better off sections also suffered. Emboldened by stoic silence of those who mattered in public eye, the British rulers, instead of initiating ameliorative actions to mitigate these human miseries, went on exploiting whatever was available, until they left the country in 1947. It was not simply that Malabar suffered the most from repeated famines, famine-led epidemics and unnatural mortalities during the imperialist rule.

References

Abrams, Mark (1946) *The Conditions of the British People, 1911– 1945* (London: Cerdric Chivers), quoted in Smales, 1975, op. cit.

Ackerman, Peter and Jack Du Vall (2000) *A Force More Powerful: A Century of Non-violent Conflict* (Palgrave Macmillan).

Adam, William (1840) *The Law and Custom of Slavery in British India* (London: Smith, Elder and Co., Cornhill).

Alamgir, M. (1980) *Famine in South Asia: Political Economy of Mass Starvation in Bangladesh* (Cambridge, Mass: Oelgeschlager, Gunn and Hain).

Allen, George (1986), 'Famines: The Bowbrick – Sen Dispute and Some Related Issues', *Food Policy*, August; pp. 259 – 263.

Ambirajan, S (1976), 'Malthusian Population Theory and Indian Famine Policy in the Nineteenth Century', *Population Studies* (30).

Arnold, David (1986), 'Cholera and Colonialism in British India', *Past and Present,* November, No.113, pp.118-151.

________(1988) *Famine: Social Crisis and Historical Change* (Oxford: Basil Blackwell).

________(1993) *Colonising the Body: State Medicine and Epidemic Disease in Nineteenth Century India* (New Delhi: Oxford University Press).

Baden-Powell, B.H. (1894) *Land Revenue and Tenure in British India* (Oxford: Clarendon Press).

Bagchi, Amiya Kumar (1972) *Private Investment in India 1900 – 1939* (New Delhi: Orient Longman).

Bailey, Christopher and Tim Harper (2004) *Forgotten Armies: Britain's Asian Empire and the War with Japan.* (London: Penguin Books).

Bandyopadhyay, Rekha (1993), 'Land System in India: A Historical Review', *Economic and Political Weekly*, December 25; pp. A. 149 – A. 155.

Bandyopadhyay, Sekhar (2004) *From Plassey to Partition: A History of Modern India* (Delhi: Orient Longman; reprinted by Orient Blackswan Private Limited, New Delhi, 2010).

Bardhan, Pranab (1974), 'On Life and Death Questions', *Economic and Political Weekly*", (Special Issue: Institutional Roadblocks), Vol. IX, Nos. 32-34, August, 10.

Barry, John (2004) *The Great Influenza: The Epic Story of the Deadliest Plague in History* (London: Penguin Books).

Basu, K, P. Patnaik and K. Suzumura (eds.) (1995) *Choice, Welfare and Development: A Festschrift in Honour of Amartya Sen* (New Delhi: Oxford University Press, published as Oxford India Paperbacks in 2000).

Beaud, Michel (1983) *A History of Capitalism* (Monthly Review Press; and South Asian edition by Aakar Books, Delhi, 2004).

Bhalla, G. S. (2007) *Indian Agriculture since Independence* (Delhi: National Book Trust of India).

Bhatia, B.M. (1963) *Famines in India: A Study of Some Aspects of Economic History of India 1860-1908* (London: Asia Publishing House; later updated to 1965 and reprinted in 1967 by the same publisher).

Bhattacharya, S. (1983), '*Eastern India*', in Dharma Kumar (ed.) op.cit. pp. 270 – 331.

Blaug, Mark (1980) *The Methodology of Economics or How Economists Explain* (U.K. Cambridge University Press; second edition, 1992).

Bottomore, et. al. (eds.) (1987) *A Dictionary of Marxist Thought* (Bail Blackwell Ltd; paperback reprint).

Bowbrick, Peter (1986), 'An Untenable Hypothesis on the Causes of Famine', *Food Policy*, (February), pp. 5 – 9.

_______(1986), 'The Causes of famine: A Refutation of Professor Sen's Theory', *Food Policy* (May), Vol 11, No 2, pp. 105 – 24.

Bradley, Keith (1994) *Slavery and Society in Rome* (London: Cambridge University Press).

Bridge, Carl (1986) *Holding India to the Empire: The British Conservative Party and the 1935 Constitution* (New Delhi: Sterling).

Brown, Judith (1994) *Modern India: Origins of an Asian Democracy* (New York: Oxford University Press).

Buchanan, James M. (1975), 'Utopia, the Minimal State, and Entitlement', *Public Choice*, Vol. 23, pp. 121-26.

Caldwell, John (1988), 'Malthus and the Less Developed World: The Pivotal Role of India', *Population and Development Review*, No. 24, December.

Chandavarkar, A.G. (1983), '*Money and Credit 1858-1947*', in Dharma Kumar (ed.) op.cit., pp. 762 – 803.

Chandra, Bipan (2009) *History of Modern India* (Delhi: Orient Black Swan; reprinted in 2011).

Chaudhuri, B (1983), "Eastern India", in Dharma Kumar (ed.); op.cit., pp. 86-176.

Chopra, P. N. (ed.) (1973) *The Gazetteer of India, Volume 2: History and Culture*, Part III: Modern India 1761-1947 (New Delhi: Publication Division).

Cohen, Bernard (1984), 'Florence Nightingale', *Scientific American*, 250 (3), March; pp. 128 – 137.

Cotton (1866), 'The Famine in India: A Lecture', The Social Science Congress, 12, October, Manchester; mimeographed; copy available in the Regional Archives, Kozhikode.

Currey, B. and G. Hugo (1984) *Famine as a Geographical Phenomenon* (Boston: D. Reidel, Geo Journal Library).

Das, Debarshi (2008), 'A Relook at the Bengal Famine', *Economic and Political Weekly*, 2 August; pp. 59-64.

Das, Tarakchandra (1949) *Bengal Famine 1943: As Revealed in a Survey of Destitutes in Calcutta* (Calcutta: University of Calcutta).

Dasgupta, Biplab (2003), 'The Colonial Political Perspective', *Social Scientist*, Vol. 31, No. 358-359; March-April; pp. 27-56.

Davis, Mike (2001) *Late Victorian Holocaust: El Nino Famine and the Making of the Third World* (London: Verso Books).

Devereux, S. (2001), 'Sen's Entitlement Approach: Critiques and Counter-critiques', *Oxford Development Studies*, Vol. 29, No. 3; pp. 246 – 263.

Digby, William (1878) *Famine Campaign in South India*, 2 Vols. (London: Longmans, Green & Co.).

_______(1901) *'Prosperous' British India* (Longmans, Green & Co., and Fisher Unwin).

Dreze, Jean and Amartya Sen (1989) *Hunger and Public Action* (New Delhi: Oxford University Press; ninth Impression, 2008).

_______and Athar Hussain (eds.) (1995) *The Political Economy of Hunger: Selected Essays* (New Delhi: Oxford University Press; third impression, 1999).

_______(1995), 'Famine Prevention in India', in Dreze, Sen, and Hussain (eds.), op. cit. pp. 69-177.

Dutt, Ramesh C. (1900) *Open Letters to Lord Curzon on Famines and Land Assessments in India* (London: Kegan Paul, Trench, Trubner & Co. Ltd. - reprinted 2005).

_______(1901) *Indian Famines: Their Causes and Prevention* (London: Kegan Paul, Trench, Trubner & Co. Ltd.).

_______(1904) *Economic History of India*, Vol. 1 (Delhi: Publication Division - First Indian edition 1960; reprinted in 1989).

Dutta, Bhabatosh (1978) *Indian Economic Thought: Twentieth Century Perspective, 1900–1950* (New Delhi: Tata McGraw Hill).

Dykes, J. W. B. (1858) *General Manual of Ryotwar Tenure* (Government of Madras, Fort St. George, Madras).

Dyson, Tim (1989) *India's Historical Demography: Studies in Famine, Disease and Society* (London: Curzon Press).

_______(1991), 'On the Demography of South Asian Famines', *Population Studies*, pp. 44-45 and 279–297.

Edkins, Jennifer (1996), 'Legality with a Vengeance: Famines and Humanitarian Relief in Complex Emergencies', *Journal of International Studies*, 25; pp. 547–575.

Esterik, P Van (1985), 'Intra-family Food Distribution: Its Relevance for Maternal and Child Nutrition', in Michael C. Latham (ed.) op.cit. pp. 73 – 149.

Ferguson, Nial (2004) *Empire: The Rise and demise of the British World Order and the Lessons for Global Power* (New York: Basic Books).

_______(2008) *The Ascent of Money: A Financial History of the World* (New Delhi: Penguin Books India Pvt Ltd.).

Ferrill, Arthur (1986) *The Fall of the Roman Empire: The Military Explanation* (New York: Thames and Hudson Ltd.).

Fieldhouse, David (1996), 'For Richer, for Poor?', *The Cambridge Illustrated History of the British Empire* (Cambridge: Cambridge University Press).

Fine, Ben (2004), 'Economics and Ethics: Amartya Sen as Point of Departure', *New School Economic Review*, Vol. 1, No. 2; pp. 95 – 103.

Floud, Roderick and Deidre McCloskey (ed.) (1994) *The Economic History of Britain since 1700*; Vol. I: 1700-1860; Vol. II: 1860-1939 (London: Cambridge University Press).

Fogel, R.W. (1992), 'Second Thoughts on the European Escape from Hunger: Famines, Chronic Malnutrition, and Mortality Rates', in Osmani (ed.) op.cit.

Frykenberg, Robert E (ed.) (1992) *Land Control and Social Structure in Indian History* (Madison: University of Wisconsin Press).

Gadgil, D.R. (1924) *The Industrial Evolution of India 1860–1939* (New Delhi: Oxford University Press; fifth Edition, eighth impression, 1988).

Galbraith, John Kenneth (1954) *The Great Crash 1929* (New York: Penguin Books and Hamish Hamilton; reprinted in 1975).

Gandhi, M.K. (1924), 'Relief Work in Malabar', reproduced in the *Collected Works of Mahatma Gandhi*, Vol. 29: 16 August, 1924 – 26 December 1924.

Ganesan, Uma (2010), 'Medicine and Modernity: The Ayurvedic Revival Movement in India, 1885 – 1947', *South Asia*, Series 4, Vol.7, No.1, Fall; pp.: 108 – 131.

Ghose, Ajit Kumar (1982), 'Food Supply and Starvation: A Study of Famines with Reference to the Indian Sub-continent', *Oxford Economic Papers*, July; pp. 368–389.

Ghose, Sanker (1993) *Jawaharlal Nehru: A Biography* (Delhi: Allied Publishers).

Ghosh, Jayati (1995), 'State Intervention in the Macroeconomy', in P. Patnaik (ed.) op.cit. pp. 146-186.

Ghosh, Santikumar (1959) *Inflation in an Underdeveloped Economy* (World Press).

Gibbon, Edward (1776) *The Decline and the Fall of the Roman Empire* (Web resource, read through Openlibrary.org in June 2013).

Gill, G (2005) *The Extraordinary Upbringing and Curious Life of Miss Florence Nightingale* (New York: Random House).

Gladstone, David (ed.) (1999) *Before Beveridge: Welfare before the Welfare State* (London: Civitas; the whole book accessed from website).

Gopalan, A.K. (1980) *Ente Jeevita Katha* (The Story of My Life) (Thiruvanathapuram: Chinta Publishers).

Goradia, Nayana (1993) *Lord Curzon: The Last of the British Moghuls* (New Delhi: Oxford University Press; fourth impression, 2007).

Gourley, G (2003) *Florence Nightingale and the Health of the Raj* (England: Aldershot Hants).

Gramsci, Antonio (1971) *Selections from the Prison Notebooks* (London: Lawrence and Wishheart).

Guha, A. (1977), 'Bureaucracy and the Ruling Class', *Economic and Political Weekly,* review of Misra (1977) op. cit, 2 July, pp. 1047-48.

Habib, Irfan (1995) *Essays in Indian History: Towards a Marxist Perception* (New Delhi: Tulika – third reprint 2000).

_______(2000), 'The Peasant in History', in his *Essays in Indian History* (Delhi: Tulika; pp 109–160).

Hall-Mathews, David (2008), 'Inaccurate Conceptions: Disputed Measures for Nutrition Needs and Famine Deaths in Colonial India', *Modern Asian Studies*, 42 (1); pp.1–24.

Harris, Jose (1992), 'Political Thought and Welfare State, 1870 –1940', *Past and Present*, Vol. 35 (May); reproduced in Gladston (1999), op.cit.

Harrison, Mark (1992), 'Quarantine, Pilgrimage, and Colonial Trade 1866–1900', *Indian Economic and Social History Review*, Vol. 29, No. 2.

Harriss, Barbara (1995), 'The Intrafamily Distribution of Hunger in South Asia', in Dreze, Sen and Hussain (eds.) op.cit. pp. 224-297.

Hasan, M. (1951) *History of Tipu Sultan* (Delhi: Aakar Books; reprint 2005).

Hasan, S. Nurul (1969), 'Zamindars under the Mughals', in R.E. Frykenberg (Ed), op.cit. pp. 17 – 31.

Hirst, Leonard Fabian (1953) *The Conquest of Plague:* A Study of the Evolution of Epidemiology (London: Clarendon Press).

Hobsbawm, Eric (1987) *The Age of Empire, 1875-1914* (Great Britain: Weidenfeld & Nicolson Ltd; reprinted by Abacus, 2009).

Howson, Richard & Kylie Smith (eds.) (2008) *Hegemony: Studies in Consensus and Coercion* (London: Routledge).

Innes, C.A. and F.B. Evans (1908) *Madras District Gazetteer*, Vol. I: Malabar and Anjengo Chapter XI: *Land Revenue Administration* (Madras: Superintendent, Government Press).

James, Lawrence (2000) *The Making and Unmaking of British India* (London: Macmillan).

Johnson, D. Gale (1973), '*Famine*', in the 1973 edition of Encyclopaedia Britannica.

Joseph, S.C. (1960) *Foodgrain Policy and Economic Development in India* (Delhi: Allied Publishers).

Kaper, James B, Glenn Morris Jr, and Myron M. Levine (1995), 'Cholera', *Clinical Microbiology Review*, 8(1), (downloaded from '*Journals. ASM. org*' on 13.09.2012).

Kenealy, Christine and Gerard Mac Alasney (1995) *The Hidden Famine: Hunger, Poverty and Sectarianism in Belfast 1840-50* (London: Pluto Press).

Klein, Ira (1973), 'Death in India, 1871 – 1921', *Journal of Asian Studies,* (August), 32 (24).

_______(1984), 'When the Rains Failed: Famine, Relief and Mortality in British India', *Indian Economic and Social History Review*, 21 (2), pp. 185 – 204.

_______(1988), 'Plague, Policy and Popular Unrest in British India', *Modern Asian Studies*, Vol. 22, No. 4, pp. 723 – 755.

Knight, Henry (1957) *Food Administration in India, 1939-1947* (New York: Stanford University Press).

Kolsky, Elizabeth (2010) *Colonial Justice in British India – White Violence and the Rule of Law* (London: Cambridge University Press).

Krause, Richard M. (2005), 'Preventive and Social Medicine: A Victorian Legacy', *Indian Journal of Community Medicine* (Vol. 30, No. 4).

Kumar, Dharma (1983), '*South India*", in Dharma Kumar (ed.) op.cit. pp. 352 – 375.

_______(Ed) (1983) *The Cambridge Economic History of India, Vol.2: c 1757 – c 2003* (London: Orient Longman & Cambridge University Press; reprint, 2008) .

Kuznets, Simon (1965) *Economic Growth and Structure* (New York: W.W. Norton and Company) pp. 244-45.

Lancaster, H.O. (1990) *Expectations of Life: A Study in the Demography, Statistics, and the History of World Mortality* (Springes-Verlag).

Latham, M.C. (ed.) (1985) *Determinants of Young Child Feeding and Their Implications for Nutritional Surveillance* (New York: Cornell University).

Lenin, V. I. (1899) *The Development of Capitalism in Russia* (Moscow: Progress Publishers) fifth printing, 1977 pp. 193-94.

Logan, William (1887) *Malabar Manual*, Vol. I and Vol. II (New Delhi: Fifth Asian Educational Service Reprint, 2010).

Loveday, Alexander (1914) *The History and Economics of Indian Famines* (London: G Bell and Sons Ltd; reprinted by Usha Publishers, Delhi, 1985).

Ludden, David (1985), 'Peasant History in South Asia', in *The New Cambridge History of India* (England: Cambridge University Press).

Mahalanobis, Mukherjee and Ghosh (1946), 'A Sample Survey of After-effects of the Bengal Famine of 1943', *Sankhya*, No. 7.

Maharatna, Arup (1996) *Demography of famine: An Indian Historical Perspective* (New Delhi: Oxford University Press).

Malthus, Robert Thomas (1878) *An Essay on the Principles of Population* (London: Reeves and Turner).

_______(1880) *An Investigation of the Cause of the Present High Price of Provisions* (London: Reeves and Turner).

Marr, David G. (1970) *Vietnamese Anticolonialism, 1885–1925* (Berkeley: University of California).

Marshall, P.J. (1968) *Problems of Empire: Britain and India, 1757–1813* (London: George Allen and Unwin).

Masefield, G.B. (1963) *Famine: Its Prevention and Relief* (London: Oxford University Press)

Mason, Philip (1985) *The Men Who Ruled India* (New Delhi: Rupa Publication India; 12th impression, 2012).

Massing, Michael (2003), 'Does Democracy Avert Famine?' *The New York Times*, 01 March.

Mayer, Jean (1975), 'Management of Famine Relief', *Science* (5), 9 May.

McAlpin, Michelle B (1983a), 'Famines, Epidemics, and Population Growth: The Case of India', *The Journal of Interdisciplinary History* (Autumn); pp. 351-366.

_______(1983b) *Subject to Famine: Food Crisis and Economic Change in Western India, 1860-1920* (New York: Princeton University Press).

_______(1979), 'Dearth, Famine, and Risk: The Changing Impact of Crop Failures in Western India, 1870–1920', *The Journal of Economic History* (March), Vol. 39, No. 1, pp. 143–157.

McDonald, Ian (2007), 'Bodily Practice, Performance Art, Competitive Sport: A Critique of Kalarippayattu, the Martial Art of Kerala', *Contributions to Indian Sociology*, (41) (2): 143–68.

Metcalf, Thomas (1979) *Land, Landlords and the British Raj: Northern India in the Nineteenth Century* (Berkely, Los Angelese & London: University of California Press).

Misra, B. B. (1977) *The Bureaucracy in India: A Historical Analysis of Development up to 1974* (New Delhi: Oxford University Press).

Mitra, Asok. K (1953) *Census of India 1951*–Volume VI, Part-1 A: Report (Delhi: Manager of Publications).

_______(1978) *India's Population: Aspects of Quality Control* (New Delhi: Office of the Registrar General of India).

_______(1989), 'Famine of 1943 in Vikrampur Dacca', *Economic and Political Weekly*, 4 February; pp. 253-264.

Mitra, Ashok (1982), 'The Meaning of Meaning', *Economic and Political Weekly*, 27 March, pp 488 – 489.

Mohandas, P (2009), 'War, Famine and Popular Resistance: Malabar 1940-45', in the Proceedings of the 29th Annual Session of the South Indian History Congress; pp. 285-286.

Mukherjee, Madhusree (2010) *Churchill's Secret War: The British Empire and the Ravaging of India during World War II* (New York: Basic·Books).

_______(2014), "Bengal Famine of 1943: An Appraisal of the Famine Inquiry Commission", *Economic and Political Weekly*, March 15 (Vol. XLIX, No.11).

_______Muqtada, M. (1981), 'Poverty and Famines in Bangladesh', *Bangladesh Development Studies*, No. 9, pp. 1 – 34.

Murton, Brian (2000), 'VI: Famines' in *Cambridge World History of Food*, Volume 2 (New York: Cambridge University Press).

Myrdal, Gunnar (1968) *Asian Drama: An Inquiry into the Poverty of Nations*, Volume III (Great Britain: Pelican Book).

Namboodiripad, E.M.S. (1937), 'The Question of Land Tenure in Malabar: Minute of Dissent to the Kuttikrishna Menon Committee Report on Malabar Tenancy Reform, 1937', reproduced in his *Selected Writings*, Vol. 2 (Calcutta: National Book Agency, 1985) pp. 224-251.

Naoroji, Dadabhai (1876) *Poverty and Un-British Rule in India* (London: Swan Sonnenschein).

Narayanan, M. G. S. (2006) *Calicut–The City of Truth Revisited* (Publication Division: University of Calicut).

Nehru, Jawaharlal (1946) *The Discovery of India* (Calcutta: Signet Press; latest edition by Oxford University Press, New Delhi, 2010).

Nozick, Robert (1974) *Anarchy, State and Utopia* (Oxford: Basil Blackwell).

O'Grada, Carmac (2009) *Famine: A Short History* (Princeton: Princeton University Press).

Orent, Wendy (2004) *The Mysterious Past and Terrifying Future of the World's Most Dangerous Disease* (New York: Free Press).

Osmani, Siddiq (1992) *Nutrition and Poverty* (New Delhi: Oxford University Press, Paperback edition, 2000).

_______(1995), 'The Entitlement Approach to Famine: An Assessment', in Basu, Pattanaik and Suzumura (eds.) op. cit; pp 253-294.

Panikkar, K.N. (1978), 'Agrarian Legislation and Social Classes: A Case Study of Malabar', *Economic and Political Weekly*, May 27; pp. 880 – 888.

Patnaik, Prabhat (1972), 'A Note on Export Markets and Capitalist Development', *The Economic Journal*, Vol. 82 (reproduced in P. Patnaik, 1995, op.cit).

_______(1973), 'On the Political Economy of Underdevelopment', *Economic and Political Weekly*, Annual Number, February (reproduced in P. Patnaik, 1995, op. cit).

_______(1995) *Whatever Happened to Imperialism and Other Essays* (New Delhi: Tulika).

_______(2001), 'Imperialism and the Diffusion of Development', *Social Scientist*, April-May; reproduced in P. Patnaik, 2003; op. cit).

_______(2003) *The Retreat to Unfreedom: Essays on the Emerging World Order* (New Delhi: Tulika).

_______(2011), 'On the Macroeconomics of a Colonial Economy', in P. Patnaik ed. op. cit.

_______(ed.) (1986), 'Introduction' to *Lenin and Imperialism: An Appraisal of Theories and Contemporary Reality* (reproduced in P. Patnaik, 1995; op.cit).

_______(ed.) (1995) *Themes in Economics: Macroeconomics* (Delhi: Oxford University Press).

_______(ed.) (2011) *Excursus in History: Essays on Some Ideas of Irfan Habib.* (New Delhi: Tulika).

Patnaik, Utsa (1975), 'Contribution to the Output and Marketable Surplus of Agricultural Products by Cultivating Groups in India, 1960-61', *Economic and Political Weekly*, (Review of Agriculture), Vol. X, 27 December, reproduced in Utsa Patnaik (1999), op. cit.

_______(1976), 'Class Differentiation within the Peasantry: An Approach to Analysis of Indian Agriculture', *Economic and Political weekly*, (Review of Agriculture), September 25.

_______(1987) *Peasant Class Differentiation: A Study in Method with Reference to Haryana* (Delhi: Oxford University Press).

_______(1991), 'Food Availability and Famine: A Longer View', *Journal of Peasant Studies*, October; (reproduced in U. Patnaik, 1999, op. cit).

_______(1999) *The Long Transition: Essays on Political Economy* (Delhi: Tulika).

_______(2000), 'The Cost of Free Trade', reproduced in U. Patnaik (2000), op. cit.

_______(2000) *The Republic of Hunger and Other Essays* (Gurgaon: Three Essays Collective).

_______(2001), 'Food Availability and Famine: A Longer View', in her *The Long Transition – Essays on Political Economy* (Delhi: Tulika).

_______(2007a), 'The Cost of Free Trade', in her *The Republic of Hunger and Other Essays* (Gurgaon: Three Essays Collective).

_______(2007b), 'The Republic of Hunger', in her *The Republic of Hunger and Other Essays* (Gurgaon: Three Essays Collective).

Paul, William (1918) *The State: Its Origin and Function* (Glasgow: Socialist Labour Press; latest edition, 2010 by Proletarian Publishing, Edinburgh).

Pavlov, V.I. (1978) *Historical Premises of India's Transition to Capitalism* (Moscow: Peoples Publishing House).

Peers, Douglas M (2006) *India under Colonial Rule 1700–1885* (London: Pearson Longman).

Potter, C.W. (2006), 'A History of Influenza', *Journal of Applied Microbiology* 91(4) pp. 572- 579.

Raghavan, M. 1985. *Movement of Administered Agricultural Prices in India since the Mid-sixties* (unpublished PhD thesis submitted to the Centre for Economic Studies and Planning, School of Social Sciences, Jawaharlal Nehru University, New Delhi).

Rajeevan, T.P. (2011), 'Charm in Rustic Languages', *The Hindu Literary Review*, November 6, p. 4.

Ram, N. (1995), "An Independent Press and Anti-hunger Strategies: Indian Experience", in Dreze, Sen and Hussain. eds. pp. 178-223; op. cit.

Rangasami, Amrita (1985), 'Failure of Exchange Entitlements Theory of Famine: A Response', *Economic and Political Weekly*, Vol. XX, No. 42, 12 and 19 October.

Ray, Satish Chandra (1909) *An Essay on the Economic Causes of Famines in India and Suggestions to Prevent Their Frequent Recurrence,* Calcutta: Baptist Mission Press and Calcutta University.

Raychoudhary, S.C. (2009) *History of India: A Detailed Study of Social, Cultural and Economic Aspects from 1760 to Present Times* (Delhi: Surjeet Publications), pp. 163-64.

Rosenberg, Charles. E (1962) *The Cholera Years: The United States in 1832, 1849 and 1866* (Chicago: Chicago University Press).

_______(1966), 'Cholera in Nineteenth-Century Europe: A Tool for Social and Economic Analysis', *Comparative Studies in Society and History*, 8(4), pp. 453 – 463 (downloaded Digital Access to Scholarship at Harvard – DASH- on 13 September 2012).

Rothermund, D. (1983) *The Indian Economy under British Rule and Other Essays* (Delhi: Manohar).

Roy, Tirthankar (2006) *The Economic History of India 1857 –1947* (New Delhi: Oxford University Press, Fourth Impression, 2010).

Sahadevan, P.C. (1966) *Rice in Kerala* (Thiruvananthapuram: Agriculture Information Centre, Kerala State).

Sarkar, Sumit (1983) *Modern India 1885–1947* (Chennai: Macmillan Publishers, 23rd impression 2010).

Satya, Laxman D. (2011), *The British Empire, Ecology and Famines in Late 19th Century Central India* (Lock Haven University of Pennsylvania; March 26; downloaded from the website: *http://www.celdf.org).*

Screpanti, Ernesto and Stefano Zamagni (2005) *An Outline of the History of Economic Thought* (Translated by David Field and Lynn Kirby; New Delhi: Oxford University Press).

Seal, S.C. (1960), 'Epidemiological Studies of Plague in India', *Bulletin of World Health Organisation*, No. 23, pp: 293-300.

Seavoy, Ronald (1986) *Famine in Peasant Societies* (New York: Greenwood Press).

Sen, Amartya (1981) *Poverty and Famines: An Essay on Entitlement and Deprivation* (New Delhi: Oxford University Press; 13th Impression, Oxford India Paperbacks, 2009).

_______(1986), 'The Causes of famine: A Reply', *Food Policy* (May), Vol. 11, No 2, pp. 125–132.

_______(1987), 'Famine and Mr Bowbrick', *Food Policy*, (February), pp. 10-14.

_______(1999), "Food, Economics and Entitlements", in Dreze, Sen. and Hussain (eds.) *The Political Economy of Hunger* (New Delhi: Oxford India Paperback; Third Impression; pp. 50 – 68)

Sen, Priyaranjan (ed.) (1937) *Florence Nightingale's Indian Letters* (Calcutta: 1, Dover Lane).

Smales, Bernard J (1975) *Economic History Made Simple* (London: Howard and Wyndham Ltd.).

Smith, Adam (1776) *Wealth of Nations* (New York: Bantam Dell, a Division of Random House Inc.).

Spear, Percival (1965) *A History of India,* Vol.II *From the Sixteenth Century to the Twentieth Century* (New Delhi: Pelican / Penguin Books – sixteenth impression 2003).

Srivastava, Hari Shankar (1968) *The History of Indian Famines and Development of Famine Policy 1858 –1918* (Agra: Sri Ram Mehra and Co.).

Stein, Burton (1969), 'Integration of Agrarian Systems of Southern India', in Robert Frykenberg (ed.), 1992 edition op.cit.

_______(2001) *A History of India* (New Delhi: Oxford India Paperback)

Stewart, Michael (1967) *Keynes and After* (U.K.: Penguin Books).

Stone, Ian (1984) *Canal Irrigation in British India* (London: Cambridge University Press).

Temple, Sir Richard (1882) *Men and Events of My Time in India* (London: John Murray).

Thorner, Alice (ed.) (2001) *Land, Labour and Rights: Daniel Thorner Memorial Lectures* (New Delhi: Tulika).

Thorner, Daniel (1955), 'Long-term Trends in Output in India', in Simon Kuznets et al (eds.) *Economic Growth: Brazil, India, Japan* (Duke University quoted in Blyn, 1966, op.cit.).

Vallee, Gerard (ed.) (2006) *Collected Works of Florence Nightingale,* Vol. 9: *Health in India*; pp. 1048 (Canada: Wilfrid Laurier University Press).

_______(ed.) (2007) *Collected Works of Florence Nightingale,* Vol. 10: *Social Change in India*; p. 976 (Canada: Wilfrid Laurier University Press).

Varier, M.R.R. (2002) *The Rediscovery of Ayurveda: The Story of Arya Vaidya Sala, Kottakkal* (New Delhi: Viking Penguin Books India).

Visaria, Leela and Pravin Visaria (1983), '*Population 1757 – 1947*', in Dharma Kumar (Ed,) Vol. II, op. cit.

Watts, Sheldon (1997) *Epidemics and History: Disease, Power and Imperialism* (Yale University: Yale University Press).

Weiss, Richard S. (2009) *Recipes for Immortality: Medicine, Religion and Community in South India* (New York: Oxford University Press).

Wheeler, E.F. (1984), 'Intra Household Food Distribution: A Review of Evidence', paper presented at meeting on *The Sharing of Food* at London School of Hygiene and Tropical Medicine (see, quoted in Harriss, 1995; op.cit).

Whitcombe, Elizabeth (1983), '*Irrigation*', in Dharma Kumar (eds.) pp. 677-736, *op.cit.*

Whiteside, Noel (1984), 'The Working Class and State 'Welfare' in Britain, 1880- 1914', *The Historical Journal*, 27(4); pp.877-900; reproduced in Gladstone (ed.) (1999); op.cit; pp. 86-116.

_______(1999), 'Private Provision and Public Welfare: Health Insurance between Wars', in Gladstone (ed.) op.cit; pp. 26-42.

William, Brian (1997) *Infectious Diseases in History: A Guide to Causes and Effects* (England: Department of Economic and Social History, University of Hull).

Winch, Donald (1969) *Economics and Policy: A Historical Survey* (U.K: Hodder and Stoughton; reprinted in paperback by Fontana, 1972).

Yawn B.P. (2008), 'Factors Accounting for Asthma Variability: Achieving Optimal System Control for Individual Patients', *Primary Care Respiratory Journal*, Vol. 17, No. 3, (September), pp. 138-142.

Index

A

Adam Smith
  on Famines, 30
  on British Performance
    - impact, 31
Agricultural/Non-Agricultural
  Population, 29
Agriculture
  British attitude to, 280
American Civil War
  - 1861...impact, 39
Army Strength Rise
  1939-1945, 106
Attachments to Demand
  Notices-Malabar, 114
Ayurveda
  suppression of, 282

B

Bangladesh Famine
  - Sen on, 138
Bengal vs Malabar
  during 1943 famine, 252
    ...Population, 253
    ...Food Production, 255-57
    ...Soil, 254-55
    ...Food Availability, 257-60
Bentinck
  Land revenue
    reduction, 161-62
Bowbric Peter
  critique on famine
    theories, 139
Britain
  19th and early 20th
    century, 238
  inter-war period, 239
  Second WW & after, 241
  role in averting
  famines, 235
  economy -1688,236
  eighteenth century, 237
British Administration
  impact,31
  imperialism
    ...and famines,32
    ...schools of thought, 30
British Attitude towards
  Malabar, 24
  Malabar Crops, 27
British Imperialism
  Features, 244-45, 248
British India
  conditions 20th Century, 73
British Indian railways
  and famine, 277
British Industrial
  penetration, 277-78
British Irrigation System, 34
British Policy on reason
  to famine, 135
Bureaucratic attitude
  to famine, 70-71

C

Canal Irrigation System
  under the British, 35
Cattle Mortality
  -1876,78, 69
Cereal Production
  Madras Presidency
    -1938-45, 110
Children sale, 43
  accounts of, 43
Cholera Epidemic
  -1943, 119
  ...spread, 120-21
  fight against, 121
  -1877-1916
  ...Mortality, 193

Churchill Winston
Role in Famine, 261
Attitude to
famine releif, 261
Denial Policy, 262
...causes, 263
Coercive Processes
- Land Revenue Collection
-Malabar, 82
-Madras, 103
Coffee Plantation
diversification, 53
Comercial Products
-Malabar, 54
Commercialization of
Agriculture, 38-39,277-79
Convicts
age-wise detention, 117
Cornwallis
as Governor general, 156
Crime Records
20th Century, 115
Crimes
during famine,46
in Malabar, 47
Crop Production trend
-British India, 146
...Thorner on, 147

D

Dalhousie
as Governor general, 162
reduction of land
revenue by, 161-62
David Arnold
Study on Grain riots, 86
Deaths
- Famine Related
-1873-78, 66
Diarrhoea & Dysentery, 203
District Collector/
other officials duties
during famine, 42-45
Draft Famine Code
(Famine Commission), 41
...intellegence system, 42
...divison of duties, 42
Dutt, R.C.,
on Permanent
Settlement, 158
on Madras Board
of Revenue, 169
suggestions to remove
sufferings of peasants
/poor, 178
to Curzon on impact
mitigation, 179
Dysentery & Diarrhoea, 201

E

E- Mapping, 223
East India Company (EIC)
entry in India, 152
...Pre 1793 system, 154
...administration, 153
...Post-1793 system, 157
...Land Revenue System
-Impact, 19
...Transfer of
Administration to
Crown Impact, 21
Endowment Bundle, 222
Enitlement Theory
Nozick vs Sen, 223-27
Critique, 227-232
Entitlement Bundle, 222
Epidemic, 39
susceptibility to, 29
causes, 39
Phase, 267
breeding of, 281
measures needed
to fight vs attitude, 213-16
works on, 183
causes, 184
British India, 186
Epidemics(All) Death
West Coast
...1911-1920, 196
Malabar
...1941-50, 197
Epidemics-Mortality
...1876-77, 68-69
Epidemic-wise Deaths
1911-1920
(West Coast), 196
1941-50
(Malabar), 197
Ethiopia Famine
Case Study, 138
Eviction
Logan on, 172

F

Factories (Malabar)
types/uses, 55
FAD
(Food Availability Decline)
as cause of famine, 48
Sen on, 221
Approach, 126
...Analysis, 282-83
Components, 129
Approach to famine, 130-51
Failure of Exchange Theory
Entitlement(FEE), 139
Theory, 139, 144
...Failure, 283
Concept, 221
Entitlement
...ways, 223
...to food, 222
Relations
-Sen on, 222
Famine
of 1727, 56
disease led
-1730, 57
of 1757, 58
18th Century, 56-58
19th century, 58
1876-78, 58
and epidemics, 185
Famine
Concept
-Sen, 227
definition, 130
causes, 149, 152
issues, 47-48
impact, 49
reasons, 53
Land revenue
as causes, 152
meaning, 274
routes of, 274
spread, 30
process of
- Adam Smith, 30
0, epidemic mortality, 118
and Mortalities, 266
largest cause of
mortality, 268
Famine Code
-1883, 64, 84,
280, 285
Famine Commission
-1880 -(Richard
Strachey), 41, 45
Famine Crimes
-Malabar, 116
Famine Enquiry
Commission-1945, 268
Famine Food, 267
Famine Insurance Funds
-Ripon,277
Famine of 1924, 87
food production/
prices impact, 88
epidemics/mortality, 89
Land Revenue Releif, 90
Gandhi Intervention, 92
Famine of 1932
symptoms, 93
monsoons, 94
Farm prices, 95
Land revenue
suspension, 101
epidemic mortality, 104-105
Famine of 1943
,105,112
impact, 106
Land Revenue, 112
Price impact, 106
Monsoons
/food production, 108
Prices/cost of living, 110
Famine Releif
Measures, 40
in budget
(20th Century
British India)91
Famine-1918
Monsoons/Epidemics
/Mortalities, 75
Famines
20th Century, 72-73
19th Century
-1876-78,68
...epidemics
/mortality, 68-69
...monsoon impact, 60,62
Famines(Malabar)
18th century, 55
Female Mortality
causes, 272

Fever, 198
  Hospital, 217
Florence Nightingale
  , 133-35
  works, 133-34
  in India, 134
  writings on
    Health & famines,136
    Views, 203
  views, 203
  on health status
    of BI, 204
  on Colonial
    Hegemony,205-207
Food Crops to Cash Crops
  diversion, 39
Food Prices (Malabar)
  20th Century
  - British India, 81, 83, 85
Food Production
  (Malabar) 1943-44, 110
Food Riots, 115
Foodcrops 1928-34
  price decline, 97
Foodgrain 1928-34
  Production value, 96-97
  Exports During famines, 38
  Output Decline
    British India(1901-41), 145
Foodgrain Prices
  (1876-78), trends, 60, 62
Foodgrain Riots, 85-86
Free Trade Ideology
  British India, 146
  Patnaik U., 146

G

Gandhi Mahatma
  intervention during
    famine, 92
Gender Disparity
  in Human Mortality
    (famine), 270
Great Depression
  (US Economy), 93
    repercussions on
      farm prices, 95

H

Haptam-Regulation VII, 160-61
Harvest Price (Rice),85
Health Care development
  British attitude, 182
Healthcare(British)
  absence, 40 apathy, 40
Hegemony
  meaning, 206-207
  Gramscian Concept, 208, 211, 213
  & famines, 279
Hospitals
  establishment overheads, 216

I

Indian Famine Commission
  -1880, 32
    ...Report, 53
  -1901, 33
Indifferent attitude
  (Britain) to Famine, 242-46
Indigenous Medicine, 213
Indigenous vs Imperialist
  State, 234
Inflammatory disorders of
  the intestines, 202
Influenza, 199
Interventional State, 232
Irish famine, 241
Irrigation Net-works
  /EIC Projecting, 33

K

Kuznets, Simon
  thesis on shifts
    in cultivation,147-48

L

Land Evictions
  -1862-80, 66
  Suspension, 102
  Additional Cess on
    - Madras, 103
  role in Famine, 263
  Collection:
    EIC, 153
    Mughals, 153
Land Survey, 163
Land Tenure System, 157
  (British), 157, 174
Land Tenure
  /Revenue System
    under British, 54
    ...impact, 55, 63
    ...assessment /collection, 64-65
Landlord Tenant Relationship
  EMS Namboodripad on, 175

Lessons learnt from
present study, 121
Logan William
...on Land Tenure, 170
...on eviction, 172
Logan's Report
-1882, 170-71
Lytton, on Temple Wage
/Charity, 68

M

Macleod Major, 169
as Principal Collector
-Malabar-1801, 169
Method - Land revenue, 169-70
Madras Famine(1876-78), 58
Madras Medical Registration
Act, 215
Mahalwari System, 160
discontinuing, 165
Major Famines (BI), 276
Major causes, 277
Malabar Model
(Land Revenue), 168-69
difference with others, 170
Malabar Tenancy
Reform Report
EMS Namboodripad on, 175
Malaria, 199
Malabar Famines
causes/factors
/strengthening,266
Male vs Female Mortality
(Famine)
views on, 270-71
Malthusian Imbalance, 126, 133
Theory of Population, 131
Market Oriented Economies, 232
Migration, 45
Miscellaneous Revenue
Demands (Land), 172
Monetisation of rent payment, 177
Monetisation, 279
Money as a medium of exchange
advantages, 177
Mortality Figures(Famine)
credibility-doubts, 269-70
Munro Thomas, 162, 166
study/work on land
settlements, 163, 165
Revenue collection under, 166
Myrdal Gunnar Theory, 133

N

Night Soil Pollution, 217
steps needed for disposal
vs attitude, 217
Nozicks Theory
of Entitlement, 223-24

O

Old Malabar
region,conditions,
drainage,monsons, 19
drought-reasons, 19
Nehru on, 20

P

Permanent Settlement
on Zamindari System, 157
Benefits-Dutt on, 153
(Bengal), 264-65
Plague
-1897-1930, 193
world mortality
-1894-1938,195
Population
Variation – Malabar
-1891-1941, 189
Decadal change 1872-1921, 188
Groups (Malabar), 23
Potato famine
Ireland, 241-42
British Attitude to, 242
Poverty and Famine
- Amartya Sen, 227, 271
Critique, 227-28 review, 228
Price Control Measures, 107
Prisoners/Prison deaths, 117

Q

Quarantine
attitude to, 281
Policy, 210-11

R

Railway
Introduction
...impact on epidemics,185
Construction in Madras
Presidency under British, 36
Development Stages, 36
Expansion & World
Development, 37
Regulating Act-1773, 156
Respiratory Diseases, 200-201

Retail Price
(Malabar) 1913-35
Paddy, 98 Rice, 99
Ragi, 99 Salt, 100
Revenue Settlement
- Ryotwari Land, 113
Rice Exports
during Famine, 260
Richard Temple
Recommendations
/Directives, 66-67
...on Famines, 66-67
...on Temple Wage
/Charity,67
Rinderpest Disease
attack on cattle, 70
Road/Rail Expansion, 38
Rupee
introduction of, 178
Ryotwari areas, 174
Ryotwari Land Revenue
assessment,80
in Madras(1874-75
-1945-46), 173
Ryotwari Revenue
- Malabar-holdings
/settlement, 103
Ryotwari System, 162, 265

S

Saharanpur Rule, 162
Salem Method
of Survey, 163
Salt Act, 135
Salt March (Gandhi), 135
Salt Price
Trends (1913-35), 100
Salt Production
(during British), 135
Sanitation &
Health care BI, 208
Scotland/Ireland famine, 241
Second World War
& Inflation, 111
Sen Amartya
critique, 139
Bowbrick on, 139-40
Omkar Goswami, 142
Madhuri Mukerjee, 143
Sen's FAD analysis, 137
flaws, 139-40
long term view, 144
Sen's Study on famines
-1940's, 137
...Case studies, 137-38
Settlement Reports
of Madras Board
of Revenue, 167
Slavery, 247
propagation
/prevalence, 43-44
types, 247
in Roman empire, 241
Social Stresses, 43
Starvation Phase, 267-68
State Role in Averting
Famines, 232
Study of Famine
Limitations, 182
...undermining
inadequacies, 182
Suez Canal
Construction
...impact, 37
Supply Components, 126
...current output, 127
...carry over stocks, 127
...Net imports, 129
Surface Soil(Malabar), 26
Surveillance Forces, 115

T

Temple Wage
/Charity, 285
...Directives, 67

V

Vaccination, 208

W

Warren Hastings
Land Revenue System, 155
as Governor general, 155-56
Womens Healthcare, 11

Y

Year/Epidemic-wise
Mortality, 117

Z

Zamindari System
(Land Revenue), 154, 157
...areas under, 166